ERNEST RICHARD HUGHES

Born in London, 5th January 1883. M.A., Oxon. Missionary in the Interior of China, 1911–29. In Shanghai, 1929-31. Reader in Chinese Religion and Philosophy in Oxford University, 1934–41; seconded to Chungking, 1942. Books include *The Invasion of China by the Western World*, 1937.

Chinese Philosophy
in
Classical Times

EDITED AND TRANSLATED BY
E. R. HUGHES

DENT: LONDON
EVERYMAN'S LIBRARY
DUTTON: NEW YORK

All rights reserved
Printed in Great Britain
by
Butler and Tanner Ltd · Frome · Somerset
for
J. M. DENT & SONS LTD
Aldine House · Bedford Street · London
First included in Everyman's Library 1942
Last reprinted 1966

PREFACE (1954)

SINCE I am now in England, it is possible for the third reprint to embody certain needed emendations. These, apart from Chapter XXII, are mainly typographical and the like small errors due to my absence in China at the time of printing. As for the improvements which I now envisage, the mechanics of the printer's task reduce these to the very barest minimum. It is perhaps just as well, for 'tinkering' so easily becomes a vice, and no translation, whatever the languages concerned, can achieve perfection. Modern studies in the evolution of languages and the behaviour of words have demonstrated this with ever increasing clarity. The meaning of a word never stays 'put' from one generation to another, and, since the living molecule of thought is not a word but a sentence, every word in a sentence is coloured by its context.

In 1942 I marked this fact by a stray footnote from time to time. I propose to go a step further now and give the reader a striking illustration of the extraordinary difficulty a translator may have to face. On pp. 13–14 Confucius is found credited with synthesizing his 'way' under one principle. Unfortunately there is no record of what he meant precisely. A disciple, however, is represented as defining the 'one string' as 'chung shu.' Now, since Han times the accepted interpretation of these two words has placed them in the field of ethics, chung to mean 'loyalty' and shu to mean 'reciprocity,' or some such moral qualities. To-day, however, the student is faced with a very complex problem, arising from the insistence by two modern critics, Chang T'ai-yen and Dr. Hu Shih, that the two terms have an epistemological content. Dr. Hu equates their meaning to 'inference,' and has made out a strong case for this. The question for the language historian now is whether by Confucius's time such a concept as 'inference' was near

enough to the surface of such a mind as his for him to be
able to express it in the two terms *chung shu*. A further
question arises, whether the rather later practice had then
begun of enriching the meaning of one term by placing
alongside it a qualifying term. There is no place here for
setting forth the evidential pros and cons: it must suffice
to say that in 1942 the ethical interpretation seemed to me
a little more likely. The same applies to making *chung* a
qualificatory adjunct to *shu*. At any rate this has the merit
of making Master Tseng less muddle-headed than otherwise
he would appear to be. One string after all is not two
strings.

This leads on to the problems connected with 'categorical
thinking.' The story of Chinese philosophy, as far as it
was unfolded in the classical era, reveals the first stages of
the search for rational categories: compare the Yin-Yang
categories and those of the Five (physico-chemical) Forces.
A discussion of 'categorical thinking' and its adjacent one,
'empirical thinking,' is to be found in a paper I gave to
the East-West Philosophers' Conference in Honolulu in
1949. (See *Essays in East-West Philosophy*, edited by
Professor Charles A. Moore, 1951.) The same volume
contains a paper by Dr. Y. P. Mei on the ethical and social
philosophy, and one by Dr. W. T. Chan on 'Syntheses in
Chinese Philosophy,' as also various reactions by distinguished American philosophers to the challenge of the
Indian and Chinese philosophies.

Sinologists will have noticed that this volume contains
no extracts from the works of Yang Hsiung (53 B.C.–A.D.
18). There are two reasons. One is that the workings of
his mind in his *T'ai Hsüan* (The Supreme Mystery) seem to
me a foreshadowing of what was to emerge more clearly in
the philosophers of the third and fourth centuries. That is
to say, he is more closely connected with a period which is
outside the scope of this volume, which is solely concerned
with what happened before Indian and Central Asian
thought began to make its impressive dint on Chinese minds.
The other reason is, quite frankly, that I am not satisfied

with my attempts to put this highly individual Szechuanese
thinker into English. His combination of Taoist and
Changes Scripture ideologies is quite baffling in places.
However, he is treated in Dr. Fung Yu-lan's *History of
Chinese Philosophy* (Chinese), vol. ii, and a translation of
this is just out from Professor Derk Bodde's competent
hands. In the same volume there appears for the first
time in the English language a comprehensive survey of all
schools of philosophic thought, including the Chinese
Buddhist, down to the nineteenth century.

Six other works can now be added to the bibliographical
list. One is three small but very pregnant volumes of
Henri Maspero's posthumous works edited by Professor
Demiéville (Paris, 1950): *Les Religions Chinoises, Le Taoisme*,
and *Études Historiques*. Most of the material goes beyond
Chinese philosophy in classical times, but the amount that is
relevant is of first importance to students. Then there is
Dr. Tjan Tjoe-som's weighty book on the *Pai Hu T'ung Yi*:
Po Hu T'ung (2 vols), Leiden 1949 and 1952. My correc-
tions in Chapter XXII stem from Dr. Tjan's magnificent
researches into the obscure apocrypha of the Han era.
Also there is the *I Ching, or Book of Changes*, Bollingen
Series, New York, 1950, a translation by Carey F. Baynes of
Richard Wilhelm's German translation. Wilhelm sat at the
feet of some ripe scholars of the late nineteenth century.
Also there are *The Spirit of Chinese Philosophy* (London
1947), a translation of Dr. Fung's *Hsin Yüan Tao*, by myself,
Dr. Fung's *A Short History of Chinese Philosophy* (New
York, 1948), and *Ho-Shang-Kung's Commentary on Lao-
Tse*, translated into English by Edward Erkes (Ascona,
1950). There is also the long anticipated history of Chinese
science by Dr. Joseph Needham and his expert assistants:
seven volumes, the first two of which are now in the press.

E. R. HUGHES.

Lincoln College,
   Oxford.

PREFACE (1942)

I ACKNOWLEDGE with a great sense of gratitude my debt to two contemporary Chinese philosophers. One is Dr. Hu Shih, now serving his country as ambassador at Washington. The reading of his famous *Chung Kuo Ku Tai Che Hsüeh Shih Ta Kang* (1921) in 1923 was an immense stimulus, and the second reading of it later suggested to me the necessity for studies in the development of the language of logic in Classical Chinese. The other is Professor Fung Yu-lan, whose *Chung Kuo Che Hsüeh Shih* (2 vols.) became another landmark in my philosophical education. Since the first volume of this work has been translated by Professor Derk Bodde, working in collaboration with the author, I also owe a debt to Dr. Bodde, which I gratefully recognize. It is inevitable and right that reference should be made to his book, *A History of Chinese Philosophy* (1939, Peiping and London), for there is no other book for the English reader to compare with it; but its value to me has been more of a general nature than of a kind to warrant an accusation of plagiarism. Yet here, as in the case of other translators, it has been my pleasure to salute from time to time *le mot juste*, and to substitute it for my own less felicitous rendering.

There is only one passage which I have taken word for word from another translator. It is Chapter XXXII in Dr. Arthur Waley's *The Way and its Power*, and I thank him and his publishers for the privilege of using that rendering. I am also grateful to Messrs. Probsthain for their permission to use Dr. Duyvendak's *Lord Shang*, and Dr. W. K. Liao's *Han Fei*, vol. i. My original intention was to take the translations I needed word for word, for that seems the only respectful course to take. I found, however, particularly in Dr. Liao's work, as to a less extent in Dr. Duyvendak's, certain roughnesses of expression which seemed better emended. I apologize, therefore, for taking these liberties with their work. If it had been feasible to communicate with them, the one in Holland and the other in China, I would have done so.

No English scholar can work in the field of Classical Chinese without owing a great debt to James Legge, the first Professor of Chinese in the University of Oxford, for his monumental labours in translating ten out of the thirteen Confucian Classics.

With regard to the innumerable debts to Chinese commentators and editors of all ages, I can only make a general recognition. And yet there are three to whom I owe most of all: Juan Yuan at the beginning of the nineteenth century for his edition of the Thirteen Confucian Classics, Sun Yi-jang at the end of the nineteenth century for his edition of the *Mo Tzu Book*, and Ma Hsü-lun in this generation for his edition of the *Chuang Tzu Book*.

E. R. HUGHES.

OXFORD,
    January 1942.

CONTENTS

PART ONE

FROM TRIBAL RELIGION TO PHILOSOPHICAL INQUIRY

PART TWO

REASONING ABOUT ETHICS AND POLITICS BECOMES A HABIT

PART THREE

THE RISE OF MATERIALISTIC UTILITARIANISM AND THE CONFUCIANIST REPLY

PART FOUR

ANALYTICAL MINDS AT WORK ON THE PROBLEMS OF KNOWLEDGE

PART FIVE

THE INDIVIDUALISTIC PHILOSOPHY OF THE TAO EXPERTS

PART SIX

FOUR DIFFERENT ATTEMPTS AT A SYNTHETIC PHILOSOPHY

PART SEVEN

RELIGIOUS PHILOSOPHIES OF EDUCATED MEN

PART EIGHT

THREE HAN CONFUCIANISTS DOGMATIZING

INTRODUCTION

THERE is something particularly appropriate about an 'Everyman' volume on Chinese Philosophy, for the Chinese people and their tradition have been impregnated with a sense of Everyman. It is true that there has been, and still is to-day, a great deal of virtuosity in their approach to matters of learning; a Chinese scholar can be ineffably highbrow. But from a quite early date in Chinese history most thinkers and scholars never succeeded in forgetting that the ordinary man, and in particular the peasant, is a vitally important member of the Great Society. So also with the exquisite art of painting in China, and with that other great art which the modern West tends to ignore, that of ritual in daily life; the plain man in the plainness of his humdrum life has always claimed in China a good share of the expert's attention. It is the Chinese sense of a common humanity; and in spite of all the inhumanities which have been perpetrated by proud aristocrats and conscienceless money-makers, this sense continued to bear fruit, has indeed been an integral part of that common sense and matter-of-factness for which the Chinese people have become famous throughout the world.

There is another aspect in which an 'Everyman' is particularly appropriate. For a very long time, dating as far back as the twelfth century and the Fukien popular printers, public opinion has always been in favour of books being published in a simple form so that the prices might be within the compass of the plain student's purse. Not only so: the later categories of Chinese literary history have been distinguished by a continual succession of 'Collectanea,' as the libraries call them, that is to say, reprints of notable works brought together in fifty, or a hundred, or even many hundreds of uniform volumes. Thus the 'Everyman' series has many counterparts in China, though not one quite so catholic in its devotion to literature in every form, including novel writing and drama.

The table of contents shows a division of this volume into eight parts, with two to four chapters to each part. In these twenty-three chapters the reader will find selections from the writings, or in some half-dozen cases the recorded sayings, of nearly thirty men who lived between the seventh century B.C. and the end of the first century A.D. The number of men quoted might have been a considerably larger one, but it became obvious that the more important thinkers should be allowed to speak for themselves at some length, and the volume not be a medley of rather scrappy quotations.

The period covered is ordinarily described as 'the Classical.' That means that the people who first began to study the development of Chinese civilization saw that in the early phases of it there was a stage which compared with the Graeco-Roman stage in the development of our Western civilization. To call that period 'the Classical,' therefore, enabled people to begin to place 'China' in their minds. In other words, they began to know something about it; for it is only by comparing, by placing the unknown in relation to the known, that we begin to know. This comparing, however, is, as both Western and Chinese philosophers have realized, a ticklish business. One has to be careful, or the result is not-knowledge but a mixture of truth and error, or even a monstrous misconception. And care entails being careful not to use unconsciously an adjective of comparison in two different senses, and in not making one of the things compared unconsciously the standard for the other.

It is a matter then of some moment that as we look round this world of ours we should have a judicious mind as much to the past as to the present. This applies particularly to the three other existent civilizations, those of the Near East, the Middle East, and the Far East, each with its Great Tradition behind it. The 'Everyman' series has realized this, and has taken steps accordingly so that alongside of this present volume of Chinese Philosophy the 'Everyman' reader has material on which to exercise his judicious mind;

he has something to compare. This raises at once the question of 'petrified civilizations,' or rather 'petrifying civilizations.' Is there any true sense in which the civilizations of Turkey and Egypt, India, and China and Japan were petrifying when our modern Western civilization thrust itself on them, and assailed the verity of their Classical traditions?

Our fathers were, for the most part, convinced that there was a real sense, and in the case of China a number of outstanding thinkers there during the last thirty years have conveyed the impression that they also felt the accusation—for accusation it undoubtedly is—to be true in fact. If that it so, there would seem to be a good deal of reason for believing that 'Classical China' has meant something different in the history of the Chinese people from what 'Classical Greece' and 'Classical Rome' have meant in the history of the West; that there was, indeed, in that era a standard set up, conformity to which was maintained for the space of eighteen centuries. On the other hand we have seen, in relation to our modern England and its Graeco-Roman heritage, that an outsider might get a very exaggerated impression of the extent of our conformity to the Classical standard. The real point to be considered is not whether the civilization of western Europe and the civilization of China are comparable in inheriting ancient formative traditions, for they both have them, but whether in the one case the people concerned were susceptible to outside and later influences, and in the other case not.

In this connection historians and others who have studied the Far East have had a good deal to say on China being in an isolated geographical position, and the Chinese people being so much the cultural and intellectual superiors of the peoples within range of contact that they experienced no challenge to their self-satisfaction: that in fact until the nineteenth century there was nothing to make them 'neither sit nor stand, but go.' It is very difficult to know precisely what is meant by this, unless it be that they were isolated from Europe; in which case the reply has to be made that Europe was equally isolated from China and India, and

very nearly as much from Arabia. And as for self-satisfaction, possibly the less we say the better. As a matter of
fact, the whole idea of China's being isolated and impervious to outside influence is plain historical nonsense
until we come to the eighteenth century. Even during the
Ming regime, which Chinese historians have regarded as a
very conservative period, the Jesuit missionaries were given
an official welcome, and two Hanlin doctors were openly
converted to the Christian religion, not to speak of the
Catholic congregations which came into existence in nearly
every province of China.

There is, however, this legitimate contrast to be made
between China and western Europe, these two cultural
areas of great antiquity. In Europe the Christian religion,
coming in from the Semitic country of Palestine, eventually
discredited the later and less inspiring products of Greek
and Roman religion and philosophy, and Christianity
became the dominant educational influence. In China the
amalgam of indigenous religious practice and philosophical
thought called 'Confucianism' was challenged by Buddhism
from India, and from the sixth to the tenth century it was
the foreign faith which was the more esteemed among live-
minded people. It evoked a rich variety of intellectual
response, and in its own way discredited the less inspiring
products of Chinese thought. In the end, however, the
indigenous tradition reasserted its power, proving able to
inspire the Sung scholars to new syntheses of the universe
and man.[1]

The moral then of this discussion is that, taking the whole
course of Chinese history into account, we have to assume
that the Chinese people are pretty much like ourselves.
They have had their ups and downs, bad times as well as
good. If anything, they have been more susceptible to
foreign influence than our Europe has been, and at any rate
were just as much impregnated with foreign blood stocks
as southern and western Europe were. Apart, therefore,
from the inherent improbability of a great civilization being

[1] Cp. my *The Great Learning*, Introduction, Chapter II.

built out of a narrow set of homogeneous elements and going on century after century without any appreciable change, the history of the Chinese people flatly contradicts the notion. The peoples who have been inbred racially and culturally are the retarded peoples, such as the aborigines of Australia. There is, of course, the conservatism of a mainly agricultural community, the attitude to life which distinguishes the French peasant of to-day so markedly from the industrial town dweller in France and England and the United States. But that conservatism is not of a cast-iron kind, either in the West or in the East. And it is an entire mistake for the townsman to think that the countryman's life is less productive of individuality. In China every province very much has its own characteristics, its own cherished names of great men, some of them with special temples in their honour, its own specialities in art and craftsmanship, in some cases in education, its own customs, both good and bad; and this is true of sections of a province, particularly where hill country and plain, or seaboard, come within its borders.

The common sense of this is that human nature is like that, East as well as West. Even primitive communities afford the clearest evidence that man has an incurable tendency to make life as interesting as he can. *Accidia* (boredom and its depression) is not only a sin in Catholic theology; it is also a biological weakness, one which statesmen have so often ignored to the desperate peril of the common weal. And this brings us to another contrast between our western Europe and China. The feudal social order in the one area gave place to a series of competing states, with the result that for the common man life has never for very long been really uninteresting. In fact, the constant wars have made life exciting to a high degree of painfulness. In the other area the stage of feudalism came a millennium and a half earlier, and broke down between the seventh and sixth centuries B.C. There ensued an epoch of the Warring States, and this led eventually to a short experiment in unified bureaucracy, and afterwards by revulsion to a compound of bureaucracy and feudalism which was the beginning of that unique institution, the Chinese State. The point here is that in spite of the country being split for generations on a north and south basis, with barbarians in control of the north, the end was a renewal of unity; and this unity became a solid determination of the people. It was part of the Great Tradition, and, in spite of periods of miserable confusion, there has been political unity in China on a territorial scale which Europe has not seen since the days of Rome. There is no need to look at this accomplishment through rose-coloured glasses and assume, as Marco Polo did from some rather superficial observation, that the Chinese were both more civilized and more blessed with happiness than any other part of the world. Close knowledge hardly sustains any such grandiose claim. On the other hand, the claim that fratricidal disunities as in Europe are a necessary concomitant of cultural vitality is definitely disproved by Chinese experience.

In conclusion, let us take these various angles of approach to China, past and present, and consider them in relation to what is so intimately connected with them, namely, the philosophy of Classical times. We can dismiss in a word the puerile sentimentality that here is some mysterious 'lore of the East,' which the crude, materialistic Westerner should reverentially receive. Neither can we allow the prejudices of insular pride to blind us to the evidences of a great accomplishment, one which may or may not be of the same ultimate value to the world as Homer and Aeschylus and Euripides on the one hand, and Socrates, Plato, and Aristotle on the other, but which is certainly not disqualified from attention because its methods of expression and inquiry, as also some of its affirmations, were different in grain. Here are matters for comparison with a judicious mind, the human-hearted mind, as China's most honoured teacher, Confucius, would urge.

In doing this a little detachment is necessary from our prepossessions about reason and its slow but sure development. Part of the value of studying Classical Chinese philosophy comes from the fact that whereas the Greek and Roman philosophers have been subtle and discerning along certain lines, their opposite numbers in China, speaking chronologically, may appear rather stupid and undiscerning on those lines. But along certain other lines the Chinese may have been quick to see certain facts where the Greeks and Romans suddenly appear to have been curiously slow. Henri Bergson discovered in the twentieth century that the intellect is a tool made and sharpened primarily for practical ends, and not speculative: not a particularly difficult discovery to make, surely! We find this discovery made in China quite early on. Again, religious utilitarianism did not achieve conscious systematic form in Europe until the eighteenth century. In China, one Mo Ti, of the fifth century B.C., worked out such a system. On the other hand, although some Classical thinkers in China used the literary device of the philosophical dialogue, none of them achieved the power with it which Plato displayed, nor, I think, did any one take analysis as far as Aristotle did. The Chinese did not discover the syllogism, and though they made a start in geometrical thinking, they lagged far behind Euclid.

We are, therefore, liable to get jolts as to the levels of rational consciousness which emerge along with new challenges to the social order. And these jolts may be taken as healthy for us, since they save us from the devil of excessive reliance on rational speculation on the one hand, and the deep sea of finding no rhyme or reason in men's experience on the other hand. Thus, for example, with regard to religious utilitarianism, a matter of very considerable moment to the people who believe in 'spiritual values,' it is not only illuminating to recognize this theory at such an early stage in an ancient society. It is also highly instructive to note that as Paley led on to Bentham and Mill, i.e. utilitarianism without the religion, so Mo Ti led on to Shang Yang and the irreligious Legalists. Our confidence is ultimately, therefore, reinforced in the existence of some

order in history, and of our being able one way and another
to get a rational apprehension of it.

IS CHINESE CIVILIZATION BASED MORE ON INTUITION AND ART THAN ON REASON AND PHILOSOPHY?

The Burlington House Exhibition of Chinese Art in 1935,
coming as it did after the admirable introductory work done
by Mr. Laurence Binyon and Mr. Hodson, did a great deal
to create among English people respect and admiration for
China. Literally a new world was opened up before their
eyes; and they were drawn into it by its human magic, by
the sublime austerity of it at one end of the scale, at the
other by its gentle sweetness and subtle responsiveness to
Nature. We had not known that men could feel like that,
and put these translucent emotions into line and colour:
in landscape painting with such convinced devotion and
delight in a bird's-eye perspective. Even those antique
bronzes, the outlandish work of craftsmen living in the
atmosphere of primitive animism, touched a chord of
sympathy and understanding: they revealed such an
exquisite sense of proportion, so bold and imagination held
in such artistic restraint.

This was not, of course, the first time that Chinese art
had touched the imagination of the English people. The
country houses of the eighteenth century were filled with
Chinese cabinets, porcelain, and paintings, testifying to the
delight with which our great-grandfathers and great-grand-
mothers welcomed these treasures from 'far Cathay.' So
there is no question in the English mind but that the Chinese
people are endowed with superb artistic gifts. And when
we turn to the poetry and painting of the T'ang epoch, the
epoch in which the Chinese themselves take especial pride
and delight, a highly intriguing question arises. Did not
the Chinese people, at this, one of the chief flowering
periods of their genius, arrive more or less consciously at
the decision that the prosaic path of reason was not worth
pursuing: that poetic intuition was the better, as it was

surely the pleasanter, guide to life's meaning? True, the Sung age followed on the T'ang; but was that not because there must be a good hard core to all sensibility, and the way to treat that necessity is to get a good, plausible system of dogma fixed up and imposed, and so be free to devote the higher energies to the refinements of life, as the Chinese did in the Ming and Ch'ing epochs? The luxury art of these later ages points to a cultivated ability to enjoy the infinite variations of artistry, whether those were revealed in the glorifying of silk and clay, of precious stone and wood, the raw materials of Nature, or in refinements of manners trimming and lacquering the rough surfaces of human relationships. Even the prosaic business of letter writing must be made to assume elaborations of style, so that it mattered less what a man said than how he said it.

And when we turn back to that early formative age, the Classical era, was it not the Taoist philosophers, the main source of inspiration for the great T'ang poets, who followed the artist's instinct as against the scientist's, who scorned all knowledge that did not come from the illumination of intuitive appreciation? Did they not show by their ribald attacks on the serious Confucianist uplifters that their pompous rationalization of society was a mere glozing of the bandit instinct for getting all one could for oneself? And is not that the real Chinese attitude, the individual worth more than society, and the individual discovering himself not by reason but by intuition?

It can be argued in this way, and it is significant that from the very earliest days, from the time when the first pieces of evidence appear, artistic power is patently displayed in China. In neolithic geological strata the 'Yang Shao Pottery' has been discovered with wonderful bold yet ordered patterns of decoration, painted with that complicated tool, a hair brush. A later variation is the 'Black Pottery,' so different that experts surmise a separate cultural influence at work. Then comes the overwhelming mass of evidence of the Bronze Age (late) culture in the heart of the Yellow River area. The excavations made at An Yang by the Academia Sinica from 1932 onwards have brought to light tens of thousands of artifacts, the nature of which demonstrate the existence of a highly developed culture in this ancient seat of Chinese civilization.[1] Here we find the archaeologist confirming the existence of a society in the second millennium B.C. which must, judging from the mere wealth of its super-chieftain, have had some sort of political organization extending over a wide area. What type of organization that was the archaeologists cannot so far tell us; we have to turn to the historians and the earliest documents on which they can set their minds. These are the writings of the Chou era authors, whom we find ascribing the feudal characteristics of their own time to an earlier Hsia regime, and back beyond that to the age of Yao and Shun, traditionally dated as 2357–2206 B.C.

The term 'formative' is very popular to-day in discussions of cultural origins: a useful term, since it recognizes that apart from extremely shattering events the accomplishments of an earlier age have a formative effect on the succeeding age, and so on all succeeding ages. Now the question before us is to what degree the Shang cultural accomplishment may be taken as formative in the development of Chinese civilization. Here was a community depending quite largely on agriculture, having domesticated the sheep and the ox and the horse and the dog: a community with special quarters in the township for bronze workers and bone workers, using writing for the recording of the oracles which they so constantly sought from on high. With their ancestor-worshipping minds and their observations of the heavens and consequent awareness of chronological times, it is even probable that these super-chieftains had started recording political events. There is a good deal to lead us to believe that the Shang Chinese were more culturally developed than the Chou border clans from the north-west who overran them in the twelfth or eleventh centuries B.C., and set up their great feudal system. And there is no question but that the Chou culture was an

[1] See Dr. H. G. Creel's *The Birth of China*. Jonathan Cape, 1936.

amalgam of Shang and Chou; so that we very reasonably surmise a hardier, ruder set of tribes or clans being civilized by the richer and more refined tribes they had mastered.

It is, however, only too easy to exaggerate the importance of the earliest known formative influence in a civilization. The problem is one of explaining how a semi-primitive society came to launch out on the highway of civilization. The solution of this problem is not to be sought merely in terms of the discovery of iron on the one hand, or on the other of feudalism leading inevitably to the birth of states and the resultant violence of competition providing the requisite spur to initiative. It is necessary to track down the quality of mind which was able to make creative use of iron, and out of internecine competition produce a determination for peace and order on a culturally stimulating scale. We are, therefore, considering one particular set of the phenomena which historians on the grand scale attempt to get into world perspective. Thus, taking for example the twenty odd major cultures which figure in the pages of these historians, and including the innumerable stunted cultures which belong to the retarded races, we find that it is in the last resort the possession of power in personality which made the former and lack of that power which made the latter. In this connection Mr. Arnold Toynbee's general idea of 'a challenge' successfully met is illuminating: not one challenge only, but a recurrent series of challenges over which a people may prove itself in the first or second instance adequate to the occasion, and then later prove inadequate. There is here no tidy line of demarcation between savage and civilized. The Greeks and Romans were part savage and part civilized, as indeed must be said of the creators and exponents of 'modern civilization.' The phenomenon is almost stupefying in its limitless variety.

What, however, is clear is that the feudal epoch, with agriculture well established and wealth for the first time accumulating on a large scale, is a key-time in the history of any people. There is a transition going on from the old tribal 'closed society' to something strikingly different, and this change reveals itself chiefly when the fixed order of overlord and feudatory and of lord and serf breaks down, and individuals have to deal with a new world in which the old values do not count. The individual under these conditions becomes far more of an individual, far more self-conscious. He gets an image of 'himself' clearly in his mind in contrast with his image of 'society,' and these two images take the place of the old comfortable blur in his mind of self-in-society and society-in-self.

It is when this happens that history comes to be made, or not made, as the case may be. And it was in the late Chou era that this took place in China, during the earlier centuries of the period covered by the quotations in this volume. Granted that the Shang culture was on a higher level than that, for example, of the Matabele at the height of their power, and that the An Yang head township was more like Mycenae than Lobengula's kraal, there is still very inadequate evidence that the Shang chiefs possessed the requisite power in personality for the step forward. We have to examine the Chou regime for indications of such power.

There we may leave this problem for the reader to make his own judgment after reading the *ipsissima verba* of the Classical thinkers. Yet as editor I have perhaps the right, as well as the duty, of stating that the longer I have studied this problem in relation to the late-Chou intellectual developments of thought, and the more I have compared these developments with those in the Greek world, the deeper has become my conviction that the first two rungs of the ladder to a higher civilization are the rungs of self-consciousness in the individual, and of the conscious use of reason. It is therefore for the reader to judge whether during the formative period in the history of the Chinese people they did or did not mount these two rungs. From this the reader will be able to go on to make a decision on the question of Art versus Science and Intuition versus Reason. We have to assume on general grounds that if a race gets things out of perspective and devotes its creative

energies too much to art or too much to science, if it relies
too much on intuition or too much on reason, it is not in
a healthy state for moving on to a higher stage of civilization.   And this assumption is supported by the history of
the Chinese people, as by the history of the Greek people.
It is supported in the Chinese case, both positively and
negatively, by its achievements and by its failures, but
it is a grave mistake to suppose that Chinese or any other
civilization could have developed as it did without possessing and using the higher rational powers of the mind.

The Breakdown of the Feudal System and what Followed

A chronological table for the Classical era is included in
this volume, for even an account in outline would demand
too much space.   But it has become increasingly clear of
late years that the study of a people's thought without
reference to their social and economic conditions inevitably
leads to misunderstanding.   Chinese philosophy first came
to birth at the breakdown of the Chou feudal order, and a
word must be added to what has already been said.

The founders of a feudal system are usually wise in their
generation as conquerors of an agricultural population.
They disturb the old order as little as possible, keeping that
population at work in its old haunts with the old family
relationships and old customs.   This the Chou lords did in
the Yellow River basin and its adjacent parts, and before
two generations were over we may surmise that things were
settling down on the basis of custom as king.   The relationship of overlord and lord, and of lord and peasant, was not
one governed by law in the jurist's sense, but by personal
services undertaken on both sides, protection on the one
hand, supply of foodstuffs on the other.   The king had no
jurisdiction outside his own demesne: the lord had power of
life and death over his serfs.   There was no private property
in land, and the holding of a fief had to be confirmed—at
any rate as a formality—at the death of a lord and the

inheritance by his son. The data is very scanty for the Western Chou period (1122?–771 B.C.), but by solid inference we can visualize an aristocratic society welded together by ritual practices of equally religious and political significance. The Royal Fane, where the Chou ancestors were worshipped on regularly recurrent occasions, was a centre of meeting until ancestral temples in the various fiefs assumed more and more importance. From the eighth century onward the kings came under the protection of one great lord after another, who either by alliance or by sheer aggrandizement were able to command the services of minor feudatories and their levies over a wide area.

The gradual collapse of the system covered four centuries, and during those centuries there was increasingly fierce competition between what were to all intents and purposes independent states. Under these conditions time-hallowed custom lost much of its effective moral influence. The code of chivalry remained in force, but it was less and less possible to conceal the treachery and time-serving which went on behind its façade of good principles and good manners. Old families went down, and new families began to come up. The size of the governing unit destroyed the personal relationship. Administration became more and more complicated, requiring the services of more and more expert assistants, men able to keep records and organize departments. Hence the growth of a new class of minister, men of non-aristocratic blood without lands on which they lived. The practice grew up of rewarding them and their heirs with 'townships' which involved no duty of service.

Thus private property in land came into being. Also money came more and more into use with the growth of inter-state trade, and with money capital in the hands of a new class in society, the merchant.

All this, of course, spelt social revolution, a backward-looking society cut adrift from its moorings and forced to look ahead. The effect of this only came home slowly because, for one thing, the divining experts and experts in temple ritual, being the masters of writing and recording, took over the new work of administering. These Ju were probably of Shang descent,[1] and therefore not members of the ruling military caste, nor of the serf class below. They acted as a sort of 'domestic chaplain' in the great houses, and came also to act as tutors to the young lordlings. They were, therefore, both repositories of traditional culture and exponents of new methods of efficiency. In their minds especially did these radical social changes produce new powers of thinking, a new consciousness of the individual. They had to justify the ways of the gods to men and the ways of men to the gods: hence a new technique of reasoning. Confucius, the father of Chinese philosophy, belonged to this class of the Ju.

DEVELOPMENT IN LANGUAGE AND LITERARY COMPOSITION

Writing in Shang times was clearly a numinous art, one of the techniques which medicine men use to give them religious prestige with the chiefs they serve. Under such conditions it is not to be expected that a written language will develop either easily or quickly. In the first Chou period, however, there would seem to have been historiographers at the capital, annalists composing bare records of events, and, an offshoot from the annalists, men who could dramatize some outstanding event and put it down in writing. That is one beginning to literary composition. The other is poetical composition, and we have fortunately in the *Book of Odes* an excellent collection of the early poetry; folk-songs, sacrificial odes, laudatory verses addressed to great lords, and poignant elegies from round about the seventh century, giving voice to the distress in men's hearts over untoward conditions. It was these poets who gave wings to men's powers of self-expression, and in these poems the individual is seen emerging into deeper consciousness of himself. Under stress of emotion this process

[1] Dr. Fu Ssu-nien and Dr. Hu Shih some ten years ago made a thorough survey of the evidence, and came to this conclusion.

acts quickly, particularly when the times create a continual succession of poignant situations.

The grammar of the *Book of Odes* is structurally simple, so simple that one of the chief hindrances to its understanding has been the failure of the Scholars to transport themselves into this semi-primitive atmosphere. Thus *ku*, the main word in succeeding ages for expressing sequence, is not found in this sense in the *Odes*. The word for expressing connection between two sets of events, one earlier and the other later, is *pi*; and the contents point to a religious meaning as the original one. Because a man did such and such, therefore to be sure (*pi*) the gods did so and so. This entails a rudimentary sense of logic, but it is a long way from the logic of a man who not only says, 'Because A happened, therefore B happened,' but also thinks of 'the cause,' and then at last achieves that triumph of philosophical sophistications 'causation' and 'causality.' The same is found with terms expressing comparison. The Chou poets had the full poetic gift of vivid designation by metaphor, and three or four words are found serving as prepositions introducing comparisons, but there is no clear distinction of language as yet between a veritable likeness and a pure figure of speech. Abstract terms are few and far between, and what there are are very simple ones.

By the time Confucius was teaching at the end of the sixth century the idea of 'because' had arrived, though there is not very clear evidence of the use of hypothesis. Comparisons were coming to be distinguished, and there are the beginnings of sustained argument. The main spur, however, to logical thinking and speaking was given by Mo Ti, who came a generation after Confucius. As reference to the quotations from the *Mo Tzu Book* will demonstrate, the language of reason advanced in his day. From that time things began to move quickly, so that in the fourth-century and third-century writers we find a highly conscious use of reason, not to speak of a delight in the use of it. All this was accompanied by refinements in grammar and syntax.

Unfortunately our study of these developments is hampered by the fact that, as the 'Great Society' became increasingly disunited, the smaller states being swallowed up by the larger so that there were in the end fewer than six great states covering the whole area down to the Yangtze, the language became less and less uniform. Local dialects there must always have been, but the new learned, administrators and teachers, in the different centres added to these differences, and extended their scope in the new written expressions.[1] With the First Emperor came a unification of the written language; although this was done by fiat, it lasted, and throughout the Han regime the process of unification continued.

Along with the language development went the discovery of new forms of literary composition. In Confucius's time apparently no one had thought of writing down his thoughts on life and the universe. The Ju had pupils—apprentices they might almost be called—varying in number according to a man's fame and official standing. There was no private teaching, and Confucius in his old age, on his return from his long exile, was probably the first private citizen to have disciples. Thus the record of his teaching comes from his disciples, and the unsystematic nature of the *Analects* demonstrates perfectly the undeveloped state of prose composition. The records of Mo Ti's teaching reveal a very different situation. There one subject at a time is treated, so that we are almost compelled to assume that the disciples who thus collected their master's teachings were responsible for that vitally important instrument of methodical thinking, the title. But when these men lived who were responsible for the quite largely methodical book we possess to-day, is a question. They may have been first generation, second generation, half a dozen generations after Mo Ti's death. Even in the fourth century B.C. teachings were still being recorded without much attention to system, and it is not until Hsun Ch'ing and Han Fei in the third century that we are sure that we have the writings of men who first

[1] Cp. development of the Romance languages in Europe.

decided what they wanted to discuss in writing, and then having written down the title proceeded to discuss it in well-connected arguments. Thus the philosophical essay came into existence in Classical China, destined to be the medium of expression for countless thinkers of later ages.

There were two other developments from the simple recording of a teacher's aphorisms with the questions and answers it provoked. One was the discovery of the philosophical dialogue. This is seen clearly in Chuang Chou's writings (fourth century B.C.), where imaginary characters are presented and most spirited dialogues take place. Also there was Kung-sun Lung with his subtle and involved discussions between himself and an opponent, revealing that quality of high intellectual honesty which Plato so admirably displayed in his dialogues. Later ages, however, were slow to make use of this literary form. The other new literary device was the *chuan* (amplification). A great teacher's recorded words formed the subjects of a disciple's teaching to his disciples. As he expounded he expanded the meaning and scope of the original. The time came when these later disciples wrote down their master's sayings, so that in a number of books we cannot tell at all when the original teacher's words end and his expositor's words begin. Confucius's grandson, Tzu Ssu, apparently was the first man to do this, though in his case it is not a disciple of his who did the recording, but he himself who, inspired by his grandfather's sayings, felt compelled to put down in black and white the new ideas which thus came to him. And then two hundred years or more later another man, who apparently wished to commend Tzu Ssu's teaching to the First Emperor, took the earlier work and added on a great section, whilst yet another hand added an introductory chapter. Thus the amplification, useful as it can be for revealing development of thought, can also, and indeed many times has been, a most fruitful source of confusion.

Space does not permit of dealing with other developments in literary composition during the Classical era, e.g. the rise of a new form of poetry. But in a book so concerned as this with the development of reason, it is impossible to ignore the development of historical composition to the point where Ssu-ma Tan and his son, Ssu-ma Ch'ien, emerge to view with their amazing *Record of History* (*Shih Chi*). It was a miracle of reason to have conceived a book of history as needing to contain, first, records of epochs and their kings and their noted official deeds; secondly, lists of officials, etc., in chronological order; thirdly, studies of great men; fourthly, essays on geography, physical and political, political economy, rituals, and customs; and fifthly, biographies of all the men with any claim to public service or distinction. This, one of the greatest literary achievements of all time and all cultures, was conceived and carried out in the second half of the second century B.C.

FROM RELIGION TO PHILOSOPHY

From Religion to Philosophy is the title of Professor F. M. Cornford's 'Study in the Origins of Western Speculation.' A provocative title to a subject which its learned author deals with in provocative fashion. I was tempted to borrow this title for Part I of this book. As a matter of fact the whole of this volume from one point of view comes under this heading. It shows, as do Plato's writings, and even the *De Rerum Natura* of Lucretius, that men who think hard and deeply, stirred by revolt against current superstitions, do not remain satisfied with negations. Some sort of spiritual philosophy comes to them in response to their persistent questions, and in many cases religion on a higher level takes possession of their souls. One of the most penetrating modern studies of this movement of the mind and soul of man from the old to the new is Bergson's *Double Origin of Morality and Religion*; and it is part of the high value of the work that it keeps before the reader's mind that the old ideas die very hard. They die very hard, yet reason will not be denied; and the result is an amalgam of old and new.

This may truly be said of Chinese Classical Philosophy. From beginning to end of this book, with but very few possible exceptions, the men cited are thinkers who lived in a highly religious social atmosphere. That does not mean a highly ethical atmosphere: very far from it! The moral sanctions of traditional religion were proving ineffectual under the more drastic tests of new conditions. With their new-won sense of individuality these thinkers ranged all heaven and earth and past and present to find a satisfying ratio to existence. The 'accepted' notion, the 'done thing,' had to stand at the bar of the individual's reason and justify itself. If it could not it was *fei* (not true), *pu k'o* (inadmissible).

Confucius was the earliest of these questing individuals whose minds broke out of the traditional mould. Considering how simple was his intellectual approach to the root questions, it must always remain a source of wonder that the more intellectual as more rational minds of Han times were able to entertain respect for him. To some extent the answer to this question must lie in the very fact that he was simple, although to this must be added the fact that he had a genius for asking questions. Something of a Socrates, like him above all in that he proved his honesty by sacrificing everything for truth's sake. Earnest-minded men, therefore, were prepared to take his views on trust, particularly as his quest was mainly one for the type of individual which made the good life in society possible. Perhaps, however, the secret of the continued respect for Confucius lies in the fact that he and his followers after him represented a 'Middle Way.' Professor Fung Yu-lan has urged this strongly in his *Chung Kuo Che Hsüeh Shih*, and it may well be that here the artistic genius of the Chinese people asserts itself, desiring in the intellectual realm expression of a sense of proportion, of balance and subtle harmony. Even in Chuang Chou, the supreme Taoist, with his transcendent power of imagination, there is still this artist's sense of an accord between eternity and this here and now.

This Classical Philosophy, therefore, is not for the most part irreligious or contra-religious in tendency. The main proof of this, I would urge, lies in two realms, the one of history, the other of political philosophy. The historical proof is that when the First Emperor (Ch'in Shih Huang Ti) made the first unification of China, bringing the peace and order men so deeply longed for, his great religiosity could not conceal the fact that unity with its power was purchased at the expense of forcing humanity into hard-set moulds. The First Emperor again and again reminds the man of to-day of Hitler and Mussolini. The Chinese people revolted against this political experiment as blasphemous.

The proof in the field of political philosophy is that Classical thinkers were plainly never able to get far away from the idea of Nature as transcendent. Although they consistently rationalized the old religious concept of a *T'ien* (Heaven) which had a will for men, the meaning of *T'ien*, and even of *Ti* (Earth), retained the idea of a sublime order of the universe, conformity to which was man's duty and happiness. And the remarkable thing is that whilst the idea of *T'ien* was less and less permeated with the idea of personality, it was through this reverence for sublime Nature that human personality was recognized as indispensable for the good life of man in society. Man must obey, but in order to be able to obey he must be free, free to be his true self.

THE TEXTS OF THE WRITINGS CITED

The reader has the right to ask two questions, in the first place whether the texts of the writings cited are to be trusted, in the second whether the translations are to be trusted. The second question will be answered in the next section. With regard to the first, all down the ages emperors and scholars have been great collectors of books: the list of imperial and famous private libraries is an impressive one. Yet the wastage of books has been nothing less than colossal, and even ancient works which were still extant in Sung times are not to be found to-day. We have two works which in particular show the extent of the earlier damage. One is the catalogue of the Imperial Library in the last decade B.C., the other the great Sung thesaurus, the *T'ai Ping Yü Lan*, a vast collection of quotations on every conceivable subject from every possible source. Examination of these two documents shows that more than three-fifths of ancient literature has perished, and the casualties have been worst among the early scientific works. Highly intriguing subdivisions in the Han catalogue are devoted to these, and they have practically all been lost; and thus, incidentally, this phase of early science cannot be compared in adequate detail with the Greek phase.

The causes of the wastage are many. There was the action of climate on paper, which resists well for one to two hundred years, but afterwards begins to get brittle and friable, thus making a manuscript easily destructible unless cherished with very great care. Then there has been the action of political disorder. Again and again capitals have been destroyed by barbarian hordes and rough soldiery, and libraries have gone up in flames, whilst when the First Emperor 'burnt the books' a great deal was lost in the first instance. Also the fortunes of a scholar family would decline, and the later descendants become peasants, so that precious manuscripts mouldered away in some cottage cupboard. But the main cause perhaps has been that fashions in literature change, and what was prized in one generation was despised in another. Scholars did not trouble to have manuscripts copied, and later, after the invention of printing, did not spend money on having them printed.

In view of all these destructive factors the wonder is that so much has survived. For this the catholic literary interests of the scholar class, with their bibliophile propensities, must be taken into account. A book was a book, however heretical it might be, particularly if it had distinction of literary style.   But the main factor has been the early invention of printing, and its vast development in the eleventh and twelfth centuries.   Manuscripts were collated then, and authoritative editions published.

To go back to the Han era (206 B.C.–A.D. 253), there were good scholars both in the first half of it and in the second, and it is through these first two bottle-necks that the ancient writings have come down to us.   These scholars had to deal with manuscripts the majority of which were made of slips of bamboo with the characters scratched on with a stylus. A bundle of slips made a chapter, a number of bundles a book.   The court librarians found that many of these manuscripts had their slips in disorder.   There are also indications that they found ancient characters with which they were not familiar.   The original text of a manuscript may well have got altered then.   Add to that the possibility that 30 B.C. was four and a half centuries distant from Confucius's death, and that we do not know when the *Analects* and the *Mo Tzu Book* and many of the others actually got put together, nor how far the amplifiers intruded their own ideas.   It is plain, therefore, that for all our cited authors allowance must be made for a real margin of error.   Finally, the copyists have to be taken into account.   They were not good scholars—copying was not a well-paid profession—and Classical works are sown with passages in which a character has obviously been miscopied.

On the other hand, there has been a prodigious amount of work in textual criticism, done in different ages from the Han to the Ch'ing dynasty (A.D. 1644–1911).   The great part of it was concentrated on the Confucian Classics, but by no means all, and in the last dynasty not only was the science of textual criticism enormously improved, but also special attention came to be paid to the non-Confucian philosophers.   All the texts, therefore, with but one or two exceptions, have been milled over again and again by men of great learning, some of whom have also been men of keen critical ability.   With regard to the Confucian Canon, on five occasions between A.D. 252 and 1803 [1] it was solemnly inscribed on stone tablets in the capital, and on two other occasions in other places. This was not done without much heart-searching among the leading scholars as to the exactly right characters to be inscribed.

The exceptions, the texts of which do leave a very great deal to be desired, are the writings of the Epistemologists (see Part Four). In their case, since to the comparative mind they are so enormously important, not only have they had to be included among the other quotations, they have also had to be edited with a greater sense of freedom. There is, therefore, on the one hand this added margin of error in the translation of them, though I need hardly assure the reader that I have made special efforts in making my emendations that they should improve the essential coherence of the argument. In all other cases where emendation has seemed to be required I have gone to the commentators and with very few exceptions have found suggestions there which saved me from trusting my own unaided judgment.

WITH REGARD TO THE TRANSLATIONS

The main part of this book is composed of translations for the correctness or incorrectness of which I must be held responsible. The reasons for my putting myself in this perilous position are (a) my dissatisfaction with the standard translations, either from the point of view of accuracy, or from the point of view of vagueness of language; (b) the fact that I have in the course of lecturing in my university had occasion to translate a number of the passages which needed to be included. In making these translations I had been to some pains in working out the principles which it seemed to me should govern translators of Chinese. Thus in undertaking an 'Everyman' volume I had the opportunity of putting these principles more strictly to the test.

[1] In A.D. 252 the Five Classics were inscribed, in 1803 the Thirteen Classics.

These principles—which in my own mind I call the rules of the game—are as follows:

1. That generally speaking, if an author is worth quoting it must be assumed that he had something clear enough in his mind to say, and that it seemed to him very important that it should be said.

2. That very often the key to a thinker's mind is to be found by asking what are the ideas which strike him most forcibly as needing to be exposed and corrected.

3. That until he be proved guilty an author should be held innocent of glaring inconsistencies, and even if such occur justice demands investigation into the reliability of the text; in other words, the chances are that writings which have been cherished for so long contain sense and not nonsense.

4. That in expressing his centrally important new ideas a thinker has to use language counters which are the current coin of interchange of thought, but which may quite easily be inadequate to express the full glory of his thought, and therefore the translator must look out for new nuances of meaning in these current counters.

5. That language is developing all the time, a statement particularly true in the case of Classical Chinese, in which new forms of grammatical expression gave expression to new powers of reasoning, and therefore it is vitally important for a translation to avoid anachronisms, i.e. expressions which are characteristic of a later stage of rational consciousness, a higher power of logical expression than the author in question had achieved.

6. That care must be exercised in seeing that full justice is done to the special meanings that the different schools of thought gave to special terms, and in distinguishing between the common use of a term and its use as a technical term.

These rules of the game are, of course, mere precautionary common sense. They are also, however, unfortunately counsels of perfection, and I hasten to add that I do not for a moment claim to have been able to apply them with

unerring precision and so been able to translate with unerring accuracy. For one thing, there are my own failings
in scholarship and in command of the resources of English;
for another the nature of the material does not allow of
perfection. This is revealed in two ways in particular.
First, if we could date all the extant works of the late-
Chou, and distinguish the hand of the amplifier at all points,
we should be in a position to distinguish the different stages
of development in the language of self-conscious reasoning.
Secondly, the key concepts of a long-established society's
language do not quite fit any term in the other language.
As Professor Malinowski shows so brilliantly in his appendix
to Ogden and Richard's *The Meaning of Meaning*, to understand one term fully it is almost necessary to study the whole
culture and physical environment of the people who coined
it. It is, of course, open to the translator to confess the
impossibility of translation, and to write the alien word in
its romanized form, and then in a glossary give suggestions
as to its meaning. But not only is this method an inconvenience to the reader, but also it does not lead to accuracy
of impression. A term such as *te*, which I have translated
in many passages as 'power in personality' or 'virtue' (in
the sense of 'by virtue of . . .'), may in some writers be given
a more mystical twist to its meaning, in other writers a
more ethical. Or again, there is *jen*, which has been
very frequently translated 'benevolence,' but which Dr.
Bodde, I think much more happily, translates as 'human-
heartedness'; for myself I should prefer 'man-to-man-
ness,' but this is too clumsy for a term which is in such
constant use.

Another difficulty arises from the fact that the author of
a statement, speaking from the standpoint of familiarity
with his own culture, a familiarity also to be assumed in
his readers, can afford to write with a succinctness which
a foreign reader two thousand years later finds entirely
cryptic. The translator, being more versed in that culture
and its language, may find the passage quite clear and understandable. The practical question then is how to incon-

venience the unversed reader as little as possible, but at the same time give the requisite explanatory addition. I think the reader will agree with me that masses of footnotes in a work which is meant for general reading, and not for close language study, are an abominable inconvenience. I have, therefore, adopted the device which the great sinologist, James Legge, used in his famous translations of the Classics. I have added in round brackets these 'paddings' to the actual text. To the best of my ability they are reliable, and if they contain certain slight errors, not, I trust, gross ones, the general reader has at any rate not been misled so badly as he would have been by the inclusion of paddings into the text, and not marking them in any way.

With regard to the rhythm of an author's style and of the progression of thought in an argument, these Classical Chinese authors have a rhythm which is different from that of writers of English. It proceeds more by short steps, and less by a flow of thought which, as it turns and eddies, is marked by commas and semicolons leading to full stops and the end of the paragraph. In order to mark this rhythm as best may be, I have used the device of the colon, and must confess that as the work of translation went on, it seemed to me very much to justify itself. But in this matter of punctuation the reader will kindly remember that Classical texts have been, like Greek texts, unpunctuated in the ordinary sense. A translator has constantly to make up his mind where the division of a sentence comes, and although there are many guides in good editions and commentaries of a text, yet there is room at a number of points for differences of opinion. When it comes to a question of using a comma or a semicolon, the guiding notion of rhythm and tempo of thinking has to be taken into account. The question is here largely one of relative complexity of thought, and if the reader is interested in this matter he may compare the translations in the earlier part of the book with those of Tung Chung-shu and Wang Ch'ung at the end.

In conclusion, the principles used in the selection of passages are as follows:

1. That a thinker's main achievements of thought should be represented.

2. That a quotation should, if possible, be long enough to show not only what the man thought, but also the way in which he arrived at his conclusions.

3. That each man should be set forth not only as himself, but also as representing a stage in intellectual development.

In trying to work on these three principles I encountered the difficulty of dealing with works such as the *Analects*, in which the material was for the most part not grouped in methodical fashion. In those circumstances it seemed by far the juster plan not to quote the material in that shape, and thereby convey the impression that a man's mind was a mere hotch-potch of unrelated ideas. I have, therefore, ventured to group the various sayings under my own headings. In doing so, I have made it clear where these titles are mine and where they are the original titles or those which early in the history of the work concerned came to be attached as titles.

Finally, in my judgment, there are valuable discoveries to be made out of the following outstanding ideological features of Classical Chinese Philosophy.

1. The chief key to the mystery of the universe, and man in it, is personality, and personality at liberty through obedience to the Given in life and to the Eternal; and this is the key to ethical achievement and the achievement of the good life in society.

2. As Tzu Ssu discovered and others later emphasized, especially Chuang Chou (and cp. Huai Nan Wang, see *Huai Nan Wang Lieh*, c. 1, *init.*), the universe of matter and so of space and time is relative to a universe of the spirit; and man *knows* this by the leap of his imagination beyond the bounds of physical space and time. This is a better starting-point than Descartes' *Cogito, ergo sum*.

3. As the *Tao Te Ching* and Chuang Chou emphasize, there is a This-knowledge and a That-knowledge, and the

temptation is to try to know only by the That path.   Therefore we need always to remind ourselves of the This path,
though in the last resort the two paths, the scientific and the
religious, are both necessary.

ADDENDUM (1954)

On p. xxx there is a reference to a man of the First
Emperor's time (third century B.C.) as adding to the *Chung
Yung*; cp. also p. 32.   Since 1942 I have made further
studies in Mid Han and Later Han literature, and the
second half of the *Chung Yung* seems to me now to be shot
through and through with evidence pointing to that part
being composed much later, viz. in the first century A.D.
in the time of the first two emperors of Later Han.   So also
with regard to *The Great Learning* (cp. p. 88), there may have
been some such text-book made in the fourth century B.C.,
but I doubt if, in its completed form, *The Great Learning*
existed before Later Han.

BIBLIOGRAPHY

PART ONE

The Chinese Classics, a translation with Critical and Exegetical Notes, Prolegomena, and Indexes by James Legge. 5 vols. in 8 parts. Oxford. 1893–5. Vols. i and iv.
The Book of Songs by Arthur Waley. Allen & Unwin. 1937.
Analects of Confucius by Arthur Waley. Allen & Unwin. 1938.
The Odes of Confucius by Cranmer Byng. Wisdom of the East Series.
The Sayings of Confucius by Lionel Giles. Wisdom of the East Series.
The Conduct of Life by Ku Hung Ming. Wisdom of the East Series.
Analects of Confucius by W. E. Soothill. World's Classics. 1937.

PART TWO

The Ethical and Political Works of Mo-tze by Y. P. Mei. London. 1929.

PART THREE

The Book of Lord Shang by J. J. Duyvendak. Probsthain's Oriental Series. London. 1928.
The Chinese Classics by James Legge. Vol. i.
Mencius by L. A. Lyall. London. 1932.
The Book of Mencius by Lionel Giles. Wisdom of the East Series.
Three Ways of Thought in Ancient China by Arthur Waley. London. 1939.
The Book of Filial Piety by Ivan Chen. Wisdom of the East Series.

PART FOUR

History of Chinese Philosophy by Dr. Fung Yu-lan, trans. by Dr. Derk Bodde. Vol. i. Allen & Unwin. 1937.
The Great Learning and The Mean-in-action by E. R. Hughes. Dent. 1942.

PART FIVE

The Way and its Power, a study of the *Tao Te Ching* by Arthur Waley. Allen & Unwin. 1934.
The Sayings of Lao Tse by Lionel Giles. Wisdom of the East Series.
Taoist Teachings of the Book of Lieh Tzu. Wisdom of the East Series.
Chuang Tzu—Mystic, Moralist, and Social Reformer by H. A. Giles. Shanghai. 1926.
Musings of a Chinese Mystic by Lionel Giles. Wisdom of the East Series.
Three Ways of Thought in Ancient China by Arthur Waley.

PART SIX

The Works of Hsün Tse by Homer Dubs. Probsthain's Oriental Series. 1928.
Han Fei Tzu by W. K. Liao. Probsthain's Oriental Series. 1939.
Three Ways of Thought in Ancient China by Arthur Waley.
The Yi King by James Legge. Sacred Books of the East. Vol. xvi. Oxford. 1882.

PART SEVEN

Tao, the Great Luminant, Essays from Huai Nan Tzu by Evan Morgan. Shanghai. 1933.

PART EIGHT

Lun Heng. Miscellaneous Essays of Wang Ch'ung. Translated by A. Forke. 2 vols. London. 1907.

B.C.	*Chinese Historical Events*	*Confucianists*	*Mohists*
c. 1500	MID SHANG DYNASTY		
1100	CHOU DYNASTY King Wen King Wu		
1000	Duke Chou		
900			
800	722. Beginning of the Ch'un Ch'iu (Spring and Autumn Period)	The *Odes, Changes,* and some books of the *History* produced during these centuries	
700			
600			
	536. First Written Law Code	Confucius (551–479)	
500		Confucius's im- mediate dis- ciples	Mo Tzu (c. 479– c. 381)
	481. End of the Ch'un Ch'iu Period	Tseng Tzu	
400	403–221. Warring States Period	Mencius (372?– 289?)	
300			
	255–207. CH'IN DYNASTY	Hsün Tzu (c. 298–c. 238).	Mohist Epistemologists
	221. Unification of China		
200	206–A.D. 220. HAN DYNASTY	Tung Chung- Shu (179?– 104?)	
	140–87. Emperor Wu		
		136. Confucian- ism made orthodox	
100 A.D.	Imperial Catalogue (c. 30–10 B.C.)		
		Liu Hsin (d. 23) Pan Ku (32–92) Wang Ch'ung (d. c. 97)	
100			

Taoists	Dialec-ticians	Legalists	Yin-Yang and Five Forces	Greece [and Rome]	India
					c. 1400–1000 Composition of the Rig-veda
					The Upani-shads (*c.* 600)
				Pythagoras (*c.* 530)	Gautama Buddha (*d.* ? 544)
Yang Chu				Heraclitus (*c.* 500)	
				Socrates (*c.* 470–399) Plato (427–347)	
Chuang Chou (369?–286?)	Hui Shih Kung-sun Lung	Shang Yang (*d.* 338) Shen Pu-hai Shen Tao Han Fei	Tsou Yen	Aristotle (384–322) Epicurus (341–270)	
Compilers of *Tao Te Ching*					
Huai-nan Wang (*d.* 122)				Cicero (106–43)	
				Seneca (*d.* 65)	

PART ONE

FROM TRIBAL RELIGION TO PHILOSOPHICAL INQUIRY

CHAPTER I: THE INITIAL STAGE

A. THE OLD ORDER CHANGING

1. *The 'Book of Odes.'*

A collection of three hundred odd poems, supposed to have been selected by Confucius from some three thousand poems current in the various states. They are a mine of information on the Chou order of society and reveal amongst other things the poignant distress of mind which that order caused in those who suffered under it. As the Introduction has outlined, the old feudal system changed vitally with the growth of the big states and the decline of the royal supremacy. Under these conditions, at any rate by the eighth century, a new power of poesy came into existence, something other than the stately sacrificial odes in commemorative praise of ancestors—the poetry of the nobility —something more individual than simple country rhymes dealing with courtship and marriage. Men—and women too—found themselves caught in an evil net; and their cries to Heaven got no answer.

> Out into the darkness I go,
> Sad my heart as sad can be:
> Bitter my poverty and want,
> For no man recks of my distress.
> Can these things be?
> 'Tis so, Heaven's veritable deed;
> And man has naught to say.
>
> *Kuo Feng*, iii. 15.

> I look beseechingly to Heaven,
> But find no pity there for me.
> For long no peace has been our lot:
> Heaven grinds us on this whetstone.
>
> . . .
>
> *Ta Ya*, iii. 10.

1

Alas, my son, that you
  Should not distinguish ill from good.
Have I not led you by the hand
  And pointed at the thing to know?
Have I not named it to your face
  And held you sharply by the ear?
Forsooth you say, 'I do not know,'
  You who have children in your arms.
You do not know the people starve!
  Full early have you known, yet do not act.

·   ·   ·   ·

Alas, my son, to you
  Have I not taught the ways of old?
Would you might listen to my words
  And ere it be too late repent.
'Tis Heaven that makes your way so hard
  And brings destruction on your land.
See then examples near at hand,
  No double mind is found in Heaven:
Let but your inward power (*te*) go back,
  And all your people suffer loss.

                                        Ta Ya, iii. **2.**

South Mountain with its beetling crags,
  Its massive height before our eyes!
So the Grand-Master's might and power
  Hold all men's eyes in trembling awe.
Our heart's distress is like a fire,
  The lightest word we dare not speak.
Whilst you [1]—it recks not you,
  The common weal has reached this pass.

South Mountain with its beetling crags,
  Rank foliage on its every slope.
The Grand-Master in his fearful might
  Spreads dire injustice through the land.

[1] The 'you' is addressed to Yin, the Grand Master. Each stanza has
this change from the third to the second person.

Calamity and woe from Heaven abound:
  Death and destruction hand in hand!
And you, our curses in your ears,
  Repent not, nor bewail your deeds.

This Yin, great officer of state,
  The prop and shield of sovereign Chou,
To hold the balance in the land
  That near and far may have one mind,
The Son of Heaven lack no support,
  And men be saved from devious paths.
Unpitying Heaven! Against all right,
  'Tis Thou hast brought us all to ruin.

.   .   .   .

Unjust, unjust the might of Heaven,
  To bring on us this black assize:
Unpitying, unpitying indeed,
  To lay on us this monstrous guilt.
O that there were true knights at hand,
  To ease our hearts, we common folk:
O that you knights would give us peace
  And banish wicked hates afar!

Hsiao Ya, iv. 7.

2. *The 'Book of History.'*

The *Shu Ching*, so well known in the West as the *Book of History*, but more properly entitled the *Scripture of Documents*, has amongst scholars to-day lost much of the religious and historical authority it once had.   The probability is that none of it was written until the Chou era, much of it only late in that era, some of it in Han times.   Yet these documents are written in an archaic style and represent certain phases of the early religious mind.   At the risk, therefore, of offending the strict historian's sense of time, two quotations are given.   The two kings, Yao and T'ang, depicted are highly legendary figures, dressed in the clothes of what the late Chou Confucianists and others called 'the Sage-kings.'   Along with the development of this 'lore of the Sage-kings' went new ideas of the state and its possibilities, possibilities which a benevolent 'Heaven' decreed should be brought into being.

The *Ti* [i.e. Yao] said, 'Who can find me a man whom in due time I can raise to work for me?'   Fang Ch'i said,

'Your son and heir, Chu, has shown himself a man of intelligence.' The *Ti* said, 'No, he is perverse and quarrelsome. Is he possible?'

The *Ti* said, 'Who can find me a man to whom I can give the charge of my affairs?' Huan Tou said, 'The Minister of Works, . . . a man of accomplishment.' The *Ti* said, 'No, he can talk (of the great things he is going to do), but when he sets to work, it is the reverse. He has only an appearance of fidelity. The floods assail the heavens.'

The *Ti* said, 'Find me a man, O Ssu Yo! The floods spread everywhere and bring ruin to the country. They spread and embrace the mountains and assault the hills. With their rearing they assail the heavens and distress my subjects. Is there a man capable of taking control?' They all said, 'Kun.' The *Ti* said, 'No, indeed no! He disregards orders and makes a bridge for his clansmen [? to get office].' The Ssu Yo said, 'Test him, and (if he fails) he may be suspended.' The *Ti* said, 'Go in reverence.' For nine years Kun persisted, but without success.

The *Ti* said, 'Find me a man, O Ssu Yo! We have reigned for seventy years. You have the capacity to put my orders into effect. We choose you for the royal throne.' Yo said, 'I have not the power in me. I am unworthy of the throne.'

The *Ti* said, 'Show me one of great or of no repute.' The answer by acclamation was, 'There is a man, unmarried, of the common people, his name is Shun of Yü.' The *Ti* said, 'Yes, I have heard of him. What of him?' Yo said, 'He is the son of a blind man, his father an utter churl, his mother doltish, (his brother) Hsiang arrogant. By filial duty he has been able to live in harmony with them, by slow degrees to bring them to order. Now they have lost the capacity for wickedness.' The *Ti* said, 'I will test him. . . .' (i. 1.)

The King [i.e. T'ang] said, 'Advance, you people, and listen to my words. I, a child, dare not start what is known as rebellion; but the Hsia are loaded with crime, and Heaven has commissioned their destruction. You now are many and you say, "Our lord has no pity for us, making us abandon our crops and cut down the Hsia." These are the words I have heard you say.

'This Hsia chief is a criminal. As I fear the Supreme Ruler [*Shang Ti*], so I dare not but put this matter right. If you say that the Hsia's crimes are no concern of yours, (I say) that the Hsia king has entirely exhausted his people's strength and ruined the Hsia townships. The people are all cold in his service and will not aid him. They say, "When will the sun cease to exist that we with our king may all die." That is what Hsia's power-in-himself [*te*] is like. It is necessary that I should go forth.

'Give your approval to aiding me, your leader [lit. the one man], to administer the punishment by Heaven. I will give you great rewards. You can trust me entirely. I do not eat my words. If you do not obey my solemn call, I shall put you and your children to death. None shall be spared.' (iv. 1.)

3. *Tso Chuan*.

This book has been traditionally ascribed to Tso Chiu-ming, a personal disciple of Confucius. It is, however, increasingly clear to-day that, although tradition is right in basing its main 'facts' on official records, its composition could not have taken place before late in the fourth century B.C. Parts of it must be dated much later. In the incident described in the quotation below the reader need not doubt that the tripods were cast in the year 536 B.C., but it is very possible that there was no correspondence between Shu Hsiang and Tzu Ch'an along the lines stated.

(At Tzu Ch'an's orders) in the third month metal tripods were cast in Cheng State with the scale of punishments inscribed on them. Shu Hsiang[1] sent a letter to Tzu Ch'an, in which he said, 'At first I esteemed you highly Now I do so no more. The former kings weighed all business with a view to right decisions, but they had no criminal statutes. They feared lest there should be a spirit

[1] Another statesman of the day. Tzu Ch'an was responsible for this new departure. A man of strongly rationalist temper, he saw clearly how the old feudal *mores* were neither efficient nor just under the new conditions.

of discussion among the people. Since crime could not be entirely avoided, they blocked the way by being just and united the people by right action. They set before them the requirements of propriety, guarded the sense of honour, and firmly held to a spirit of fellowship.[1] They instituted the different grades of emolument and status, thereby encouraging the tractable, and the different severe penalties, thereby awing the uncontrolled. Fearing the insufficiency of this, they admonished the people by their integrity, stimulated them by their conduct, enlightened them by their devotion to duty, set them tasks in a spirit of reasonableness, exercised oversight with respect (for the common people), and inspected with firmness and gave judgment with rigour. Further, they sought out the best of the wise men, discerning officers, reliable elders, and tender-hearted teachers. Thus it was possible for them to bear the responsibility of the nation, and not cause distress and disorder.

'If the common people come to know that these are hard and fast rules, they will not shun those in authority and at the same time will have contentious minds. They will bring evidence to bear on the wording of the law, hoping by good luck (to evade the penalty). Thus nothing can be done with them. It was when the Hsia regime fell into disorder that the Yü penalties were made, when the Shang regime fell into disorder that the T'ang codes were composed. All three developments came at the end of an age.

'To-day, my lord, you are chief minister in Cheng State, and you have fixed the lines of demarcation, thus instituting a highly questionable form of government with your systematizing of penalties and committing of the law to writing. You aim to tranquillize the people: instead of which are you not creating difficulties? . . . Why should there be a code at all? Once the people know the grounds for contention they will discard all sense of propriety, take their stand on the wording of the law, and dispute to the bitter end over the

---

[1] Confucius's special term *jen* (man-to-man-ness) appears here. Since the composition of this passage probably dates from long after Confucius the translator can justify an anachronistic rendering.

point of an awl. Disorderly litigations will abound, and with them bribery and corruption. The end of your age, my lord, will it not mean the downfall of Cheng State? The gossip goes round, "When a country is on the verge of ruin, it is sure to take endless measures." Does not this apply to you?'

Tzu Ch'an wrote a reply, 'With regard to your words, my lord, I am not a man of talent and I (act for the moment) not for future generations. My aim is to save this generation. Although I cannot obey your behests, I do not presume to forget your great kindness.' (*Duke Chao*, sixth year.)

B. REFINING THE PRIMITIVE ART OF DIVINATION

Study of the Yin Oracles (cp. Introduction, p. xxi) and of the earliest surviving books reveals that divination played a very important part in early Chinese religion. In this respect the Chinese people have shown the same sort of religious mind as all other races. Where they have differed from some has been in their persistent belief in divination long after the development of the individual's power of reasoning. This was largely due to the fact that during the First Han Era Confucianist scholars threw the mantle of intellectual respectability over the more reputable forms of divination. Indeed, as will appear later (cp. c. 18), the most popular book of oracles was changed by later amplifications into a guide to a rational understanding of the universe. Needless to say, there was a strong ethical side to this development.

Here we are concerned with the first manifestations of this moralizing tendency, and, as a first step to that, the systematization of the art of divining. This latter was first brought about by the invention of a stylized system of broken and unbroken lines by which the significance of the divining stalks and tortoise-shell lines could be more accurately discerned. Modern criticism is making it clearer and clearer that, in spite of the traditional beliefs about the great antiquity of this system, it did not come into existence until the first half of the Chou era. The basis of it was eight trigrams:

(1) ☰ (2) ☷ (3) ☳ (4) ☴ (5) ☵ (6) ☲ (7) ☶ (8) ☱

To these at some period not yet known to us was attached a series of symbols:

(1) The heavens, (2) the earth, (3) thunder, (4) wood and wind, (5) water, (6) fire, (7) hills, (8) low [?marshy] ground.

By using two trigrams together, one on the top of the other, a total of sixty-four hexagrams was obtained, with a correspondingly wider range of application for the diviner with his art.   At the dawn of reliable Chinese history these sixty-four hexagrams were in use, and collections of standard oracles were being compiled on the basis of them.   Examples of these appear in a book, the *Yi*, commonly known as the *Book of Changes*, though 'phases' would to my mind be the more correct term.   By the time Confucius lived this book, in its earliest unamplified form, had attained high religious sanctity.   When some hundred to two hundred years after Confucius men began to speak of *Ching* (a Sacred Book, a Scripture), the *Yi* was given the name before any other of the Confucianist Scriptures.

There follow three sets of quotations, the first set showing the original tenor of the book.

Under Hexagram I. ☰   [The oracle of the hexagram taken as a whole.] Supreme blessing: an augury of advantage.

[The oracle of each line according to its position in relation to the others.]

1. A dragon lies hid: there should be no expenditure [?].

2. Discloses a dragon in a field: advantageous to have audience of the great man.

3. A knight goes vigorously throughout the day (but) at night is more or less cautious: danger, (but) not of misfortune.

4. Something leaping up in an abyss: no misfortune.

5. A dragon flying in the heavens: advantageous to have audience of the great man.

6. An overbearing dragon, there is cause for censure (? repentance).

Under Hexagram II. ☷   [The oracle of the hexagram as a whole.] Supreme blessing: an augury of the mare's profit: a knight has the means of advance: at first going astray, later getting (his) advantage from his lord: in the south-west getting friends, in the north-west losing them: an augury of peace: good fortune.

[The oracle of each line.]

1. Treading on cat-ice: solid ice will come.

2. Straight, square, and great: without repeated efforts, in every way advantageous.

3. Concealing its marked appearance [?], (but) containing the possibility of augury: if there be a following up of the king's business, no complete success, (but) brought to a conclusion.

4. Held in a bag: no misfortune, (but) no redounding of glory.

5. A yellow robe: supreme good fortune.

6. A dragon fighting in open country, its blood dark-yellow . . . an unchanging augury of advantage.

And so on for the sixty-four hexagrams, with a separate oracle for each hexagram and one for every line in it, making a total of at least four hundred and forty-eight and probably a much bigger one, since later oracles appear to have got added on to the earlier ones. For the most part the meaning is not clear, nor does study of the commentators bring much light, since from their scholars' standpoint they gave refined symbolic meanings to terms which expressed primitive symbolization. E.g., the 'dragon' in the above oracles is surely a term belonging to early Chinese animism.

The second set of quotations is taken from the *Hsiang Chuan* (Symbolic Amplification). Tradition has ascribed this work, as it has ascribed the rest of the amplifications known as the 'Ten Wings,' to Confucius. Modern critical scholarship makes this tradition more and more dubious. Further, it is doubtful whether this *Symbolic Amplification* was written until some time after Confucius, but it shows the new sense of ethical need which was felt in his day and which he did so much to stimulate.

The symbolism is of a simple kind, each hexagram being regarded as consisting of two trigrams, each of which is a symbolic force acting in relation to the other force in juxtaposition to it. Further, each hexagram here has a name, and this is taken to be symbolically significant. Finally, politico-ethical exhortation is dragged in and borrows the numinous authority of these sacred symbols of 'the heavens, the earth, thunder,' etc.

Under Hexagram X. The heavens ☰ above and low ground ☱ below: this is *Li* [progressive action]: in accordance with this a good governor clearly distinguishes the ranks in society and stabilizes the people's will.

XX. The wind ☴ moving above the earth ☷: this is *Kuan* [making observation]: in accordance with this the former kings made inspections of all parts of the kingdom, made observation of the people, and put their principled teaching into force.

XXX. Brightness duplicated ☲ on ☲: this is *Li* [dispersing]: in accordance with this a great man develops a light which sheds itself over the four quarters of the land.

XL. Thunder ☳ making rain ☵: this is *Chieh* [releasing]: in accordance with this a good governor forgives errors and is lenient over offences.

L. Above wood ☴ there is fire ☲: this is *Ting* [a tripod securely based]: in accordance with this a good governor rectifies the high position he holds and consolidates his commission from Heaven.

XVI. Thunder ☳ bursting out of the earth ☷: this is *Yü* [preparation in advance]: in accordance with this the former kings invented music and made their power of personality [*te*] worthy of worship. . . .

XXIX. Water ☵ on water ☵, flowing everywhere: this is *Hsi K'an* [repeated water—presumably regarded as a great fertilizing influence]: in accordance with this a good governor's unchanging spiritual power is repeatedly in action, in all matters connected with his principles.

LIX. Wind ☴ active on top of water ☵: this is *Huan* [wide dispersion]: in accordance with this the former kings made offerings to (*Shang*) *Ti* [the High Ruler] and established their ancestral temples.

The third set of quotations is from the Fourth Wing, sometimes printed in along with the *Hsiang Chuan* (i.e. the Third Wing). There would appear to be no connection between the two. It is enough to cite the statements—ethical judgments now, not oracles—attached to the lines of Hexagrams I and II.

Under Hexagram I.

1. 'A dragon lies hid and there should be no expenditure': an active [*yang*] influence underlying.

2. 'Discloses a dragon in a field': spiritual power is widely diffused.

3. 'Vigorously throughout the day': going back to the right (moral) way.

4. 'Something leaping up in an abyss': advancing without any retributive misfortune.

5. 'A dragon flying in the heavens': the great man originates.

6. An overbearing dragon, there is cause for censure (? repentance): fullness cannot endure for long.

Under Hexagram II.

1. 'Treading on cat-ice and solid ice about to come': the beginning of the *Yin* influence is coagulation, and the gradual attainment of the Way is (like) ice becoming hard.

2. The movement of the second line is from the straight to the square: 'without repeated efforts in every way advantageous' is the light of the Way in the Earth.

3. 'Concealing its marked appearance, but containing the possibility of augury' is to be timely in one's official advancement: 'if there be a following out of the king's business,' great is the glory of the wisdom shown.

4. 'Held in a bag and no retributive misfortune': to be cautious is not harmful.

5. 'A yellow robe and supreme good fortune': ornament at the centre.

6. 'A dragon fighting in open country': its course is exhausted.

CHAPTER II: NEW POWERS OF REASONING COMING INTO PLAY

A. CONFUCIUS AND THE DISCOVERY OF THE SELF-CONSCIOUS MORAL INDIVIDUAL

Confucius (551–479 B.C.), as the Introduction has shown, is the greatest name in 'Chinese Philosophy.' Yet there is very little in his recorded teaching—such of it as we can rely on as being his and not what later generations thought that he should and must have taught—which gives the impression of his having been a philosopher in the modern or even the Greek sense. He was a great teacher, but not a systematic thinker.

Of the various sources which claim to give details of his life and teaching the *Lun Yü* (lit. discussions and sayings) is the only one which the best Chinese scholarship of the past has allowed to be really authoritative.[1] This book (known in the English world as the *Analects*) is, however, a very composite work, containing material of very varied authenticity. Not much more than half can be really trusted even as good second-hand evidence. Yet the man speaks to us through it with unmistakable personal force.

The records in the *Analects* were made by different groups of disciples' disciples, and finally amalgamated into this one book It shows how in Confucius's day the art of book-making, i.e. of consecutive writing, was far behind the stage it reached by the third century B.C. At first sight there appears to be little or no arrangement in it; but closer examination shows that the different groups of these disciples had different interests, anecdotal, religious, political, and so forth, so that the material has been roughly arranged. But this arranging is so rough that a clear idea of Confucius's teaching cannot be obtained by reading it straight along. For this reason the following quotations are arranged under different headings. The first heading deals with Confucius himself as a man and an influence, for it is under this heading that the main bulk of the *Analects* material comes.

1. *Confucius the Man as People saw Him.*

'At fifteen I set my heart on learning. At thirty I knew where I stood [lit. I took my stand]. At forty I had no more doubts. At fifty I understood the decrees of Heaven.

[1] The quotations under 'The Master said' in the *Mean-in-action* (cp. p. 32) may be taken as equally authoritative, and should be taken into account in an estimate of Confucius's teaching.

At sixty my ear was obedient (to their call). At seventy I followed my heart's [1] desire, for I did not overstep the boundaries of the right.' (ii. 4.)

Someone asked Master K'ung [2] how it was he was not taking part in the administration of the country. The Master said, 'The Book (of Documents) says, "Be filial, only be filial and friendly with your brothers, and you will be helping in the administration of the country." This also is taking part in the administration. . . . It is not necessary deliberately to take part.' (ii. 21.)

A disciple asked what the meaning was of

> O the dimples of her winning smile,
> The lovely black and white of her eyes!
> O fair is she in her plain simplicity!

The Master said, '(In painting) the plain ground first, the colours second.' Tzu Hsia said, 'Then ritual comes second?' The Master said, 'You set me going. Now at last I have someone with whom I can speak of the *Odes*.' (iii. 8.)

'The possession of high station without generosity, the conduct of ritual without reverence, the discharge of mourning duties without grief, these are things I cannot bear to see.' (iii. 26.)

'It is human-heartedness in a place which makes it beautiful. If a man does not elect to live in a human-hearted place, how can he become wise?' (iv. 1.)

The Master said, 'In the morning to hear the Way, in the evening to die: there's nothing wrong about that.' [3] (iv. 8.)

The Master said, 'Shen! My way has one string which threads it all together.' Master Tseng [i.e. Shen] agreed, and when the Master had gone out and the disciples asked

---

[1] *Hsin* more often to be translated as 'mind.' The early Chinese psychology.

[2] K'ung was Confucius's surname. 'Confucius' is the seventeenth-century Jesuit missionaries' Latinization of *K'ung-fu-tze* (Master K'ung).

[3] Sometimes nothing but the homely punch of colloquial speech gives the right feel of Confucius's thinking. And that was Confucius with no affectation about him, when speaking to people immensely candid, and when he did not know refusing to be drawn.

what this meant, he replied, 'The Master's Way is simply this, to be undeviating in his reciprocity.' (iv. 15.)

(The disciple) Tzu Kung said, 'The Master's views on the fine externals of culture we often have the privilege of hearing, but not his views on man's nature or the ways of Heaven.'[1] (v. 12.)

When the Master (in exile) was in Ch'en, he said, 'We must go home, we must go home. My children [i.e. disciples] there are ambitious and careless. Versed as they are in the fine externals of culture, they do not know what makes for (moral) judgment.' (v. 21.)

The Master said, 'In a hamlet of ten households you would certainly find somebody as conscientious and trustworthy as I am, but not one as devoted to learning as I am.'[2] (v. 27.)

The Master said, 'For a man to live he must be upright. If he is not upright and keeps alive, it is a stroke of luck in escaping (death).' (vi. 17.)

The Master said, 'I am a transmitter and not a creator. I believe in and have a passion for the Ancients. . . . In silence I get to know: I keep on learning without being satiated: I go on teaching without becoming wearied. What more is there to be said of me? . . . That I have not fully cultivated the spiritual power in me, that I have not fully expounded what I have learnt, that I have been unable to visit just men of whom I have heard, that I have been unable to reform bad men of whom I have heard: these are the things which make me unhappy.' (vii. 1.)

The Duke of She asked Tzu Lu about Confucius, but Tzu Lu made no reply. The Master said, 'Why did you not say something about this being the kind of man he is: in his ardour forgetting to eat, happy in forgetting his

[1] There was plainly an inner core of sensitive shyness about Confucius. He did not speak easily on deep subjects. The prevailing opinion among Chinese scholars to-day is that he was not religiously minded. To me this is very doubtful, although it is clear that he revolted against much of the religion of his day.
[2] There can be little question but that what Confucius meant by learning was learning about the past, learning the principles and practice of ritual, and careful study of good poetry. Cp. Introduction for the extent of literature in his day.

misery, and not knowing that old age is close at hand.'
(vii. 18.)

The Master never spoke of prodigies, feats of strength,
political disorders or spirits [? miracles].   (vii. 20.)

The Master said, 'Heaven begat the power-in-me [*te*].
What is Han T'ui [1] to me?'   (vii. 22.)

The Master fished with a hook but not with a net, and
when fowling did not shoot sitting birds.[2]   (vii. 26.)

There were four things which the Master was set on
eradicating [? in himself]: a biased mind, arbitrary judgments, obstinacy, and self-centredness.   (ix. 4.)

The Master said, 'If, for example, a man is making a
mound of earth and stops short by one basketful of completing it, I stop also.   If, for example, the ground is still
level with only one basketful tilted on to it, but he is going
on with the work, then I also go to it.' [3]   (ix. 18.)

> The beauty of the cherry blossom!
> But its branch springs back from my hand!
> Do I not think constantly of you, (my love)?
> But your home is too far away (for me to see you).

The Master said, 'He did not really think of her.   (If he
did,) how was it her home was too far?'   (ix. 30.)

At home in his village his manner was unassuming like
a man who had no gift of speech; but in the ancestral
temple [? of the Duke] and at court he spoke easily although
with care. . . .[4]   (x. 1.)

(The disciple) Chi Lu asked how the spirits of the dead
and the other spirits should be served.   The Master said,
'If you fail to serve men alive, how can you serve their
spirits?'   Tzu Lu then asked about death, and the Master
replied, 'If you do not understand life, how can you
understand death?'   (xi. 11.)

---

[1] According to tradition, at one time when Confucius and his disciples
were in exile, this official sent soldiers to deal with them, and Confucius
was in serious danger of being killed.
[2] Cp. Mencius, who stressed the principle of the close season.
[3] One mark of teaching genius.
[4] In this Book x the desire to make a sage of him is very apparent.   He
is portrayed in all sorts of stained-glass attitudes, but this one reference
looks true enough.

The head of the Chi family was richer than Duke Chou ever was and yet (the disciple) Ch'iu collected his imposts for him and made them larger and larger. The Master said, 'He is no disciple of mine. My children, you have my permission to beat the drum and attack him.' (xi. 16.)

Tzu Kung asked, saying, 'How about the men who are liked by all their fellow villagers?' The Master said, 'They won't do.' 'Then how about the men who are hated by all their fellow villagers?' The Master said, 'They won't do. They do not come up to the level of the men who are liked by the good and hated by the bad.' (xiii. 24.)

The disciple Kung was prone to criticize people. The Master said, 'What an admirable person he must be! For myself I have no leisure for this.' (xiv. 31.)

Tzu Lu was spending the night at Shih Men, and the gate-keeper asked him where he came from. He answered that he came from Confucius's (house). The gatekeeper said, 'He is the man, isn't he, who knows that it cannot be done and yet goes on doing it.' (xiv. 41.)

Chang Chu and Chieh Ni were at work together plough-ing when Confucius came that way and sent Tzu Lu to inquire about the ford there. Chang Chu asked Tzu Lu for whom he was acting as driver, and he replied that it was Confucius. 'What, Confucius of Lu State?' 'Yes,' said Tzu Lu, to which the other replied, 'He knows where the ford is.' [1] Tzu Lu then asked Chieh Ni, and he asked Tzu Lu . . . whether he was not a disciple of Confucius. Tzu Lu replied that he was, whereat Chieh Ni said, 'This swelling flood (of anarchy) spreading over the whole country—no one can change it. As for you, you put yourself under a leader who merely withdraws from the common ruck of men. You had much better put yourself under one who withdraws from the world altogether.' With this he fell to covering up the seed. Tzu Lu went and told the Master. He sighed and said, 'It is no good

---

[1] Book XVIII is clearly a later compilation showing a romancing tendency. This remark here would seem to mean that since he is a sage he knows everything.

to try and herd with birds and beasts. If I cannot live amongst my fellow men, what can I live with? If the Way prevailed in the Great Society, there would be no occasion for me to try to change it.' (xviii. 6.)

2. *Confucius's Preoccupation with the Individual.*

(a) *His Careful Study of the Individual.*

The disciple Tsai Yü used to sleep during the day. The Master said, 'Rotten wood is no good for carving. . . . What is the use of reproving him? . . . In the beginning I used to listen to what people said and trust them to act. Now I both listen to what people say and observe what they do. It was my experience with Tsai Yü which made me change.' (v. 9.)

The Master said, 'So! I have never seen any one[1] who could see his own faults and press the charge home in his own breast.' (v. 26.)

The Master said, 'I have never seen a man who was really resolute.'[2] Someone said that there was Shen Ch'eng, to which the Master replied, 'Ch'eng! Why, he is all desires. How could he become resolute?' (v. 10.)

The Master said, 'For my part I have never seen any one with a real passion for human-heartedness and a real hatred of what is inhuman. A man with a real passion for human-heartedness will not put anything above it. A man with a real hatred of what is inhuman will become human-hearted to the extent that he will not deliberately have anything inhuman affecting his self. Are there any who are able to devote their strength for a single day to being human-hearted? I have never seen any. (Nevertheless) I have never seen any who had not the strength to achieve this.' (iv. 6.)

The Master said, 'Is human-heartedness something

[1] The appeal to personal experience seems to have been a characteristic of Confucius's way of thinking, and is one of the ways in which he laid an indelible mark on his people's minds.
[2] *Kan* was chiefly used in connection with the courage of soldiers. Confucius came to be aware of what we call 'moral courage.'

remote? If I want to be human-hearted, behold, human-heartedness has arrived.' (vii. 29.)

The Master said, 'You can rob the three levies (of Lu State) of their due control, but you cannot rob the humblest man of his aims.' [1] (ix. 25.)

The Master said, 'A wise man does not get perplexed: a human-hearted man does not get unhappy: a courageous man does not get frightened.' (ix. 28.)

Fan Ch'ih was strolling with the Master below the Rain Dance altars, and he asked about filling up the measure of his spiritual power, the disciplining of the vice in him, and the discernment of states of delusion. The Master said, 'What admirable questions! To put service first and reward second, that, I suppose, is not filling up the measure of your spiritual power! To attack your own evil without attacking other people's, that, I suppose, is not disciplining the vice in you! In a passing fit of rage to be regardless of your own safety *and* that of your parent, that, I suppose, is not a state of delusion!' [2] (xii. 21.)

The Master said, 'A man of real power in personality is sure to have the gift of speech, but a man with the gift of speech not necessarily has the real power of personality. A human-hearted man is sure to have courage, but a brave man not necessarily has human-heartedness. (xiv. 5.)

Tzu Lu asked about becoming a complete man, and the Master said, 'If one had the wisdom of Tsang Wu Chung, the freedom from private desires of Kung Ch'o, the courage of Chung Tzu of P'ien, and the skill of Jan Ch'iu in the arts,[3] and refined these (qualities) by means of ritual and music, that is good enough to make a complete man.' He added, 'But how can we insist on this to-day? When a man sees the chance of profit to think of the right, when he

---

[1] The control of the Lu State militia was at this time usurped by three dominant clans. They divided the levies into three parts. *Chih* (aims): it is tempting to translate this by 'will,' but this abstraction of faculty psychology is at odds with the Chinese *hsin* (mind-heart) psychology.

[2] We have to suppose a sarcastic quirk here. Cp. xiii. 19. Confucius describes Fan Ch'ih as a *hsiao jen* (small man), and small men he regarded as very often morally pretentious men.

[3] Archery, charioteering, etc.

sees danger ahead (for his prince or parents) to throw his life into the scale, in a long-drawn-out emergency [1] not to forget his lifelong professions, that also is good enough to make a complete man.' (xiv. 13.)

The Master said, 'In their nature at birth [2] men are nearly alike, in their habits they are vastly different.' (xvii. 2.)

The Master said, 'It is only the wisest and the stupidest who do not change.' (xvii. 3.)

(b) *His Discovery of the Virtue of Human-heartedness.*

The Master said, 'It is only the human-hearted man who is capable of really liking men and really disliking them.' (iv. 3.)

The Master said, 'If a man be really bent on human-heartedness, then there is no wickedness (in him).' (iv. 4.)

Tzu Kung asked, if (a ruler) wished to include all his people in his benefits and was actually able to bring aid to every one of them, what then? Might he be described as human-hearted? The Master said, 'This has not much to do with human-heartedness. He would undoubtedly be a sage. Even Yao and Shun were distressed (at not reaching this level). A human-hearted ruler wants security for himself, and so he makes others secure. He wishes to get a wider sphere of influence, and so he extends other people's sphere of influence. The ability to draw parallels from matters very near to oneself may be called the art of human-heartedness.' (vi. 28.)

Chung Kung asked about human-heartedness, and the Master said, 'In public behave as you would in the presence of an honoured guest. Set the people their public tasks as if you were conducting a great sacrifice. The treatment you would not have for yourself, do not hand out to other people. Then there will be no resentment against you in the state, no resentment in your clan.' (xii. 2.)

(The Sung official) Ssu-ma Niu asked about human-

---

[1] An alternative rendering is 'a bond of long standing.'
[2] For 'congenital nature' (*hsing*) cp. Mencius and Hsun Ch'ing. The term *hsing* occurs only twice in the *Analects*, in Confucius's mouth only here.

C 972

heartedness, and the Master said, 'The human-hearted man is cautious in what he says.' Niu asked whether he really meant that human-heartedness was this, and the Master replied, 'Since doing is so difficult, can a man be otherwise than cautious in speaking?' (xiv. 3.)

(Somebody stated that) to refrain entirely from love of mastery, from boasting of one's accomplishments, from resentments and from covetous desires, (these qualities) warranted the description of human-heartedness: whereat the Master said, 'They warrant one's saying that they are difficult to do. But if you say "human-hearted," then I am not sure.' (xiv. 2.)

The Master said, 'The man bent on public service,[1] if he be the human-hearted kind of man, under no circumstances will he seek to live at the expense of his human-heartedness. There are occasions when he will lay down his life to preserve his human-heartedness.' (xv. 8.)

(c) *His Reinterpretation of Good Breeding and a Sense of Honour.*[2]

Wealth and high station, these are what men would like to have; but if they cannot be obtained in conformity with principle [*Tao*] they must not be held. Poverty and low station, these are what men dislike; but if they cannot be avoided [3] without contravention of principle, they must be accepted. If a man of honour discards human-heartedness, how can he ever continue to bear the name? Not even while he is eating does a man of honour ignore human-heartedness. Whatever the urgency, whatever the danger, he sticks to it. (iv. 5.)

The Master said, 'If the man of breeding be light-minded, people will not look up to him, and what he learns will not stay by him. The first thing is loyalty and keeping his

---

[1] It should be remembered that Confucius as a teacher was largely engaged in training men who were aiming at state service.

[2] The quotations under this heading could have been made twice as many. Presumably on most occasions the remarks were addressed to the men whom Confucius was training. No one statement should be taken as a definition. Rather he has an idea and tries it out.

[3] The sense demands *mien*, or some such word, for *te* (obtain).

word. He will have no friends who do not come up to his standard; and if he does wrong, he will not shirk mending his ways.' (i. 8.)

The Master said, 'A man of honour is not a mere tool.' (ii. 12.)

The Master said, 'Amongst men of honour there is nothing to cause selfish rivalry. This is certainly the case even with archery.[1] It is with a bow and a gesture of giving precedence that (the competitors) advance to shoot and then when they retire and drink to each other. Their rivalry is one between men of honour.' (iii. 7.)

The Master said, 'The true man of honour in relation to the Great Society has no private preferences, or otherwise. He sees these matters in relation to the right.' (iv. 10.)

The Master said, 'A man of true breeding sets his heart on spiritual power in himself: the man of no breeding sets his heart on land. . . .' (iv. 11.)

The Master said, 'The desire of a man of honour is to be slow in speech and quick in action.' (iv. 24.)

The Master said, 'Moral power does not live alone. It is sure to have neighbours.' (iv. 25.)

The Master described Tzu Ch'an [2] as having four (characteristics) of the Way of a man of honour. In his private capacity he was modest, in the service of his superiors respectful, in his provision to meet the people's needs benevolent, in his organization of their forced labour just. (v. 15.)

The Master said [? to his disciples], 'Be trustworthy in every respect, be devoted to the acquisition of learning, steadfast unto death for the Good. Do not enter any area which is running dangerous risks, nor live in one where the people are in rebellion. If the Way prevails among the states, you can make yourselves prominent; but if it does not prevail, then keep in retirement. If it prevails in

[1] These archery meetings had been held since the early days of the Chou regime. Duke Chou, for whom Confucius had so deep a veneration, seems to have established them in order to bring the feudatories together. The code of honour for them, as in the tourneys of Western chivalry, was an elaborate one.
[2] A famous statesman of a neighbouring state. His life overlapped that of Confucius. Cp. Part One, Chapter I, the quotation from the *Tso Chuan*.

your area, it is a disgrace to be poor and humble. If it does not prevail, it is a disgrace to be rich and honoured.' (viii. 13.)

A high official of Sung asked about 'men of honour,' and the Master said, 'A man of honour has no self-pity and no fears.' The official replied, 'Is that all that it means?' The Master said, 'When he examines his heart and finds no taint, what cause has he for self-pity or for fear?' (xii. 4.)

The Master said, 'Men of true breeding are in harmony with people, although they do not agree with them; but men of no breeding agree with people, and yet are not in harmony with them.' (xiii. 23.)

The Master said, 'A man of true breeding is easy to serve but hard to please; for if you try to please him by any other means than the Way, he is not pleased. When he sets men their tasks, it is as appropriate tools for appropriate jobs. A man of no breeding is hard to serve but easy to please: for you can please him by other means than the Way. But when it is a matter of setting men tasks, he expects them to be ready for anything.' (xiii. 25.)

The Master said, 'Men of true breeding have dignity but are not arrogant. Men of no breeding are arrogant but have no dignity.' (xiii. 26.)

The Master said, 'Men of true breeding are ashamed for their words to go beyond their deeds.' (xiv. 29.)

Tzu Lu asked about men of true breeding, and the Master said, 'They bring their personality into flower with a view to reverent action.' Tzu Lu asked if this were all, and the Master said, 'They bring their personality into flower in order that they may bring peace to other men.' Tzu Lu again asked whether this was all, and the Master said, 'They bring their personality into flower in order that they may bring peace to every family and clan. If they do that, could even Yao or Shun find fault with them?' (xiv. 45.)

Once when Confucius was in Ch'en State, the supply of food was exhausted, and his followers became so weak that they could not stand up. Tzu Lu came to the Master in a rage, saying, 'Then men of breeding have also (to suffer) utter penury?' The Master said, 'Men of breeding can endure penury. Men without breeding in such circumstances are immediately swept off their feet.' (xv. i.)

The Master said, 'The man of honour who uses the right as his raw material and ritual as the means for putting it into effect, who modestly sets to work on what is right and faithfully carries it to completion, what a sense of honour he has!' (xv. 17.)

The Master said, 'The man of honour makes demands on himself: the man without a sense of honour makes demands on others.' (xv. 20.)

Tzu Kung asked whether men of honour also hate, and the Master said, 'They do. They hate those who proclaim abroad other men's evil. They hate those vulgar fellows who slander those above them. They hate those who are bold in action but have no idea of good form [lit. ritual]. They hate those who are presumptuous and obstructive.' (xvii. 24.)

3. *Confucius on the Relationship between Governor and Governed.*

Tzu Kung asked about governing, and the Master said 'Adequate supplies of food, adequate stores of munitions, and the confidence of the people.' Tzu Kung said, 'Suppose you unavoidably had to dispense with one of these, which would you forgo? The Master said, 'Munitions.' Thereat Tzu Kung asked if of the remaining two he had to dispense with one, which he would forgo. The Master said, 'Food; for all down history death has come to all men, (and yet society survives); but the people who have no confidence (in their rulers) are undone.' (xii. 7.)

Chi K'ang Tzu [a leader in the dominant clan of Confucius's state] asked Master K'ung[1] about governing. Master K'ung replied, 'Sir, to rule is to straighten things out. If you should take the lead in straightening things out, who would dare to unstraighten them?' (xii. 17.)

Chi K'ang Tzu asked Master K'ung about governing,

---

[1] Certain passages in the *Analects* and other books use 'Master K'ung' and not just 'the Master.' There is some evidence to show that the 'Master K'ung' was a later practice; but it may only indicate the practice of one school among his followers.

saying, 'Suppose I were to kill the people without principles in order to bring over to me the people with principles, what then?' Master K'ung answered, 'Sir, you have the office of ruling. Can you do this by dint of killing? Let your desires be good and the people will be good. The wind is the characteristic [*te*] of the ruling class, the grass of the plebeian class. When the grass encounters the wind, it is bound to bend.' (xii. 19.)

Chi K'ang Tzu asked what could be done by way of encouraging the people and so inducing them to be reverent and loyal (to their rulers). The Master said, 'If with dignity you make your official approach to them, then they will reverence you. If you are dutiful to your parents and kind to your children, then they will be loyal to you. If you put good men into office and so teach those who are incompetent, then they will be encouraged.' (ii. 20.)

Tzu Lu asked about governing, and the Master said, 'Be their leader and work hard for them.' Tzu Lu asked for something more, and the Master said, 'In no circumstances get tired of doing this.' (xiii. 1.)

Tzu Lu said, 'Sir, the Prince of Wei is waiting for you to assume the administration. What will you do first?' The Master said, 'The essential thing is to rectify the use of terms.' Tzu Lu said, 'What, sir! You are speaking off the point. What has such a rectification to do with government?' The Master said, 'How unmannerly you are, Yu! When a man of breeding comes on anything he does not understand, he more or less blames himself. If names be not used correctly,[1] then speech gets tied up in knots; and if speech be so, then business comes to a standstill. If that should happen, then the (order of) ritual and the (harmony of) music could not flourish; and if that should happen, the administration of justice would be wide of the mark; and if that should happen, the people would be tied hand and foot.' (xiii. 3.)

[1] For what Confucius had actually in mind see the next quotation. Names must correspond to realities. Thus his constant reference to *chun tzu* (man of breeding) was an effort to make clear that *chun tzu* must mean much more than a member of the aristocracy.

Duke Ching of Ch'i State asked Master K'ung about governing. Master K'ung replied, 'Let a sovereign BE a sovereign, a minister BE a minister, a father BE a father, a son BE a son.' The Duke said, 'Good! It is true that if a sovereign be not a sovereign, a minister not a minister, a father not a father, a son not a son, we might have (any amount of) grain (in the store-houses)—but should we ever succeed in eating it?' (xii. 11.)

Duke Ting (of Lu State)[1] asked for advice on a sovereign's employment of his ministers and a minister's service of his sovereign. Master K'ung replied, 'A sovereign is able to employ his ministers by means of the traditional ritual. A minister (then) serves his sovereign by loyal (obedience).' (iii. 19.)

The Master said, 'If we assume that the making of a state depends on our capacity for the mutual yielding (which is embodied) in the traditional rituals, what is the conclusion to be drawn? If we assume that it does not depend on such a capacity, what is the use of the rituals?' (iv. 13.)

The Master said, 'If those in the higher ranks of society be devoted to ritual, then none of the common people can dare not to venerate them. If they be lovers of justice, then none of the common people can dare not to obey them. If they be worthy of confidence, then none of the common people can dare to prevaricate. If that be the state of affairs (in a country), then the common people will come to it from all parts, carrying their babies on their backs.' (xiii. 4.)

The Master said, 'When a ruler is right in himself, things will get done without his giving orders. When he is not right in himself, he may give orders, but they will not be obeyed.' (xiii. 6.)

When the Master went to Wei, Jan Yu was driver of the carriage. The Master said, 'What a big population!' Jan Yu said, 'When the numbers have increased, what next

---

[1] A weak ruler who could not hold his own against the dominant 'Three Han' clan. Confucius's advice amounted to this, that the duke should insist on his traditional rights as duke, and act with the traditional rituals of courtesy towards these presumptuous barons.

requires to be done?' The reply was, 'Enrich them.'
When Jan Yu asked what further required to be done, the
reply was, 'Give them good teaching.'   (xiii. 9.)

The Master said, 'Given a true king (on the Chou throne),
within a generation human-heartedness would undoubtedly
prevail.'   (xiii. 12.)

When Tzu Hsia was Warden of Chu Fu, he asked for
advice on governing it.   The Master said, 'Do not hanker
after quick results, nor visualize petty profits.   If you do
the first, you will not have any great influence.   If you do
the second, the really important things will not get done.'
(xiii. 17.)

The Duke of She in conversation with Master K'ung said,
'In my parts there are conscientious men.   For instance, if
a man does not return a stray sheep to its owner, his son
will give evidence against him.'   Master K'ung said, 'In
my parts a conscientious man is very different from that.
A father screens his son, and a son screens his father.   Con-
scientiousness lies there somewhere.'[1]   (xiii. 18.)

The Master said, 'If you try to lead the people by means
of regulations and to order their life by means of punishments, they will try to avoid them without any conscience
whatever.   If, however, you try to lead them by your own
moral power and to order their life by means of rituals,
both their consciences will act, and they will flock round
you.'   (ii. 3.)

4. *Confucius's Belief in Heaven and the Moral Order of the Universe.*

Someone asked to have the Great Sacrifice (in the Royal
Ancestral Temple) explained, and the Master said, 'I do
not know.   The man who could explain that would have
everything in this world of ours as plainly revealed as this';
and he pointed to the palm of his hand.   (iii. 11.)

'To sacrifice is like being in company, to sacrifice to the

---

[1] The categorical imperative of parental and filial love was not, in the
eyes of Confucius, or of his followers, one which should give way to the
demands of legal justice.

spirits of one's ancestors is like being in the company of the spirits.' (With regard to this saying) the Master said, 'Not to be in their company in the sacrifice is like having no sacrifice.'¹ (iii. 12.)

Wang Sun Chia [the commander-in-chief of Wei State] asked what one was to make of the saying, 'It is better to pay court to the spirit by the cooking stove than to the spirits in the shrine.'² The Master said, 'It is not true. The man who sins against Heaven has nowhere where he can pray.' (iii. 13.)

When Yen Yuan [his 'beloved disciple'] died, the Master cried in anguish, 'Heaven is destroying me, Heaven is destroying me.' (xi. 8.)

When (his disciple) Po Niu was ill, the Master went to see him. He took his hand through the window³ and said, 'It is killing him. It is the will of Heaven. But that such a man should have such a disease!' (vi. 8.)

One Kung-po Liao slandered Tzu Lu to the (dominant) Chi clan, and Tzu-fu Ching-po informed the Master, saying, 'Undoubtedly my master [the head of the Chi clan] has been led astray by Kung-po Liao, but I am still strong enough to get him executed.' The Master said, 'If the Way is to prevail, it is the Will of Heaven. If it is to be discarded, it is the Will of Heaven. Can Kung-po Liao do anything apart from the Will of Heaven?' (xiv. 38.)

5. *The Past in Relation to the Present.*

The Master said, 'I have transmitted and do not create anew.⁴ I am faithful to the men of old and love them.'

The Master said, 'How utterly I am falling back! It is long since I dreamt that I saw the Duke of Chou.' (vii. 1, 5.)

What sublime majesty was that of Shun and Yü! The

---

¹ My interpretation is not on all fours with Mr. Arthur Waley's, but I none the less owe a great deal to him here. This applies also to the next quotation.
² Clearly a cynical remark which had become current in that cynical if still superstitious age.
³ Tradition gives the disease as leprosy.
⁴ By 'transmitting,' as he did, with new emphasis on the individual, Confucius was creating more than perhaps he realized.

*C 973

Great Society was theirs, but they were not trammelled by
it. How great was Yao as a sovereign! The sublime
majesty of him! Only Heaven is great: only Yao copied
it. (This spiritual power) going beyond all bounds, so
that no man may give a name to it! Sublime majesty, with
its sublime achievements of civilization, all glorious to
view! (viii. 18, 19.)

The Chou era could look back on the two preceding
ones. How great then is its civilization! I follow Chou.
(iii. 14.)

Tzu Chang asked whether the state of affairs could be
known ten generations ahead. The Master said, 'To what
extent the Yin House added to and subtracted from the
Hsia ritual, it is possible to know: also to what extent
the Chou House added to and subtracted from the Yin.
Thus it is possible to know about the successors to the
Chou House, even though a hundred generations elapse.'[1]
(ii. 23.)

The Master said, 'I could speak about the Hsia ritual,
but Chi[2] cannot sufficiently attest my words. I could
speak of the Yin ritual, but Sung cannot attest my words.
For these states lack both documents and men of learning.
If there were enough of these, I could give them as evidence.'
(iii. 9.)

The Master said, 'In the old days men studied (the past)
with a view to their self-improvement. Nowadays they
study with an eye on other people [i.e. to getting a reputa-
tion].' (xiv. 25.)

Tzu Kung said, 'Kuan Chung was the opposite to human-
hearted, was he not? When Duke Huan killed Prince
Chiu, Kuan Chung did not seek death with him and on
the contrary became Duke Huan's chief minister!' The
Master said, 'As a minister he made Duke Huan head of
the feudal lords, uniting in good order the Great Society.

[1] This statement hardly agrees with the next one.
[2] Chi State was originally a fief to which the Chou overlord entrusted the
duty of perpetuating the sacrifices of the old royal house of Hsia. Sung
did the same for the royal house of the Shang-Yin era.

To the present day we enjoy his bounty, for, were it not for
Kuan Chung, we should be wearing our hair unbound and
our clothes buttoning on the left side.' [1]   (xiv. 18.)

6. *With Regard to Knowledge.*

The Master said, 'I am not one who was born with knowledge. I am one who loves the past and earnestly seeks
to know it.' (vii. 19.)

The Master said, 'There may be those who act without
knowledge. I do not. Hearing much and selecting what
is good in what I hear and following this; seeing much and
making note of it: this is the secondary kind of knowledge.' [2]

The Master said, 'I have spent the whole day without
food and the whole night without sleep in order that I
might meditate. I gained nothing from doing so. It is
not so good as learning.' (xv. 30.)

The Master said, 'Am I really a wise man? I do not
know. But if the sheerest bumpkin asks me a question,
. . . I set the matter forth from beginning to end, for and
against.' (ix. 7.)

The Master said, 'If a man learns but does not think,
then he is nothing. If he thinks but does not learn, then
he is in a dangerous state.' (ii. 15.)

The Master said, 'Yu [i.e. Tzu Lu], shall I teach you what
knowledge is? When you know a thing, to recognize that
you know it; and when you do not know a thing, to recognize that you do not know it. That is knowledge.' (ii. 17.)

The Master said, 'A man should stir himself with poetry,
stand firm in ritual, and complete himself in music.' (viii. 8.)

The Master said, 'Learn as if you could never get there,
(but) were afraid of losing it.' (viii. 17.)

The Master said, 'The man who reanimates the old and
so gets to know the new is fit to be a teacher.' (ii. 11.)

[1] In other words, he saved us from being conquered by the barbarians,
and having to follow their customs.
[2] Mr. Waley suggests that this is a sarcastic reference to the people who
prided themselves on 'innate knowledge.' The great question is what
Confucius had in mind when he thought of 'knowledge.'

7. *Five Ethical Judgments.*[1]

Tzu Kung asked whether there was one word which a man's whole life might be spent in practising. The Master said, 'Is not reciprocity such a word? What you do not wish done to yourself, do not do to others.' (xv. 23.)

The Master said, 'While a man's father is alive, observe the bent of his mind. When his father dies, observe his actions. If during three years [? the years of mourning] he makes no alterations in his father's way, he may be called a filial son.' [2] (i. 11.)

The Master said, 'The life of a man consists in his honesty. If he is not honest, it is sheer luck that he keeps alive.' (vi. 17.)

The Master said, 'To be a man and not to keep one's word—I do not know how this may be. How can a heavy carriage move without a yoke-bar (for the oxen), and a light carriage without a cross-bar (for the horse)?' (ii. 22.)

The Master said, 'How admirable was Hui! [3] With just a modicum of food and a gourd of water, and living in a mean alley-way: other men could not endure the misery of it, but Hui was not affected. He remained quite happy. Admirable indeed!' (vi. 9.)

8. *Confucius, the Authority on Ritual.*[4]

Master Kung said, 'To deal with the dead to enhance their deadness (to us) would be inhuman [not *jen*] and so indefensible. To enhance (a sense of) their being alive would show a want of knowledge and so be indefensible. Thus it is that the bamboo vessels (placed in the coffin) are

[1] To be considered in the light of the material already given.

[2] The old idea was that Confucius was an arch-exponent of the extreme filial piety which became so striking and permanent a feature of Chinese civilization. There would seem to be no evidence for this idea in the *Analects*, although some evidence in less reliable sources. Tseng Shen was more the founder of ethical religious filial piety.

[3] Confucius's favourite disciple. He died young, to his master's great distress.

[4] The *Li Chi* picture of Confucius differs from that of the *Analects*, but is not incompatible with it. By training he had the expert liturgist's sensitiveness to the importance of rites and the scrupulous practice of them. But he went further than that.

not fit for use, the earthenware vessels are not fit for drinking from . . . the lutes and pipes are out of tune, the bells and musical stones without their stands. Thus these things are [? to be] called "radiant" [1] implements, implements with spirit radiance.' (*Li Chi, T'an Kung*, i. 3.)

Tzu Lu said, 'How shocking to be a poor man! When his parents are alive he has no means of feeding them properly, and when they die he has no means of carrying out the proper rites.' Master Kung said, '(Merely) to suck up bean soup and water can please a man's parents completely, and so this can be called filial service. Just wrapping the body from head to foot and burying it without a coffin, if this is in keeping with a man's means, may be called the proper rite.' (*Li Chi, T'an Kung*, ii. 2.)

At Pien there was a man who on the death of his mother wept with the abandon of a child. Master K'ung said, 'Grief! This is indeed grief. The difficulty is to keep on like this. The Ritual exists in order to make a tradition which is handed on. That is why "wailing" and "leaping" are moderated.' (*Li Chi, T'an Kung*, i. 2.)

Tzu Kung asked about the mourning rites (for parents). The Master said, 'To be reverent is the most important. The feeling of grief is second to it and emaciation (of the body) is least important of all.' (*Li Chi, S'a Chi*, ii. 1.)

B. TZU SSU: A PHILOSOPHICAL MIND SEARCHES FOR REALITY

Under this heading come passages from the book which has been long known to the West as *The Doctrine of the Mean*. In the Chinese there is no 'doctrine.' There are just two words, one, *chung*, meaning normally 'the centre,' but here more probably approximating to what philosophers mean by 'the Mean'; the other, *yung*, the word used for denoting a common workman or the tasks which such a man performs. The idea, therefore, seems to be of a Mean to be found in all types of action. Since the material universe is included in the author's purview, 'the

---

[1] It is possible Confucius invented this adjective *ming* (radiant) to go with these implements, or it may be the technical term was the old numinous word for such numinous objects.

[2] Change to 'Tzu Lu appears several times in the *Analects* as prone to get off on the wrong foot with the Master. Cp. p. 24.

Mean-in-action' is about as near to the Chinese as we can get.
'The function of the Mean' or 'the functioning Mean' is tempting, but 'function' and 'functioning' have too many modern
scientific associations for them to be advisable in this connection.

This book and its title first appear in history in the collection
called the *Li Chi*, the *Record of Rites*, a work compiled towards
the end of the first century B.C.: cp. *The Great Learning*. On
the other hand, tradition has consistently attributed the book to
Tzu Ssu, a grandson of Confucius, and there is good reason for
believing that tradition here is right—up to a certain point.
That point is where in the latter half of the book a mass of terms
come which are extremely characteristic of certain phases of the
thought of the middle of the third century B.C. Modern critics
also have grounds for doubting whether the opening paragraphs
are not the work of a later hand. So far, so good: granted that a
later writer has been at work amplifying the original. But then
another question arises. In the middle of the book come a
series of statements in which the term *ch'eng* is the motif. *Ch'eng*
is usually translated by 'sincerity,' by which is meant 'moral
sincerity.' This, however, does not do justice at all to the plainly
metaphysical implications it has in some of these statements,
nor does it take into account that in the *Analects ch'eng* means
'truly.' 'Reality' is the proper translation; although the reader
must be warned that for the author the reality of the universe
could be reproduced in the character of a man. Indeed, to make
people see this was probably the main reason why the author
wrote what he did.

If it be assumed—and there is good ground for doing so—that
some at any rate of these *ch'eng* statements came from Confucius's grandson, then we have here the reflections of a profoundly philosophical mind; e.g. he got down to the idea of the
material universe as a thing in time and space, and so limited
and relative to something beyond itself, a spiritual reality. The
following quotations are to be taken as all coming from Tzu Ssu.

To the student the book as a whole is vastly important. It
proved a profound source of inspiration to the critics of the
Sung era, and they placed it third in the series of the Four
Books which they set up as containing the quintessence of the
Confucianists' system of faith.

(*Section II. Tzu Ssu invokes Confucius's Authority for the
idea of the Mean in Action.*)

Chung-ni [Confucius] said, 'The man of true breeding is
the mean [1] in action. The man of no breeding is the

[1] Assuming that Confucius coined the phrase, it is better here to avoid
printing it as a technical term. We may say that in Tzu Ssu's vocabulary
it became a technical term.

reverse. The relation of the man of true breeding to the mean in action is that, being a man of true breeding, he consistently holds to the Mean. The reverse relationship of the man of no breeding is that, being what he is, he has no sense of moral caution.'

The Master said, 'Perfect is the mean in action, and for a long time now very few people have had the capacity for it.'

The Master said, 'I know why the Way is not pursued. (It is because) the learned run to excess and the ignorant fall short. I know why the Way is not understood. The good run to excess and the bad fall short. . . .'

The Master said, 'Alas, this failure to pursue the Way!'

The Master said, 'Consider Shun, the man of great wisdom. He loved to ask advice and to examine plain speech. He never referred to what was evil, and publicly praised what was good. By grasping these two extremes he put into effect the Mean among his people. In this way he was Shun [i.e. a sage-emperor], was he not?'

The Master said, 'All men say "I know," but they are driven into nets, caught in traps, fall into pitfalls, and not one knows how to avoid this. All men say "I know," but, should they choose the mean in action, they could not persist in it for a round month.'

The Master said, 'Hui, a real man! He chose the mean in action, and, if he succeeded in one element of good, he grasped it firmly, cherished it in his bosom, and never let it go.'

The Master said, 'The states and families of the Great Society might have equal divisions of land: men might refuse noble station and the wealth that goes with it: they might trample the naked sword under foot; but the mean in action, it is impossible for them to achieve that.'

Tzu Lu inquired about strong men, and the Master said, 'Is it strong men of the southern kind, or strong men of the northern kind, or, maybe, making yourself strong (that you have in mind)? The (typical) strong man of the south is magnanimous and gentle in instructing people, and he takes no revenge for being treated vilely: it is the habit of a man of true breeding to be like this. The (typical) strong man of the north lives under arms and dies without a murmur: it is the habit of a man of true force to be like this. Hence the man of true breeding, how steadfast he is in his strength, having a spirit of concord and not giving way to pressure. He takes up a central position, and does not waver one way or another. How steadfast his strength, for, when there is good government, he does not change his original principles, and, when there is vile government, he does not change, even though his life be at stake.'

(Section III. The Material World is limited, the Way unlimited.)

The Way of the enlightened man [*chun tzu*] is widely apparent and yet hidden. Thus the ordinary man and woman, ignorant though they are, can yet have some knowledge of it; and yet in its perfection even a sage finds that there is something there which he does not know. Take the vast size of heaven-and-earth; men can still find room for criticism of it. Hence, when the enlightened man speaks of supreme bigness, it cannot be contained within the world of our experience; nor, when he speaks of supreme smallness, can it be split up in the world of our experience into nothing. As is said in the *Odes*: 'The hawk beats its way up to the height of heaven, the fish dives down into the abyss.' That refers to things being examined from above and from below. Thus the Way of the enlightened man, its early shoots coming into existence in the ordinary man and woman, but in its ultimate extent to be examined in the light of heaven-and-earth.

(Section IV. Confucius's Authority invoked to show that the Way of the Mean is one which involves an Unlimited Demand on every sort of Individual, and also is mixed up with Religion.)

The Master said, 'The Way is not far removed from men. If a man pursues a way which removes him from men, he cannot be in the Way. In the *Odes* there is the word,

"When hewing an axe-handle, hew an axe-handle. The
pattern of it is close at hand." You grasp an axe-handle
to hew an axe-handle, although, when you look from the
one to the other [i.e. from the axe in your hand to the block
of wood], they are very different.' [1] Therefore the right
kind of ruler uses men to control men and attempts nothing
beyond their correction; and fidelity and mutual service
(these two human qualities) cannot be outside the scope of
the Way. The treatment which you do not like for yourself
you must not hand out to others. . . .

The acts of the enlightened man agree with the station in
life in which he finds himself, and he is not concerned with
matters outside that station. If he is a man of wealth and
high position, he acts as such. If he is a poor man and low
in the social scale, he acts accordingly. So also if he is
among barbarians, or if he meets trouble. In fact, there is
no situation into which he comes in which he is not himself.
In a high station he does not disdain those beneath him.
In a low station he does not cling round those above him.
He puts himself in the right and seeks no favours. Thus he
is free from ill will, having no resentment against either
Heaven or men. He preserves an easy mind, as he awaits
the will of Heaven: (in contrast to) the man who is not
true, who walks in perilous paths and hopes for good luck.

The Way of the enlightened man is like a long journey,
since it must begin with the near at hand. It is like the
ascent of a high mountain, since it must begin with the low
ground. As is said in the *Odes*:

> The happy union with wife and child
> Is like the music of lutes and harps.
> When concord grows between brother and brother,
> The harmony is sweet and intimate.
> The ordering of your household!
> Your joy in wife and child!

The Master said, 'How greatly parents are served in

[1] It is often difficult to decide where a quotation ends and an amplification begins. In the absence of reliable evidence that Confucius made
long speeches, it is wiser to assume that a quotation does not run to any
length. On the other hand, in the succeeding remarks some are definitely
traceable as coming from Confucius.

this!' He also said, 'How irrepressible is the spiritual power in the spirits of the great dead! Look for them, and they are not to be seen. Listen for them, and they are not to be heard. They are in things, and there is nothing without them. They stir all the people in the Great Society to fast and purify themselves and wear their ritual robes, in order that they may sacrifice to them. They fill the air, as if above, as if on the left, as if on the right. The *Odes* has it, "The coming of the Spirits! Incalculable! And yet they cannot be disregarded."' Even so is the manifestation of the imperceptible and the impossibility of hiding the real [*ch'eng*].

(*Section V. Outstanding Personality cannot but have Wide and Continuing Influence, as is proved by the Hero-Saints of Tradition.*)

The Master said, 'Consider Shun, the man of superb filial piety. By the virtue in him he was a sage: in his dignity he was Son of Heaven: in his wealth he owned all within the Four Seas. Temple sacrifices were made to him, and his memory was cherished by his descendants. Thus it is that outstanding personality is bound to obtain its position of authority, its wealth, its fame, and its lasting life. For thus it is that Heaven, as it gives life to all creatures, can be surely trusted to give to each what is due to its basic capacity. And thus it is that the well-planted is nourished and the ill-planted falls prostrate. . . . Thus it is that the man of superb personality is bound to receive the Great Commission.'

The Master said, 'The one man who has been without sorrow is King Wen. He had King Chi for father and King Wu for son.[1] The father laid the foundation, and the son built on it. King Wu thus inherited from a line of kingly men, the T'ai King, King Chi, and King Wen. Once he

---

[1] All of them examples of great filial piety. This emphasis on filial piety may strike a Western reader as rather fantastic. But Tzu Ssu's age was one of great political changes, and he was searching for a principle of continuity. He finds it in a spiritual continuity, one of accumulative power in personality, as the father passes it on to the son and he enhances it.

had buckled on his armour, the world was his, for, (although he rebelled,) he suffered no loss to his world-wide reputation. In dignity he became Son of Heaven, in wealth he owned all within the Four Seas. Temple sacrifices were made to him, and his memory was cherished by his descendants.' It was in his old age that King Wu received the Commission, and it was Duke Chou who carried to completion the virtue in King Wen and King Wu. . . .

As the Master said, 'How wide an influence King Wu's and Duke Chou's filial piety had.' Filial men are those who are well able to follow up what other men have willed, and preserve what they have undertaken. . . .

Let men only grasp the significance of the rites at the altars of Heaven and Earth and those in the ancestral temple, and government will become (as easy) as pointing to the palm of the hand.[1] For the rites to Heaven and Earth are the means by which service is rendered to *Shang Ti* [the High Ruler], the rites in the temple are the means by which (grateful) offerings are made to those from whom we have sprung.

(Section VI. The Question of Government one of Moral Personality in Ruler and Ruled.)

The Duke Ai asked advice as to governing, and the Master said, 'King Wen's and King Wu's system of government is revealed in the historical records. With their kind of men the system worked: without their kind of men it comes to an end. Man's right way is to be prompt in good government, as the earth's way is to be prompt in making things grow. Thus good government is like the speed with which *p'u lu* reeds grow. Thus it is that good government depends on men.

Men are obtainable on the basis of personality. The cultivation of personality is on the basis of the Way. The cultivation of the Way is on the basis of human-heartedness.

---

[1] A good illustration of what we may surely assume happened often enough, namely, that the dictum of 'the Master' became the dictum of his disciple, though in a slightly different form.

To be human-hearted is to be a man, and the chief element
in human-heartedness is loving one's parents.   So it is with
justice: it is to put things right, and the chief element in it is
employing worthy men in public service. . . .

Thus it is that enlightened men must not fail to cultivate
their personalities; and, having it in mind to do this, they
must not fail to serve their parents; and having it in mind to
do this, they must not fail to have knowledge of men; and,
having it in mind to have this knowledge, they must not fail
to have knowledge of Heaven.

There are five things which concern everybody in the
Great Society, as also do the three means by which these
five things are accomplished.   To explain, the relationship
between sovereign and subject, between father and son,
between husband and wife, between elder and younger
brother, and the equal intercourse between friend and
friend, these five relationships concern everybody in the
Great Society.   Knowledge, human-heartedness, and fortitude, these three are the means; for these qualities are the
spiritual power in society as a whole.   The means by which
this power is made effective is unity.

Some people know these relationships by the light of
nature.   Others know them by learning about them from
a teacher.   Others again know them through hard experience.   But once they all do know them, there is unity.
Some people practise these relationships with a natural
ease.   Others derive worldly advantage from their practice
of them.   Others again have to force themselves to practise
them.   But once they all have achieved success in practising
them, there is unity.'

The Master said, 'To love to learn is to be near to having
knowledge.   To put into practice vigorously is to be near
to being human-hearted.   To know the stings of shame is
to be near to fortitude.   So we may infer that the man who
knows these three things, knows how to cultivate his self.
When he knows how to do that, it may be inferred that he
knows how to rule other individuals.   And when he knows
how to do that, it may be inferred that he knows how to

rule the whole of the Great Society with its states and families.'

(*Section VI. The Necessity for Unremitting Effort and for Truth and Reality in the Self.*)

In the transaction of business success depends on preparation beforehand: without preparation there will be failure. If you decide beforehand what you are going to say, (when the time comes) you will not stutter and stammer; and if you are decided on what you are setting out to do, you will fall into no quandaries.   Decide (therefore) beforehand what conduct should be, and then there will be no regrets: decide beforehand what the Way is, and then there will be no limit to the result [? spiritual results].   Thus, unless those in the higher ranks of society can capture the confidence of those in the lower ranks, it is impossible for them to gain the support of the people for their administrative measures. But there is only one way by which this confidence may be captured; for, if friends cannot trust each other, there can be no confidence in the men in the higher ranks.   But there is only one way by which friends can come to trust each other; for, if men are not dutiful to their parents, there can be no trust between them as friends.   But there is only one way for men to be dutiful to their parents; for, if in rounding in on themselves they are not true [*ch'eng*], they cannot be dutiful to their parents.   But there is only one way for a man to have a true and real [*ch'eng*] [1] self; for, if he does not understand the good, he cannot be true and real in himself.

(*Section VII. Reality in Heaven and Realness in Man.*)

It is the characteristic of Heaven to BE the Real.   It is the characteristic of man to be coming-to-be-real.   (For a man) to be real [i.e. to have achieved realness] is to hit the Mean without effort, to have it without thinking of it, entirely naturally to be centred in the Way: (in other words) to be a sage.

[1] Assuming as I do that some of the *ch'eng* passages come from Tzu Ssu's pen, this is the turning-point in his argument as to the metaphysical significance of personality.   *Ch'eng* = 'true and real' here.

To be coming-to-be-real is to choose the good and to hold fast to it. This involves learning all about the good, asking about it, thinking it over carefully, getting it clear by contrast, and faithfully putting it into practice. If there is any part about which he has not learnt or asked questions, which he has not thought over and got clear by contrast, or which he has not put into practice, he sets to work to learn and ask and think and get clear and put into practice. If he does not get the required result, he still does not give up working. When he sees other men succeeding by one effort, or it may be a hundred, he is prepared to add a hundredfold to his own efforts. The man who can last this course, although he is stupid, will come to understand, although he is weak, will become strong.

[To (be able to) proceed from (the capacity for) realness to understanding is to be ascribed to the nature of man. To proceed from understanding to realness is to be ascribed to instruction in truth. Logically, realness involves understanding and understanding involves realness.][1]

(*Section VIII. Human Realness in Action: its Power to bring Completion in Development.*)

It is only the man who is entirely real in his world of experience who has the power to give full development to his own nature. If he has that power, it follows that he has the power to give full development to other men's natures. If he has that power, it follows that he has the power to give full development to the natures of all creatures. Thus it is possible for him to be assisting the transforming and nourishing work of heaven and earth. That being so, it is possible for him to be part of a trinity of power (heaven, earth, and himself). . . .

(*Section IX. Human Realness in Action: the Ability to Foreknow.*)

A characteristic of the entirely real man is that he is able

[1] This passage is perhaps an amplification by a later hand, so I enclose it in brackets.

to foreknow. When a country is about to flourish, there are bound to be omens of good. When it is about to perish, there are bound to be omens of evil fortune. These are revealed in the milfoil and (the lines on the shell of) the tortoise. They affect the four limbs. When disasters or blessings are on the way, the morally good and the morally evil (elements) in a country are bound to be known first of all. Thus the entirely real man has a likeness to the divine.[1]

(*Section X. Realness again in Relation to Completion of Things.*)

Realness is self-completing, and the way of it is to be self-directing. Realness is the end as well as the beginning of things, for without realness there would be no things at all; which is the reason why the true man prizes above everything coming-to-be-real. Realness is not merely a matter of an individual completing himself. It is also that by which things in general are completed. The completing of the individual self involves man-to-man-ness [*jen*]. The completing of things in general involves knowledge. Man-to-man-ness and knowledge are spiritual powers [*te*] inherent in man, and they are the bridge [lit. *tao*, way] bringing together the outer and the inner. Hence it is self-evidently right that realness should function [2] continuously.

(*Section XI. Realness transcends the Material.*)

The result is that entire realness never ceases for a moment. Now if that be so, then it must be extended in time: if extended in time, then capable of proof: if capable of proof, then extended in space-length: if extended in length, then extended in area: if extended in area, then extended in height-visibility.[3] And this quality of extension

---

[1] The primitive religious art of divination was beginning to be ethicized and rationalized in Tzu Ssu's age. It is interesting and important to note how Tzu Ssu's religion retained its hold in so good a philosophic mind as his.

[2] The temptation to use 'function' proves irresistible.

[3] I take *kao-ming* as Tzu Ssu's attempt, with the language at his disposal, to express the third dimension. Three dimensions are necessary before 'form,' i.e. visibility, is possible.

in area is what makes material things supportable from below: this quality of extension in height-visibility is what makes things coverable from above: whilst the extension in time is what makes them capable of completion. Thus area pairs with earth, height-visibility pairs with heaven, and space plus time makes limitlessness. This being its nature, realness is not visible and yet clearly visible, does not (deliberately) stir things and yet changes them, takes no action and yet completes them.

(*Section XVIII. Tzu Ssu links Human Realness to the Spiritual Power of Heaven.*)

It is only the man who is entirely real in his world of men who can make the warp and woof of the great web of civilized life, who can establish the great foundations of civilized society, and who can understand the nourishing processes of heaven and earth. Can there be any variableness in him? His human-heartedness how insistent! His depths how unfathomable! His superhumanness how overwhelming! Who is there who can comprehend this unless he possesses acute intelligence and sage-like wisdom, unless he reaches out to the spiritual power of Heaven?

PART TWO

Reasoning about Ethics and Politics becomes a Habit

Chapter III: Mo Ti, the Rise of Religious Utilitarianism

The philosopher known as Mo Ti—for even his name is doubt-ful—cannot be dated with accuracy. Some of the evidence points to his having been born a few years after Confucius's death, whilst there is reason to suppose he was alive during the first decade or two of the fourth century B.C. His name figures prominently in the controversies of that and the third century; and there can be no question but that his teaching and the teach-ings of his different groups of followers were major forces in the amazing intellectual developments of those years. Bands of Mohists are mentioned as existing in all parts of the 'Great Society,' even in Ch'in, the less civilized state in the west. They are the only school of thought which is known to have had some sort of group organization, and what appear to have been regular meetings, for chanting their Master's words. They figure in the books of the first century B.C., but after that there are no references to them as an existent body of opinion. The learned Confucian editors of the *Ssu Ku Chuan Shu T'i Yao* (eighteenth century) say of them: 'Because of Mencius's exposure of him, nobody was willing to come under Mo Ti's name, but the Buddhists . . . with their sense of compassion got something from Mohism.' [1]

The *Mo Tzu Book* originally contained seventy-one chapters. To-day eighteen of these are missing, nine of them from the section dealing with defensive warfare: for Mo Ti's genius also ran to mechanical invention and military tactics. Of the extant chapters six are of great technical philosophic interest, but are not cited here because they plainly belong to the later ages of Mohist thought (cp. c. 11). The quotations here are taken mainly from what may be called the 'synoptic chapters,' since they come in groups of three, one subject to each group. Since these subjects represent Mo Ti's main tenets, both through the features any three chapters have in common and through those they have in contrast to each other, we get a synoptic view of these lines of thought. They approximate to essays—the first methodically argued essays in Chinese literature—but

---

[1] English students of philosophy would do well to note that religious utilitarianism does not appear in our own history of thought until the eighteenth century.

are actually records of teaching given. Thus they are not the products of Mo Ti's own pen. What is more, examination of terminology gives the impression of different strata in the synoptic record, a shorter, simpler, and so probably earlier record, and longer and therefore later ones. Yet the obvious veneration for Mo Ti, together with the studied repetition of the sentences, leads to the belief that these records are very near to Mo Ti's *ipsissima verba*. This is important, for, as will appear in the quotations, Mo Ti's mind was not only superbly logical but also brilliantly dialectical. He may be taken as the father of several new forms of reasoning, in this respect contributing much more than Confucius did, although at the outset of his career he owed much to Confucius in intellectual and moral stimulus.

Chapter 4.   On Standard Patterns.

[By way of general introduction to Mo Ti's style of thinking.]

Our Master Mo said: Any one in the Great Society who takes any business in hand, cannot dispense with a standard pattern. For there to be no standard and the business to succeed, this just does not happen. Even the best experts who act as generals and councillors - of - state, all have standards (of action); and so also even with the best crafts-men. They use a carpenter's square for making squares and compasses for making circles: a piece of string for making straight lines and a plumb line for getting the perpendicular. It makes no difference whether a crafts-man is skilled or not: all alike use these five (devices) as standards, only the skilled are accurate. But, although the unskilled fail to be accurate, they nevertheless get much better results if they follow these standards in the work which they do. Thus it is that craftsmen in their work have the measurements which these standards give.

Now take the great ones who rule our Great Society, and the less great ones who rule the different states, but who have no standards of measurement (for their actions). In this they are less critically minded than the craftsman. That being so, what standard may be taken as suitable for ruling? Will it do if everybody imitates his father and mother? The number of fathers and mothers in the Great Society is large, but the number of human-hearted [*jen*] ones is small. If everybody were to imitate his father and mother, this standard would not be a human-hearted one. For a standard, however, to be not human-hearted makes it impossible for it to be a standard. Will it do then if everybody imitates his teacher?[1] The number of teachers is large, but the number of human-hearted ones is small. If everybody were to imitate his teacher . . . this standard would not be a human-hearted one. Will it do then if everybody imitates his sovereign? The number of princes is large, but the number of human-hearted ones is small. If everybody imitated his sovereign, this standard would not be a human-hearted one. Hence, fathers and mothers, teachers and sovereigns cannot be taken as standards for ruling.

That being so, what standard may be taken as suitable for ruling? The answer is that nothing is equal to imitating Heaven. Heaven's actions are all-inclusive and not private-minded, its[2] blessings substantial and unceasing, its revelations abiding and incorruptible. Thus it was that the Sage-kings imitated it. Having taken Heaven as their standard, their every movement and every action was bound to be measured in relation to Heaven. What Heaven wanted, that they did: what Heaven did not want, that they stopped doing.

The question now is, what does Heaven want and what does it hate? Heaven wants men to love[3] and be profitable to each other, and does not want men to hate and maltreat each other. How do we know that Heaven wants men to love and be profitable to each other? Because it embraces all in its love of them, embraces all in its benefits to them.

[1] It is a distinctive feature of Mo Ti's reasoning that he was not afraid of repetition. The argument is given in exactly the same words in relation to different sets of people, etc. Where this becomes boring to the reader it will be omitted.

[2] It seems best to translate by 'it' and 'its.' Yet, as modern Chinese philosophers generally affirm, Mo Ti's 'Heaven' is equivalent to a Being or even a Person with a Will. Cp. below where Heaven is described as 'embracing all men in its love of them.'

[3] Mo Ti seldom used Confucius's word jen (man-to-man-ness, human-heartedness). His word ai is one expressing rather the feeling of love. On the other hand, his utilitarian mind made him construe love in terms of doing good, being useful to your fellow men.

How do we know that Heaven embraces all . . . ?   Because
it embraces all in its possession of them and in its gifts
of food.

Take then the Great Society.   There are no large or small
states: all are Heaven's townships.   Take men.   There are
no young men or old, no patricians or plebeians: all are
Heaven's subjects.   This is so, for there is no one who does
not fatten oxen and sheep and dogs and pigs and make
pure wine and sacrificial cakes with which to do reverence
and service to Heaven.   Can this be anything else than
Heaven owning all and giving food to all?   Assuming then
that Heaven embraces all and gives food to all, how could
it be said that it does not want men to love and benefit
each other?

Hence I say that Heaven is sure to give happiness to
those who love and benefit other men, and is sure to bring
calamities on those who hate and maltreat other men.   I
maintain that the man who murders an innocent person
will meet with misfortune.   What other explanation is
there of the fact that when men murder each other, Heaven
brings calamity on them?   This is the way in which we
know that Heaven wants men to love and benefit each other
and does not want them to hate and maltreat each other.

The above chapter not only shows clearly that Mo Ti had a
logical mind: it also introduces us to the three main characteristics of his teaching.   These are, first, the logic of belief in
Heaven and the spirits; second, the logic of all-embracing love;
third, the logic of profit.   A fourth is his insistence on political
unity, not to say uniformity.   Four sets of quotations follow
under these headings.

1. The Logic of Belief in Heaven and the Spirits.

Chapter 28. On the Will of Heaven.

The word of our Master Mo: [1]   What is the explanation
of the disorder everywhere?   It is that our leaders in
society are clear about less important matters and not clear

---

[1] This introductory expression occurs frequently, and makes one wonder
whether these writings may not have been written for liturgical purposes.

about more important matters. How do we know that they are clear about less important matters and not clear about more important? Because they are not clear about Heaven's purposes. How do we know that they are not clear about Heaven's purposes? By taking family life we know it. Take the case of a man who has offended the head of his family. He can still find another family in which to take refuge. None the less fathers and elder brothers are constantly warning the young, bidding them be careful in the family. . . . And then take the case of a man who misconducts himself in his country. He can still find another country in which to take refuge. None the less fathers and elder brothers are constantly warning the young. . . . Now, however, take the case of all men living under the sky and serving Heaven. If they offend against Heaven, there is no place where they can take refuge. And yet people have not the knowledge to warn each other. By this I [1] know that if a matter is supremely important no one knows about it.

Thus it is that our Master Mo has the word: Be careful! You must do what Heaven wants and avoid what Heaven hates. He (then) said: What does Heaven want and what does it hate? Heaven wants righteousness and hates what is to it unrighteous. How do we know that this is so? The answer is that righteousness is rectifying. [2] (Then) how is it known that righteousness is making right? (By the fact that) if the Great Society possesses righteousness it is well ordered, and if it does not possess righteousness it is in confusion. By this means we know that righteousness is rectifying, but, on the other hand, that there is no rectifying

[1] The actual character for 'I' seldom occurs in classical writings. It does occur from time to time in the *Mo Tzu Book*. I take *wu* to mean 'I,' and *wo* to mean 'we,' but there are contexts where this does not work.
[2] In the argument which follows it becomes clear that *cheng* (making right) refers both to making the individual right and making the whole community right. The second of the synoptic records (c. 27) here makes Mo Ti mean 'rectifying the government of the country,' and that was a current Confucian definition of government, but the evidence of c. 26 as of this c. 28 points to Mo Ti very much having the individual in mind. Dr. Mei Yi-pao's translation 'righteousness is the standard' does not seem warranted, well as it fits in with Mo Ti's emphasis on uniformity and the necessity for having a standard.

of those above (socially) by those below. Rectification must be from above downwards.

This being so, the fact is that the common people are unsuccessful if they follow their own inclinations in making right.[1] There are the minor officials who make them right. Also the minor officials are unsuccessful if they follow their own inclinations in making right. There are the high officials who make them right. Also the high officials are unsuccessful . . . There are the feudal lords who make them right. Also the feudal lords are unsuccessful . . . There are the Three Dukes who make them right. The Three Dukes are unsuccessful . . . There is the Son of Heaven who makes them right. The Son of Heaven is unsuccessful if he follows his own inclinations in making right. There is Heaven which makes him right.

.   .   .   .   .

Take the leaders in society who want to act righteously. It follows (logically) that they must not fail to obey the Will of Heaven. The question then is: what is the Will of Heaven like? The answer is: to love all men everywhere alike. How is this known? By the fact that Heaven gives food to all men alike. How is this known? (By the fact that) from ancient times to the present day there has been no remote, isolated, barbarian country but has fattened oxen and sheep and dogs and pigs and prepared sacrificial cakes and wine in order to sacrifice to the High Ruler [*Shang Ti*] and the mountains and river and the spirits. By this means it is known that (Heaven) gives food to all alike. Assuming that it gives food to all alike, it follows that it must love all alike. . . . Further, that Heaven loves the hundred clans is proved not merely by this. Take all the countries with their grain-eating people. For every innocent man murdered there is bound to be some calamity. Who does the murdering? The answer is, man. Who

[1] All the evidence points to Mo Ti having a profound love of the common man; but in his political opinions he was the very reverse of democratic.

sends the calamity? The answer is, Heaven. If it be not exactly true that Heaven loves these people, for what reason does Heaven send calamities for the murder of innocent men? [1]

I maintain that a wise and good man is sure to reward good and punish wickedness. How do I know this? I know it by means of the Sage-kings of the Three Eras, because in those past days Yao, Shun, Yü, T'ang, Wen, and Wu loved all alike in the Great Society and followed this up by benefiting their hundred clans, changing their purposes, taking the lead in worshipping the High Ruler, the mountains and streams, and the spirits. Heaven saw this as loving and benefiting what it loved, so it loved and benefited these (Sage-kings). Thus it rewarded these kings, setting them up in the supreme position of Son of Heaven in order that they might be a pattern to all. They are named 'sage men,' and by this is learnt the proof [2] of goodness and its reward.

This argument from history is completed by a presentation of the reverse action in connection with the wicked kings of the past, Chieh, Chou, Yu, and Li, who hated every one and took the lead in blaspheming the High Ruler, etc. They all came to a bad end; and 'by this is learnt the proof of wickedness and its punishment.' There follows a similar double-sided argument demonstrating that Heaven approves of government by righteousness as against government by force. The latter is developed as follows:

What is it like to have government by force? The answer is: the big logically will attack the small, the strong will plunder the weak, the majority will maltreat the minority, the clever will deceive the simple, the patricians will despise the plebeians, the rich will disdain the poor, and the young will rob the old. Thus all the states in our Great Society

[1] The use of the rhetorical question came to play a great part in Chinese prose. Confucius clearly was an adept at using it, but it was Mo Ti who gave this literary device its sharply logical force, using it to make a *reductio ad absurdum*.

[2] *Cheng* (evidence) occurs only once in the *Analects*, and then with the meaning of giving evidence about a crime. Here we find it in an argument used as proof. We cannot be sure that Mo Ti started this use, but it is clear that sooner or later his followers had it.

will injure each other grievously, precisely by the use of water, fire, poison, and lethal weapons. In this way there will be no profit to heaven above or to the spirits in the middle sphere or to men below—three no-profits making no profit anyway, a state of affairs to be described as armed violence against Heaven.

The subsequent paragraphs do not add materially to our understanding of Mo Ti's belief in Heaven. They are concerned with proving the illogicality of the 'leaders in society.' On the one hand, they denounce those who rob on a small scale, whilst, on the other, they claim as righteous something which is 'several million times worse,' namely the attacking of a weak country by a strong. There occurs here a characteristic example of Mo Ti's power of sarcasm.

This is something which confuses us. According to this, what is the difference between confusing the distinction between black and white and (confusing that between) sweet and bitter. Take the case of a man who when he is shown a few black objects calls them black, but when he is shown a large number of black objects calls them white. He would have to admit that his eyesight was in disorder and that he did not know the difference between black and white. Take also the case of a man given a few sweet things to taste. . . .

The final conclusion is that 'the Will of Heaven is the warp and woof [*ching*] of righteousness.' To what extent this uncompromising ethical emphasis is characteristic of the old religion in Mo Ti's day is a question. On the other hand there can be no question but that Mo Ti used his dialectical skill in defending certain features of the old religion. This is clear from the chapters dealing with the spirits of the dead and a rising cult of unethical fatalism.

Chapter 31. On the (Moral) Intelligence of Spirits.

C. 31 is the only chapter in the book on this subject. It is supposed to be the third of the synoptic records on this subject.

The word of our Master Mo: Reach back to the past of the Three Eras and to the time when the Sage-kings were no more. The Great Society lost righteousness and the feudal lords made might to be right. This meant that sovereigns and their ministers . . . became harsh and disloyal, fathers and sons uncompassionate and unfilial . . . leaders careless in administering justice, the low-born careless over their tasks. . . . Starting from this the Great Society began to be in a state of confusion. What were the causes which made it so?[1] Logically they are doubts as to the difference made by spirits existing or not existing,[2] and the failure to realize the power of the spirits to reward the worthy and punish the violently bad. Supposing now that all men believed in the spirits having power so to reward and so to punish, how could society be in confusion? The people to-day who deny the existence of spirits and from morn to night teach all and sundry that of course there are no spirits, cause people to doubt whether the existence of spirits makes any difference; and this is the way in which society falls into chaos.

This is why our Master Mo affirmed that since kings and dukes and leaders in society actually do seek to profit society and remove its injurious elements, therefore this question whether the existence of spirits makes any difference is one which must on no account escape investigation. If, however, the question is precisely of that nature, how can we properly investigate it?

The word of our Master Mo: The universally true way of learning by investigation whether a thing exists or not, is, without question, by means of the actual knowledge (on the evidence) of everybody's ears and eyes. This is the criterion of whether a thing exists or not. If it has been heard and seen, then it undoubtedly is to be taken as existing. If no one has heard of it or seen it, then it undoubtedly is to be taken as non-existing. In such a case, why not go to some village or district and make inquiries? If from the

---

[1] When a man arrives at the stage where he says 'because' and 'therefore' he has begun to reason self-consciously. When he begins to say 'this is a cause' and 'that is an effect,' he has gone a step further and has started to reason about reasoning. It is a little doubtful whether Mo Ti had reached this second stage. Some of his recorders certainly had, as we see here.

[2] On the evidence of this chapter the reference here is mainly to spirits of the dead, but not entirely. Also, the writer was thinking not merely of manes, i.e. the dead who were known in their lifetime, but also of queer sorts of ghosts and spectres.

beginning of man down to the present, spirit-like things
have been seen and their voices heard, how can it be asserted
that they do not exist?   But if they have not been seen and
heard, how can it be asserted that they do exist?   Now
take the words of those who maintain that there are no
spirits.   They say that there are any number of people who
think that they have heard and seen spirit-like things, but
surely there is no one who has heard or seen a spirit thing
which (both) exists and at the same time does not exist.

The word of our Master Mo: If we take only what every
one has both heard and seen in common, then there is the
case of Tu Po.   The Chou King Hsüan [1] put to death his
minister, Tu Po, although he was innocent of any crime.
Tu Po said: 'Our sovereign puts me to death although I am
an innocent man.   If a dead person has no consciousness,[2]
then there is an end of me.   But if I still have consciousness
when dead, before three years are out I shall certainly make
our sovereign know this!'   In the third year King Hsüan
assembled the feudal lords at P'u T'un.   There were several
hundred chariots there, and several thousand attendants
all about the place.   At noon Tu Po, riding in a plain
chariot drawn by a white horse and wearing red clothes
and a red hat and holding a red bow with red arrows, pursued the king and shot him in his chariot.   The arrow
pierced his heart. . . . Not a man of the Chou attendants
present but saw it, and of distant places not one but heard
of it, whilst a record of it was made in the Chou Annals.
. . . Taking what this book has as one's angle of vision, how
can there be doubts about the existence of spirits?

There follow four other illustrations from the annals of one
state and another, each leading to the same final remark as the
one above, and later in the chapter the author goes back to
records in silk and bronze of the Sage-kings as proving that
these sages believed in the existence of spirits and that the records
of their lives and of the lives of their wicked descendants prove
the existence of spirits.

[1] 827–783 B.C.
[2] So Dr. Mei Yi-pao (*Works of Motse*, p. 162).   The character *chioh*,
usually translated 'knowledge,' seems in a few classical contexts to require
the idea of 'consciousness.'

The new cult of unethical fatalism was that 'if a man's fate is to be rich, then he will be rich: if his fate is to be poor, then he will be poor, and nothing can be gained by wrestling with fate.' The three synoptic chapters have survived. They are of great interest to the historian of legend and literary critic, but in relation to Mo Ti's religious beliefs contain nothing very distinctive from what has already been illustrated. Mo Ti and his followers, with their intense if narrow convictions about the moral order of the universe, were, of course, strongly opposed to this kind of rationalism. On the other hand, one passage is of very great interest to the student of pure philosophy. It is as follows:

Chapter 35. *Against Fatalism.*

It is very necessary that the statements of these believers in fate should be clearly differentiated. Nevertheless how this theory is to be clearly differentiated is a difficult question.

The word of our Master Mo: A standard must be set up. A statement without a standard (of reference) is like fixing the quarters in which the sun will rise and set by means of a revolving potter's wheel. Since that is not the way to attain a clear knowledge of the distinctions between what is right and wrong and beneficial and injurious, therefore a statement must pass three tests. What is meant by 'three tests'? In the words of our Master Mo, there is the test of a solid foundation (to a statement), the test of its verifiability, and the test of its applicability. In what way can a foundation be given? By building the statement on the facts about the ancient Sage-kings. In what way can it be verified? By ascertaining the facts about what people generally have heard with their own ears and seen with their own eyes. In what way can a statement be applied? By adopting it for the purposes of disciplinary government and observing what there is of profit to the state and to the people.

II. *The Logic of All-embracing Love.*

Chapter 14. *On All-embracing love.*

[From the second of the synoptic records on this subject.]

The sage man who takes in hand the ordering of the Great

Society must know what it is that gives rise to disorder: only so can he put it in order. If he does not know what gives rise to disorder, then he cannot make order. This is illustrated by the physician and his attack on men's diseases. He must know what it is that gives rise to disease. Only so can he attack it. If he does not know this, then he cannot attack it.

Why should the ordering of disorder in the state be unique in not being like this? . . . The sage man who has the ordering of the Great Society cannot but examine into what gives rise to disorder. When this examination is made, the rise of disorder is (found to be) people not loving each other, ministers of state and sons not being filial to their sovereigns and fathers: that is what is called disorder. Sons love themselves and not their fathers: and the result is that they injure their fathers in profiting themselves. Younger brothers love themselves and not their elder brothers; and the result is . . . Ministers love themselves and not their sovereigns: and the result is . . . So in the case of fathers who have no compassion for their sons, and elder brothers for their younger brothers, and sovereigns for their ministers. This also is universally described as disorder. Fathers love themselves and not their sons: and the result is they injure their sons in profiting themselves. . . .

If we go to the robbers all over the country, it is just the same. Robbers love their households and do not love the households of different kinds of people. The result is that they rob these other households in order to profit their own. And the same applies to the great officers who throw each other's clans into confusion and the feudal lords who attack each other's countries. . . . Examine all this as to its origin: it all comes from failure to love one another. . . . If the whole of society had mutual love without discrimination, country would not attack country, clan would not throw clan into confusion: there would be no robbers: sovereigns and ministers, fathers and sons, all would be compassionate and filial. In this state of affairs it follows that the Great Society would be well ordered. . . . Thus it was that our

Master Mo said that he could not but urge that men should be loved. This is his word.

The above gives in shortened form the whole argument of c. 14. In the second and third synoptic accounts the treatment is in very much the same language, though the order is different and there is more of the thrust and counterthrust of sharp debate. This feature is now illustrated.

Chapter 15. On All-embracing Love.

[From the third synoptic record.]

The knights and gentlemen everywhere to-day, however, say that although in theory this kind of all-embracingness is very good, none the less it is very difficult for universal application. The word of our Master Mo is: The leaders in society simply do not understand what is to their profit, nor do they distinguish the facts.[1] Take the case of besieging a city. To fight in the fields, to achieve fame at the cost of one's life: this is what all men everywhere find very difficult. Yet if their sovereign calls for it, then the whole body of knights are able to do it. How very different from this is mutual all-embracing love and the mutual exchange of profit. To love and benefit another is to have him follow on and love and benefit you. To hate and injure another is to have him follow on and hate and injure you. What is there difficult in this? The fact is simply that no ruler has embodied it in his government and no knight has embodied it in his conduct.

Formerly Duke Ling of Ch'u State liked his knights to have small waists. Thus it was that his court officers all limited themselves to one meal a day. Having exhaled their breath they tightened their belts. It was only by leaning against a wall that they could stand up. Within a year the whole court was black in the face. There is the fact: the sovereign called for it, and the ministers were able

[1] Emending *pien* (to argue) to *pien* (to distinguish). The text in any case requires emendation. Another question is whether *ch'i ku*, translated as 'their facts,' is not rather 'their reasons,' in which case Mo Ti, or his early disciples, had reached that pitch of abstract analysis which enables a logician to say 'this is a cause' and 'that is an effect.'

to do it. . . . This is the kind of thing which people find to be difficult. . . .

None the less, the knights and gentlemen everywhere say that it [i.e. all-embracing love] cannot be put into practice. To illustrate this they say it would be like picking up Mount T'ai and stepping over the river Ch'i. The word of our Master Mo denounces this as an illustration. He said that picking up Mount T'ai and stepping over the river Ch'i should be described as beyond the limit of human strength, and from antiquity down to the present day there never had been a man who could do this. How different is mutual all-embracing love and the mutual exchange of benefits! In the old days the Sage-kings put it into practice. As to how it is known that this was so,[1] in the old days when Yü [2] brought the Great Society into order, he dug out the West River and Yu Tou River in order to drain off the waters of the Ch'ü, Sun, and Huang Rivers. In the north he dammed the Yuan and Ku Rivers in order to fill up the Hou Chih Ti and Hu Chih basins. He made a watershed of the Ti Chu (range) and made a tunnel through Mount Nung Men. He did this to benefit the people of the Yui, Tai, Hu, and Ho tribes together with the people west of the Yellow River. . . . This expresses what Yü did. I, to-day, can practise all-embracingness.

Chapter 16. On All-embracing Love.

[From the third synoptic record.]

Our Master Mo said that the man who criticizes others must have something as an alternative. To criticize without an alternative is like using fire to put out a fire. The (idea) the man expresses is logically indefensible.

I regard all-embracingness as exactly right. In this way quick ears and clear eyes co-operate in hearing and seeing,

---

[1] In c. 16 there is an interesting variant of this: 'We are not contemporaries of theirs: we have not heard their voices nor seen their faces. We know by means of what is written on bamboo and silk (strips) and what is engraved in metal and stone and handed down to later generations.'
[2] He was the patron saint, so to speak, of the Mohists, as Yao and Shun were of the Confucianists.

arms and legs are immeasurably strengthened to co-operate in movement and action, whilst those who possess the Way co-operate untiringly in teaching it. In this way those who are old and without wife and child have their bodily needs served so that they complete their tale of years, whilst the helpless young, children who are fatherless and motherless, have something they can trust so that their bodies can grow big and strong. . . .

It is incomprehensible what it is that makes the knights on hearing about all-inclusiveness oppose it. What are the facts of the case? As it is, the words of these knightly opponents do not stop at denunciation. They say, It is excellent, but none the less it is unusable.

The word of our Master Mo: If it is unusable, even I will oppose it. How can it be both good and unusable? Let us go forward along two lines. Suppose there are two knights, one of them holding fast to discrimination (in love), the other to all-embracingness. The result will be that the one who discriminates will make the following statement: It would be absurd for me to regard my friend's body as I regard my own, to regard his parents as I do my own. The result would be that when he observed his friend to be hungry and cold, he would not feed him or clothe him: when his friend was ill, he would not tend him: when his friend died, he would not bury him. These would be the words of the man who discriminates, and also his deeds. The knight who is all-embracing would not speak or act like that. He would say: I have heard that the high-minded knight in the Great Society must regard his friend's body as his own, his friend's parents as his own: only then can he be regarded as a high-minded knight. The result would be that when he observed his friend to be hungry and cold, he would feed and clothe him. . . .

Now if we come to the point that the words of the two knights contradict each other and their actions are diametrically opposed, we have to assume that both speak the truth and both act accordingly, so that each man's words and actions agree like the two halves of a tally: not a word

is spoken which is not put into practice.   In that case the
question may well be put: Suppose a great stretch of country
here and a man putting on his harness for going out on
campaign in which the scale of life and death cannot be
known. . . . Do you know or do you not know to whom
he would entrust his household and his parents and the
care of his wife and children?   Would it be to the friend who
was all-embracing or the friend who discriminated?   I think
that on such an occasion as this there are no fools anywhere,
whether men or women.   Even though he were opposed
to the all-embracing man, he would still put him in charge.

III. The Logic of Profit.

As a corollary to this categorical imperative of all-embracing
love, Mo Ti denounced wars of aggression, the vice to which his
age, as the age before him, was so prone.   He also denounced
extravagant expenditure in the conduct of mourning rites, a
practice which the Confucians, both then and later, greatly
encouraged.   He also set his face against the luxury in court
circles, involving as it did the unremunerative use of state funds.
His objection was particularly strong against the art of music,
to him a shocking waste of time, money, and labour.   Behind
all this lay a strictly utilitarian mind, which is revealed not only
in its rational strength, but also in its rational limitation, namely
its preoccupation with material prosperity.

Chapter 18. In Condemnation of Aggressive Warfare.
[From the second synoptic record.]

There is an old proverb: If your plans fail, learn the future
from the past, learn the invisible from the visible.   With
plans of this nature one may be both successful and wise.

Take the case of a country about to go to war.   In winter
the cold is to be feared, in summer the heat.   This means
that neither winter nor summer is the time for such
action.   But if in the spring, then the people miss their
sowing and planting: if in the autumn, then they miss reaping and harvesting.   If they miss only one season, then the
number of people who will die of cold and hunger is incalculable.   Now let us reckon the army's equipment, the
arrows, standards, tents, armour, shields, and sword hilts:
the number of these which will break and perish and not

come back is beyond reckoning. So also with the spears, lances, swords, daggers, war chariots, and baggage wagons: the number of those which will get smashed and ruined and never come back is beyond reckoning. So also with oxen and horses who go out fat and come back lean, or die there and do not come back at all: a number beyond reckoning. So also with people: the incalculable number who die, owing to the food supply being cut off or failing through the distance of transport; the number who, living under bad conditions with irregular meals and excesses of hunger and repletion, fall sick by the road and die. The army casualties also are incalculably large, perhaps whole armies perishing. Hence the spirits lose their worshippers, again to an incalculable extent, whilst the state robs the people of their incomes and diminishes their sources of profit.

All this is so: and why? The answer in defence of it is: we covet the fame and the profit of being victors in war. That is why it takes place. And the word of our Master Mo in reply is: Reckon up what they win for themselves: it is nothing of any use. Reckon up what they gain: it is the exact opposite of profit; far less than the loss. Take the case of an attack on a town with its inner wall one mile, its outer two miles, in circumference. To capture this without the thrust of a spear or the death of a man would be an empty achievement. As it is, however, the deaths at most must be reckoned by the ten thousand, at least by the thousand, and all that can be obtained is one or two miles of township. And all the time the great states have empty [i.e. half-populated] townships to be reckoned by the thousand—waiting to be occupied peacefully—and uncultivated lands to be reckoned by the ten thousand—waiting to be opened up peacefully. Thus then the amount of land waiting to be possessed is in excess, the population waiting to be ruled in true kingly fashion insufficient. Now then: to bring the people to death and to aggravate the troubles of high and low in order to quarrel over a half-populated township, this logically is to throw away that of which you have too little and to double that of which you have too

much.   To put the affairs of state right in this fashion is
directly counter to the interests of the state.

Chapter 25. On Moderation in the Rites of Mourning.

[The only surviving essay of the three synoptic essays.]

The word of our Master Mo . . . When in the past ages
of the Three Dynasties the Sage-kings were no more, the
Great Society lost hold of righteousness, and some later
leaders in society regarded elaborate funerals and prolonged mourning periods as signs of human - hearted
righteousness and the duty of filial sons.   Others regarded
the elaborate funerals and prolonged mourning periods as
not human-heartedness, not righteousness, and not the duty
of filial sons. . . .

Since there are doubts arising from the contentions of
both sides, let us look into the matter from the angle of the
rectification of the state, the family, and the people in them.
Reckon up whether elaborate funerals and prolonged
mourning fits in with these three benefits.   It is my opinion
that if by the application of these principles the poor can
really be enriched, the population be increased, social in-
stability be changed to stability, and disorder be made good
order, then elaborate funerals and prolonged mourning
periods will be signs of human-heartedness [*jen*], righteousness, and the duty of filial sons, and those who plan on
behalf of man must on no account refrain from advocating
these practices.   A *jen* sovereign will promote them throughout society, making them into institutions which the people
must believe and observe from the cradle to the grave.   My
opinion, however, also is that if by applying these principles
the poor cannot really be enriched, nor the population increased . . . then elaborate funerals will not be . . . the
duty of filial sons, and those who plan on behalf of men must
on no account refrain from prohibiting these practices.   A
jen sovereign will seek to eradicate them from society. . . .
For the fact is that the promotion of profit and the eradi-
cation of injury throughout society as a means to bring

state and people into confusion, this has never happened in the history of man.

There follows a detailed description of a great lord's funeral with the moral that in the case of 'a common hind dying, the resources of the family are in danger of being exhausted,' whilst the death of a lord empties the state treasury before gold and jade and pearls can be placed by the body and the mound be filled with carts and horses and bundles of silk. . . .

When to this is added the physical strain of ritual mourning with its bouts of weeping, abstention from food, and other mortification of the flesh, it is clear that 'elaborate funerals involve the burial of wealth and prolonged mourning prevents people from getting on with their work,' whether they be princes or peasants. Also 'child-bearing is delayed and even stopped altogether. With poverty prevalent, banditry breaks out on all sides and all society is in disorder.' Thus by this triple, utilitarian test, elaborate funerals and the like are not profit but injury to men.

The argument goes on to a perfect illustration of the religious utilitarian mind: the profit motive attributed without any compunction to Heaven and the spirits.

If the country be stricken with poverty, the sacrificial cakes and wine will be adulterated. If the population drop, there will be few to worship the High Ruler and the spirits. If the country be in disorder, sacrifices will not be made at the proper time. Not only so: there are cases of the worship of the High Ruler and the spirits being forbidden by the Government. In these circumstances the High Ruler and the spirits will begin to follow on by taking control of the matter. They will ask whether it is better to have men or not to have them. Then logically the High Ruler and the spirits will send down judgment on their crimes, will visit them with calamities, will punish them and cast them out. Is not this logically the situation which arises?

Chapter 21. On Moderation in Spending.

[The second of the two surviving essays.]

. . . In ancient times the regulations of the Sage-kings made standards of moderation to the effect that all the artisans in the Great Society, the wheelwrights, tanners, potters, carpenters, should take in hand what they best could do, and that when they had met the needs of the common people they should stop. Whatever meant extra expense without extra profit to the people, that the Sage-kings refused to have made. . . . Thus with regard to standards for eating and drinking, the regulations were that no one should go beyond what satisfied hunger and prolonged the power of breathing, what strengthened legs and arms and made keen the powers of hearing and seeing. People were not to go to the length of blending the five flavours and harmonizing the different perfumes, or to pro-cure rare delicacies from distant countries. How we come to know that this was so is through Yao. He ruled from Chiao Tu in the south to Yu Tu in the north, from where the sun rose in the east to where it set in the west. There were none who did not come and do homage to him. Turning to the meals he most liked to have, they were those without two kinds of millet and soup with a second course of meat. He ate out of an earthen bowl and drank from an earthen cup. . . . The Sage-king did not practise the strict observance of the social code with its bowing and scraping and passing the wine cup round.

. . . So with the regulations about clothes, the standard was not to go beyond dark purple silks in the winter, seeing that they are both light and warm, or in the summer beyond linen clothes, seeing that they are both light and cool. Thus whatever added to the expense but did not add to profit, the Sage-kings refused to have made.

The same principle is applied to weapons, carriages, boats, and houses. Thus the requirements of a carriage are given as 'safety for riding in, speed in arriving.' This is its 'profit.' The idea of 'function,' fulfilment of the basic purposes for which a thing was made, seems clearly to have crossed the rational consciousness of Mo Ti and his disciples. On the other hand, not merely luxury art, but all art, is abhorrent to them.

IV. On Political Unity.

The fourth side to Mo Ti's teaching demonstrates even more clearly the systematic contours to his mind. He had indeed a system of thought in a sense which cannot be ascribed to Confucius's ways of thinking. This estimate is not only praise, but also criticism, for Mo Ti was to a dangerous degree at the mercy of his two principles, the authority of Heaven and the profit of man.

Thus in facing the outworn feudalism of his day with its twin curses, the employment of court favourites as administrators and the breakdown of loyalty and political cohesion, Mo Ti's logical mind drove him to make not one but two emphases. The first aimed at being humane; the second, a corollary to the first, was likely to have an opposite effect. Mo Ti, the religious utilitarian, could not see this.

Emphasis I. The Exaltation of Men of Worth.

   Chapter 8.

[The first of the synoptics.]

The word of our Master Mo: To-day kings, dukes, and the big men in society, in making systems of government in their states, all want the country to be rich, the population big, and the administration of justice such as to produce order. But instead of getting wealth they get poverty, instead of a big population a small one, instead of order disorder. This then is basically to miss what they want and get what they hate. What are the facts about this matter?

The word of our Master Mo: Disorder consists in the failure of the kings, dukes, and big men . . . to promote men of worth and use the services of able men in administration. The facts are that if a country has plenty of worthy officers, then the order provided by the state is an unbreakable one, but if it has few such officers, then its order is easily broken. Thus it is that the business of the big men consists primarily in increasing the number of men of worth; and the question then is what is the (right) method for doing this.

The word of our Master Mo: To illustrate, if you want to increase the number of expert archers and drivers in the country, you will certainly have to enrich them, elevate their social status, honour them, and praise them before

you can obtain a full complement of them.[1]   How much
more this applies to worthy officers, to men of solid virtue,
with a command of language, learned in the method of the
Way!   These, to be sure are the treasures of the state, the
assistants of its guardian deities.   These also must be
enriched, have their social status enhanced, should be
honoured and praised before a country's full complement
of worthy officers can be reached.

When the Sage-kings of antiquity began to govern their
word was: The unrighteous shall not be enriched, the unrighteous shall not be ennobled, the unrighteous shall not
have court favour, the unrighteous shall not stand near the
royal person.   The rich and noble, when they heard this,
all retired and consulted to this effect: We originally depended on our wealth and station, and now our lord
promotes the righteous regardless of whether they are poor
and base-born.   That being so, it follows that we must on
no account be unrighteous.

Court favourites are dealt with in the same language, and then
the common people and half-civilized people on the borders,
and the conclusion drawn is that all ranks of society emulated
each other in achieving righteousness.

In those days, therefore, there was a hierarchy of virtue
and rewards on the basis of work done. . . . Officials were
not permanently ennobled and the rank and file not endlessly
at the bottom of the social scale.   The man of ability was
elevated, the man of no ability put below him: public spirit
was encouraged, and personal grudges put away.

In the second essay (c. 9) the criticism of present-day rulers is
based on their intelligence in trifles and their inconceivable
stupidity over matters of grave import. Thus:

They cannot make their own clothes, so they are sure to
employ expert tailors. . . . They have not learnt to exalt
worth and employ ability in the work of government. . . .
Accordingly relatives of the men who with cause are rich

---

[1] The *a fortiori* device of dialectic is of common occurrence in these
essays.   This is the first time it appears in Chinese literature.

and of high station, and handsome engaging fellows, these are employed. Is there any guarantee that they will be wise and prudent? This is to employ the unwise and imprudent to order the state.

Emphasis II. On Unity.

Chapter 2.

[The first of the synoptic trilogy.]

The word of our Master Mo: In the old days when human life was beginning and there was no government by punishment, the tendency in talking was to express different (ideas of) righteousness.[1] Thus one man and so one righteousness, two men two righteousnesses, ten men ten righteousnesses. Whatever the number of men, so many different (ideas) there were of righteousness. And thus everybody maintained that his righteousness was true and the other man's was false. Thus it was that they exchanged mutual disapprovals, and inside the family, fathers and sons, elder and younger brothers came to be hostile. Each went his own way and was unable to agree with the other. People everywhere used fire and water and poison to do malicious injury. Things came to such a pass that surplus energy could not be spent in mutual labour, surplus wealth could not be shared out, and good ways of life were kept concealed and not communicated (to a man's neighbour). The chaos everywhere was like that of birds and beasts.

It became clear that the way in which this chaos came about was through there being no controlling head. The result was that a man of sufficient worth was chosen out of the whole population [2] and set up as Son of Heaven. He, finding his strength inadequate, selected from the whole population three men and officially appointed them to act

[1] Care is necessary in translation not to assume more than a writer expresses. This writer apparently was very near to the stage of conscious distinction between 'a thing' and 'the idea of a thing,' but he did not quite reach it. Cp. the section on the Mohist logicians, Chapter XI.

[2] It is curious that both here and in the parallel passage in c. 13 this choosing is not directly ascribed to Heaven. In c. 13 Heaven is made the subject of the parallel sentence.

as the Three Dukes. After these two steps, seeing that the
Great Society was so vast that among the people of distant
countries and differing lands their distinctions of right and
wrong, and profit and loss, could not be intelligently known
like adding up one and two, therefore myriad countries
were plotted out and the feudal lords set up as sovereign
rulers in each of them. . . . Because their strength was
inadequate they chose those in the country who were sufficiently worthy and officially appointed them as heads.
All then being completed the Son of Heaven gave his word
to the peoples: On hearing of good or evil, all shall report
it to the (officers) above them, and what they call right all
shall call right: what they call wrong, all shall call wrong.
If an officer be at fault, a remonstrance shall be made to
him in due form.[1] If among those below there is any (one
specially) good, the onlookers shall acclaim it. To be of
one mind with those above and not to make factions below,
this shall be rewarded by those above and praised by those
below. On the other hand, if on hearing of good or evil,
no report be made to those above . . . and those below
make factions and are not of one mind with those above,
this shall be punished by those above and renounced by
those below. By this means the rewards and punishments
are open to clear investigation and produce well-evidenced
confidence.

Hence a village head was the (most) human-hearted man
in the village, and he made an official statement: news of
good or evil must be reported to the district head and what
he calls right all shall call right. . . . Remove from your
speech and your actions everything that is wrong and learn
the district head's good speech and actions. Then the
district cannot be described as in a state of disorder.

The same form of words describes the same situation on the
larger scale of the district in relation to the country and finally
on the scale of the country in relation to the Great Society. The

---

[1] It is curious that the term used is of an inferior giving advice to a
superior, in other words the remonstrance apparently is to come from
below. The next sentence also gives the idea that the ordinary man
was to have some freedom in expressing his views.

sovereign rulers of the countries are referred to as 'the countries' (most) human-hearted men.' From the Son of Heaven the argument goes on to deal with Heaven.

If all below are of one mind with the man above, but are not of one mind with Heaven, then the jungle (of political chaos) still remains. In the event of devastating winds and rains coming one after the other, these are the means by which Heaven punishes the whole population for not being of one mind with Heaven.[1]

---

[1] These sentences appear to belong to a supplementary section dealing with the present and not with the past age of the Sage-kings. This is clearly the case in c. 12, whilst c. 13 has no parallel. The argument sidesteps the question whether the Son of Heaven himself may not be responsible for this lack of identification with the Will of Heaven. This is curious, since the reasoning is generally so closely worked out. Also, the Confucian tradition was quite clear that the blame might fall on the Son of Heaven. It was only the Legalists who maintained that the king could do no wrong.

CHAPTER IV: CONFUCIUS'S DISCIPLES: THE TRADITION OF 'THE MASTER' EVOLVING

The doings and sayings of Confucius's disciples [1] are, for the most part, recorded in works which scholars cannot as yet date with any confidence as having been produced before Han times. (Cp. Introduction, pp. xxxiii–xxxiv.) The tradition, however, is consistent in making seventy to seventy-seven as the number of real disciples, and there is more or less reliable information about some twenty of them. Amongst them a few stand out as very real persons, men of character and individual bent along lines either of thought or of action. There is no doubt that before long there were three or four kinds of vigorous expositions of 'the Master's' teaching. Han Fei, the Legalist writer (third century B.C.), speaks of eight varieties in his day. Unfortunately, the earlier history of 'Confucius's Door' is lacking in clear details. We can only distinguish three varieties of tradition with any accuracy.

The more spiritual and deeply ethical side to the teaching was upheld and developed by Tseng Shen and his disciples, possibly with Tzu Hsia and Tzu Yiu and their disciples in close affiliation. This section of the Confucian school tended to lay heavy emphasis on ritual observance, both religious and social. They were rather like the Pharisees in the Gospels with their good and their bad qualities. Then there was a more political side emphasized by others whom we can less certainly name. Doubtless they were too busy governing to leave time for writing. Tzu Chang, who figures prominently in the *Analects* and is mentioned at the head of Han Fei's list, is not placeable as a particular influence, though he and Tzu Kung had a supreme veneration for 'the Master.' But from the point of view of pure philosophy Tzu Ssu, whose *Mean-in-action* has been quoted above, is the most important of them all.

In the following quotations Tzu Ssu does not appear. Neither do the politically minded, for Mencius (fourth century) and the *Great Learning*, which I assign to the early fourth century, are their great representatives. Thus there is only need here to illustrate the teaching of Tseng Shen and closely allied groups.

Tzu Hsia said, 'The man who treats men of worth as such, who makes light [?] of sexual pleasure, who knows how to serve his father and mother with might and main, and to serve his prince with his life, who in his friendships is true to his word, he may be spoken of as without (the

[1] To judge from the Imperial Catalogue (*c.* 30 B.C.) three or four of them wrote books. These have not survived under their own names.

refinement of) book learning, but I should certainly describe him as having that learning.' (*Analects* i. 7.)

Ssu-ma Niu was so unhappy that he said, 'Other men all have brothers, I alone have not.' Tzu Hsia said, 'I have heard it said that life and death are by Heaven's decree, and wealth and rank also are from Heaven: if a man of breeding pays due reverence and is not idle,[1] if he is courteous as custom [lit. the Rituals] demands, then all within the Four Seas are his brothers. How can a man of breeding be unhappy because he has no brothers?' (*Analects* xii. 5.)

The disciples of Tzu Hsia asked Tzu Chang about friendly intercourse with people, and he said, 'What has Tzu Hsia to say?' They replied, 'Associate with those with whom you may, keep away from those with whom you should not have dealings.' Tzu Chang said, 'This is different from what I have been told, namely that a man of breeding pays honour to men of worth but is tolerant with everybody, takes delight in the good but pities the incompetent. Take me, (assuming) I have great worth: how can I not tolerate other men? And if I am not a man of worth, other men will reject me. How can we have this rejecting of men?' (*Analects* xix. 3.)

Tzu Yiu said, 'The disciples of Tzu Hsia are like children. If discipleship be only a matter of cleaning and sweeping, of making the proper answers to questions, and (the etiquette of) entering and retiring, then they pass muster. But these are matters of no importance. The question is, how they would manage, if they were put on to matters of basic importance.' Tzu Hsia, hearing of this, said, 'Yen Yiu [i.e. Tzu Yiu] is wrong. If the Way for men of honour be expounded to a man before he is ripe for it, he will be tired of it after he is ripe; (as is seen) for example in the different treatment given to the various plants and trees. Surely one may not fool one's disciples! Presumably the man who has both the initial and the final stages (of the Way) in him, is a sage and no less.' (*Analects* xix. 12.)

There was a drought, and Duke Mu [of Lu, 408–375 B.C.]

[1] Accepting Mr. Waley's suggested emendation.

summoned Master Hsien to give him advice. The Duke said, 'Heaven has given no rain for a long time, and I want to expose a cripple to death from the sun. What do you think?' The answer was, 'Heaven is responsible for there being no rain, and to expose some other man's sick son would be an act of cruelty. It does not seem to me that it could have an effect.' 'In that case I will expose a witch,' said the Duke, 'how about that?' The answer was, 'Heaven is responsible for there being no rain; and to pin your hopes to (the suffering of) a foolish woman seems to me rather wide of the mark.' 'Suppose, then, I move the market-place: how about that?' The answer was, 'When the Son of Heaven dies, markets are held in side lanes for seven days, and when a great feudatory dies, the same is done for three days. Under the circumstances to move the market seems to me something which might be done.' (*Li Chi, T'an Kung, ad fin.*)

Yu Tzu and Tzu Yiu [two of Confucius's more intimate disciples] were standing together when they saw a mourner abandoned in his grief like a child. Yu Tzu said to Tzu Yiu, 'I simply do not comprehend the frenzied leaping in the burial rites, and I have long wished to do away with it. Genuine emotion involves doing away with it, does it not?' Tzu Yiu said, 'There is in ritual the (element of) lessening emotion and the (element of) deliberately fostering the material side. For emotion to have free play and move straight to action is after the manner of the Jung and the Ti [the barbarian peoples]. But ritual is not like that at all. If men are pleased, they sing. From singing they pass to swaying their bodies, from that to dancing, from that to a state of wild excitement, from that to feeling unhappy, from that to sighing, from that to beating the breast, and from that to throwing themselves about.[1] A guide to moderation is needed here, that is to say, ritual. A corpse is a hateful object. Its impotency revolts people. This is

[1] Some textual critics in the eighteenth century questioned the text with its transition of joy to sorrow. To the modern psychologist this presents no difficulty.

why it is wrapped in a shroud and drapings and plumes are used, that people may not find the dead man hateful. Further, from the time the death takes place, dried and salted meat-offerings are prepared, and these are dispatched to the grave-side. But as for their being eaten after the burial, no one has ever seen (the dead) tasting them. And yet, from the earliest times to the present, this practice has never been abandoned. This is because it stops people from being revolted (at a dead man).[1] Thus what you criticize in ritual is not a defect in it.' (*Li Chi, T'an Kung* ii. 2.)

MASTER TSENG

Master Tseng, as Tseng Shen is always called in the *Analects*,[2] had two main sides to his teaching. He was the first of a new type of ritualist, the scholar-ritualist, to which Confucius's teaching and influence gave birth, along with the scholar-administrator type. Both had a new sense of the individual, the ethical individual, and whilst the scholar-administrators faced the moral issues of the individual in relation to government, the scholar-ritualists were deeply concerned with the daily task of self-cultivation. The cultivation of the moral self, that was Tseng Shen's passion, and along with it went his passion for perfect filial service of parents both when alive and after their death. This is the point where the deeply ethical Chinese religion of filial piety as an emergent form of primitive ancestor-worship first makes its appearance; and Tseng Shen probably was much more responsible for this development than Confucius was.

The following quotations are grouped under the two headings: the cultivation of the moral self, and filial piety. They are taken from three sources.

1. *The Cultivation of the Moral Self.*

Master Tseng said, 'Every day I examine myself in three ways: whether in my transacting of business for other men I have been faithful to them; whether in my intercourse with my friends I have been true in word; whether I have not passed on teachings which I have not mastered.' (*Analects* i. 4.)

Master Tseng said, 'Gifted, yet seeking advice from the

[1] Cp. B. Malinowski in *Science, Religion, and Reality* (1925), p. 47 et seq.
[2] The only explanation of this which appeals to me is that his disciples had a hand in compiling the *Analects*, and thought their teacher as great a man as Confucius.

not gifted: possessed of much, yet seeking instruction from those possessed of little: having, as though he had not, full as if he were empty: badly treated, yet not protesting—I once had a friend whose habit of life was this.'[1]

Master Tseng said, 'A man with public duties cannot afford not to be both large-hearted and stout-hearted. His burden is heavy and his course a long one. He must make human-heartedness his burden of responsibility; and that surely is a heavy load! Only with death does his course come to an end; and that surely is a long road.' (*Analects* viii. 7.)

Master Tseng said, 'The man of honour attacks the evil in himself, seeks out his faults, forces himself over what he fails to accomplish, expels his selfish desires, persistently obeys (the demands of) righteousness [*yi*]: so he may be said to be a man who learns.

The man of honour loves day by day to learn and when the time comes to put into practice, he never avoids the difficult or follows the easy path. In righteousness alone he abides. At break of day he addresses himself to his vocation, and when the night comes he examines within, meditating on the dangers to his self. So, he may also be said to guard his vocation.

The man of honour learns from the very compulsion of his vocation. He always asks for methodical instruction, and when it is not positive, he takes time to observe the features in the matter so that he may go into it again. Even if he cannot get it expounded, he does not force the issue.

To the man of honour it is a source of grief if, when he has studied a matter, his study of it is not comprehensive: if, when he has studied it comprehensively, he does not get it by heart: if, when he has got it by heart he does not really know it: if, when he has really got to know it, he fails to put it into practice: if, when he has not failed to put it into practice, he fails to be sweetly reasonable[2] over it.

This is the point to which he carries his studies. Since he keeps a painful watch on their being comprehensive, his

[1] Commentators have wondered whether the reference is to Yen Hui.
[2] The New Testament ἐπιείκεια is the exact counterpart of the Chinese *jang* in some of its uses.

actions are sure, although his words may be insignificant. In his actions he is sure to get ahead of other people, whilst in words he is sure to be behind them. And, since his whole life long he guards this with painful care, his actions are not with a view to a speedy reputation nor his undertakings with a view to quick achievement. The very man himself being in his words and deeds, men publish the words abroad and uphold the deeds. And, since his whole life long he guards this apprehensively, he does not destroy the small, insignificant things [1] (in life). In action he makes himself, not other men, insignificant—and, if they realize this, they have a good will towards him, whilst if they do not realize it, (he says,) "I none the less know myself." And, since his whole life long he vigorously takes this into account, calamity is to him an object of anxiety, disgrace an object of fear. So, when he sees the good, he is afraid of missing a share in it; when he sees the bad, he is afraid of its getting inside him. The result is that his life is one of suspense. When he sees an advantage to be gained, he thinks of dishonour: when he sees evil, he thinks of being fouled by it; when he longs for anything, he thinks of the disgrace (attached to it): when he is angry, he thinks of the calamity (that will ensue). And, since his whole life long he watches out for this in dread, he directs his thoughts to mastering his vital energy [ch'i]. . . .

The man of principle being himself good rejoices in the goodness of others, himself having ability rejoices in the ability of others, and should he have inabilities he does not pass them on to others. And whilst he loves men to be good, he does not push them to it: whilst he hates men being bad, he does not get wrought up about it, or where he does get wrought up over wrongdoing, he does not patch things up. But then he adorns what is beautiful (in the culprit) and does not attack him: for there is nothing gained by attacking and no reform comes from patching things up. . . . He keeps silent about men's faults and completes what is beautiful in them. Coming and going, if in the morning

[1] Cp. the biblical 'the smoking flax shall he not quench . . .'

a man does wrong and at night reforms, the man of principle is with him . . .; for the righteousness in him logically is an unvarying righteousness, the goodness in him a neighbourly goodness. Seeing his neighbour's one small point (of goodness) he hopes for two, and big points at that; for he does not make capital for himself at the expense of the other man with his lack of moral personality [*te*]. . . . He, indeed, may be described as having knowledge.

.　　.　　.　　.　　.

This is the reason why the man of principle both in speech and action is frightened, feeling the need of encouragement to avoid offence.[1] And this is the reason why he . . . sees himself as not yet perfect in preparation, although he may be so; nor dare he give his mind to being as he is. He can serve his father: so it is possible to serve his prince. He can serve his brother: so it is possible to serve his teachers and elders. To set a son to work is like setting a minister his tasks. . . . The man who can accept friendship can accept the colleagues who rank with him in government business. To be kind to one's household is like giving rewards for state service. . . . And this is the reason why goodness of necessity begins in the family. When a man of influence outside the family has bitter feelings against him in his family, he is (morally) insecure. . . .' (*Ta Tai Li*, c. 49.)

2. *The Implications of Filial Piety.*

When Master Tseng was ill (and near to death), he called his disciples and said, 'Uncover my feet, uncover my hands. In the *Odes* is the word:

> In constant fear and trembling,
> With unceasing vigilance,
> As if on the edge of a precipice,
> As if I were treading thin ice.

---

[1] *Tsui*, the old feudal term for an offence against one's lord, and so later used in the sense of a crime, an offence against the law. The Christian reader needs to avoid confusing the classical *tsui* with 'sin' in the religious sense. There are classical words which have that significance, but *tsui* is not one of them.

From now on, my children, I know that I am safely through.'[1] (*Analects* viii. 3.)

Master Tseng said, 'When special attention is given to those who are finished [i.e. the dead] and they are long remembered, the moral power [*te*] of the people has become a solid reality.' (*Analects* i. 9.)

Master Tseng said, 'With regard to a filial son's "nourishing his aged parents," he makes their hearts glad and does not go against their wishes. He makes pleasure for their eyes and ears and makes their bedroom comfortable. He faithfully provides them with food and drink. With regard to the filial son's "continuing for life," this is not to the end of his father's and mother's lives but to the end of his own life. This is the reason why he loves what they loved, reverences what they reverenced, even to their dogs and horses without exception. How much more with regard to the people (whom they loved and reverenced)!' (*Li Chi, Nei Tse* ii.)

Master Tseng said, 'Men of principle lay down filial piety as fidelity in action, as ritual at its noblest. Thus it is that, in the case of a son failing in his filial duty to his father, we dare not say that it is a case of the father having failed to nurture his son. In the case of a younger brother failing to acknowledge his elder brother, we dare not say that it is a case of the elder brother having failed to instruct his younger brother. . . . Therefore fathers talking with fathers [2] (may) speak of "taking care," (but) sons talking with sons (should only) speak of filial duty: elder brothers talking with elder brothers (may) speak of "instructing," but younger brothers talking with younger brothers (should only) speak of "acknowledging." . . .

The man of principle's filial piety is as follows: with

---

[1] i.e. through with the lifelong duty of not harming the body my parents gave me.

[2] The passage is a key one, because it shows that extreme feature of filial-piety religion, that the son has only duties and not rights as against his father, however bad the latter may be. Some Confucian moralists have disagreed with this, and maintained that a father's duty to his son is also a categorical imperative.

devoted love [1] and reverence that is the direct opposite to licence. Along with the dedication of his bodily strength there is decorum [*li*], along with his attitude of deference a sense of peace. Unwearied in his subtle urging of the right (on his father) he is obedient, and that in no laggard fashion. So, when there is smiling joy over the good faith of devoted service, this may be said to be filial piety.' (*Ta Tai Li*, c. 51.)

Master Tseng said, 'There are three kinds of filial piety. Great filial piety is bringing honour to one's parents. Next to it is not disgracing them. The lowest is being able to provide food for them.' (His disciple) Kung Ming Yi asked him, saying, 'Master, may you be called filial?' Master Tseng said, 'What is this you are saying? What is this you are saying? What a man of principle means by a filial son is a man who before he makes up his mind does the right thing by asking his father's and mother's advice. I am only a food-providing man. How can I be (really) filial? This body of mine is the limbs and body handed down by my parents. In using one's parents' handed-down limbs, dare one be without reverence? Therefore to lack deference when at home is unfilial: to be unfaithful in the service of one's prince is unfilial: to be an irresponsible official is unfilial: to go back on one's word with friends is unfilial: to be a coward in battle is unfilial. In these five cases calamity forthwith falls on one's body. Dare one be reverent?'

Master Tseng said, 'Establish filial piety, and it will fill all the space between the heavens and the earth. Spread it out, and it will extend to the Four Seas. Hand it down to future ages, and morning and evening it will be observed. Develop it to the Eastern Sea, the Western Sea, the Southern Sea, the Northern Sea, and it will be the standard (of conduct). As is said in the *Odes*:

> From west to east, from north to south
> No thought but what was submissive.'
>
> (*Ta Tai Li*, c. 52.)

---

[1] *Ai*, the word which expresses the emotional warmth of affection.

PART THREE

THE RISE OF MATERIALISTIC UTILITARIANISM AND THE CONFUCIANIST REPLY

CHAPTER V: SHANG YANG: THE TOTALITARIAN

The Legalist School's thought and political practice were in every way counter to the early Confucian School, whilst its gross utilitarianism was in some ways the logical outcome to Mo Ti's benevolent utilitarianism. Shang Yang (*d.* 338 B.C.), the first great Legalist thinker, was a native of Wei State. Finding no opening for his abilities there, he went to Ch'in, the backward state in the far west. There he gained the support of the reigning duke for a policy of radical changes in the body politic. He was a realist of realists, devoted to the material strength of the state and that alone. Behind his policy lay a philosophy of the common man which closely resembles that in Hitler's *Mein Kampf*. On the other hand, he saw more clearly than any previous statesman or thinker that the coming of the bureaucratic state meant the systematic development of law. Thus he was the founder of what Han dynasty writers called the *Fa Chia*, Legalist School. Although Lord Shang came to a bad end, he initiated a work in Ch'in State which brought it, a hundred years later, to supremacy over all the other states. The then king of Ch'in became First Emperor of China (*Shih Huang Ti*), and as such inaugurated a totalitarian regime, highly efficient, but utterly ruthless. This lasted only for a generation. (Cp. Introduction, p. xxxii.)

Three brands of Legalist thinking emerged during these two centuries, Shang Yang's emphasizing *fa* (law), Shen Pu-hai's emphasizing *shih* (autocratic power), Han Fei's emphasizing *shu* (statecraft).

With regard to the *Book of Lord Shang*,[1] it is impossible to say how much of it was written by Lord Shang himself. In those parts of it which have survived some essays are plainly by later hands.[1]

Chapter 1. The Reform of the Law.

Duke Hsiao discussed his policy. The three Great Officers, Lord Shang, Kan Lung, and Tu Chih, were in

---

[1] Cp. Dr. Duyvendak's *Book of Lord Shang* (London, 1928). The following translations are taken with but very few alterations from this work. Cp. Preface, p. vii.

attendance on the prince. Their thoughts dwelt on the vicissitudes of the world's affairs; and they discussed the principles of rectifying the law, seeking for a way of directing the people. The prince said, 'I intend now to alter the laws, so as to obtain orderly government, and to reform the rites so as to teach the people; but I am afraid the empire [1] will criticize me.' Lord Shang said, 'I have heard it said that he who hesitates in action does not accomplish anything, and he who hesitates in affairs gains no merit. Let Your Highness settle your thoughts quickly about altering the laws and perhaps not heed the criticism of the empire.'

Lord Shang said, '. . . There is more than one way to govern the world, and there is no necessity to imitate antiquity, in order to take appropriate measures for the state. T'ang and Wu succeeded in attaining supremacy without following antiquity, and, as for the downfall of Yin and Hsia, they were ruined without rites having been altered. Consequently, those who act counter to antiquity, do not necessarily deserve blame, nor do those who follow established rites merit much praise. Let Your Highness not hesitate.' Duke Hsiao said, '. . . One should, in one's plans, be directed by the needs of the times—I have no doubts about it.' Thereupon, in consequence, he issued the order to bring waste lands under cultivation.

Chapter 2. An Order to Cultivate Waste Lands.

[There are twenty arguments adduced, of which the following are selected.]

.   .   .   .   .

3. If dignities are not conferred nor offices given according to deviating standards,[2] then the people will not prize learning, nor besides will they hold agriculture cheap. If they do not prize learning, they will be stupid, and being stupid, they will have no interest in outside things. When

---

[1] What Dr. Duyvendak calls 'the empire' I in my translations of pre-Ch'in works have called 'the Great Society.'

[2] Extraneous standards, i.e. extraneous to the basic political requirements of agriculture and military strength (Ed.).

they have no interest in outside things, the country will exert itself in agriculture and not neglect it; and when the people do not hold agriculture cheap, the country will be peaceful and free from peril. If the country is peaceful and free from peril, exerts itself in agriculture and does not neglect it, then it is certain waste lands will be brought under cultivation.

4. If government salaries are liberal and consequently taxes numerous, then the large number of persons who live on others involves ruin for agriculture; but if they are assessed according to a calculated [i.e. very limited] number of persons who live on others, and if people are made to work hard, then the wicked and licentious, the idle and lazy will have nothing on which to live and they will take up agriculture. When they take up agriculture, then it is certain waste lands will be brought under cultivation.

5. Do not allow merchants to buy grain or farmers to sell grain. If farmers may not sell their grain, then the lazy and inactive ones will exert themselves and be energetic; and if merchants may not buy grain, then they will have no particular joy over abundant years. Having no particular joy over abundant years, they do not make copious profits in years of famine; and making no copious profits, merchants are fearful, and being fearful, they desire to turn farmers. If lazy and inactive farmers exert themselves and become energetic, and if merchants desire to turn farmers, then it is certain waste lands will be brought under cultivation.

7. If it is impossible to hire servants, great prefects and heads of families are not supported, and beloved sons cannot eat in laziness. . . . Then it is certain waste lands will be brought under cultivation.

9. If mountains and moors are brought into one hand [under one control], then the people who hate agriculture, the tardy and lazy, and those who desire double profits,[1] will have no means of subsistence. This being so, they will certainly become farmers, and so it is certain waste lands will be brought under cultivation.

[1] i.e. are averse to working unless there is prospect of double profit.

10. If the prices of wine and meat are made high and the taxes on them so heavy that they amount to ten times the cost of production, then merchants and retailers will be few, farmers will not be able to enjoy drinking bouts, and officials will not over-eat. . . . Then it is certain waste lands will be brought under cultivation.

16. If the administration of all the districts is of one pattern, then (people) will be obedient; eccentric men will not be able to be ostentatious, and successive officials will not dare to make changes; and if they act wrongly and abolish (the existing administration), it will be impossible to keep their actions hidden. . . . Then the official appurtenances will be few,[1] and the people will not be harassed . . . taxes will not be troublesome. . . . Then it is certain waste lands will be brought under cultivation.

Chapter 3. Agriculture and War.

The means whereby a ruler of men encourages the people are office and rank: the means whereby a country is made prosperous are agriculture and war.

.   .   .   .   .

The people say, 'We till diligently, first to fill the public granaries, and then to keep the rest for the nourishment of our parents. For the sake of our superiors we forget our love of life and fight for the honour of the ruler and for the peace of the country. But if the granaries are empty, the ruler debased, and the family poor, then it is best to seek office. Let us then combine relatives and friends and think of other plans.' Eminent men will then apply themselves to the study of the Odes and History and pursue these improper standards: insignificant individuals will occupy themselves with trade and practise arts and crafts, all in order to avoid farming and fighting. Where the people are given to such teachings, how can the grain be anything but scarce and the soldiers anything but weak?

.   .   .   .

[1] The official class will be a small one (Ed.).

If, in a country, there are the following ten things: the *Odes* and *History*, rites and music, virtue and the cultivation thereof, benevolence and integrity, and sophistry and intelligence, then the ruler has no one whom he can employ for defence and warfare. If a country be governed by means of these ten things, it will be dismembered as soon as an enemy approaches, and even if no enemy approaches, it will be poor. But if a country banish these ten things, enemies will not dare to approach, and even if they should, they would be driven back. When it mobilizes its army and attacks, it will gain victories; when it holds the army in reserve and does not attack, it will be rich. . . . Therefore sages and intelligent princes are what they are, not because they are able to get to the bottom of everything, but because they understand what is essential [1] in everything.

·　　·　　·　　·　　·

If (the people's) attention is devoted to agriculture, then they will be simple, and being simple, they may be made correct. . . . Being single-minded,[2] their careers may be made dependent on rewards and penalties: being single-minded, they may be used abroad.

Chapter 4. The Elimination of Strength.

·　　·　　·　　·　　·

Thirteen kinds of statistics [3] are known in a strong country: the number of granaries within its borders, the number of able-bodied men and women, the number of old and weak people, the number of officials and officers, the number of those making a livelihood by talking, the number of useful people, the number of horses and oxen, the quantity of fodder and straw.

---

[1] From a purely utilitarian point of view (Ed.).
[2] i.e. thinking only of profit and loss (Ed.).
[3] In c. 6 reference is made to 'the statistical method of administering a country.'

Chapter 6. The Calculation of Land.

.   .   .   .   .

It is the nature of the people, when they are hungry, to
strive for food: when they are tired, to strive for rest: when
they suffer hardship, to seek enjoyment: when they are in a
state of humiliation, to strive for honour. . . . Therefore
it is said, 'Where fame and profit meet, that is the way the
people will follow.' . . . If the profit comes from the soil,
the people will use their strength to the full; if fame results
from war, then they will fight to the death.

Chapter 8. On Unification.

Now, a true sage, in establishing laws, alters old customs
and causes the people to be engaged in agriculture night
and day. It is necessary to understand this.

.   .   .   .   .

A true sage, in administering a country, is able to con-
solidate its strength and to reduce it. . . . Therefore, for
one who administers a country, the way in which he consolidates its strength is by making the country rich and its
soldiers strong: the way in which he reduces the people's
force is by attacking the country's enemies, and so encouraging the people to die for their country. . . . So an intelligent
ruler who knows how to combine these two principles will
be strong, but the country of the one who does not know
how to combine these two will come to be dismembered.

Chapter 9. The Employment of Laws.

I have heard that when the intelligent princes of antiquity
established laws,[1] the people ceased to be wicked: when they
undertook an enterprise, the required ability was spontaneously forthcoming: when they distributed rewards, the army
became strong. These three principles were the root of
government. Indeed, the reason why people were not
wicked when laws were established was that the laws were

[1] Laws (*fa*) in the sense of this book are not old inherited customs with
the force of law, but a carefully arranged system of rewards and punishments for specifically defined acts. This system an intelligent ruler should
think out and publish abroad and put into force without fear or favour (Ed.).

clear and the people generally profited by them: the reason
why the required ability was forthcoming spontaneously
when an enterprise was undertaken was that the desired
achievement was clearly defined; and because this was so,
the people exerted their strength. . . .

For a prince there exists the fact that people have likes
and dislikes; and therefore, for it to be possible to govern
the people, it is necessary that the prince should examine
these likes and dislikes. Likes and dislikes are the basis
of rewards and punishments. Now the nature of man is
to like titles and emoluments and to dislike punishments
and penalties. A prince institutes these two in order to
guide men's wills; and so he establishes what they desire.
Now if titles follow upon the people's exertion of strength,
if rewards follow upon their acquisition of merit, and if the
prince succeeds in making people believe in this as firmly
as they do in the shining of sun and moon, then his army
will have no equal.

Further, if the law has neither measures nor figures,[1] then
affairs will daily become more complicated, and, although
laws have been established, yet the result will be that the
administration will be in disorder. Therefore an intelligent
prince, in directing his people, will so direct them that they
will exert their strength to the utmost, in order to strive for
a particular merit; and if, when they have acquired merit,
riches and honour follow upon it, there will be no bravery
in private causes. . . . Therefore, in general, an intelligent
prince in his administration relies on force and not on virtue.
. . . Laws are the means whereby success (in administration)
is obtained.

Chapter 13. Making Orders Strict.

In applying punishments, light offences should be
punished heavily: if light offences do not appear, heavy

[1] i.e. an exact grading of merits and demerits, with a clear statement as
to how much the reward or punishment will be.

E 973

offences will not come. This is said to be abolishing
penalties by means of penalties; and if penalties are
abolished, affairs will succeed. If crimes are serious and
penalties light, penalties will appear and trouble will arise.
This is said to be bringing about penalties by means of
penalties, and such a state will surely come to be dismembered.

.   .   .   .   .

Chapter 14. The Cultivation of Fixed Standards.

Orderly government is brought about in a state by three
things. The first is law, the second good faith, and the
third fixed standards. Law is administered in common by
the prince and his ministers. Good faith is established in
common by the prince and his ministers. The right standard is fixed by the prince alone. If a ruler of men fail to
observe, there will be danger: if prince and ministers neglect
the law and act according to their own self-interest, disorder
will be the inevitable result. Therefore, if law is established,
rights and duties are made clear, and self-interest does not
harm the law: then there is orderly government. If the
fixing of the right standard is decided by the prince alone,
there is prestige. If the people have faith in his rewards,
then their activities will achieve results, and if they have
faith in his penalties, then wickedness will have no starting-
point. Only an intelligent ruler loves fixed standards and
values good faith, and will not, for the sake of self-interest,
harm the law. For if a ruler speaks many liberal words
but cuts down his rewards, then his subjects will not be of
service to him, and if he issues one severe order after
another, but does not apply the penalties, people will
despise the death penalty.

.   .   .   .   .

Those who are engaged in governing in the world are for
the most part lax in regard to law, and place reliance on
private appraisal,[1] and this is what brings disorder in a state.

[1] This is an attack on the Confucianists and their emphasis on moral
influence exercised by the prince and his officials.

The early kings hung up scales with standard weights, and fixed the length of feet and inches, and to the present day these are followed as models because their divisions were clear. Now suppose the standard scale were abolished but a decision had to be made on the weight of something, and suppose feet and inches were abolished but a decision had to be made about length, even an intelligent merchant would not apply this system, because it lacked definiteness. Now, if the back be turned on models and measures, and reliance be placed on private appraisal, in all those cases there will be a lack of definiteness. Only a Yao would be able to judge knowledge and ability, worth or unworth, without a model. But the world does not consist exclusively of Yaos! Therefore the ancient kings understood that no reliance should be placed on individual opinions or biased approval, so they set up models and made the distinctions clear. Those who fulfilled the standard were rewarded, those who harmed the public interest were punished. The standards for rewards and punishments were not wrong in their appraisals, and therefore people did not dispute them. But if the bestowal of office and the granting of rank are not carried out according to the labour borne, then loyal ministers have no advancement; and if in awarding rewards and giving emoluments the respective merits are not weighed, then fighting soldiers will not serve their prince.

Chapter 23. Prince and Minister.

.   .   .   .   .

I have heard that the gate through which the people are guided depends on where their superiors lead. Therefore, whether one succeeds in making people farm or fight, or in making them into travelling politicians, or in making them into scholars, depends on what their superiors encourage. If their superiors encourage merit and labour, people will fight; if they encourage the *Odes* and the *History*, people will become scholars. For people's attitude towards profit is just like the tendency of water to flow downwards, without preference for any of the four sides. The people are only interested in obtaining profit, and what they will do depends on what their superiors encourage. If men with angry eyes, who clench their fists and call themselves brave, are successful; if men in flowing robes, who idly talk, are successful; if men who waste their time and spend their days in idleness, and save their efforts for obtaining benefit through private channels, are successful—if these three kinds of people, though they have no merit, all obtain respectful treatment, then people will leave off farming and fighting and do this: either they will extort it by practising flattery or they will struggle for it by acts of bravery. Thus farmers and fighters will dwindle daily, and itinerant office-seekers will increase more and more, with the result that the country will fall into disorder, the land will be dismembered, the army will be weak, and the ruler debased. This would be the result of relaxing laws and regulations and placing reliance on men of fame and reputation. Therefore an intelligent ruler is cautious with regard to laws and regulations: he does not hearken to words which are not in accordance with the laws (which he has promulgated): he does not exalt actions which are not in accordance with the laws: he (himself) does not perform deeds which are not in accordance with the laws. But he hearkens to words which are in accordance with the law: he exalts actions which are in accordance with the law: he performs deeds which are in accordance with the law. Thus the state will enjoy order, the land will be wide, the army will be strong, and the ruler will be honoured. This is the climax of good government, and it is imperative for a ruler of men to examine it.

Chapter 25. Attention to Law.

A country of a thousand chariots is able to preserve itself by defence, and a country of ten thousand chariots is able to round itself off by fighting [i.e. wars of aggression]—even (a bad ruler like) Chieh, unwilling (as he would be) to whittle down a word of this statement, would yet be able to subdue his enemies. And if abroad one is incapable of waging war and at home one is incapable of defence, then even (a good ruler like) Yao could not pacify for any misbehaviour a country that (normally) would be no match for him. Looking at it from this point of view, that through which the country is important and that through which the ruler is honoured is force. Force being the basis of both, how is it then that no ruler on earth succeeds in developing force? Bring about a condition where people find it bitter not to till the soil, and where they find it dangerous not to fight. These are two things which filial sons, though they dislike them, do for their fathers' sake, and loyal ministers, though they dislike them, do for their sovereign's sake. Nowadays, if you wish to stimulate the multitude of people, to make them do what even filial sons and loyal ministers dislike doing, I think it is useless, unless you compel them by means of punishments and stimulate them by means of rewards. . . . Therefore my teaching is to issue such orders that people, if they are desirous of profit, can attain their aim only by agriculture, and if they want to avoid harm, can escape it only by war.

CHAPTER VI: THE 'GREAT LEARNING'

This book first appears in history in the collection called the *Record of Rites*, compiled at the end of the first century B.C. There it remained for one thousand two hundred years, part of the Confucian canon, but not attracting any special attention. Then the critics of the Sung era were inspired by it, and it was made the first among the Four Books which (cp. Introduction) came to be regarded as containing the quintessence of the Great Tradition. The same school of thought in Sung times which exalted it was responsible for rearranging the order of its component chapters and for propounding the theory that the opening section came from Confucius himself, the rest of the book from Tseng Shen, the filial-pietist. There seems very little evidence for this theory, and to-day most scholars confess that we do not know who was the author. My own theory, built on internal evidence, is that it, or the main part of it, was compiled by some court tutor during Shang Yang's later years with a view to instructing his young aristocrats of pupils in the goodness of the Confucian faith and the wickedness of the new materialism.

That by Sung times the text of the book was in disorder is clear enough. Fortunately we have the version which the Sung Scholars rearranged, and, since we are not burdened with some of their predilections, we may make a less radical rearrangement which none the less makes very good sense. In the following quotation this is the order followed.[1]

The *Great Learning* is interesting from a literary point of view. It is neither a collection of sayings and anecdotes, nor an essay or collection of essays. It is essentially a text-book, composed with a view to being easy to learn off by heart, and presupposing a teacher who expounds the section which his pupils have learnt. In this respect it resembles the *Tao Te Ching*.

Chapter 1. (*A Statement of the Theme of the Book*.)

The Way [*Tao*] of learning to be great consists in shining with the illustrious power of moral personality [*te*], in making a new people, in abiding in the highest goodness. To know one's abiding-place leads to fixity of purpose, fixity of purpose to calmness of mind, calmness of mind to serenity of life, serenity of life to careful consideration of means, careful consideration of means to the achievement of the end.

[1] In the *Chinese Classics*, by James Legge, vol. i (Clarendon Press, 1893), the order is the one which the Sung Scholars made.

Things have their roots and branches, human affairs their endings as well as beginnings. So to know what comes first and what comes afterwards leads one near to the Way. The men of old who wished to shine with the illustrious power of personality throughout the Great Society, first had to govern their own fiefs [*kuo*] efficiently. Wishing to do this, they first had to make an ordered harmony in their own families. Wishing to do this, they first had to cultivate their individual selves [*hsiu sheng*]. Wishing to do this, they first had to put their minds right. Wishing to do this, they first had to make their purposes genuine. Wishing to do this, they first had to extend their knowledge to the utmost. Such extension of knowledge consists in appreciating the nature of things.[1] For with the appreciation of the nature of things knowledge reaches its height. With the completion of knowledge purposes become genuine. With purposes genuine the mind becomes right. With the mind right the individual self comes into flower [*hsiu sheng*].[2] With the self in flower the family becomes an ordered harmony. With the families ordered harmonies the state [*kuo*] is efficiently governed. With the states efficiently governed the Great Society is at peace.

Thus from the Son of Heaven right down to the common people there is unity in this, that for everybody the bringing of the individual self to flower is to be taken as the root [i.e. the essential thing]. (Since that is so,) for the root to be out of order and the branches to be in order is an impossibility. For a man to despise what he should respect and then be respected for having what he despises, is contrary to man's experience. This is what people speak of as 'knowing the root.'

---

[1] *Ko*=appreciating the nature of, *wu*=things, i.e. material things, affairs, events in history, traditions, doctrines, anything which, as we should say, can be an object of consciousness. In its earlier usage, *ko*, I urge, is more the artist's term 'appreciate' than the scientist's 'investigate.'

[2] *Hsiu* came to have a moralistic disciplinary meaning, but in its earlier usage had not necessarily that significance. Philologically the form of the ideograph looks like a combination of 'process' and 'the feathers of the full-grown bird.'

Chapter 2. (On Knowing the Root.)

(With regard to the meaning of knowing the root,)[1] it means the height of knowledge.   In the *Odes* it is said:

> See there, the Ch'i River with its winding course,
> Its bamboos all lush and green!
> Even so our accomplished prince!
> The bone is carved and the ivory polished;
> The jade is cut and the granite ground smooth.
> So he, like the music of strings, yet with a martial air,
> Stern yet debonair.
> So accomplished a prince,
> Ever to be held in memory!

That carving and polishing means learning. That cutting and grinding means the cultivation of the self. 'Like the music of strings'—so he trembles within himself. 'Stern yet debonair'—so he is the very pattern of majesty. 'Ever to be held in memory'—abounding power of personality and the height of goodness are what the common people can never forget. . . .

In the *K'ang Kao*[2] it is said, 'He has the gifts of illustrious power of personality.'   In the *T'ai Chia*[2] it is said, 'He guards this illustrious charge from Heaven.'   In the *Ti Tien*[2] it is said, 'He has the gifts for shedding lustre on his outstanding power of personality.'   These three are cases of the self shedding lustre.   On King T'ang's bath-tub there was an inscription: 'If on one day there may be a renovation, then every day there may be, indeed daily there must be.'   So in the *K'ang Kao* it is said, 'Making a new people,' and in the *Odes* is the saying, 'The fief which Chou held was an ancient one, but the charge from heaven was new.'   The true man, therefore, in everything uses his supreme endeavours.

. . . In the *Odes* it is said, '*Ming-mang* goes the oriole's song, as it rests on a corner of a mound'; and the Master

[1] I submit that the copyists responsible for the surviving text omitted *so wei chih pen* after they had written *tz'u wei chih pen*.

[2] The *K'ang Kao* is in the *History* (*Shang Shu*) and is the charge given by King Wu to one of his brothers.   We may imagine the author of the *Great Learning* enlarging on the Sage-kings and their power of personality.   The *T'ai Chia* and the *Ti Tien* also come in the *History*.

[Confucius] said, 'As to resting, the bird knows where it can rest—is it right as a man to be less than a bird?'

In the *Odes* it is said:

> Hail to King Wen
> And the glorious homage he paid to abiding!
> As a monarch he abode in human-heartedness,
> As a minister he abode in reverence,
> As a son he abode in filial piety,
> As a father he abode in kindness,
> With his fellow countrymen he abode in good faith.

.   .   .   .

All this means knowing the root.

Chapter 3. (*On Making Purposes Genuine.*)

What is described as 'making one's purposes genuine' is as follows. Beware of self-deception. It is to be compared to hating a bad smell and loving a lovely sight; this is what is called self-fulfilment. Thus it is that the true man is sure to be on guard when he is alone. The man who is not true, in his privacy has the habit of setting no limit to the badness of his actions. Then when he comes into the presence of a true man he is abashed. He conceals his bad qualities and displays his good. But he gains nothing by doing so, for (under these conditions) a man sees himself as if he saw his own liver and reins. This means that what is really within will take on form without. That is why the true man is sure to be on guard when he is alone. . . .

Chapter 4. (*On the Relation of the Rectification of the Mind to the Cultivation of the Self.*)

As to the meaning of 'the cultivation of the self consists in the rectification of the mind,' if the self is angry about anything, or frightened, or delighted over anything, or unhappily perturbed about anything, in each case it follows that it cannot get itself right. When the mind is away, we gaze at things and do not see them: sounds come to our ears and we do not hear them: we eat and do not discern the flavours. This is what is meant by 'the cultivation of the self consists in the rectification of the mind.'

*E 973

Chapter 5. (On the Relation of the Cultivation of the Self to the Bringing of an Ordered Harmony in the Family.)

As to the meaning of 'the bringing of the members of the family into an ordered harmony consists in cultivating the self,' men are prejudiced about those whom they love, prejudiced about those whom they hate, prejudiced about those whom they revere, prejudiced about those whom they pity, prejudiced about those whom they despise. There are very few people in the world who are awake to the evil in the object of their liking and awake to the attractiveness in the object of their dislike. Hence, as the proverb puts it, 'Men are not aware of the evil of their sons nor of the fertility of their fields.' This means that there can be no bringing of the members of the family into an ordered harmony unless there is cultivation of the self.

Chapter 6. (On the Relation between Bringing the Family into an Ordered Harmony and the Efficient Ruling of the State.)

As to the meaning of 'the efficient ruling of a state of necessity consists in bringing its families into an ordered harmony,' it is not the case that a man can fail in instilling good principles into his own family and at the same time succeed in instilling those principles into men outside it. Thus it is that a true man without going outside his family brings good principles into being throughout the country. Filial piety is the means by which the prince is served. Deference to an elder brother is the means by which the elder generation is served. The exercise of parental kindness is the means by which a whole population is influenced. In the *K'ang Kao* it is said, 'Act as if you were watching over an infant.' If your mind is truly set on your action, although you may miss your mark, you will not go far astray. A young woman has never had to learn to suckle an infant before she got married.

If one family be human-hearted, human-heartedness will grow in the whole country. If the members of one family give way to each other, the spirit of giving way will grow in the whole country. If one man be incontinently wicked, he will cause anarchy in the whole country. The mechanism of the situation is like that. This means that one remark may throw public business into disorder, or one man may consolidate a country. . . .

Thus it is that what the true man has in himself, that he can require from others: what he has not in himself, that he cannot require from others. There never has been a man who had no store of reciprocity in himself and yet was able to communicate it to other men. Hence the ruling of a state consists in ordered harmony in the family. . . .

Chapter 7. (On the Relation between the Government of States and Universal Peace.) [1]

1. (The Way of the Measuring Square.)

As to the meaning of 'the attainment of peace in the Great Society consists in the efficient government of the states,' if those in high places treat old age as old age should be treated, the people develop the filial spirit. If those in high places treat their seniors as seniors should be treated, the people develop the younger-brotherly spirit. If they have pity on orphans, the people will not go counter to them. Thus there is for the true man the Way of the Measuring Square. [2] What a man dislikes in those above him, he must not bring to bear on those beneath him. What he dislikes in those beneath him, he must not bring to the service of those above him. What he dislikes in his forbears, he must not do in advance for his descendants. What he would dislike in his descendants, he must not do as following his forbears. The treatment which he dislikes from (his neighbours on) the right, he must not give to (those on) the left. The treatment which he dislikes from (his neighbours on) the left, he must not give to (those on)

---

[1] The argument in this section is an extensive one and is divisible into five subsections.

[2] The measuring square was a carpenter's tool. This metaphor for the principle of reciprocity is not found in the *Analects*. Our author may be the man who coined the expression.

the right. This is what is meant by the Way of the Measuring Square.

2. (What being Father and Mother to the People entails.)

In the *Odes* is the saying, 'Blessings on our true man, father and mother to his people.' To like what the people like and to hate what the people hate, this is the meaning of being father and mother. . . .

Again, as the *Odes* say:

> Before they lost their people's (hearts)
> The Yin kings stood at God's right hand,
> The Yin kings stand before our eyes (as proof):
> God's high commission is hard to keep.

It is that: win the people, and the country is won: lose the people, and the country is lost. This is why the true man is first concerned with the power of moral personality. Possessing the power in himself, he possesses men. Possessing men, he possesses the soil. Possessing the soil, he possesses wealth. Possessing wealth, he possesses the means for governing.

3. (Power of Personality is the Root, Wealth is the Branch.)

This moral power is the root; wealth is but a branch. If the root be discounted and the branch be prized, there will be quarrelling, and the people will be incited to steal. This is why the people will disperse if the wealth be amassed in the ruler's hands, and the reason why the people mass round the ruler if the wealth be dispersed among them. And if the ruler's words go forth in injustice, it is the reason why injustice will come home to roost. If injustice enters (the palace) with the produce of the country, injustice will take that produce away. It is said in the *K'ang Kao*, 'The charge from Heaven itself is not unchangeable.' This means that goodness brings it to a man, and evil takes it away from him.

.   .   .   .   .

5. (On the National Scale Justice [1] is Gain.)

For the creation of wealth there is a supremely right Way. If those who create the wealth be many, those who consume it few, and if the accumulating departments be zealous, the spending departments economical, then there will be a permanent sufficiency of wealth.

For the human-hearted man wealth is the means by which the individual self is expanded. For the non-human-hearted man the individual is a tool for the expansion of wealth. There never has been a case in which those in high places were devoted to human-heartedness and those beneath them were not devoted to justice. There never has been a case in which there was devotion to justice and state affairs failed of completion. There never has been a case in which (in these circumstances) there was opposition to the wealth being in the Government's storehouses.

. . . The man at the head of a country's administration who is only concerned with wealth and expenditure is himself a base fellow. He may think he is doing good, but his ways of getting things done are those of a base fellow. Calamity from Heaven and injury from men both ensue, and although there may be good men in the country, they can do nothing to stop this. This means that on the national scale gain is not (real) gain: justice is gain.

[1] I use 'justice' for *yi*, justice in the wide Platonic sense with its implication that righteousness has at its centre the idea of equity and fair dealing.

CHAPTER VII: MENCIUS: POLITICAL PHILOSOPHER AND PSYCHOLOGIST

Mencius (Meng K'o) was a member of the governing class of Lu State, but appears to have had nothing much to do with politics, either there or in its semi-dependent neighbour, Tsou, with which he had close ties. But politics was his master passion, and at more than one of the great courts he was regarded with great respect. Aristocrat though he was, his intense admiration for Confucius plus his own fine political sense gave him a deep appreciation of the importance of the people in the body politic. More than that, he had an eye for the psychological side of things, for the motives which induce action, and the deeds which can only be accomplished under certain ethical conditions. He had, therefore, much to say on the psychology of good politics and of good ethics. From the point of view of Western political realists his thinking was idealistic, from the point of view of the idealists it was realistic.

In Hsun Ch'ing's book (mid third century B.C.) Mencius is referred to as following the Tzu Ssu variety of the Confucian tradition. There are various indications that this is correct, notably a reproduction of a passage in the *Mean-in-action*, but on the whole there is curiously little to show any close connection. This may be accounted for by the fact that Tzu Ssu and Mencius were such very different men. From the point of view of Mencius's importance in the history of Chinese philosophy it is important to note that it was not until the Sung era that his book achieved full canonical status. Before that it received a fair amount of attention, but nothing like what it received after Chu Hsi made so much of it. As a thinker, Mencius has for the last hundred years been the most popular among Western students of China.

The record of Mencius's teaching is found in the book under his name. This, according to an early tradition, was compiled by him in his old age with the help of a disciple. But it looks rather as if most of the seven books into which this record was divided have got later additions. The arrangement of the book is that of a series of conversations with his disciples and others, including rulers of states or kings, as most of them styled themselves in Mencius's day. The conversations are for the most part longer than those in the *Analects*; but none the less this arrangement of the book makes it discursive. The plan, therefore, followed in quotations here is the same as that used for the *Analects*, namely, bringing salient passages under various headings.

1. *Illustrations of the Theories and Dialectical Methods of Mencius and his Contemporaries.*

Master Meng said, '. . . The means by which the men of old became greatly superior to (ordinary) men was no other than this, that they, to be sure, were well able to extend the scope of their actions. Now here is a case in which, Sire, your mercy is sufficient to include animals but does not include the people. Why this anomaly? After weighing we know the light and the heavy: after measuring we know the long and the short. This applies to matters of all kinds and particularly to the mind. I beg you, Sire, to measure up this matter of yours. Having increased your armaments, endangered your soldiers and servants, and excited the resentment of your fellow princes, are you pleased in your mind? . . . If that be the case, then we know exactly what it is you greatly desire. You wish to enlarge your territories, to have Ch'in and Chu States in attendance at your court, to overrun the Middle Kingdom, and pacify the barbarian tribes in all quarters. But to seek to satisfy such a desire by means of such action is like "climbing a tree and looking for fish."' [1]   (i A. 7.)

Master Meng said, '. . . That is why I maintain that in the relation of the mouth to flavours in food men have a like sense of taste, in the relation of the ear to singing a like sense of hearing, in the relation of the eye to colour a like sense of beauty. Applying this to minds, do they disagree and so form an exception? What are the things in which minds agree? In reason and in righteousness. The sages had in advance what our minds agree on. That is where the pleasure which reason and righteousness afford our minds is like the pleasure which the flesh of grass-fed and grain-fed animals afford our mouths.'   (vi A. 7.)

Master Meng said, '. . . Master Yang takes his stand on "every one for himself." He would not pluck out a single

[1] That Mencius here idealizes 'the men of old' must not blind us to the logical interest of his argument. It contains an illustration of generalization, the rejection of other possible causes in favour of one single cause, the recognition of exceptions, the scientific method of 'dial readings,' the use of the *reductio ad absurdum* in dialectical reasoning.

hair although it would benefit the whole of society. Master
Mo (on the other hand) loved all inclusively and wore
himself out from his head to his heels. Whatever benefited
society, that he did. Tzu Mo laid hold of the mean and in
doing so came near to the right. (And yet even) holding
the mean without balancing considerations is like having
a one-track mind. And that is what I hate, for to take up
one point and disregard a hundred others is an outrage to
truth [*Tao*].' (vii A. 26.)

Master Meng said, '. . . The words of Yang Chu and
Mo Ti fill the country. Everywhere if people's words are
not wholly taken up with Yang, they are with Mo. Now
Yang maintains "every one for himself," [1] that is to say, no
sovereign lord. Mo maintains "all-inclusive love," that is
to say, no father. To be without a father and a sovereign
is to be an animal. . . . If the principles of Yang and Mo
be not stopped, Confucius's principles will not shine forth.
That is to say, these scandalous theories will delude the
people, and the path of human-heartedness and righteousness will be blocked. If that happens, then beasts will be
encouraged to devour men and men will become cannibals.
. . . Any one who can denounce Yang and Mo is a disciple
of the sages.' (iii B. 9.)

Master Kao said that that which is born in men is their
nature [*hsing*], and when Master Meng asked him whether
the meaning of this statement was like the meaning of
'white is white,' Kao answered that that was his meaning.

Master Kao said, 'Men's nature is like a current of water.
If you open a channel for the current to the east, it will flow
east. If you open a channel to the west, it will flow west.
Men's nature makes no distinction between the good and
the not good, just as water makes no distinction between
east and west.' Master Meng replied, 'Water can be trusted
not to make a distinction between east and west: but is this
so in relation to up and down? Men's natural tendency

---

[1] Mencius's description of Yang Chu's philosophy no more does justice
to it than the modern meaning of 'epicurean' does justice to Epicurus's
teaching. Yang Chu goes further than our English seventeenth-century
Hobbes.

towards goodness is like the water's tendency to find the lower level. Now if, for example, you strike the water and make it leap up, it is possible to force it over your head. . . . But this surely is not the nature of water, and it is only if force is applied that it acts in this way. That men can be made to do evil is due to their nature also being like this.'

Master Kao said, 'It is men's nature to enjoy food and sex. Human-heartedness is subjective, not objective,[1] and righteousness is objective, not subjective.' Master Meng asked what he meant by this distinction and he answered, 'Suppose a man there older than I am, and I pay respect to him as such. It is not that there is any respecting of him in me. It is as if he were white and I recognized he was white in accordance with the external fact of his whiteness. That is why I say it is objective.' Master Meng replied, 'A white horse's whiteness is no different from a white man's whiteness, but I wonder whether you treat an old horse with the same respect with which you treat an old man! And further, is righteousness a matter of the man being old or a matter of the respect you pay?' Kao replied, 'If a man is my younger brother, then I love him; but if he is the younger brother of a man of Ch'in, then I do not love him. That is, it is a matter of feeling in myself. That is why I say it is subjective. To an old man of Ch'u I pay respect as I do to an old man of my own people. That is, it is a matter of feeling with regard to age. That is why I say that it is objective.'

Master Meng replied, 'Our enjoyment of meat roasted by a man of Ch'in is no different from our enjoyment of meat roasted by ourselves. Taking things generally, they are also like that. Assuming that to be the case, is our enjoyment of roast meat also objective? . . .' (vi A. 2–4.)

[1] The contrast in the Chinese is between *nei* and *wei* (lit. internal and external). Hence 'subjective' in the artists' sense of depending on the individual feeling and point of view, and 'objective' in the sense of not so depending. That seems clear, but this rendering makes human-heartedness and righteousness not clear. It would seem that the contrast is between human-heartedness as representing individual morality and righteousness as representing social morality.

2. *Mencius's Ethic and his Psychological Approach to Ethical Problems.*

Master Meng said, 'Of all duties to men which is the greatest? The duties to one's parents are the greatest of all. Of all responsibilities which is the greatest? Responsibility for one's self is the greatest of all.' (iv. A. 10.)

Kung Tu [a disciple of Mencius] said, 'Master Kao says that men's nature is neither good nor evil . . . whilst there are others who say that some men have a good nature and some have an evil nature. . . . Now you [i.e. Mencius] say that men's nature is good. If this is the case, then are all these others wrong?'

Master Meng replied, 'Speaking realistically, it is possible for men to be good, and that is what I mean when I say that (men's nature) is good. If they become evil, it is not the fault of their natural powers. Thus all men have a sense [1] of compassion, also a sense of shame over wickedness, a sense of reverence, and a sense of truth and error. The sense of compassion is equivalent to individual morality [*jen*], the sense of shame to public morality [*yi*], the sense of reverence to ritual propriety, and the sense of right and wrong equals wisdom. These four, individual morality, public morality, ritual propriety, and wisdom, are not fused into us from without. We invariably are possessed of them, and that without reflecting on them. This is why I maintain that if we seek for them, then we find them: if we neglect them, we lose them. That contrasts can be made between men of twice and five times and even to an incalculable degree is due to the fact that men fail fully to carry out their natural powers. . . .' (vi A. 6.)

Master Meng said, 'All men have the sense [*hsin*] of compassion for others. The former kings, having this sense of compassion, thereby ruled compassionately. Having the sense of compassion and practising this compassionate rule,

[1] The Chinese here and in the three following instances is *hsin*, commonly to be translated as 'mind,' though 'heart' sometimes fits our usage more nearly. The question is whether *hsin* includes the idea of consciousness. I think it does, and therefore see no reason for discarding our English idiom of 'a sense of.'

their control of the Great Society was as easy as rolling things in the hand. What I mean by all men having a sense of compassion is that if, for instance, a child is suddenly seen to be on the point of falling into a well, everybody without exception will have a sense of distress. It is not by reason of any close intimacy with the parents of the child, nor by reason of a desire for the praise of neighbours and friends, nor by reason of disliking to be known as the kind of man (who is not moved by compassion). From this point of view we observe that it is inhuman to have no sense of compassion, inhuman to have no sense of shame over wickedness, inhuman to have no sense of modesty and the need for yielding place to a better man, inhuman not to distinguish right and wrong. The sense of compassion represents the tender shoot of individual morality, the sense of shame that of public morality, the sense of modesty that of ritual propriety, the sense of truth and error that of wisdom. Men have these four tender shoots just as they have their four limbs; and the man who in spite of having these tender shoots in him says of his own accord "I am unable," that man plays the thief with himself; and when he says it of his ruler, he plays the thief with his ruler. . . . Every "I" with these four tender shoots knows how to nourish and expand them, just like fire bursting into flame and a spring gushing forth on all sides. Let them expand to the full, and they alone suffice to protect all within the Four Seas.[1] Should they be prevented from expansion, they do not suffice for the service of a man's father and mother.' (ii A. 6.)

Master Meng said, '. . . With those who do violence to themselves it is impossible to converse, with those who throw themselves away it is impossible to act. The meaning of doing violence to oneself is contravention of ritual and righteousness, the meaning of throwing oneself away is inability in oneself to dwell in human-heartedness and follow

[1] An expression often used by Mencius, though not peculiar to him (cf. pp. 36, 37). It denotes the Chou territory, plus the surrounding country, or possibly the whole earth. Mencius's age was waking up to a geographical world of which China was only a part. Cp. Tsou Yen's ideas, Chapter XV.

righteousness. For human-heartedness is man's abode of
peace and righteousness is man's true path. Alas, that that
abode is left empty and desolate and that path is abandoned
and not followed!' (iv A. 10.)

Kung-sun Ch'ou [a disciple] asked if he might learn from
his Master what his idea of an unperturbed mind was and
what Master Kao's was. The reply was, 'Kao's idea is,
do not try to get in the mind what you cannot put into
words: do not try to get from the vital energy in you
[*ch'i*] what you cannot get from your mind. Now the
second statement is permissible but the first is not. Purpose in the mind is the teaching power (needed by) the vital
energy, as this energy is the power developing cohesion
(needed by) the body; and of these purpose is of the first
importance, the vital energy of secondary importance. The
result is that I maintain that we have to hold fast to our
purposes, but not if these injure the vital energy in us. . . .
If the purposes be integrated, they can stir up the vital
energy in us; and (equally) if the vital energy in our limbs
be integrated, it can stir up purpose in the mind. For
example, when a man stumbles or gets hurried, this is due
to (unintegrated) energy in his limbs, and it has a reversing
[? paralysing] effect on the mind.'

Kung-sun Ch'ou then asked in what way (spiritual)
growth was achieved. The reply was, 'By our understanding (the significance of) speech, and by skill in nourishing the vast-flowing vital energy in man.' When Kung-sun
Ch'ou asked him what he meant by 'the vast-flowing
energy,' the reply was, 'It is difficult to put it into words.
Such is the nature of this energy that it is immensely great
and immensely strong, and if it be nourished by uprightness
and so sustain no injury, then it pervades the whole space
between the heavens and the earth.[1] Such is the nature of
this force that it marries righteousness with truth [*Tao*] and

[1] Mencius certainly did find his idea difficult to express. If, however,
we remember that he was in Tzu Ssu's tradition (cp. the *Mean-in-action*,
the later sections), his linking of the physical and metaphysical with the
spiritual and ethical becomes more understandable. *Ch'i* as animating
force is comparable with 'élan vital,' whilst Mencius's development of the
idea brings its meaning near to 'soul.'

without it (material and spiritual) corruption would set in.
It is the product of accumulated righteousness, though not
of a righteousness handed down and casually caught at.
(For) if human conduct be possessed of no (divine) dis-
content in the mind, then corruption would set in. . . .
Here is a duty which must be accomplished, and that without
ceasing. The mind must not forget it. And yet the mind
must not deliberately help the growth, as the Sung farmer
did. There was a man there who was vexed with his
growing corn because it was not tall; so he pulled it up.
When he returned home in a state of exhaustion he told his
people, "I am very tired to-day: I have been helping the
corn to grow." His son ran out to see—the corn of course
was all withered away. Now in our Great Society there
are very few who (in relation to the vast-flowing vital
energy) either do not help the corn to grow, or neglect it
as being of no use. . . . The people who help the vast-
flowing vital energy to grow are the people who pull it up.
Not only is their labour in vain, it is actually injurious.'
(ii A. 2.)

Master Meng said, 'Those who have the Mean nurture
those who have not, and those who have natural gifts
nurture those who have not. Thus it is that men are glad
over the possession of worthy fathers and elder brothers.
If those who had the Mean and natural gifts were to forsake
those who had not, the difference between the worthy and
unworthy could not amount to the space of an inch.'
(iv. B. 7.)

Master Meng said, '. . . An enlightened man builds on
the deep foundation of the Way [Tao]. His wish is to
possess it of himself. If he comes to possess it, then he
dwells at peace in it and so comes to have a profound confidence in it, and so gets it on every hand and makes contact
with its bubbling spring. This is the cause of an enlightened man's wishing to possess it of himself.' (iv B. 14.)

Master Meng said, 'When Shun [the Sage-king] was
living in the deep mountains amongst the trees and the
rocks, wandering among the deer and the swine, there was

apparently hardly any difference between him and the un-civilized men of the hills, but directly he heard one good word, directly he saw one good action, he was like a river bursting its banks and flowing out in an irresistible flood.'[1] (vii A. 16.)

Master Meng said, 'When any one told Tzu Lu [one of Confucius's disciples] that he had a fault, he was delighted; and when Yü [the Sage-king] heard good words he bowed. The great Shun had his great characteristic: he regarded goodness as the common property of himself and others. He would discard his own way and follow others. To have joy in choosing (the good) in others, this was to him goodness.' (ii A. 8.)

3. *Mencius's Political Theories.*

Duke Wen of T'eng asked for advice on the way to con-solidate his territory. Master Meng said, 'Neglect of what concerns your people's (welfare) will not do. . . . The people constitute the Way [*Tao*]. Thus the hearts of those who have a stake in the country are fixed, and the hearts of those who have no stake in the country are not fixed; and if their hearts are not fixed they let themselves go in vice and extravagance. There is nothing they will not do. If after that they are betrayed into crimes and you follow this up with punishment, this is just catching the people in a trap. Surely, if a human-hearted man be at the head, there can be no entrapping of the people. . . .'

Under the Hsia rule (the system was) fifty *mou* [Chinese acres] of land to a family and 'tribute' paid. Under the Yin rule it was seventy *mou* and a 'contribution' made to the State [i.e. not more than so much in a good year and in a bad year less], under the Chou rule it became a hundred *mou* and a 'fixed exaction.' Although as a matter of fact the amount in the three systems came to one part in ten, yet 'a fixed exaction' [*ch'e*] means a skinning [*ch'e*] and a

[1] To Mencius Shun was the greatest of the Sage-kings. He refers frequently to him, and discusses his peculiar virtues in great detail. The idealistic side of Mencius's ethic cannot be appreciated without realizing the actuality which the early kings imparted to it.

'contribution' means mutual dependence. As Master Lung said, 'For the administration of the land there is nothing better than "contributions," nothing worse than "tribute."' 'Tribute' involves striking an average on a few years yield as representing the permanent yield. But then in good years when there is any amount of grain, a heavy toll would not be a tyrannical proceeding. In proportion it would be a small amount. On the other hand, in bad years when there is not enough to manure the fields, the result could only be the taking of the whole crop. For the 'father and mother of his people' [i.e. the ruler] to give them careworn faces, to make them after the labour of the year have no food for their fathers and mothers and take to borrowing to make things better, so that the old people and the children are found lying in the ditches—is this consistent with his position? . . .

The Duke sent Pi Chan [his new minister] to ask advice on the nine-square [1] land system. Master Meng said, 'Your lord proposes to practise human-hearted government and has chosen you, sir, for this task. You will certainly have to exert yourself to the utmost. The necessary beginning of human-hearted government is marking out the boundaries yourself, for if the boundaries are not right, the sections are not properly adjusted and the bounty of the crops is inequitably distributed. That is why tyrannical princes and their base underlings neglect fixing the boundaries. Once these boundaries are made right, the division of the (good and bad fields) and the organization of stipendiary allowances for officials can be fixed at your ease as you sit.

Now, although T'eng has but little rich agricultural land, you doubtless propose to have a gentleman class [2] [*chun tsu*]

---

[1] 'Nine-square' is adopted from the ideograph for a well, 井. Mencius so describes the system in this passage that one suspects it is his own invention; but some of his and other writers' remarks point to something of the sort being actually in existence, or rather a feature of old West Chou feudalism. Apart from Mencius's idealistic embroidery, such a system is characteristic of feudal land tenures in many countries.

[2] Mencius was strongly opposed to a proletarian theory put forward in his day that the whole of the community should engage in agriculture, since the essentials of human-hearted government could be carried out by the abler peasants in their spare time.

and a peasant class, for without the gentleman the peasant cannot be governed and without the peasant the gentlemen has nothing to eat. My advice, if you please, is that for the outlands [i.e. less certainly fertile land which required clearing] one part in nine of the crops should be taken and that as a "contribution to the state." For the more central part of the country one part in ten should be exacted. . . .

Where there are more males than one in a family, each should have twenty-five *mou*. In cases of removal owing to death, the family should not go into another district; for within one neighbourhood with its fields belonging to the same nine-square there will be constant interchange of friendliness, mutual help in watch and ward, mutual relief in times of sickness, and consequently the hundred clans living in affectionate concord.

One square mile [Chinese] makes a nine-square, and one nine-square comprises nine hundred *mou*. The centre square is the public field and eight families have each a hundred *mou*; and the distinction between one set of peasants and another consists in the extent to which together they improve the fertility of the public field and not until that is done presume to attend to their private business.

Here is the outline of the system. It depends on your prince and you, sir, to make it richly beneficial. (iii A. 3.)

King [1] Hsüan of Ch'i asked Master Meng what kind of power in personality should lead to the exercise of royal authority. The reply was, 'Protect the people, and nothing can stop you from exercising this authority. . . .'

Master Meng said, 'Supposing a man were to inform you, Sire, that he had the strength to lift more than a ton, but not to lift a feather . . . would you let it pass?' The answer was 'No,' whereat Master Meng said, '. . . As a matter of fact, inability to lift a feather is due to a man not using the strength he has . . . and lack of protection for

---

[1] The rulers of the larger states in Mencius's day had arrogated to themselves the title of king, strictly a title confined to the Son of Heaven. King Hsüan had his eye on the chance of becoming Son of Heaven, and at the time of this conversation Mencius apparently thought him the most likely one among the state rulers to have kingly qualities.

your people is due to mercy not being used. Thus it is that your failure to exercise royal authority is due not to your inability to exercise it, but to the fact that you do not exercise it.'

When the king inquired what the difference in form was between 'not doing' and 'not being able to do,' the reply was, 'With regard to taking the T'ai Mountain under your arm and jumping over the North Sea, if you say to people that you cannot do it, your words represent the truth that you cannot. (On the other hand) with regard to helping an older man break off the branch of a tree, if you say to people that you cannot, this is "I do not," not "I cannot." Thus it is that your failure to exercise royal authority is not in the class of picking up the T'ai Mountain and jumping over the North Sea, but it is in the class of not breaking off a branch.'

'Extend the principle of "respect to the aged in my family" to the aged in other men's families, and the principle of "tender care for those of tender years in my family" to those of tender years in other men's families, and the Great Society may be "rolled in the palm of your hand." . . . Thus it is that with the expansion of the scope of your mercy, it is sufficient to protect all within the Four Seas, with the non-extension of its scope it is insufficient to protect your own wife and children.' . . .

'Plant mulberry trees round every five-*mou* homestead, and people of fifty may be clothed in silk. Do not miss the breeding times of domestic fowls and pigs [*t'un*] and dogs and swine [*chih*], and people of seventy may have meat to eat. Do not (by calling out the militia for wars) deprive the hundred-*mou* fields of the seasonal work they require, and the families of several mouths may not go hungry. Give close attention to schools [1] and the principles taught in them, emphasizing the great moral obligation [*yi*] of filial

---

[1] Tradition has assigned the foundation of schools to the Sage-kings, but the critical historian to-day is sceptical about this. In Mencius's time there were educational institutions of some sort in the state capitals, and in the works of the third century B.C. writers we find evidence of country teachers and their pupils.

piety and younger-brotherly submission, and grey-beards will not (be found) carrying burdens on the roads. Given this state of affairs . . . it is unprecedented for a state ruler not to exercise royal authority.' 'Suppose, Sire, your administration were to diffuse human-heartedness, it would make all the officials everywhere wish to have a place in your court, all the farmers wish to till the land of your country-side, all the merchants wish to store their goods in your markets, all strangers wish to travel on your roads, and all those who have grievances against their rulers wish to come and lay them before you, Sire. In those circumstances who can stop them coming?' (i A. 7.)

Master Meng said, 'Do not interfere with the seasons of husbandry, nor allow close-meshed nets in the ponds: then the grain and fish and turtles will be more than can be consumed. Have the axes and bills enter the mountain woods only in due season: then the wealth of timber will be more than can be used. This will enable the people to nourish the living and bury the dead without ill will against any man; and that is the first step to royal authority.' (i A. 3.)

Master Meng said, 'When men are subdued by force, they do not submit in their minds, but only because their strength is inadequate. When men are subdued by power in personality, they are pleased to their very heart's core and do really submit.' (ii A. 3.)

Master Meng said, 'In the annals of the states there are no righteous wars. As for that war being better than this one, there are such cases. With regard to "taking measures against bad fief-holders," this is the over-lord punishing his subjects by force of arms. Enemy states, however, cannot (be said to) "take measures" against each other.' (vii B. 2.)

King Hsüan of Ch'i inquired whether it was true that T'ang had banished Chieh [1] and King Wu warred down Chow. Master Meng replied that so tradition had it. The

---

[1] Chieh was the last of the Hsia line, and Chow the last of the Yin line. Owing to their crimes against Heaven and men T'ang and Wu received Heaven's commission to destroy them.

king then asked whether a subject might put his overlord
to death, and the reply was, 'To act the robber with one's
human-heartedness is rightly described as being a robber,
and to act the robber with one's righteousness is rightly
described as being a ruffian. A man who is a ruffian and a
robber is rightly described as a man of no account; and what
I have heard is that one Chow, a man of no account, was
executed. I have not heard of it as regicide.'[1]   (i B. 8.)

4. *Mencius's Attitude to Heaven.*[2]

Wan Chang asked whether it was true that Yao gave (the
sovereignty of) the Great Society to Shun. Master Meng
said that it was not true, for the Son of Heaven was not
competent to give (the sovereignty of) the Great Society
to another. To this Wan Chang's reply was, 'Very well:
but then, since Shun did have the sovereignty, who gave it
to him?' To this the answer was, 'Heaven gave it to him.'
'Heaven gave it to him,' said Wan Chang: 'Did Heaven
give explicit orders to him?' The reply was, 'No: Heaven
does not speak. The only thing it does is to reveal by deeds
and events.' 'Reveal by deeds and events!' said Wan
Chang. 'How did it do that?' The reply was, 'The Son of
Heaven is competent to recommend a man to Heaven, but
he cannot cause Heaven to give that man the sovereignty.
The great fief-holders can recommend a man to the Son of
Heaven, but they are not competent to cause the Son of
Heaven to give that man a fief. . . . In that bygone age
Yao recommended Shun to Heaven, and Heaven accepted
him, discovered him to the people, and the people accepted
him. This is why I say that Heaven does not speak: all it
does is to reveal by deeds and events.'
Wan Chang said, 'I venture to ask in what way Yao
recommended Shun to Heaven, and Heaven accepted him,
discovered him to the people, and they accepted him.' The

---

[1] Behind this lies the Confucian theory of the people's right to rebel
against an inhuman king. The reader can imagine the influence of this
saying in the history of China.
[2] As Professor Feng Yu-lan and other scholars have pointed out, there is
no strict logical coherence about Mencius's references to Heaven.

reply was, 'He made him preside over the sacrifices and the hundred spirits vouchsafed their approval. Thus Heaven accepted him. Yao put him in charge of affairs of state with the result that they were effectively managed and the hundred clans were at peace with him. Thus the people accepted him. Thus Heaven gave him the throne and the people gave it. . . . Shun was assistant to Yao for twenty-eight years, and this was more than man could do: it was from Heaven. When Yao died and the three years' mourning was completed, Shun left Yao's son in the south of the South River. All the great fief-holders whose duty it was to appear at court did not go to Yao's son, but to Shun. Those with cases requiring arbitration did not go to Yao's son, but to Shun. The minstrels did not celebrate Yao's son, but Shun. That is why I say it was Heaven. If at that late hour Shun had gone to the capital [1] and trampled his way to the seat of the Son of Heaven, taking possession of Yao's palace and ejecting his son, that would have been usurpation, and not the gift of Heaven. This is the meaning of what is written in the *T'ai Shih*,[2] "Heaven looks from the angle from which my people look, Heaven hears from what my people hear."' (v A. 5.)

Master Meng said, 'Shun came from being a farmer: Fu Yueh was called to office from the building of walls, Chiao Ko from salting fish, Kuan Yi-wu from being in prison, Sun-shu Ao from the sea, and Pai Li Hsi from the market-place. The fact is that when Heaven proposes to impose a great responsibility on a man, it is sure first to discipline his purposes by suffering, and his bones and sinews by bodily toil, to starve his limbs and flesh, to empty his very self, confounding all his undertakings. Thereby it stirs his mind, toughens his nature, and makes good his disabilities. Men regularly have to make mistakes before they are able to reform, have to be troubled in mind and perplexed in thought before they can communicate it. Without lawless families and arrogant officers within and

---

[1] Emending *chung kuo* to *kuo chung*.
[2] The *T'ai Shih* is in the *History*.

hostile states and anxieties abroad, countries constantly go
to ruin. By this we come to know that life is in relation
to sorrow and affliction, and death is in relation to peace
and joy.' (vi B. 15.)

Master Meng said, 'Those who exercise their minds [i.e.
mind-heart] to the full come to understand their congenital
nature; and if they understand their nature they understand
Heaven. They keep their minds alive and nourish their
nature and so serve Heaven. Untimely death and long
life are not two different things for them, for they cultivate
their selves as they await the issue; and so they take their
stand on destiny. . . . There is nothing that is not destiny.
Therefore accept obediently your true destiny. Thus the
man who comprehends destiny does not stand under an
overhanging wall. To die because of complete fidelity to
one's principles is a true destiny. To die because one is a
criminal in chains is not a true destiny.'

Master Meng said, 'If we strive, then we obtain, and if we
neglect, then we lose (what we have). According to this,
striving has an effect on our obtaining, and the power to
strive is in us. (But) there are right and wrong ways of
striving, and destiny comes into obtaining. According to
this, striving has no effect on our gaining, and the power of
striving is something outside us.' (vii A. 1 and 2.)

Master Meng said, 'In every instance bad and good
fortune come from men's own seeking. As the *Ode* has it,

Constantly saying, "Match yourself with the great commission,"
 Yourselves strive for many blessings.

And it is written in the *T'ai Chia*, "When Heaven is manu-
facturing evils, it is still possible to escape them. But
when you manufacture evils for yourself, it is not possible
to keep alive."' (ii A, 4.)

CHAPTER VIII: THE FILIAL-PIETY SCRIPTURE

A Westerner will never really come to understand the Chinese traditional approach to the state unless amongst other things he really tries to grasp how much the approach was conditioned by the exaltation of the family above the state. This Chinese principle, one held with a conviction which has, in the past at any rate, been essentially religious, is set forth in all the clarity of its logic in the *Hsiao Ching (Classic of Filial Piety)*. The following quotations are from this book.

In this book Confucius is made the great exponent of the doctrine, but there can be very little doubt that 'the Master' never delivered himself of the sentiments found here. Like some of the books in the *Record of Rites*, the *Classic of Filial Piety* is to be ascribed to the Master Tseng branch of the Confucian school, and to judge by certain tokens of thought and style it belongs, in part at any rate, to mid-Han times (cp. *Ssu Ku Ch'üan Shu Tsung Mu T'i Yao*, chüan 32). Yet a *Classic of Filial Piety* is quoted in a book produced in the middle of the third century B.C. The unavoidable conclusion is that an earlier version was drastically revised by some Han filial-pietist.

The book is consummately moralistic in its terse, bald way; and at some points is open to damaging criticism as camouflaging a mundane and selfish ethic. Yet it has individual touches not found elsewhere, and even flashes of poetry in its thinking. What is more, it puts all classes in society on a level, as first and foremost presented with a categorical imperative, a supreme duty, not to the state, but to the authors of their being.

Chapter 1. Introducing the Central Idea and Explaining the Principle.[1]

Chung Ni [i.e. Confucius] was in his house with Master Tseng [2] in attendance. The Master said to him, 'The first kings had both supreme moral power [*te*] and a vital doctrine with which they made the whole Great Society docilely obedient. The people, through using this doctrine, developed a spirit of concord, and the upper and lower ranks of society bore no ill will against each other. Do you know what this doctrine was?'

---

[1] This and the other headings are the traditional ones.
[2] I take it that this book was written by a later disciple of the Tseng school. Thus the following doctrines are not to be taken as emanating from Confucius, but as a type of teaching current by the third century B.C.

Master Tseng rose from his mat and said, 'Stupid as I am, how could I be adequate to knowing this?' The Master said, 'It was filial piety which was the root of power and of that (process) by which enlightened teaching[1] came to birth. Sit down again, and I will explain this to you. The body with its limbs and hair and skin comes to a man from his father and mother, and it is on no account to be spoiled or injured. That is the first thing about filial piety. To establish the self [? the moral self], to walk in the Way, and to make oneself famous in later generations, thereby glorifying one's father and mother: this is the last word about filial piety. Filial piety at the outset consists in service to one's parents, in the middle of one's path in service to one's sovereign, in the end in establishing one's self. In the *Ta Ya Ode* is the word:

> With your ancestors ever in mind
> Cultivate the virtue in you.

Chapter 2. The Son of Heaven.

The Master said, 'One who loves his parents dare not incur the hate of men, one who reverences his parents dare not suffer indignity from men.' He [i.e. the Son of Heaven] loves and reverences his parents in the fullness of service and thereby extends the teaching influence of the power in him among the hundred clans. It is a pattern to all within the Four Seas. Such is the filial piety of the Son of Heaven. In the *Fu Hsing* is the word, 'The One Man is blessed; and the masses of the people depend on him.'

Chapter 3. The Great Feudatories.

To be above men without being arrogant is to be exalted and yet to avoid peril. To have a policy of strictly limited economy is to be full and yet not to waste that fullness. To be exalted and yet avoid peril is the means by which

---

[1] I suspect that in a number of contexts *chiao* (enlightened teaching) might be more accurately translated as 'religious teaching.' In any case it means, as here, teaching based on definite principles held with a religious kind of conviction. Cp. c. 7, where it is translated 'dogma.'

noble station is permanently preserved. To be full and yet not waste that fullness is the means by which wealth is permanently preserved. With these attached to one's person the state altars can be protected and the harmony of the people secured. Such is the filial piety of the great feudatories. In the *Odes* is the word:

> That they must be apprehensive, must be cautious,
> As standing on the edge of a deep abyss,
> As treading on thin ice.

Chapter 4. The Ministers and Officers of State.

Robes which the first kings did not prescribe, those they dare not wear. Words which the first kings did not prescribe, those they dare not speak. Deeds of virtue which the first kings did not prescribe, those they dare not do. Thus with none of their words against the rules, none of their deeds against the right [*Tao*], neither in speech nor action do they show private preference. The Great Society may be full of their words and yet no mouth denounce them, may be full of their deeds and yet no man bear malice. With robes and speech and conduct scrupulously correct, then they can maintain their ancestral temples. Such is the filial piety of ministers and officers of state. In the *Odes* is the word:

> Never idle day or night
> In serving the One Man.

Chapter 5. The Under Officers.

The same spirit of service which they use towards their fathers should be used for their mothers, that there may be no discrimination in affection. The same spirit of service which they use towards their fathers should be used towards their sovereign, that there may be no discrimination in reverence. The truth is, the mother captures the affections (of a son), the sovereign captures the reverence (of an officer), and the one who captures both is the father. Therefore (for under officers) to serve one's sovereign by

being a filial son, that is loyalty. To serve one's political
superior by being reverent, that is obedience. With their
loyalty and obedience thus unfailing in their service of
those over them, their official grants and positions can be
secure and their sacrifices (to ancestors) be preserved. Such
is the filial piety of under officers. In the *Odes* is the word:

> Rising early, and going to bed late,
> Do not disgrace those who gave you birth.

Chapter 6. *The Common People.*

To follow the course of heaven (in the revolving seasons)
and distinguish the advantages afforded by (different soils),[1]
and then by rigorous economy in personal expenditure to
have food for their fathers and mothers: this is the filial
piety of the common people.

There never has been a case in any class, from the Son of
Heaven to the common people below, of one whose filial
piety had neither beginning nor end and yet never suffered
calamity.

Chapter 7. *The 'Three Powers'* (*Heaven, Earth, and Man*).

Master Tseng said, 'How supreme is filial piety!' The
Master said, 'Filial piety is the unchanging truth of Heaven,
the unfailing equity of Earth, the (universal) practice of
Man. If the people pattern themselves on this truth of
Heaven and Earth, then the light of Heaven leads on to the
benefits of Earth, so that the Great Society of states becomes
ready to obey. In this way the mere dogma produces
results without (the exercise of) severity, its rectifying brings
order without (the repression) of awe.'

The first kings saw this possibility of transforming the
people by means of teaching. Therefore by their all-
embracing love they put this (principle) in the forefront so

---

[1] This is James Legge's interpretation, and he has great scholars' names
behind him. Personally I find this interpretation difficult to approve.
'Share' is the more natural meaning of *fen* here. If that be correct, then
'the *Tao* of Heaven' may well refer to Heaven's impartiality in providing
for all. Thus as an alternative rendering: 'put into common use Heaven's
Way (of the common good), share out the benefits of Earth.'

that no man might neglect his parents. By their personal justice they set it before the people's eyes so that they rose up and practised it. By their reverence [? towards men as men] and courtesy they led the way to it so that the people did not quarrel. By their rituals and music they gave expression to it so that the people were harmoniously attached to each other. By their likes and dislikes they made it clear so that the people knew what was forbidden. In the *Odes* is the word:

> So the Grand Master's might and power [1]
> Hold all men's eyes in trembling awe.

Chapter 8. Filial-Piety Government.

The Master said, 'In bygone days when enlightened kings governed the Great Society by means of filial piety, on no account would they keep the ministers of small countries waiting for an audience—how much more in the case of dukes and marquesses and counts and barons! Thus it was that they won the hearts of a myriad states to delight in serving at the sacrifices [2] to their royal forbears.'

Those governing the states would on no account treat wifeless men and widows with contempt—how much more in the case of under officers and ordinary people! Thus it was that they won the hearts of the hundred clans to delight in serving at the sacrifices to their princely predecessors.

Those governing their families would on no account misdemean themselves with servants and concubines—how much more in the case of their wives and children! Thus it was that they won the hearts of men to delight in serving at the sacrifices to their parents.

[1] The author is unfortunate, not to say careless, in his clinching quotation. The people trembled before the Grand Master in question because he was wickedly tyrannical, not because he was supremely benevolent. Cp. c. i, *init.*

[2] There are a few passages, of which this is one, in classical literature, which lead us to think that in the Chou feudal society the serfs were given a share of some sort in their lord's ancestral sacrifices. It is possible, however, that this pleasant get-together feature is more the idea which the Han ritualists propagated of what ought to have been the case.

In these circumstances, whilst they were alive, parents were in a state of great comfort: after their death when they were being sacrificed to, their ghosts [*kuei*] enjoyed the offerings. In this way harmony and peace prevailed throughout our Great Society, no divine judgment fell on it, no disaster of rebellion was brewed in it. Thus it was that enlightened kings governed the Great Society by means of filial piety. In the *Odes* is the word,

> With virtue so arresting
> All parts do homage to him.'

Chapter 9. *The Government of the Sages.*

Master Tseng said, 'I venture to ask whether the virtue in a sage has anything more in it than filial piety.' The Master said, 'It is the nature [*hsing*] of Heaven and Earth to have man as the most honourable of all creatures; and of all human conduct none is so (morally) great as filial piety.

'In filial piety there is nothing so great as honouring the father. In doing this there is no (achievement) so great as making him "Associate[1] of Heaven": and Duke Chou was the man who succeeded in this achievement. In the days that are gone Duke Chou sacrificed to his high ancestor, Hou Chi, in the suburbs[2] as "Associate of Heaven" and set up King Wen's [his father's] tablet in the Ming T'ang as "Associate of Shang Ti [High God]." The result was that from all the lands within the Four Seas came (princes) each with his tribute (to join in) the sacrificing. How then could there be anything more in a sage's virtue than filial piety?'

The fact is that family feeling, being born at the parents'

---

[1] Arguments, based on such passages as this, that Confucianists really believed that man could be on an equality with God, seem to me rather unimaginative. *Pei* was used of the relation of husband and wife, and the wife was not regarded as a mechanical equal of her husband. The users of the expression *pei t'ien* (Heaven) or *pei Shang Ti* were thinking of bygone saints and heroes whose glory of personality and abiding merit they commemorated in high sacrifice.

[2] In the southern suburb of the Chou capital was the altar to Heaven, in the northern the altar to Earth. As to the royal 'Hall of Brilliance,' the date of its inauguration is very uncertain. However, Han historians argue that from very early times there was such a hall and that in it sacrifices were made to Shang Ti and to the first ancestor of the royal line.

knees, comes daily, through the work of caring for them, to be more and more a looking up to them; and what the sages did was to follow along this line by giving authoritative teaching on being reverent; and to follow along the line of this feeling of family affection by giving authoritative teaching on being loving. The dogma of the sages produces results without (the exercise of) severity, its rectifying brings order without (the repression) of awe. Thus the Way of fathers and sons being that of the Heaven-endowed nature [*hsing*] is also that of the equity (which must prevail) between sovereigns and subjects. Indeed there is nothing so great as the handing on of life by the father and mother, nothing of such import as the wealth of condescension which they, the sovereign and parents, bestow. Therefore to be without love of parents and to love other men (in their place) means being 'a rebel against virtue': to be without reverence for parents and to reverence other men means being a 'rebel against sacred custom [*li*].' Should, then, disobedience be after the pattern of obedience, the people would have no pattern to go by. Such a pattern would not come within the scope of a good power of virtue; high-minded men cannot prize it.

A high-minded ruler is not like this. In his condescension to his people his thoughts about speaking are consistent with the truth, his thoughts about action with what brings joy, his equity in virtue with what brings him honour, his schemes in action with being imitated, his demeanour with being observed by all men, his movements (in the temple service) with the rules. In this way he brings his people to fear and love him, to make him their model and the symbol (of right living). And thus it is that he becomes able to form his authoritative teaching from the virtue in himself, and so is able to put into effect the fiats of his true governing. In the *Odes* is the word,

> This limpid man, (our) princely one,
> In all his bearing flawless.[1]

---

[1] The stanza ends with: 'He rectifies the four quarters of the state.'

PART FOUR

ANALYTICAL MINDS AT WORK ON THE PROBLEMS OF KNOWLEDGE

Apparently Confucius was the first to raise doubts whether all that was supposed to be knowledge was really knowledge. This he did with his ethical emphasis on the high social importance of terms representing the truth about things, particularly about actions and events. Tzu Ssu by his emphasis on the relativity of the time-space universe opened the door for higher flights of reasoning on the nature of the universe and man's knowledge of it, whilst Mo Ti gave men the tools of practical logic. Within a hundred and fifty years of Confucius's death there was a regular galaxy of thinkers working away at the new problems presented to consciousness. Through *Chuang Tzu* (c. 33), the *Lü Shih Ch'un Ch'iu, Hsun Tzu*, the Imperial Catalogue, and other sources we know the names of a considerable number of these men, and have some idea of what they taught. We have also works purporting to be written by some of them, books which are unfortunately suspect as coming from later hands. With regard, however, to those who were more purely epistemologists, they were more subject to neglect than to being edited, and of the names which have come down two only, apart from the Taoist thinkers (cp. Part Five), really stand out as men whose minds we can study. One is Hui Shih, the other Kung-sun Lung; and of these two Hui Shih has to be studied in the pages of other men's works. There is, however, a further work, a well-defined section in the *Mo-Tzu Book*, consisting of six chapters which are almost entirely concerned with epistemological and kindred questions. This Part Four, therefore, is divided into three parts, a chapter on Hui Shih, a chapter on Kung-sun Lung, and a chapter on the later Mohist logicians.

Although the concentrated study of knowledge *qua* knowledge did not attract the more dogmatically inclined Han era, the effects of the earlier investigations and speculations, together with the enhanced riches of logical language, can be traced in the Han writers.

In these chapters I have resisted for the most part the temptation to make cross-references to complementary ideas in the classical, medieval, and modern philosophies of the West. I found that once I started it was impossible to estimate which points were more important and which less, and the number of foot-notes grew beyond all reason.

CHAPTER IX: HUI SHIH

Hui Shih bears the distinction of being the one opponent whom Chuang Chou, the most brilliant mind the Chinese race ever produced, acclaimed as a foe worthy of his steel. He appears to have been somewhat older than Chuang Chou, so that his death must have been somewhere about the end of the fourth century B.C.

Hui Shih appears in various chapters of Chuang Chou's writings, but nowhere with clearer indication of his views than in chapter 33 of the *Chuang Tzu Book*. There he is given as the author of the ten following aphorisms, some of them being highly paradoxical ones. Of these aphorisms nothing need be said further than that they stand in the true line of development from Tzu Ssu and his sense of relativity, and that Hui Shih was immensely sensitive to the element of unceasing change in Nature.

Hui Shih explored the significance of things . . . and said:

1. That beyond which there is nothing greater should be called the great unit. That beyond which there is nothing smaller should be called the small unit.

2. That which has no thickness cannot be increased in thickness, (but) its size can be a thousand miles (long).

3. The heavens are as low as the earth, mountains on the same level as marshes.

4. The sun exactly at noon is exactly (beginning to) go down. And a creature exactly when he is born is exactly (beginning to) die.

5. A great similarity compared with a small similarity is very different. This state of affairs should be described as a small similarity-in-dissimilarity. The myriad things in Nature are both completely similar and completely dissimilar. This state of affairs should be described as a great similarity-in-dissimilarity.

6. The Southern region (beyond the borders of China and not fully explored) has no limit and yet has a limit.

7. To-day I go to Yueh State and I arrive there in the past.[1]

8. Linked rings can be sundered.[1]

9. I know that the hub of the world is north of Yen State and south of Yueh State.[2]

10. Love all things equally: the heavens and the earth are one composite body.

---

[1] In these two statements the key to the puzzle is presumably in the passage of time by which my action to-day becomes an event of the past, and the rings decay and fall apart.

[2] i.e. Position in space is purely relative to the point of view from which one is looking. It is perhaps relevant to note that when Matteo Ricci in the seventeenth century made a map of the two hemispheres to interest Chinese literati he drew it in such fashion as to make China indeed the Middle Kingdom.

CHAPTER X: KUNG-SUN LUNG

Kung-sun Lung, a scion of the ruling house of Chao State, is known to have been a disciple of Hui Shih, and as having early in the third century B.C. urged his own king and the king of Yen State not to make war on each other. There can, however, be little doubt that the dominating interest of his life was the problems of pure philosophy. In the first chapter of the *Kung-sun Lung Book*, which is a biography of him, he is recorded as saying that his reputation had been gained from his 'Discussion on White Horses,' and that if he were deprived of that he had nothing to give men.

This discussion is, therefore, given below in full. It reveals the difficulties with which the thinkers of those times had to wrestle in making language the adequate medium of their thought. (Cp. Introduction, p. xxxvi.) That Kung-sun Lung refused to be beaten by his limitations is evidence not merely of intellectual acumen, but also of the urgency with which the problems of knowledge presented themselves. Further, the fact that he put the results of his investigations into dialogue form gives us an insight into his intellectual honesty. He was unsatisfied until he had put the arguments against as well as the arguments for. In this respect Kung-sun Lung represents the highest achievement of philosophical writing in classical times, for the interlocutor in his dialogues is never a mere puppet set up to make futile objections.

Chapter 2. A Discussion on White Horses.

A. (You say that) a white horse is not a horse: is this (logically [1]) admissible?

B. It is.

A. How can that be so?

B. The term 'horse' is the means by which a bodily form is named. The term 'white' is the means by which a colour is named. The naming of a colour is not the naming of a form. Therefore I say that a white horse is not a horse.

A. Since there are white horses in existence, it is not

---

[1] I take it that *k'o* in this kind of connection both in this author and others of his age can only be rendered by an expression such as 'logically admissible,' though 'logically' of course must not be taken to have the same content as the modern Western philosopher's 'formal logic.'

admissible [1] to say that there are no horses in existence, (and so) it is not admissible to say that the said white [2] horses are not horses. (If you grant that) white horses exist, how do you make out that they are not horses?

B. If you want to get a horse, a yellow horse or a black one will do perfectly well; but if you want to get a white horse, a yellow horse or a black one will not do. On the assumption that a white horse is a horse, what you are wanting to get is one thing, namely a white horse which is not different from a horse (generally). In that case, how is it that a yellow horse or a black one will do (from one point of view) and will not do (from another point of view)? If a thing both will do and will not do, its image (in the mind) is not clearly defined.[3] The fact is, yellow horses and black ones (represent) the one-ness of horse-ness and may (logically) be used as corroborative of the fact that horses exist: but they may not (logically) be used as corroborative of the fact that white horses exist. This proves that white horses are not horses.

A. You make out that a horse's having colour makes it not a horse; but in the world of experience [lit. heaven below] there are no horses which have not colour. Is it admissible then to say that there are no horses in the world?

B. To be sure horses have colour and therefore there are white horses in existence. Suppose, however, that horses did not have colour, there would without question still be horses, and it would be entirely beside the mark to cite white horses as instances. Therefore white horses are not horses. (Further) your 'white horse' is horse-ness plus white-ness. That being so, I therefore say a white horse is not a horse.

A. (Granted that) horse-ness does not require the addition of white-ness, and that white-ness does not require the addition of horse-ness to make white-ness; but we can make a harmony of horse-ness and white-ness with the double name 'white horse.' Whether the two qualities

[1] 'Logically' is omitted here and later for the sake of brevity.
[2] Emending *wu* to *pai*.
[3] Compare the 'undistributed middle' of modern formal logic.
*F 973

blend or not, the making of the name is admissible.[1]   Therefore I say that it is not admissible to maintain that a white
horse is not a horse.

B. To take the existence of white horses as equal to the
existence of horses (generally) is to hold that the existence
of white horses is equal to the existence of yellow horses.
Is that admissible?

A. It is not admissible.

B. Then, to take the existence of horses (generally) as
different from the existence of yellow horses, this is differ-
entiating yellow horses from horses (generally); and to do
that is to regard yellow horses as not horses; and to do that
and at the same time regard white horses as horses, this is
equal to a flying creature going into a pond (like a fish), to
an inner and outer coffin being in different places.   It is an
instance of speech which is universally recognized as self-
contradictory, as a subversive statement.

A. My statement that if there are white horses it is inadmissible to say that there are no horses in existence, this
was made irrespective of the whiteness.   Although [2] it is
irrespective, there still are white horses and it is inadmissible
to say there are no [3] horses.   Therefore (my statement) is
a means of getting at the existence of horses.   It is nothing
more than using horse-ness for getting at the existence
of horses.   It is not regarding white horses as horses
(generally).   Therefore with regard to your view of white [4]
horses, it is inadmissible to say they are not horses.[5]

B. Whiteness does not determine what it whitens, so
that it is admissible to disregard it.   But the name 'white
horse' equals saying that whiteness does determine what it
whitens and determines the thing which is not whitened as
not white.   The name 'horse' does not take colour into
account one way or the other, and for this reason yellow
horses and black horses are admissible as representatives

                    [1] Eliding *wei.*
                    [2] Emending *shih* to *sui* and *chieh* to *yi* or some such copula.
                    [3] Emending *yu* to *wu.*
                    [4] Emending *yu* to *pai.*
                    [5] Emending the first *ma* to *fei.*

of it. The name 'white horse' (on the other hand) is in relation to the rejection and acceptance of colour; and, because yellow and black horses are all cases in which the colour concerned is rejected, therefore white horses are the only ones which are admissible as representatives. Not rejecting is the antithesis to rejecting. Therefore I say that white horses are not horses.

In this book there are also: (1) A Discussion on Universals and Things; (2) A Discussion on All-pervasive Change; (3) A Discussion on Hardness and Whiteness; (4) A Discussion on Names and Actualities. Unfortunately the text in these chapters is, speaking generally, less reliable than the text of chapter 2, which the reader has already discovered from the foot-notes to be unsatisfactory. The problems thus raised for the critics are not necessarily insoluble, so that we may hope for the fruits of the old and new commentators' labours to emerge before long. The titles given are sufficient evidence that the basic questions in metaphysics and epistemology were being asked in those last generations of the Chou era.

Dr. Feng Yu-lan in his *Che Hsüeh Shih* (*History of Chinese Philosophy*), vol. i (cp. Dr. Bodde's translation, pp. 204–14), devotes fifteen pages to careful exposition of selected quotations from these chapters. Two passages alone can be cited here, one to introduce 'Everyman's' readers to Dr. Feng's highly significant conclusions about Kung-sun Lung's *chih*, 'pointers'—or, as Dr. Feng suggests they should be called, 'universals'—the other for the light which these two passages throw on Kung-sun Lung's position in chapter 2, and on his final attitude to the possibility of knowledge.

Things in every instance involve universals,[1] but universals do not point to the material world. If there were no universals, things could not be described as 'things.'

Since universals [2] do not point to the material world, is it admissible to describe things as universals? For universals are what do not exist in the material world and things are what do exist in the material world, and it is not logically admissible to make what exists equal to what does not exist.

[1] I accept Dr. Feng's interpretation of *chih* as 'universal.' But the reader should bear in mind that *chih* in its literal sense means 'finger' or 'pointer,' and he would do well to read over the passage substituting 'pointer' for 'universal.'

[2] Adding *chih* before *fei* and regulating *chieh* and *erh* accordingly. As it stands the sentence is ungrammatical

(Now,) if the material world has no universals and things may not be described as universals, this very denial of things as universals is a negative universal. If there are negative universals, (it is still admissible to say that) things in every instance equal universals. And if we should deny that there are negative universals, that denial itself would be a universal, so that (it would still be admissible to say that) things in every instance involve universals though the universals are negative ones.

The fact that the material world has no universals springs from each single thing having a name. A name in itself is not a universal. To call it a universal is to make 'universal' mean what it does not mean; and that is inadmissible.[1] To go, however, a step further, universals are what all men hold in common. There are no universals in the material world, but it is inadmissible to describe things as not having universals. That statement entails a denial that there are negative universals, and that statement entails things in every instance involving universals. . . .[2]

(*Kung-sun Lung*, c. 2.)

These 'universals' or 'pointers' beyond the material world bear a resemblance, as Dr. Feng points out, to Plato's 'ideas.' On the other hand, the next passage points to Kung-sun Lung's attitude towards knowledge being a more sceptical one. With regard to 'hardness,' and 'whiteness' he raises the issue which brought the seventeenth-century Western natural philosophers to distinguish between primary and secondary qualities.

A. 'Hardness,' 'whiteness,' and 'stone' involve three separate affirmations—is this logically admissible?

B. It is not admissible.

A. Is it admissible for there to be two?

B. Yes, it is.

A. How is this so?

B. When one finds whiteness without hardness, the affirmations entailed number two; and when one finds

---

[1] A name being the counterpart in the mind to the actuality of the thing.
[2] The text presents great difficulties here, but this is the best sense I can make, though it makes Kung-sun Lung guilty of begging the question. Presumably he thought this was self-evident.

hardness without whiteness, the affirmations entailed number two.

A. If one finds a white (element) in an object, it is not admissible to say that there is no whiteness there, and if one finds a hard (element) in an object, it is not admissible to say that there is no hardness there; so that with regard to the stone (which is both white and hard) surely there are three (affirmations).

B. Seeing does not find the hard (element) in the object, but does find the white (element) without the hard. Feeling with the hand does not find the white (element) in it, but does find the hard (element) without the white.

A. If there were no whiteness in the material world, it would be impossible to see the stone, and if there were no hardness it would be impossible to feel the stone. Since whiteness and stone are not mutually exclusive, is it admissible to make the three concepts unrelated to each other? [1]

B. They are of their nature unrelated, not made to be unrelated.

A. With its whiteness and its hardness the stone of necessity finds these (two qualities) complementary to each other. How, then, can they be unrelated?

B. The finding of the whiteness and the finding of the hardness in the stone involve a seeing and a not-seeing which are irrespective of each other. . . . Since one and one are not complementary to each other, therefore they are irrespective of each other. Being irrespective equals being unrelated. (*Kung-sun Lung*, c. 5.)

Some of this is obscure enough, but one thing seems fairly clear, namely, that Kung-sun Lung would not allow that analysis of an object into its component qualities could bring us to understanding its whole composition. To him what each sense gives is out of relation to what the other senses give; and therefore what is known through one channel is essentially out of relation to what is known through any other channels. That being so, knowledge in any real sense is not obtainable through the

---

[1] *Ts'ang*, lit. hidden. This character became a technical term for the Dialecticians, denoting a logical situation in which two or more concepts could not be related to each other.

senses. The question is whether Kung-sun Lung believed that knowledge consisted of universals. Presumably he did, but we are as yet, I think, unable to state positively that this was so. This element of doubt is increased by the study of the famous, not to say notorious, 'Twenty-one Paradoxes,' which the *T'ien Hsia Pien* (*Chuang Tzu*, c. 33) attributes to him and his associates. Some of these have serious philosophical interest (cp. Group 1 below), some seem merely frivolous (cp. Group 2), warranting the judgment passed on Kung-sun Lung by later ages, that he confused the distinction between truth and error and right and wrong.

Group 1.

Fire is not hot [i.e. the sensation of heat is in us and not in the fire].

Eyes do not see [i.e. it is the mind which perceives by means of the eye and light].

T-squares are not square, and compasses cannot make circles [i.e. T-squares and compasses cannot be relied on to make the perfect square and the perfect circle as visualized by the mind].

The shadow of a flying bird never moves.

Group 2.

An egg has hair [? meaning that an egg produces a feathery, hairy creature].

A chicken has three legs [? meaning that the statement about it having two legs introduces a third element of leg-ness into the concept 'chicken'].

A dog can be a sheep [? meaning that since everything is in process of changing into something else, therefore a dog can become a sheep].

An orphan colt has never had a mother [? meaning that an orphan is a child which has no mother].

CHAPTER XI: LATER MOHIST THINKERS

We have no information as to who these thinkers were or when they lived. The only evidence as to date that there is to go on is the general historical evidence of the decline of Mohism in Han times and the internal evidence which these six chapters in the *Mo Tzu Book* themselves afford. The last is fortunately clear enough. These thinkers, belonging to a society with a religiously serious and altruistic tradition, carried this spirit into their reflections on the state of affairs which the speculations of the Dialecticians, e.g. Hui Shih and Kung-sun Lung, revealed. They were true Mohists, convinced of the need for authority and for that authority to be based on practical considerations of men's welfare. From this point of view it was essential that men should be able to use their reason in reliable fashion. They set themselves, therefore, the task of providing the tools of practical logic for honest inquiring minds.

Of these six chapters, the first two, *Mo Ching* 1 and 2 (Canons [1] 1 and 2) go together, and may well be by the same author. Canon 1 is a series of ninety to one hundred definitions—the state of the text makes exact calculation difficult—in a great variety of fields, logic, metaphysics, geometry, ethics, politics, etc. Canon 2 is a series of eighty to ninety propositions with the addition to each of a *shuo* (explanatory) statement, giving a clue to the significance of the proposition. This idea of a *shuo* was followed up by some later writer or writers who added on two chapters, *Ching Shuo* 1 and 2, giving illustrative expositions of the definitions and propositions given in Canons 1 and 2. Finally some third hand, or set of hands, wrote a *Ta Chü* (Great Selections) chapter, in which the main position taken in the other four chapters is expounded in consecutive arguments.

The text of these chapters has unfortunately come down to us in a bad state of preservation. The best consecutive one is that of the *Hsiao Chü* (Small Selections), and that is given below in full. The quotations of Canons 1 and 2 and the Expositions 1 and 2 are dictated by two considerations, one in relation to the importance of the matter dealt with and its intrinsic philosophical interest, the other in relation to the text being reliable for both Canon and Exposition.[2]

---

[1] The term 'canon' (*ching*) was being used in this era for any authoritative work which gave the tenets of a school of thought of whatever complexion.

[2] The only serious omission from the quotations is that of the geometrical definitions. For references to these in English see Dr. Hu Shih's *Development of the Logical Method in Ancient China* and Dr. Bodde (*op. cit.*).

Some Definitions Relating to Knowledge and Dialectic.

Canon 1 and Expositions.

A Cause = that which something gets and by which it proceeds to become.

In re causes, a minor cause is one which, where it exists, does not involve of necessity a thing becoming what it is, but which where it does not exist involves that the thing cannot become what it is: for example, a point in a line.[1] A major cause is one which, where it exists, involves of necessity that a thing becomes what it is, and where it does not exist, involves that the thing cannot become what it is: for example, the disclosing of a thing to view producing the sight of it.

Knowing = a faculty.

In re knowing = a faculty: this faculty = that by means of which one knows, that which does not necessarily entail actual knowing: as in the case of stupidity.[2]

Concentration of the mind = searching for.

In re concentration of the mind: this = a person using his faculty of knowing to search for (something), but not necessarily finding it: merely catching a glimpse of (something).

Knowing = establishing contact with the external world.

In re establishing contacts:[3] this = a person using his power of concentration to establish contact with an object and so being able to apprehend its outward form: as in the case of seeing (a thing) properly.

Mind-knowledge[4] = understanding [*ming*].

In re mind-knowledge: this = a person using his contacted knowledge (as a basis) for discussion of an object so that the person's knowledge of it is all clear: as in the case of understanding.

[1] Without a point to start from there can be no line; but a point does not necessarily go on to make a line.
[2] Emending *ming* to *pu ming*.
[3] Emending *chih* to *chieh*.
[4] A single ideograph consisting of the ordinary *chih* (to know) plus *hsin* (the mind). These Mohist epistemologists apparently invented this term, but it did not catch on, curiously enough, and so is not part of the current coin of the written language.

Hardness and whiteness = (two qualities which are) not mutually exclusive.

If hardness and whiteness are in different places [i.e. different objects], they are not complementary; but mutual incompatibility = being mutually exclusive (and that is not what hardness and whiteness are). . . . The interpenetration of hardness and whiteness (in the same object) is complete.

Interpenetration = mutually getting.

The parts of a body interpenetrate but not completely.

Similarity = in some respects interpenetrating, in some respects not.

A standard model [*fa*] = that according to which a thing gets the sum of its characteristic qualities [lit. its so-ness].

A standard model = (for example) either the idea (of a perfect circle) or the compasses (which make a circle) or an actual circle.

Being alive = a material form + continuity of knowing.[1]

The life of the material form cannot be guaranteed to continue.

A 'that' [i.e. a proposition, a subject for dialectical discussion] must not be two different things if it is to be [2] allowed (as a subject of discussion).

In re a 'that': (for example) 'All cows are not-cows': [3] to have two concepts (of the proposition) is in all cases wrong.

Dialectic = contending over a 'that,' and in dialectic the right wins.

In re dialectic: (for example) one party says that is a cow and another party says it is not a cow; this is contending over a 'that' and the parties cannot both be right. Since they are not both right, one of them must be wrong.

Benefit [4] = being pleased with what you get.

[1] *Chih* in a number of passages, of which this may be one, might well be translated 'to be conscious of.'

[2] Emending the final *pu* to *erh.*

[3] Sun Yi-jang confesses himself entirely bothered by this and the next passage. Here is my attempt: emend *chü* to *wu* (not), and in the next sentence emend *yi* to *pu* (not).

[4] These Mohist logicians approved Mo Ti's utilitarianism and in consequence introduce the utilitarian psychology into questions of knowledge. Cp. the explanation of 'harm.'

Harm = disliking what you get.

In re mind-knowledge: not to know the harm from anything is a crime in mind-knowledge: in regard to knowledge, there should be care about this. To have no way
of escaping (greater) harm except by wanting something
unpleasant is to be forced in the matter. Or, take the matter
of eating dried (and rather putrid) meat and then being
upset by it, the benefit and the harm cannot really be
known. To have an appetite for the dried meat and then
to be upset by it is a case of failing to use your feeling of
doubt in the matter to prevent your appetite. Abnormal
benefit and harm cannot be known. But if a man has to
run to get what he wants and he does not run, this is a case
of using the feeling of doubt in the matter to prevent the
appetite.

To set a person on to doing something = making a
cause.

In re setting on to doing: this involves its being very unlikely to produce free action. *In re* 'cause,' this=certain
expectation of the completion of the action entailed.

Names = names of universal application, names which
classify, and private names.

In re names: 'thing' is a name of universal application.[1]
There are actualities (corresponding to 'things') and these
actualities are of necessity conditioned by the multitude of
their individual characteristics [*wen*]. 'Horse' is a classifying name. The actualities of that kind necessarily bear
this name. 'Tsang'[2] is a private name, and its use is
restricted to the actuality concerned.

To state a (categorical) proposition = making a judgment
about actualities; and speech = what emerges from (cate-

---

[1] Dr. Feng Yu-lan (op. cit., p. 286) compares this with *summum genus*.

[2] 'Tsang' appears to have been the name by which any house-born slave
was called, as 'Huo' was the name by which a captive was called. According to this, a 'private name' cannot be taken as the equivalent to the proper
noun in English grammar. On the other hand, the Mohists advocated
universal brotherhood, and we may assume here that the author is incidentally stressing that a slave is a brother man by name Tsang, not
merely a *tsang*. I take it, therefore, that 'private name' *is* the equivalent
of the English proper noun.

gorical) propositions; and speech in general = saying so-and-so.

In re propositions: information conveyed involves the use of delineatory names for the stating of a proposition about the actuality of a 'that' [i.e. any subject of discussion]. Therefore any speaking, whatever the mouth which gives vent to it, emerges from the act of naming; and a name, for example of a tiger, is equivalent to the picturing of a tiger. Also *in re* speech, we may say that its characteristic is the height of rockiness.[1] (For example,) when we face the future we say 'about to be,' and when we face the past we say 'having been'—words which are as clear-cut in meaning as a rock is in shape.

Knowing = hearing about something, making an explanation of it, experiencing it personally: a harmonizing of names with their actualities and then action. Hearing about = the passing on of (someone else's) personal experience. Seeing (for oneself) = every part of the object seen.

In re knowing: to receive by transmission is (the characteristic of) hearing about, position in space no obstacle (the characteristic of) an explanation,[2] making one's own observation (the characteristic of) experiencing personally. The means by which a thing is described is its name, the thing described is the actuality, the yoking of the name and actuality together the harmony (required), and purpose plus movement the action (required). To hear about something involves someone reporting on it, and that is the second-hand element. But someone observed the thing for himself, and that is personal experience. To see involves a time element and scrutiny of the parts of the thing.

Action = preserving, destroying, exchanging, lessening, increasing, or transforming.

In re action: to fortify a rampart is (characteristic of) preserving, to contaminate (characteristic of) destruction,

[1] Eliding *chieh*.
[2] The expositor would seem to have had in his mind the fact that explanation involves classifying and that the classification of a thing links it with all the other things in that class wherever they may be.

to buy and sell (characteristic of) exchanging, to smelt ore of diminishing, to grow bigger of increasing, frogs becoming rats [1] of transforming.

Likeness = that of duplication, of parts in a whole, of concord, of being classifiable together, (any one of these four kinds).

In re likeness: where there are two names to one actuality, there is a duplicating likeness. Where (the parts) are restricted to the whole, there then is a likeness of the parts to each other. Where several people live together in one house, there then is concord. Where there are some points of likeness, there then is the likeness according to class.

Unlikeness = that of duality, of not coalescing, of disagreeing in spirit, of not being classifiable together in any respect [i.e. incompatible].

In re unlikeness: two (separate things) are bound to be unlike (in some respect, however slight), and that is duality. Where things are not linked together (in one organism), that is not being parts of a whole. Where things cannot be in the same place together, that is disagreement. Where there are no points of likeness, that is incompatibility.

Likeness and unlikeness taken together = disclosing to view what exists in a thing and what does not.

In re likeness and unlikeness taken together: for example, the practice in rich families of achieving reciprocity in the exchange of the good things they possess for those they do not. They compare and measure quantities, allowing so many oysters in return for so many silkworms. . . .[2]

Canon 2 with Expositions.

'To get to know but not by the five roads of sense': the explanation lies in duration of time.

It is by means of the eye that we see [*chien*] and it is by

---

[1] There is more than one instance in the classical books of the belief that metamorphoses of this kind took place. Cp. the evolutionary passage quoted from *Chuang Tzu*, p. 208.

[2] The idea is of an infinite variety of things not easily comparable, and involving an infinite gradation of likeness and unlikeness.

means of the fire that the eye perceives; [1] the fire is not perceived except through the five roads of sense. But the knowledge (gained thereby) after a period of time, is not related to the eye seeing as if an actual fire was there.[2]

'Fire is not hot': the explanation lies in perception.

When we perceive fire, we describe the fire as hot, but this is not (merely) through the fire being hot. It is we who have an accordant power of perception, i.e. a (faculty of) knowing.

'For a man to know what he does not know': the explanation lies in selection and rejection by means of names.

Mix up what a man knows with what he does not know and ask him (which is which). If he is then able to say certainly, 'This I know' and 'This I do not know,' it is through a double power of selecting one lot of (classifying) names as right and rejecting another lot as wrong. This is two ways of getting to know.

'What a thing actually is and what I know it to be, and what it is when another man is made to know, these are not necessarily the same': the explanation lies in flaws (in knowledge).

(For example) somebody injures something: that is the state the thing is in. I see the event: that is my knowledge of it. I tell someone else: that is making him know.

'Non-existence is not necessarily conditioned by existence': [3] the explanation lies in the matter under consideration.

In re non-existence: if a thing arrives at non-existence, then it first existed and afterwards ceased to exist, as for

[1] It is interesting to note that the English 'perception' and 'to perceive' are used in relation to all the senses, though particularly in relation to seeing. The Chinese *chien* clearly is used in the same way.

[2] Why the expositor in so obvious a reference to memory does not mention it makes a very interesting question. There were terms there waiting to be used. Did he refrain because duration of time (and ? consciousness) was the essential point for him, and he did not want to confuse his readers with an extra faculty of memory?

[3] Cp. *Tao Te Ching*, c. 2, where existence and non-existence are described as conditioning each other. I take this passage with its exposition as a good example of the fair-mindedness as well as the acumen with which these Mohist logicians treated their opponents.

example, if horses ceased to exist. But if the sky fell down, there would be now existence piled on non-existence.

'Doubt begins [1] in an unexpected turn of events or in happening on some violation of right which blocks the concentration of the mind on not doubting': the explanation lies in whether (the source of doubt) is really existent or not.

In re doubt and unexpected (turns of events and violations of right) : [2] . . . A cow house being made in the summer is because there is a cold spell. It is (not) really unexpected. If you make a rational proposition [*chü*] of the matter, then it is of little consequence. If you ignore it, it becomes a burden: you have no strength to deal with it. . . . Like the grindstone and the feathers [3] . . . like a brawler getting killed by misadventure owing to drinking wine during the public market. Is that an unaccountable event? Or is it a case of folly? Does an intelligent man regard himself as that sort of person? (If he does,) he is a fool. [4]

'The justice of Yao [the Sage-king] is imposed on the present but belongs to ancient and very different times': the explanation lies in 'justice' having more than one meaning. [5]

In re Yao and being a great eater: some people view a man on the basis of his reputation, others on the basis of his actuality. To introduce a friend as a rich merchant is to view him on the basis of his reputation: to point him out as a great eater is to view him on the basis of his actuality. So with the justice of Yao, it is of great repute at the present day, whilst the actuality of the justice designated belongs to ancient times.

'Non-existence is possible, but once a thing exists it is

[1] Emending *shuo*, which quite clearly is wrong, to *ch'i*, which suits the sense.
[2] The text is in bad condition, but such parts as one can get clear have great intrinsic interest.
[3] i.e. feathers flying up for no apparent cause, but actually because the turning of a grindstone near by creates a draught.
[4] Our Mohist logician is true to the puritan tradition his master created.
[5] An attack on the Confucianists for their excessive and undiscriminating laudation of Yao. The point is that he may have been a good king according to the standards of his age, but he would not necessarily be so in a more civilized age.

impossible for it to be ejected': the explanation lies in its
having been so.

In re the possibility of non-existence: if a thing has been
supplied (to the universe), it stands as such. It is impossible for it not to be. In course of time it is exhausted
and yet [1] not exhausted.

Hsiao Ch'ü.

With regard to dialectic, it sets out to make clear the
dividing line between truth and error, [and so] to discriminate the different threads which constitute order and disorder: [2] to make clear the relative positions of likeness and
unlikeness, and to examine the logic of names in relation
to actualities, [? and so] to distinguish between the beneficial and the harmful and to resolve doubts.

How is the so-ness of the things in creation to be marked
out? In discussions to work out comparisons between
different kinds of argument by means of names designating
actualities, by means of propositions expressing ideas, by
means of explanations setting forth causes, by means of
classification selecting and rejecting.[3] What applies to
oneself is not to be opposed in others, and what does not
apply to oneself is not to be expected from others. Where
there is uncertainty, an argument [4] cannot be conclusive.
Where a hypothesis is set up, the argument is about what is
at the time not so. To work to a pattern (in an argument)
is to have a criterion, for a pattern is the means by which
an argument goes according to rule. The result is that if
an argument sticks to the pattern, it is right: if it does not
stick to the pattern, it is wrong. This is working to a pattern.

To illustrate is to bring forward some other thing with a

[1] Adding *erh*. The point of the passage is the one which Bergson made
between clock time and 'durée.'

[2] This probably refers to political order and disorder, but it is not necessarily restricted to it. These later Mohists were deeply convinced of the
need for order in thinking as a condition for order in society.

[3] Does this mean taking this phenomenon to belong to this class and
conceding that phenomenon to belong to that class?

[4] This sentence has no subject, but in subsequent sentences the pronoun
chih (it) turns up. I think the reference must be to the *yen* (speech, argument) mentioned in the previous paragraph.

view to illuminating an argument. To argue by parallel is to compare propositions consistently throughout and find them on all fours with each other. To argue by analogy is to say, 'You, sir, are so, and it stands to reason that I also may be so.' To argue by extension [1] is to take cases which have not been cited as similar to the cases which have been cited. To concede this is like making a statement to the effect that they are similar and it is out of the question for us to say they are different.

With regard to things [i.e. the subjects of propositions], there are those which in their similarity do not conform to the parallelism of similar propositions. The similarity between them only reaches a certain point and stops there. Besides [2] the so-ness of two or more things, there are also the processes by which they become so, and these things may be similar in their so-ness but not in the processes by which they respectively become so. (Further,) besides making a thing the subject of a proposition, there is also the purpose for which it is made the subject, and (two or more things) may be similarly adduced but not for the same purpose. The result of all this is that illustrative, parallel, analogical, and extensional, (these four forms of) propositions, may in practice be badly wrong, have a topsy-turvy effect, be very far from the truth, go sliding along and become entirely divorced from the root (of the real). [3] In that case they must be subjected to examination. It is impossible for them to be used with mechanical accuracy. Thus it is that if an argument shows all sorts of skill with abnormal classifications and extraordinary logical reasons given, then it is not to be regarded with favour. The subject of a proposition may be right generally and actually so (at the time) or it may be not actually so (at the time). It may be all-inclusive in one respect and not all-inclusive

---

[1] The temptation is to translate by 'induction,' but Dr. Fung Yu-lan's translator, Dr. Bodde, uses 'extension.' This is wiser, for the writer might have in mind the generalization which is found in the major premiss of a deduction.

[2] Emending *yeh* to *yu* (besides, also) and doing the same in the succeeding sentence.

[3] Our writer attacking his *bêtes noires*, the sophists.

in another. It may be right in one respect and not in another. There cannot be a mechanically accurate usage. This is why an argument which shows all sorts of skill with abnormal classifications and extraordinary logical reasons given is not to be regarded with favour. It is because it is not true.

(For example,) a white horse is a horse, and to ride a white horse is to ride a horse; a fleet horse is a horse, and to ride a fleet horse is to ride a horse. (Again,) the son by a captive woman is a human being, and (for her master) to love such a son is to love a human being. The son of a slave woman is a human being, and to love such a son is to love a human being. This is right and is a case of what is actually so. Such a son of a captive woman is a man, and as a man he serves his father. He does not serve just a man. So with a man's younger brother being handsome. The man loves him as his younger brother: he does not love him first as a handsome man. A carriage is made of wood, but to ride in a carriage is not to ride in wood. . . . A robber is a man, but the more robbers there are is not the more men there are. For there to be no robbers is not for there to be no men. How is this to be made clear? To hate there being more robbers is not to hate there being more men. To wish there should be no robbers is not to wish there should be no men.

Public opinion is agreed that the right is along this line: with the conclusion that, although a robber is a man, yet to love robbers is not to love men, and not to love robbers is not not-loving men, to kill robbers is not to kill men. There is no difficulty here—and yet there is a difficulty [1]— for the 'this' [i.e. men] and the 'that' [i.e. robbers] belong to the same category. Public opinion holds to the 'that' and does not regard itself as self-contradictory. The Mohists hold to the 'this' and are opposed to the other position as being without ground [ku] to it: a case of what

[1] The text here gives trouble. Sun Yi-jang suggests the elision of *tao wu nan* altogether. Agreed that those words do not make sense, but the writer's argument surely requires something which expresses that there is a difficulty.

is called 'prejudiced within and illogical without,' not making sense in the mind: is not this so? To be prejudiced within and make no explanation, this is a case of a (conclusion) being right but not what it sets out to be. For instance, also, 'to read books is not to love books: to love reading books is to love books. To go in for cock-fighting is not loving cocks but loving cock-fighting.' . . .[1]

In loving men you do not wait till you love all men before you take it that you love one. In not loving men you do not wait till you do not love all men. Not having universal love for man is based in not loving (certain) men. In horse-riding you do not wait till you have ridden all horses before you can regard yourself as a horse-rider. When you come to not being a horse-rider, you do not wait until you have failed to ride all horses before you take it that you are not a horse-rider. This is a case of being all-inclusive in one respect and not being all-inclusive in another respect. Take living in an organized state, it involves having an organized state to live in. But the existence of one house does not make an organized state, for 'the fruit of the peach-tree is peaches, and the fruit of thorns [2] is not dates.' To visit a sick man is to visit a man, but to hate a man's sickness is not to hate the man. Men's ghosts are not men, but your elder brother's ghost is your elder brother. Thus to sacrifice to the ghost of a man is not to sacrifice to a man, and yet to sacrifice to your elder brother's ghost is to sacrifice to your elder brother. As for the horse and the fiery glance of its eye, we may say that the horse is fiery-glancing; but because its eyes are big, we may not say that the horse is big. . . . One horse equals 'horse' and two horses equal 'horse.' A horse is a being with four feet, i.e. there are four feet to every horse, and (we may not say) two 'horses' have only four feet. The horse may be a being which is white, and there may be two horses which

---

[1] The text again is difficult, but it is so worth while doing the best we can with it.
[2] The emblem of land being uncultivated, and so of there being no organized community. The statement would appear to be a well-known proverb.

are white, but we may not say that any one horse must be white.

'If a (categorical) proposition is a fallacy, then it is impossible to know similarities and differences': the explanation lies in the fact that such a proposition is not (logically) admissible.[1] 'The fact that an ox-horse [2] is not an ox is compatible with the admission of their similarity': the explanation lies in inclusiveness. 'Hold to the This and hold to the This plus That, for these are similar': the explanation lies in dissimilarity.

In re (categorical) propositions being fallacious: an ox and a horse are different, but to use an ox's possession of teeth and a horse's possession of a tail as explaining a cow's non-horseness is (logically) inadmissible. They both have teeth and tails: and although oxen and horses are neither in all cases with teeth and tails nor without them, we can still say that an ox and horse are not of the same species. It is through an ox having horns and a horse not having horns that they are not of the same species. If the proposition be made that oxen have teeth and horses have not, and from this regard them as not similar, that is a fallacy. It is like saying that oxen have teeth and horses have tails, in which case some may actually be oxen and some may not. According to this it is admissible to say that some are oxen and some are not oxen but horses.

The fact is, to say an ox-horse is not an ox is not admissible; also to say that it is an ox is not admissible. (According to this) then, with a proposition which is partly admissible and partly inadmissible, (you cannot) go on and say that the proposition 'an ox-horse is an ox' is inadmissible. In fact ox-ness is not a duality, nor is horse-ness, but ox-horse-ness is a duality. According to this, then, oxen cannot but be oxen, horses cannot but be horses, and ox-horses cannot but be ox-horses. Q.E.D. [lit. no difficulty there].

To have a that and a this is admissible. The thats of a

[1] Emending *chio* to *ch'ih*.
[2] ? the name for a yak.

that abide in their that-ness, and the thises of a this abide in their this-ness. To be both a this and a that is not admissible. But a that (may be) about to become a this, and (in that case) 'to be a that and a this' is also admissible, and the that-this-ness abides in its that-this-ness. According to this, and following on with the that-this, then it is also about to become a (complete) this.[1]

'If one hears that something which is not known is like something which is known, then both things are known': the explanation lies in the conveying of information.

In re hearsay: (for instance,) if you are standing outside (a room) the things outside are the things you know.[2] If someone says to you that the colour inside the room is like this colour (outside), this equals the thing you do not know being like the thing you do know. With the question whether the colour is black or white, which colour would win? It would be the one which is like the colour outside. If that were white, the colour inside would be bound to be white. On the assumption that we know the colour to be white in this one case, we therefore know the colour to be white in the other case.

In general names are used with the purpose of getting a valid understanding of what is not known, not with the purpose of having what we do not know create doubts about what we do understand. It is like using a foot-rule to measure an unknown length. With regard to things outside the room, there is knowledge by personal experience; with regard to the things inside the room, there is knowledge by explanation.[3]

---

[1] At first sight the contention here may appear to be merely a generalization of the previous one; but that is not so. There was no question there of an ox-horse being on the way to become an ox or a horse. Here the author is concerned with things in process of changing. Through it all he sticks stoutly to his conviction that speech must retain its stoniness, that knowledge must be clear-cut, i.e. no statement or concept must be allowed to have two different meanings.

[2] Accepting Teng Kao-ching's emendation (cp. Dr. Feng Yu-lan, op. cit., p. 294).

[3] Dr. Bodde (*ad loc.*) translates by 'inference.' According to the sense of the passage this is of course entirely admissible, but, since *shuo*, i.e. the term used for 'explanation,' is the term used here, I feel hesitant.

'To regard all speech as misleading is misleading':[1] the explanation lies in the nature of what is said.

In re (regarding all speech as) misleading: speech which plays hide-and-seek may be taken as misleading. This (judgment) is not misleading. But then (according to this) there are (statements) which are (logically) inadmissible. But suppose we take as tenable a man's speech which is (logically) inadmissible, surely we have no sense of discrimination.

'(The idea of) infinity does no harm to (the idea of) including every one': the explanation lies in filling up an infinite area.[2]

Given a southern region (beyond the borders of China) which is finite, then it is possible to get the totals about it. But if it is infinite, then it is not possible to get the totals. If we cannot know whether it is finite or infinite, then we cannot know whether we can get at the totals or not, and we cannot know whether men fill up the whole region or not, and so of necessity it is misleading to think that we can love the whole population.[3] (On the other hand,) if the population does not fill an infinite area, then the total of men is limited and there is no difficulty about totalling what is limited. (Also) if the population fill an infinite area, its infinity is completed. Being completed, it is finite. There is no difficulty about that.

[1] An attack on Chuang Chou's position (cp. Part Five, Chapter XIII).
[2] Emending *fou chih* to *wu chung*, thus making sense and putting it on all fours with the exposition.
[3] On the ground apparently that 'filling up' entails the idea of a limit. Our Mohist friend, usually so pertinacious in his common sense, here would appear to be rather chopping logic. But the point at issue obviously is whether the Mohists can really claim to love all men, seeing that they do not know how many people live in the world.

PART FIVE

The Individualistic Philosophy of the Tao Experts

Chapter XII: 'Tao Te Ching': A Text-book on Man's Freedom in his Natural Environment

This book, a *ching* (authoritative book) on the *Tao* (Way) and its *te* (distinctive power), is one of the most famous in China, varying in its popularity from age to age, but none the less, in spite of its teaching running counter to Confucianist orthodoxy, appealing permanently to something very deep in Chinese hearts. Until the art of literary and historical criticism began to become a science there was an unquestioned belief that the book was written by one Lao Tan, a contemporary of Confucius; and it is often spoken of as *Lao Tzu*. To-day scholarly opinion tends to regard it as the work of a much later mind (? late fourth century B.C.), and indeed a very composite work, containing old fragments embedded in much later contexts. It looks very much like a text-book put into the hands of Taoist disciples when they came to learn the Way from a master. In any case the book is full of cryptic allusions, which the initiate would explain to the uninitiate. The style is in most chapters poetical, and as such extremely succinct. In a word, it is poetry in the fullest sense, mystic poetry at that, for all its common sense.

To ascribe the work to a later age than that of Confucius (551–479 B.C.) creates a problem. When did the Taoist movement begin? Men must have been thinking more or less in this way long before the first Taoist book we can date, viz. the authentic parts of *Chuang Tzu* (fourth to third century B.C.). The high refinement of thought in that work presupposes earlier attempts to get behind the mystery of time and change.

PART ONE

Chapter 1.

If the Tao could be comprised in words, it would not be the unchangeable Tao:

(For) if a name may be named, it is not an unchangeable name.

When the Tao had no name, that was the starting-point of
   heaven and earth:
Then when it had a name, this was 'mother of all creation.'

[1]

Because all this is so, to be constantly without desire is the
   way to have a vision of the mystery (of heaven and earth):
For constantly to have desire is the means by which their
   limitations are seen.
These two entities although they have different names
   emerged together;
And (emerging) together means 'in the very beginning.'
But the very beginning has also a beginning before it began—.
This door into all mystery!

Chapter 2.

The whole world knows that beauty is beauty: and this is
   (to know) ugliness.
Every one knows that goodness is goodness: and this is (to
   know) what is not good.
Thus it is: existence and non-existence give birth to each
   other:
The hard and the easy complete each other:
The long and the short are comparatively so:
The high and the less high are so by testing:
The orchestra and the choir make a harmony:
And the earlier and the later follow on each other.

This is why the sage abides by actionless activity,
And puts into practice wordless teaching.
Since all things have been made, he does not turn his back
   on them:
Since they have life, he does not own them:
Since they act, he does not entrust himself to them.
When he has achieved any success, he does not stay by it.
In this not staying by his success he is unique;
And this is why he is not deprived of it.

[1] In almost every one of the chapters there comes a point in the argument
which corresponds rather to the division of a sonnet. For this reason I
make this space.

Chapter 3.

Let there be no putting of the best people into office: this will stop vicious rivalry among the people. Let there be no prizing of rare merchandise; this will stop robbing among the people. Let nothing desirable be visible; this will save the people's minds from (moral) confusion.

This is why the sage's form of government
Empties the people's minds and fills their stomachs,
Weakens their ambitions and strengthens their bones,
Unfailingly makes the ordinary man ignorant and passionless,
The wise man afraid to take action.
(For,) if action is actionless, there is nothing not under control.

Chapter 4.

The Tao is hollow: use it and there is no overflowing.
How fathomless it is! It makes one think of a common ancestor to all creatures,
One who blunts their cutting edges, unties their knots,
Makes a harmony of the lights (in the heavens) and lays the dust [1] (of this grimy world).
How limpid it is, as if it would stay so for ever! [2]

And yet we do not know whose son (this common ancestor could be),
This image of something before the High God!

Chapter 5.

Heaven and earth are not human-hearted: for them all creatures are but straw dogs. [3]

[1] The Western reader needs to remember that in north China sandstorms and clouds of dust are a feature of the climate. Hence this Taoist imagery of the world men live in.
[2] It is open to conjecture whether this sentence is not a gloss which early crept into the text.
[3] Straw dogs were used in sacrifices. They might be very carefully made, but when the sacrifice was over they were thrown away.

A sage also is not human-hearted: for him also the hundred clans are but straw dogs.

Here is this space between heaven and earth, a bellows as it were,

Which is empty but does not buckle up, which the more it is worked the more it gives forth.

But, however many words are used, the number comes to an end.

It is better (to say nothing and) to hold fast to the mean (between too much and too little confidence in heaven and earth).

Chapter 6.

The spirit [? divine significance] of a valley is to be undying.

It is what is called 'the Original Female,' [1]

And the Doorway of the Original Female is called 'the root from which heaven and earth sprang.'

On, on goes this spirit for ever, functioning without any special effort.

Chapter 7.

The heavens continue, and the earth endures;
And that in them which makes them so permanent
Is that they do not live for themselves.
Thus it is that they can live so long.

This is why a sage puts himself second and then (finds) himself in the forefront;

Puts himself outside (of things and events) and survives in them.

Surely it is because he has no personal desires that he is able to fulfil his desires.

---

[1] I take it that there is reference here to some early myth about the genesis of the world, a myth which later became rationalized under the Yin-Yang concept. The Yin is the female, the Yang the male in all creation. It is like the Taoists to make use of the simplest material. Here they work it into their idea of the valley symbolizing the power of being empty and receptive.

Chapter 8.

The higher form of goodness is like water;
For water has the skill of profiting all creatures
Without striving with them.
It puts itself in the (lowly) place which everybody hates.
So near the Tao is it.

The goodness of houses consists in their being on the ground:
The goodness of men's minds consists in their being pro-
    found:
The goodness of companionship consists in human-hearted
    ness:
The goodness of speech consists in its being reliable:
The goodness of government consists in bringing good order:
The goodness of any business consists in its being efficiently
    done:
The goodness of any movement consists in its being timely.
Only in all this there must be no striving,
For thus only can nothing go wrong.

Chapter 9.

To set out deliberately to be full to the brim [i.e. satisfy
    every desire] is not so good as (to know when) to stop.
If you are thorough in sharpening (a sword), you cannot pre-
    serve its edge for long.
If you fill your hall with gold and jade, there is no way by
    which you can guard it.
If you are rich and of exalted station, you become proud,
    and thus abandon yourself to unavoidable ruin.

When everything goes well, put yourself in the background:
That is the way Heaven acts.

Chapter 10.

Are you able, as you carry on with the restless physical soul,[1]
    to embrace the oneness (of the universe) without ever
    losing hold?

[1] There are two souls in a man, according to Chinese thinking of those
days and since, the spirit soul (*hun*) and the physical soul (*po*).

Are you able as you control your breathing and make it more
and more gentle, to become an (unself-conscious) babe?

Are you able, as you cleanse the Mysterious Mirroring [1]
(through consciousness), to leave no scratches (of misconception)?

Are you able to love the people and rule a state, without
being known to men?

Are you able, whether Heaven's Door is open or closed, [2]
to be the (passive, receptive) Female?

Are you able to have a right understanding of all quarters
and never interfere?

Give life to them and nourish them;
(For) to give life but not to own, to make but not depend on,
To be chief amongst but not to order about,
This is what is meant by 'the Dark Power' (of unconscious
influence).

Chapter 11.

Thirty spokes together make one wheel;
And they fit into 'nothing' (at the centre):
Herein lies the usefulness of a carriage.
The clay is moulded to make a pot;
And the clay fits round 'nothing':
Herein lies the usefulness of the pot.
Doors and windows are pierced in the walls of a house,
And they fit round 'nothing':
Herein lies the usefulness of the house.

Thus it is that, while it must be taken to be advantageous
to have something there,
It must also be taken as useful to have 'nothing' there.

Chapter 12.

(Indulgence in) the five colours makes men blind,
(Indulgence in) the five notes (of music) makes men deaf,

[1] Cp. *Shu* v, 10 for 'mirroring in water.' The author seems to pose consciousness *in re* vision. Cp. p. 271 on the 'L' Ho Shang Kung (second
century B.C.) comments, 'The mind dwells in a dark place.'
[2] This cryptic phase is explained by Wang Pi as referring to conditions
of peace and confusion in society.

(Indulgence in) the five flavours destroys the palate,
(Indulgence in) riding and hunting drives men's minds mad,
(Indulgence in) rare merchandise makes obstacles to right
  action.

This is why a sage is concerned with what is inside him (*lit.*
  the stomach), not with what he can see (outside).
Thus it is that he abandons 'the That' [i.e. the external world]
  and lays hold of 'the This.'

Chapter 14.

The object you look at and cannot see is called 'invisible';
The sound you listen to but cannot hear is called 'inaudible';
The thing you try to grasp but cannot get hold of is called
  'intangible';
These three (qualities) it is impossible to investigate to the
  end;
And thus it is that they blend and make One.
This oneness on its upper side is not light,
On its under side is not dark.
It has unbroken succession (in time),
For it goes right back to the (time when there was) nothing.
Thus it is called the 'form of the formless,' the 'image of the
  non-material.'
Thus it is called 'indistinguishable,'
For if you go to meet it, you can see no front to it,
If you follow after it, you can see no back.

Lay hold of (this) ancient truth.
By it you can be master of your present existence,
You can know how antiquity began,
And that is a clue to the Tao.

Chapter 16.

Go on to the limit of emptiness:
Hold fast to the stability of stillness.
(For) all things were made by one process,
And, as our eyes demonstrate to us, they all turn back.

They may flourish abundantly,
But each turns and goes home to the root from which it came.
Home to the root, home, I affirm, to the stillness.
This means, to turn back is destiny;
And the destiny of turning back, I affirm, can never be changed.

To know the never-changing is to have the Light;
As not to know the never-changing is blindly to breed calamity.
To know the never-changing is to have capacity,
To have capacity is to be impartial,
And to be impartial is the power of kingship.
The power of kingship is of Heaven,
And to be of Heaven is to be of the Tao.
To be of the Tao is to continue—
With a mortal body to be free of danger.

Chapter 17.

The king who is really over all his subjects is the one who is merely known to be there,
Next to such a king is the one whom they love and praise,
Next to him is the one they fear,
And next to him the one they despise.
If (the king) does not trust (his people) enough,
They indeed do not trust him.

How remote is (the true king), his speech how rare a treasure!
For, when success attends him and all things go well,
The hundred clans all say, 'All this comes to us of itself.'

Chapter 19.

Away with these 'sages'! [1]   Away with these 'wise men'!

[1] The later years of the Chou era saw an 'Age of Enlightenment' when it became a little easy for a man with a new theory about life and the universe to be regarded as a sage. The attack in this section is primarily but by no means exclusively directed against the Confucianists. That late-Chou era was much under the impression, as the English Victorian age was, that there was great virtue in the development of material civilization.

The profit to the people will be a hundred per cent.
Away with these 'human-hearted men'! Away with these
    'just men'!
The people will turn back to filial piety and (plain) kindness.
Away with these skilful artisans! Away with these profit-
    making merchants!
Thieves and robbers will cease to exist.

These three classes of men make out that we are not
    civilized enough:
What actually happens is, more edicts added on.
Give people Simplicity to look at, the Uncarved Block to
    hold:
Make few their self-centred desires.

Chapter 22.

If you adapt yourself, then you (remain) part of the whole:
(For) if a thing is forced, it will get straight (again);
If the ground is low, it will be filled.
If you are ruined, then you can (start) afresh;
For if there is little (in hand), there is (the opportunity) for
    acquiring,
Whilst if there is much, it leads one astray.

This is why the sage embraces oneness,
Makes it the test of everything in society.
He does not display himself:
Thus it is that he is brilliantly displayed.
He does not count himself right:
Thus it is that his rightness is made manifest.
He does not fight his own cause:
Thus it is that he is victorious.
He does not boast of his achievements:
Thus it is that he becomes leader.
He alone does not strive with men:
And thus it is that all men are unable to strive with him.
(So then) this ancient saying, 'If you adapt yourself, then

you remain part of the whole,' is by no means empty words.   Reality (in man) is being part of the whole, and so belonging to it.

Chapter 25.

Before heaven and earth were produced,
There was Something, without form (and yet) all complete.
Silent!   Empty!
Sufficient unto itself!   Unchanging!
Moving everywhere, but never exhausted [?]!
This indeed might well be the mother of all below heaven.
We do not know its real name (to classify it).
That we may have it in writing we say Tao (the Way).
If we have to classify it, we say 'Supreme.'
'Supreme' involves breaking away (from the general mass),
Breaking away involves being removed from,
Being removed from involves coming back (to the mass).

Thus it is that the Tao is supreme,
Heaven is supreme, and Earth is supreme;
And a king also is supreme.
Within his territory there are four supremacies,
And the (true) king abides in the union of them.
Man models himself on the earth,
The earth on heaven,
Heaven on the Tao;
Whilst the Tao models itself on itself being what it is.

Chapter 29.

The men who set out to capture all under heaven and
    make it their own, according to my observation do not
    succeed.
What is under heaven is a sacred vessel,
Not to be treated in such fashion,
And those who do so bring it to ruin.
Those who hold on to it, lose it.
The truth is that some creatures go before and others follow
    behind,

Some breathe one way, and others breathe another,
Some feel strong, and others feel weak,
Some like constructing,[1] and others like destroying.
This is why the sage has nothing to do with the excessive,
     the extravagant, or with being exalted.

Chapter 30.

The man who uses the Tao in the service of an autocrat
Does not war down the states by force of arms.
His business is to long for the return (to peace and inaction):
For where soldiers are, there thorns and brambles grow:
After the passing of a great army,
The harvest is sure to be bad.
A really able commander stops when he has some success:
He dare not exploit his command of force.
Having some success he must not be elated:
Yes, having some success, he must not boast:
Yes, having some success, he must not become un-
     governably proud.

That success may have been an unavoidable step,
But the (real) success must not be one of force;
For the weakness of old age accompanies the vigour of
     youth.
The explanation is this: (force) is not of the Tao;
And what is not of the Tao quickly perishes.

Chapter 32.[2]

Tao is eternal, but has no fame (name);
The Uncarved Block, though seemingly of small account,
Is greater than anything that is under heaven.
If kings and barons would but possess themselves of it,
The ten thousand creatures would flock to do them homage.
Heaven-and-earth would conspire
To send Sweet Dew,

[1] Reading *tsai*.
[2] By permission I use Dr. Arthur Waley's admirable translation for this
chapter.

Without law or compulsion, men would dwell in harmony.
Once the block is carved, there will be names,
And so soon as there are names
Know that it is time to stop.
Only by knowing when it is time to stop can danger be
avoided.
To Tao all under heaven will come
As streams and torrents flow into a great river or sea.

Chapter 33.

To know men is to be wise:
To know one's self is to be illumined.
To conquer men is to have strength:
To conquer one's self is to be stronger still,
And to know when you have enough is to be rich:
For vigorous action may bring a man what he is determined
to have,
But to keep one's place (in the order of the universe) is to
endure;
And to die and not be lost, this is the real blessing [1] of long
life.

Chapter 34.

The Supreme Tao, how it floods in every direction!
This way and that, there is no place where it may not go.
All things look to it for life, and it refuses none of them:
(Yet) when it has done its work, it has no fame to be [2] its
distinctive clothing.
(For) while it nourishes all things, it does not lord it over
them.

Since unfailingly it has no wants toward them,
It may be classed among things of low estate:

[1] Both then and down the ages since long life has been popularly conceived as one of the great blessings which crown man's life. The Taoists
(cp. Chuang Chou) saw deeper than this.
[2] It is open to conjecture that the *yu* of 'to be' should be emended to
pu, 'no,' and thus the meaning become 'with no (distinctive) clothing to it.'
*G 973

Since all things belong to it, but it does not lord it over
  them,
It may be named the Supreme:
But — to say the last word — it does not arrogate
  supremacy to itself,
And thus it is that it is able to fulfil its supremacy.

Chapter 35.

If you grasp the Supreme Symbol (of nothingness) [1] and go
  all over the country,
There will be no harm (to any one) in your going.
Indeed, the peace and quiet will be beyond bounds:
Music and cakes and ale,
And the passing stranger (made to) stop.

(Yet) the words from the mouth of the Tao, how insipid
  they are!
There is no taste to them at all.
Look for the Tao, and it is not enough to be seen,
Listen for the Tao, and it is not enough to be heard.
(Ah, but) use the Tao and it is not enough to come to a stop.

PART TWO

Chapter 38.

The high exponent of power in personality is without
  power [i.e. power personal to him]; and this is why he
  has (real) power in personality.
The inferior exponent is (set on) not losing his power; and
  this is why he has no (real) power in personality.
The high exponent taking no action has no ulterior ends,
Whilst the inferior exponent has ulterior ends to his activity.
(Thus) the high exponent of human-heartedness has no
  ulterior ends to his activity,
Whilst the high exponent of justice has.

---

[1] Cp. cc. 4 and 14. What human beings can grasp is only an image, not
the supreme reality of *Tao* in its ultimate mystery.

(Thus) the high exponent of ritual [i.e. social and religious conventions], when he acts and fails to get the due response,
Bares his arm and uses force.
Thus it is that when the Tao is lost, there is personal power,
When that is lost, there is human-heartedness;
And when that is lost, there is justice;
And when that is lost, there are the conventions of ritual.
In relation to sincerity of heart and speech, ritual only goes skin-deep, and is thus the starting-point of moral anarchy;
And foreknowledge of events to come [1] is but a pretentious display of the Tao, and is thus the door to benightedness.
This is why the really grown man concentrates on the core of things and not the husk,
And thus it is that he rejects 'the That' and lays hold of 'the This.' [2]

Chapter 43.

The most yielding thing [? the Tao] in our world of experience can master the most immovable:
Since it is 'nothing' [i.e. immaterial], it can penetrate 'no-space' [i.e. the material].

Hence we know that inaction is the profitable course.
(Yet) the truths which cannot be compassed in words,
And the profit which comes from inaction,
These men rarely grasp.

Chapter 47.

Not to go out of the house is to know the world of men,
Not to look out of the window is to know the ways of the heavens; [3]

[1] The exponents of Confucianism—and the author has them very much in mind in this passage—claimed that their type of moral wisdom enabled them to foretell what would happen to states and men
[2] Cp. Part Four, Chapters. X and XI, *passim*, where the logicians are mainly concerned with emphasizing the distinction between this proposition and that. Cp. also below, cc. 54, 57, 72, and *Chuang Tzu*, c. 2. This last passage is the most important, cp. Introduction, p. xxvii.
[3] ? The *Tao* of Heaven.

For the further a man travels,
The less he knows.

This is how the sage knows without going anywhere,
Can name things without seeing them,
Can bring them to completion without doing anything (to
    them).

Chapter 48.
The business of learning is one of day by day acquiring more,
The business of the Tao one of day by day dealing with less.
Yes, dealing with less and less,
Until you arrive at inaction.

If you practise inaction, nothing will be left undone:
For the way to acquire (lordship) over society is by in-
    variably not interfering.
If you interfere in any way, you are inadequate to lording
    over society.

Chapter 49.
The sage has no unalterable mind:
He makes the mind of the people his mind.
Thus, the good I treat as good:
I (must) also treat the evil as good;
For thus I obtain goodness (from them).
Truth-speakers I treat as truth-speakers:
Liars also I (must) treat as truth-speakers,
For thus I obtain truth-speaking (from them).

The sage in the midst of society is constantly absorbing:
For the sake of society he muddles his mind.
Thus the people all pay heed with their ears and eyes,
And he can treat them all as babes.

Chapter 54.
The firmly rooted cannot be torn up:
The firmly grasped cannot slip out of your hand.

(Just as) there is no remission in the ancestral sacrifices
   which sons and grandsons make,
So foster it [i.e. the Tao] in yourself,
And the power of your personality will be true power:
Foster it in relation to your family,
And the power of it will be enough and to spare:
Foster it in relation to your country,
And the power of it will go from strength to strength.
Foster it in relation to the Great Society,
And the power of it will be everywhere.

For thus it is that in yourself you see other selves,
In your family you see other families,
In your district you see other districts,
In your country you see other countries,
In your society as a whole you see the Great Society of man.
How otherwise am I to know that the Great Society is
   what it is?
Only by means of 'the This.'

Chapter 55.
How solid and impervious is the spiritual power which
   contains!
It is to be compared to a babe.
Neither insect nor serpent stings it,
Nor savage beast seizes it,
Nor bird of prey clutches it.
Its bones are soft and its sinews weak;
Yet the grasp of its hands is strong.
It has not yet experienced the mating of male and female;
But it is complete in this respect,
The supreme example of vital energy.
(Also) it can cry all day and not get hoarse;
The supreme example of harmony [? between a creature
   and its functioning organs].
To know this harmony means to know the never-changing
   (element in life),
To know the never-changing means to have the Light.

(On the other hand) to keep on increasing your living
   power, that, I say, is an omen of ill:
For the mind to make the vital energy its servant, that, I
   say, is the use of force.
And, since the weakness of old age accompanies the vigour
   of youth,
This means, violence is not of the Tao.
To be not of the Tao is to perish quickly.

Chapter 57.

'The ruling of a country is achieved by the rectifying of it,
The successful use of arms by their cunning contrivance,
The possession of the Great Society by not interfering.'
But how can we know that these things are so?
(The only way) is by 'the This.'
The more taboos there are in society,
The poorer the people will be:
The more weapons the people have,
The more will the darkness of evil be over state and family:
The more forms of skill men have,
The more monstrous inventions there will be:
The more laws there are promulgated,
The more thieves and robbers there will be.
Hence the saying by a sage:
'Let me do nothing and the people will transform themselves.
Let me love quiescence, and the people will put themselves
   right.
Let me not interfere, and the people will of themselves
   grow rich.
Let me have no desires, and the people will of themselves
   come to be an uncarved block.'

Chapter 61.

The big state is a matter of flowing down (like water).
In the relationships between states in the Great Society a
big state plays the female part; for the female in all cases
by quiescence triumphs over the male, and this happens
because her quiescence puts her beneath the male. Thus

it is that if a big state puts itself beneath a small state [i.e. at its service], and if a small state puts itself beneath a big state, each wins the other. As a matter of fact, the one puts itself below in order to win, the other is below and wins. It is nothing more than that the big state wants to add to the population it supports and the small state wants to come into the service of other men [i.e. avoid poverty-stricken isolation]. Thus both attain their respective desires: but the bigger one of the two must take up a lowly position.

Chapter 65.

In the old days those who were capable of practising the
    Tao, did not use it to enlighten the people:
They set out to make them ignorant.
The people are hard to govern because they are too clever.
Hence to use cleverness in governing a country
Is to destroy authority in it.
Not to use cleverness is a blessing to a country.

To know (by experience) both these states,
Is, moreover, to have a standard for comparison;
And to discern this standard unfailingly
Is to have the 'Numinous Power' (by which the universe
    came to be),
The 'Numinous Power' which goes so deep and so far,
That joins with all creatures in turning back,
And so brings them to the Great Obedience.

Chapter 67.

Men everywhere declare that our tenets are in appearance
    supremely paradoxical.[1]
It is, however, just because the Tao is supreme that it
    appears paradoxical.
As for the conventions [i.e. non-paradoxical], they are just
    of long standing,—and what trifles they are!

[1] *Pu hsiao* was a term much used among filial-pietists. It meant that a son was not like his father, i.e. not what he ought to be. I suggest that it must mean 'paradoxical' here.

We have three treasures; so keep hold of them and guard
    them. The first is kindness, the second thrift, the third
    not presuming to be first among men.
Be kind, and thus you can be brave:
Be thrifty, and thus you can be generous:
Do not presume to be first, and thus you can become the
    chief of all the appliances (for governing).
To-day kindness is discarded: and how much more bravery!
Thrift is abandoned: and how much more generosity!
(Qualities) of the second rank: and how much more
    (qualities) of the first!
This is death.

.   .   .   .   .

Chapter 68.
A really expert advance guard does not intimidate: [1]
Really expert fighters do not display any rage:
Really expert conquerors are victorious without joining battle:
And really expert users of men put themselves below them.

This is what is called 'the spiritual power in not striving
    with men,'
What is called 'vigour in the using of men,'
What in ancient times was the height (of praise) and was
    called 'being the mate of Heaven.'

Chapter 69 [concluding statement].

.   .   .   .   .

Thus it is that when armies are joined in battle, the side
    which deplores (the fighting) will be the victor.

Chapter 71.
To know what is not (true) knowledge is the better part:
Not to know what is (true) knowledge is to be a sick man;

---

[1] The frequent references to war and military tactics tell their own tale
of that age which went from one sanguinary war to another. They also
illustrate the realistic nature of the Taoist mind which saw in everything,
good and bad alike, symbols of life's actualities.

And it is only by seeing sickness as sickness
That one can cease to be sick.

The sage is not a sick man;
And it was because he saw sickness as sickness
That he ceased to be sick.

Chapter 72.

If the people are not overawed by majesty,
Then supreme majesty has arrived.
There must be no scorn of what makes home for them,
No contempt for what means life to them.
Only if you do not despise them will they not despise you.

This is why the sage knows himself, and does not display
    himself,
Has his self-love but does not over-value himself.
The truth is, he rejects 'the That' and lays hold of 'the
    This.'

Chapter 73.

If courage goes with daring, then (the man) may get killed.
If courage goes with not daring, (the man) may live:
Both of these may sometimes bring profit, sometimes bring
    loss;
And, since there is no one who knows the ground of
    Heaven's condemnation
The sage for this reason sees this matter as fraught with
    difficulty.

The Way [Tao] of Heaven is not to contend and yet to
    be able to conquer,
Not to declare its will and yet to get a response,
Not to summon but have things come spontaneously,
To work very slowly with well-laid plans.
Heaven's net is vast with wide meshes:
Yet nothing is lost.

Chapter 80.

Take a small country with a small population. It might
well be that there were machines which saved labour ten
times or a hundred times, and yet the people would not
use them. It might well be that the people had to die
twice over (in defence of their country), and yet they would
not emigrate to distant countries. Although there might
be carriages and boats, no one would ride in them. Although there might be weapons of war, no one would issue
them. It might well be that people would go back to using
knotted cords.[1]

Make the people's food sweet, their clothes beautiful,
their houses comfortable, their daily life a source of pleasure. Then the people will look at the country over the
border, will hear the cocks crowing and the dogs barking
there, but right down to old age and the day of their death,
they will not trouble to pass to and fro.

Chapter 81.

True speech has no beauty to it;
And beautiful speech has no truth to it.
Good people do not go in for dialectics;
And dialecticians are not good people.
Real knowledge is not knowing everything;
And the know-alls have not got real knowledge.

A sage does not hoard.
Having used what he has on behalf of other men,
He has the more in himself:
Having given that away,
He is all the richer.
This is the Way [*Tao*] of Heaven:
A profit which involves no loss.
This is the way of a sage:
His actions involve no quarrelling (over what is his and
    what is other men's).

[1] One tradition as to the first attempt men made at writing.

CHAPTER XIII: CHUANG CHOU, THE POET OF FREEDOM

Chuang Chou, the greatest of the Taoist thinkers, is a man about whose life we know very little. Even his date is uncertain, though he must have died somewhere about 286–275 B.C. Nevertheless through the *Chuang Tzu Book* we come to know him well: his sense of humour and illuminating wit, the sweep of his imagination, his underlying earnestness and devotion to truth. Ssu-ma Ch'ien (145–*c*. 86 B.C.) said of him that he 'so flayed the Confucianists and Mohists that the scholars of his day were quite unable to refute his criticisms.' He did, indeed, do a great deal of 'debunking'; and yet he was constructive as well as destructive. He could beat people like Hui Shih at their own game; though one imagines that he was not really concerned about niceties of logic. Logic was his tool and not his master. This was because he was at heart a poet, enthralled by visions of time in eternity. In contrast to the authors of the *Tao Te Ching*, who had a great deal to say on the true government of society, he was a philosophical anarchist, not only discounting civilization and its arts, but also willing for all society to go so that the soul and body of the individual man might be free.

He is said to have written prolifically, but the *Chuang Tzu Book* of to-day contains only thirty-three chapters, and there can be little doubt that more than half of them were written by men who doubtless counted as his followers, but whose minds, good as they were, moved on a different plane from his.

Chapter 1. Excursions into Freedom.

In the Northern Ocean there is a fish, its name the Kun [Leviathan], its size I know not how many *li*.[1] By metamorphosis it becomes a bird called the P'eng ['Roc'], with a back I know not how many *li* in extent. When it rouses itself and flies, its wings darken the sky like clouds. With the sea in motion this bird transports itself to the Southern Ocean, the Lake of Heaven. In the words of Ch'i Hsieh, a recorder of marvels, 'When the P'eng transports itself to the Southern Ocean, it thrashes the water for three thousand *li*, and mounts in a whirlwind to the height of ninety thousand *li*, and flies continuously for six months before it comes to rest.'

A mote in a sunbeam (that in one sense is all that this

---

[1] *Li*—the Chinese mile, roughly a third of the English mile.

vast Roc is): flying dust which living creatures breathe in
and out! And that blueness of the sky! Is it an actual
colour, or is it the measureless depth of the heavens which
we gaze at from below and see as 'blue,' just like that
and nothing more? Again take water, without the dense
accumulation of which there is no power for the floating of
a great ship. And (think of) a cup of water upset in a
corner of the hall. A tiny mustard seed becomes a ship
(afloat), but the cup which held the water will remain
aground because of the shallowness of the water and the
size of the cup as a ship.

So with the accumulation of wind, without sufficient
density [1] it has no power to float huge wings. Thus it is
that the P'eng has to rise ninety thousand *li* and cut off
the wind beneath it. Then and not before, the bird, borne
up by the down-pressed wind, floats in the azure heavens
with secure support. Then and not before, it can start on
its journey south.

A cicada and a young dove giggled together over the
P'eng. The cicada said, 'When we exert ourselves to fly
up on to the tall elms, we sometimes fail to get there and
are pulled back to the ground; and that is that. Why then
should any one mount up ninety thousand *li* in order to go
south?' Well, the man who goes out to the grassy country
near by takes only three meals with him and comes back
with his stomach well filled. But the man who has to
travel a hundred *li* grinds flour for one night on the way;
and the man who has to travel a thousand *li* requires food
for three months. These two little creatures (the cicada
and the dove), what can they know?

Small knowledge is not equal to great knowledge, just as
a short life is not equal to a long one. How do we know
this to be so? The mushroom with one brief morning's
existence has no knowledge of the duration of a month.
The chrysalis knows nothing of the spring and the autumn.
This is due to their short life. In the south of Ch'u State

---

[1] 'Density' seems the only word to represent the Chinese. This is an
admirable example of the realistic way in which a really great poet's
imagination works.

there is a Ming-ling tree whose springs and autumns make five hundred years. In the old days there was a Ta-ch'un tree whose springs and autumns made eight thousand years. Right down to the present Grandfather P'eng [1] is famed for his immense age—although if all men matched him, how wretched they would be! . . .

A variant version of the story of the Leviathan and the Roc is here given, winding up with a quail laughing at the P'eng and describing its flight among the bushes as 'the perfection of flight.' Chuang Chou says that this is due to the difference between small and great. He then continues:

Thus it is that the knowledge of some men qualifies them for a small office and for effecting unity in one district, whilst the moral power of another man fits him to be a ruler and proves itself throughout a whole country. These men have a view of themselves which is like the quail's view of himself.

On the other hand, Master Yung of Sung State just laughs at these men. If the whole world should admire or criticize him, he would neither be encouraged nor discouraged. Having determined the difference between what is intrinsic and what extrinsic, he disputed the accepted boundaries of honour and dishonour. In this he was himself, and there are very few such men in the world. Nevertheless he was not really rooted.

Take Master Lieh. He could drive the wind as a team and go, borne aloft, away for fifteen days before returning. Such a man attains a happiness which few possess. Yet in this, although he had no need to walk, there was still something on which he was dependent [viz. the wind]. Supposing, however, that he were borne on the normality of the heavens and earth, driving a team of the six elements in their changes, and thus wandered freely in infinity-eternity, would there be anything then on which he was dependent?

Thus it is that I say, 'The perfect man has no self, the spirit-endowed man no achievements, the sage no reputation.'

[1] The Methuselah of Chinese tradition.

(The Emptiness of Fame.)

Take the Sage-king Yao, who wished to abdicate his throne in favour of the recluse Hsü Yu. Yao said, 'When the sun or the moon is shining, if you should keep a torch alight, it surely would be difficult for it to give light. When the seasonal rain is falling, if you should keep on watering the ground, that would surely be waste of labour. Do you, my Teacher, establish yourself on the throne and the Great Society will be ordered. I am but a dead body. I see myself as incompetent. Pray then, reach out for the Great Society.'

Hsü Yu replied, 'You, Sire, in ordering the Great Society have brought it to perfect order. If I should now take your place, it surely would be only for fame. But fame is only the transient part of the actual. Am I to act for a transient end? The tit builds its nest in the deep forest, but that nest takes up no more room than a twig. The tapir drinks from a great river, but it only fills its belly. Return and take your kingship easily. For my part there is no way by which I can be of use to the Great Society. If a cook cannot cope with his kitchen (and prepare the sacrificial meats), the impersonator of the dead or the liturgist in the hall does not seize the cups and stand and take the cook's place.'

(The Spiritual Man and the Inability of the Non-spiritual to understand him.)

Chien Wu [an inquirer about the Taoist Way] inquired from Lien Shu, saying, 'I heard Chieh Yü say something which went too far and is not really true. It carried one out, but did not bring one back, so its likeness to the bound-less Milky Way frightened me. It was grossly deceptive, removed from human experience. . . . He said that a spirit man lived on the Miao-ku-she mountain. His flesh and skin were like ice and snow: his delicate grace like a girl's. His food was not that of ordinary men, for he breathed in the wind and drank the dew. He mounted the clouds in the air and drove a team of flying dragons, wandering out beyond the Four Seas. His spirit was congealed. Yet he delivered living things from corruption and every year made the crops ripen. For me this was a wild tale, and I did not believe him.'

'So,' said Lien Shu, 'the blind man has no conception of the beauty of art, nor the deaf man of the music of the bells and drums. Blindness and deafness are by no means confined to material things. These defects also exist in relation to things of the mind [lit. to knowledge], and these words of yours make it appear that you are defective in this way. The virtue in that spirit man is such that all things are of little worth to him: they are all one to him. The world may be anxious to be governed: but why should he bother himself about society? That man, nothing can injure him. If there were a flood reaching to the sky, he would not be drowned. If there were a great drought and the metals and stones became liquid and the soil of the mountains were burnt up, he would not be hot. Why, the very refuse of his body would serve to manufacture a great sage-emperor.

(How Greater Knowledge changes a Man's Sense of Values.)

A man of Sung State took some sacrificial caps to the State of Yueh[1] to sell. But the people of Yueh wore their hair short and adorned their bodies [? when they sacrificed], so that they had no use for the caps. In the same way the Sage-king Yao, who ruled the peoples of the Great Society and who had brought peace to all within the Four Seas, went to see the Four Masters of Miao-ku-she mountain. On his return to his capital, his Great Society no longer existed for him.

(The sophist) Master Hui[2] in conversation with Master Chang said, 'The King of Wei sent me the seed of a great gourd. I planted it and the result was a gourd as big as a five-bushel measure. When I used it for holding water, it

[1] Yueh was a country on the borders of Chinese civilization.
[2] This is Hui Shih, who is dealt with in Part Four, Chapter IX.

was not rigid enough to bear lifting. If I had cut it up to make ladles, they would have been too shallow for the purpose. There was indeed no purpose for which it was not too big, so I broke it to pieces as useless.'

Master Chuang said, 'Sir, you were stupid over the use of big things. For example, there was a man of Sung State who possessed a salve which healed chapped hands. His family, one generation after another, had been washers of silk. A stranger who had heard of this salve offered him a hundred ounces of gold for it. The clan, when called together to consider the matter, said, "We have been washing silk for generations and have only made a few ounces of gold. Now in one morning we can make a hundred ounces. Let us sell the salve." The stranger, having obtained the salve, went and told the King of Wu, who was having trouble with Yueh State and had made the unknown man commander of his ships. He engaged the men of Yueh in winter time [when hands get chapped], and in the battle on the water he defeated the Yueh forces. For this he was rewarded with land and made a noble. The ability to heal chapped hands was in both cases the same, but in the one case it meant a title of nobility, in the other it meant being tied down to washing silk. The difference lay in the way of using the salve. Now, Master Hui, you possessed a gourd as big as a five-bushel measure. Why then did you not consider it as a huge cup in which you could float on the rivers and lakes? instead of which you were distressed that it was too shallow to be a ladle. The conclusion, sir, is that it looks as if you had a dull mind, doesn't it?'

Master Hui said, 'I have a huge tree. . . . Its great trunk is so knobby and its small branches so twisted that you cannot put the measuring tools square on them. It stands by the public road, but no carpenter casts a glance at it. Now, Master Chuang, your words are big but of no use. Every one agrees in rejecting them.'

Master Chuang said, 'Have you never seen a wild cat, its body crouching low as it waits for its prey? It springs from

this side to that, now high, now low—and it gets caught in
a trap and dies in a net! There is the yak, so big that it
looms over one like a cloud in the sky. That is being really
big; and yet it is no use for catching mice. Now, sir, you
have a huge tree and you are distressed because it is of no
use. Why do you not plant it in the village of non-existence, in the open country of nothingness. Beside it you
could wander in inaction; and beneath it you could be
free to sleep. No axe would cut it down, nothing would
injure it, for there would be no purpose for which it might
be used. Would you not be free from trouble then?'

Chapter 2. The (Inner) Harmony of (Opposing) Things.[1]

Tzŭ Ch'i, a man from Nan Kuo, leant against a low
table as he sat on the ground. He looked up to heaven, and
his breath died down. Without a sound he seemed to lose
his partnership (of soul and body). Yen Ch'eng Tzŭ Yu,
who was standing before him in attendance, said, 'How is
this, that you can make your body like a sapless tree and
your mind like dead ashes? At this moment the person
leaning against the table is not the person who was leaning
against it before.'

Tzŭ Ch'i said, 'Yen, this is a good question you are asking.
At the moment, you must understand, my self was gone
clean away. You have listened to the music which man
makes, but you have not listened to the music of the earth;
or you may have listened to the music of the earth, but you
have not listened to the music of Heaven.'

Tzŭ Yu said, 'May I ask you for an explanation of this?'

Tzŭ Ch'i said, 'The great mass of breath (in the atmosphere) is called the wind. There are times when the wind
does not move. When it does move, a myriad apertures
are aroused to make sounds. Have you never listened to
the *liao liao* of the wind? You know the cavities and holes
in the rugged heights of the mountains and the woods—
with trees a hundred spans in girth. There are, as it were,

---

[1] 'Things' in this chapter, as often elsewhere, includes not only things in
Nature, but also institutions and ideas of every kind.

noses and mouths and ears, square sockets and round depressions, mortars and ditches and pools. So there is a roaring and a snoring, a whistling and a sizzling, a howling and a yowling. The wind dies down and there is a tiny melody: it comes at full blast and there is a great diapason. There is a lull and every hole is devoid of sound. . . .'

Tzŭ Yu said, 'Since the music of the earth is just a matter of all kinds of holes, and human music a matter of pipes, may I ask what the music of Heaven is?'

Tzŭ Ch'i said, 'All this blowing varies in a myriad ways. Who then can there be who excites all this and makes each way be itself and all of them be self-produced?'

(Supreme Knowledge and Partial Knowledge, and the Conditions under which they arise.)

Great knowledge includes everything: small knowledge is restricted. Great speech has no pungency to it: small speech (may be pungent but) it is just chatter.

Whether men are asleep and soul has communion with soul, or whether they are awake and the body is freed and its contacts are the basis of intercourse, the mind is day by day engaged in struggle. There are indecisions, griefs, reservations, small fears giving rise to perturbation, great fears giving rise to recklessness.

Consider the mind. In some men it shoots forth like a bolt from a cross-bow, assuming mastery of right and wrong. In others it holds back, merely guarding (the opinions) they have won. In others it decays like the decline of the year, in other words, day by day crumbling away to nothing. In others it is sunk in creaturely activity from which it cannot be drawn back. In others it is sealed with hates, in other words like an old drain (choked with muck). Thus the mind has one foot in the grave, and there is no way of reviving it [lit. bringing it back to the light of the sun].

(Consider the emotions.) Joy and anger, sorrow and delight, anxiety and regret, the fire of sex passion [1] and the

_____
[1] Emending the character *pien* to *luan*.

(subsequent) feeling of contentment: evanescent moods, like the music coming from emptiness, like mushrooms coming from damp heat. Day and night alternate before our eyes, and there is no knowing what they may bring forth. (An emotion) gone, is gone, and to-morrow can by no means [1] reproduce it.

What is the cause of the emotions? It is near to the truth to say that without them there is no 'I,' and without an 'I' they have nothing to take hold of. But we are ignorant as to what makes this so. There must be a True Lord, but we are least able to discover traces of His existence. We may act in the belief that He exists, but we cannot see His form, for the Reality that exists has no form.

(Consider the body and its parts,) its nine apertures and six internal organs, all in their places. Which of them shall we like best? Or are we to be pleased with them all alike? (As a matter of fact) each has its personal function, and thus all are in the position of servants: is that not so? As servants they have not the power to control each other: is that not so? Then can they take turn and turn about in being master and servant? (As a matter of fact) they have a true ruler in his place [viz. the 'I']; and whether they try or not to find out his reality does not add to or subtract from the truth about him.

Once this 'I' has received its complete form and so long as it awaits the completion of its span, it cannot be non-existent. But as it rubs and fights against the material world it is moving towards this completion with the speed of a galloping horse; and nothing can stop this. Alas, alas, to be throughout one's life dispatched on service, but to see no achievement coming from it! To be wearied with one's service and not to know what is its final object! Surely we are right in lamenting this. And nothing is gained by men affirming that there is no physical death. The body decomposes, and the mind decomposes with it. And surely we are right in affirming that this is supremely

[1] Emending *mu* to *mo*.

lamentable. Thus man's life is like a passing dream,[1] is it
not? Unless it be that I alone am dreaming and other
men are not dreaming.

Men follow the dictates of their made-up minds, and
there is no one who does not do this. But how can *a
priori* knowledge take the place of the mind choosing for
itself? This does happen, but it is the ignorant who allow
it to happen. To make the distinction between right and
wrong apart from the making up of the mind is equivalent
to 'going to Yüeh to-day and arriving there in the past.'[2]
It amounts to making nothing be something. But if
nothing can be something, even a divine Yü[3] could not
have knowledge, and there would be nothing we could do
about it.

Take speech. It is not just an emission of breath. The
man who speaks has something to say, and what he has to
say is by no means absolutely predetermined [i.e. apart
from the speaker]. Are we to infer that the words exist
(waiting to be said) or that they do not exist until they
are said? And this is a question of whether we can prove
a distinction between human speech and the chirping of
fledgelings.

The question has to be asked: how the Tao becomes
obscured so that there is the distinction of true and false.
Also, how is speech obscured so that there is the distinction
of right and wrong? The Tao cannot go away (for a
moment) and cease to be here; neither can words be here
[i.e. have been spoken] and be impossible. The obscuring
of the Tao is in relation to one-sided thinking, and the
obscuring of speech is in relation to the embroidery of
eloquence. Thus it is that there are the distinctions of right
and wrong made by the Confucianists and the Mohists, the
one affirming what the other denies, and denying what the
other affirms. If then we want to affirm what they (both)
deny and deny what they affirm, there is no other way than
that of a clearer understanding.

[1] Emending the character *man* to *meng*.
[2] The famous paradox by Hui Shih. Cp. Part Four, Chapter IX.
[3] The Sage-king Yü.

(We have to realize that) a thing is both a 'That' and a 'This,' and it cannot see itself as a 'That.' If you know yourself, then you know. (Otherwise you do not know.) Thus it is that I maintain that the 'That' proceeds from the 'This,' also that the 'This' is linked to the 'That.' The 'That' and the 'This' together, life interpreted under conditions (of time)! After all, now there is life, now death; now death, now life. What is possible at one time is impossible at another: and what is impossible at one time is possible at another. Being linked to the right is being linked to the wrong, and being linked to the wrong is being linked to the right. That is why the sages do not follow these distinctions and so become enlightened by Heaven,[1] and are linked to the 'This.'

(As has already been stated) a 'This' is also a 'That,' and a 'That' is also a 'This.' Then in addition, a 'That,' as also a 'This,' is equally affirmable and deniable, with the result that we cannot infer either that they exist, or that they do not exist. Do not let them get to the point of being a pair of opposites. This is called (reaching) the axis of the Tao; for an axis from the outset is in position at the centre of a circle and meets the requirements of every change endlessly. Since both the right and the wrong are endlessly (changing), therefore I maintain that there is no other way than that of illumination. . . .

The possibility of the possible and the impossibility of the impossible—it is the Tao in action which brings this about. Thus a thing is described as being so [i.e. what it is]. How is it just what it is? Through the so-ness in its being just what it is. How is it not what it is? Through the not-so-ness in its being just so. A thing never varies in having what makes it what it is, nor in having what makes it possible. There is not anything which is not what it is, nor which is impossible. Thus it is that there are roof-slats alongside of solid pillars, ugliness alongside of beauty, and to be great [kuei], to alter [kuei], to flatter [kuei], to be

---

[1] *T'ien*, the transcendental side to Nature.

marvellous [*kuei*]; [1] all these through Tao have the unity of mutual interpenetration. For a thing to be separated out (from the mass) is for it to become a thing. For it to become a (complete) thing is for it to de-become. Every single thing both becomes and de-becomes, [2] both processes being to and fro in the unity of mutual interpenetration.

Only the man of all-embracing intelligence knows this unity of mutual interpenetration. Because he has this intelligence, he cannot be made use of but takes up his abode in its common functioning. His functioning has utility, for to be of (real) use is to interpenetrate and be interpenetrated; and to penetrate and be interpenetrated is to achieve. To arrive at achievement is about all a man can do. Following on from that comes stopping; and to stop without knowing that one is stopping that is—Tao.

For a man to wear out his spirit and intelligence in an effort to *make* a unity of things, and to be ignorant of the fact that they are in agreement, this is to be described by 'The Morning Three.' What do I mean by that? Well, there was a certain monkey-keeper who had charge of their diet of acorns. He ordered three in the morning and four at night for each one. The monkeys were all angry about this. The keeper said, 'Very well, then, you can have four in the morning and three at night.' The monkeys were all pleased. Thus in name there was actually no change for the worse, whilst scope was given to feelings of pleasure and anger and the arrangement was in conformity with those feelings. It is in this way that sages by means of the surface distinctions of 'the right' and 'the wrong' make harmony, and yet take their ease in Heaven's levelling out. By levelling out I mean going two ways at once.

[1] The modern pronunciation of these four characters given here as *kuei* is as follows: *k'uei, kuei, ch'üeh*, and *kuai*. The traditional rhyme of the first is *k'uei*. Chuang Chou's selection of these four somewhat unconnectable concepts here is with a view to showing that there must be some connection since the ideographs exist and, what is more, are expressed by the same sound in speech. *N.B.*—I have no reason to suppose that that sound was actually *kuei*, but it must have been something like it.

[2] The text is emended, a *pu* being added to the *wei* to make a double negative. Without this sense seems hardly possible.

The knowledge which the men of old had was perfect in one respect. How this was so, is as follows. There were men who held that before there began to be (so many) things (in the world), that was perfection, a state of completion to which nothing could be added. Then there came a second stage in which there were a large number of things, but they had not begun to be carefully differentiated. Next to this came a stage when things were differentiated, but there had not begun to be a distinction between right (things) and wrong (things). This ornamentation (of things) as right and wrong was the process which brought about the waning of the Tao in the world, and the same process brought about the rise of personal preference. And it is equally out of the question to infer either that there really is progress and regress or that there is not. If we say there is, it is a case of 'Chao's fine playing of the lute.' If we say there is not, it is a case of 'Chao's inability to play the lute.' [1] Chao Wen's playing and Shih Huang's wielding of the conductor's baton and Master Hui's leaning against a Wu tree: the three experts' knowledge was just more or less. Hence each went on till the last year of his life; but it was only they who prized their knowledge and regarded it as extraordinary compared to any one else's. Because they prized it they wanted to enlighten people with it. But other people were opposed to their enlightening and enlightening. The result was the confusion worse confounded of Master Hui's argument about hardness and whiteness—his son (you know) tried for his whole life to reach the conclusion of the argument and failed. If that is the meaning of progress, then I too (in this argument) am adding to the progress. If, however, it may not be described as progress, then there is no progress, not even with me (and my arguing!). These are the reasons why sages aim at the glorious light which comes from slippery doubts. It is why they cannot be used and on the contrary make

[1] Chao Wen is said to have been a music master in Cheng State. The reference here seems to be to a divided opinion about him, some, including himself, saying he was a fine player, and some that he was not.

their abode in common functioning. I describe this as increasing one's intelligence.

I will illustrate. Here are some words, and I do not know whether they are classifiable or not as right—for any things to be classifiable and not classifiable is for them together to make a new class, and then they are in the same position as the other classified things. However that may be, allow me to try and say what I want to say. Since there is such a thing as the beginning, there is also such a thing as a beginning before the beginning, and there is also such a thing as a beginning to before the beginning to before the beginning. Since there is such a thing as something, there is also such a thing as nothing; and then, since there is such a thing as before the beginning of something and nothing, there is also such a thing as a beginning to before the beginning of something and nothing. There we are! And I do not know which of the two, something and nothing, is something and which is nothing. Coming to myself and what I have just described, presumably it is a description of something, but I do not know whether it is really something or whether it is really nothing.

(It has been argued that) [1] 'in the world of our experience (there is a sense in which) there is nothing bigger than the tip of a new-grown hair, whilst a great mountain is a tiny thing: that there is no greater age than that of a baby cut off in infancy, whilst Grandfather P'eng (with his 700 years) died in his youth: that heaven and earth were born at the same time that I was, and so all things in nature and I are one and the same thing.' Since they are one, you can still find words to express it, can you? [2] And since it has been expressed, can it still be unexpressed? 'One plus the words about it makes two, and two plus the oneness (of the two) makes three.' If we go on like this, even the cleverest reckoner breaks down: and how much more the ordinary run of men!

[1] There follow quotations from Master Hui and his fellow sophists.
[2] Chuang Chou's position is that the use of words invariably involves comparison.

Thus it is that by going on from nothing to something we arrive at three. How much more if we go on from something to something! Don't let us go on! Let us stop here!

The Tao has never begun to have mutually exclusive distinctions. Words, on the other hand, have never begun to have permanency. Because this is so there are lines of division. With your permission I will mention them. The left involves the right. Reasoned statements (about a thing being on the left or the right, etc. etc.) involve judgments. Then divisions of opinion involve arguments. Then controversies involve quarrels. These may be called the Eight To-and-Fro's.[1] What is beyond the world of space, the sage holds within himself, but he does not reason about it. What is within the world of space he reasons about, but he does not make any judgment on it. About the annals and the records of past kings he makes a judgment, but he does not argue, with the result that division of opinion is not really division of opinion, nor arguing really arguing. How that comes about is by reason of the sage embracing all things. The mass of men argue with a view to demonstrating to each other; which is why I say that arguing is not a revealing process.

The supreme [2] Tao cannot be talked about, and the supreme [2] argument does not require speech. (So also) supreme benevolence is not just being charitable, supreme purity not just being disinterested, and supreme courage not just brute violence. If the Tao were to glitter, it would not be the Tao. The speech which argues comes short of what it might be. The benevolence that is stereotyped does not succeed. The purity that is flawless does not engage confidence. The courage that is absolutely unyielding defeats its own end. . . .

Thus it is that he who knows how to stop at what he does not know is perfect. Who can know the argument which is not put into speech and the Tao that has no name? If

---

[1] Emending the text as Ma Hsü-lun suggests.
[2] The character *ta* (big) in many contexts conveys the impression of meaning authoritative or transcendent.

there should be the ability to know in this way, this knowledge might be described as 'the Store of Heaven.' Pour into it and it does not overflow. Pour out from it and it does not become empty. It does not know the source of its knowing. This is the meaning of 'storing up the light.'

.   .   .   .   .

(A Further Discussion of Rightness and Wrongness.)

Yueh Ch'ueh asked Wang Yi if he knew what there was that things had in common. He said, 'How should I know? Perhaps you know what there is that you do not know?' Yueh Ch'ueh said, 'How should I know about that? Does it follow that things are not known?'

Wang Yi said, 'How should I know? However it may be, I will try and put the matter into speech. Can there be any way by which I may know that what I call knowledge is not really not-knowledge? And can there be any way by which I can know that what I call not-knowledge is not really knowledge? Let me try to ask you some questions. If the people sleep in damp places their loins will hurt and one side of their bodies will be dead. But is that the case with an eel? If a man stays up in a tree, he will get frightened and go all of a tremble. But is that the case with a monkey? Which of these three knows the right place in which to live? Men eat flesh, deer feed on grass, centipedes find snakes sweet, and owls and crows guzzle mice. Which of these four knows the right taste? Monkey mates with monkey, and the buck with the doe. Mao Ch'iang and Li Ch'i [the two famous beauties] are regarded as very beautiful; and yet at the sight of them, fish dived deep into the water, birds flew high into the air, and deer fled from their presence. From my personal point of view, the basic principles of benevolence and justice and all the little tracks of rightness and wrongness are so inextricably confused that it is impossible for me to know how to differentiate them.'

Yueh Ch'ueh said, 'If you do not know what is profit

and what loss, then a perfect man, to be sure, does not know. Is not that so?'

Wang Yi said, 'The perfect man [1] is a mystery. The great pools might be all scorched up, but he could not feel hot. The great rivers might be all frozen hard, but he could not feel cold. Thunder might split the mountains and the wind lash the sea, but he could have no fear. A man of that kind could mount the clouds and the air and ride the sun and the moon, wandering away beyond the bounds of the Four Seas. Neither Death nor Life brings change in him himself. How much less then can (so-called) principles of profit and loss?'

Master Chü Ch'iao approached Master Chang Wu with a question, saying, 'I heard from the lips of the Master [Confucius] that when (it is said that) the sage does not occupy himself with mundane affairs: does not seek profit or avoid loss, has no pleasure in the conscious pursuit (of things), does not play the official with the Tao, says nothing and says something, says something and says nothing, and wanders into the beyond, free of the dust and grime of the world: then for him, the Master, these words were quite fantastic. For me, on the other hand, they denote the practice of the mysterious Tao. In what sort of way do you regard this, my dear sir?'

Master Chang Wu said, 'This is a matter about which the Yellow Emperor [2] was perplexed. How then is Confucius competent to have knowledge on it? Not only so: you also are too hasty in your calculations. . . . You see a cross-bow and immediately expect broiled duck. I will speak to you inconsequentially on the matter. You listen inconsequentially.

'Sitting by the sun and the moon! Cradling space and

---

[1] *Re chih jen*, which I have translated as 'perfect man'; but this is rather unsatisfactory, in spite of the fact that, as the term got into general circulation, it came to have much this meaning. The Taoists invented the term, and I cannot help thinking that the men who first used it thought of *chih* in its literal sense of 'arrive'; hence the 'man who has reached the great objective.'

[2] The mythical Sage-emperor whom the Taoists exalted as the first to know the Tao.

time in one's arms! Blending and harmonizing them!
Getting rid of the slippery uncertainties of distinctions and
putting menials alongside honourable persons! Everybody
babbling away, but the sage a blockhead (with nothing to
say), as he mingles a myriad years (in himself) and becomes
integrated, complete, balanced, whilst things, as they are,
all go on pursuing their courses.'

How do I know that to love life is not to be in a state of
illusion? How do I know that to hate death is not like a
man who was lost in his childhood and now does not know
his way home? Li Chi was the daughter of the warden at
Ai. When Chin State first captured her her tears rained
down and drenched her coat. But after she had arrived
at the palace and had shared the king's (luxurious) bed
and fed on all the rich food, she repented of her tears. How,
sir, do you know that the dead do not repent of their
original craving for life? The man who dreams at night
that he is carousing, may when the morning comes be
weeping, whilst the man who dreams he is weeping, may
when the morning comes be out hunting. In a dream you
do not know that you are dreaming, and you can even
divine the dream you are dreaming. It is only when you
wake up that you know you have been dreaming.

Not only so: there is the great awakening, and then we
shall know that all this (present experience) is a great dream.
Fools, however, regard themselves as awake now — so
personal is their knowledge. It may be as a prince or it
may be as a herdsman, but so sure of themselves! Both
the Master (Confucius) and you are dreaming; and when I
describe you as dreaming, I am also dreaming. And these
words of mine are paradoxical: that is the name for them.
And a myriad generations will pass before we meet a sage
who can explain this, and when we meet him it will be the
evening of our little day.

Suppose you and I have our argument. If I cannot beat
you and you beat me, does it follow that you are right and
I am wrong? If you cannot beat me but I beat you, does
it follow that I am right and you are wrong? Is one some-

times right and sometimes wrong, or are both of us right or both of us wrong? If you and I do not have a common knowledge (about the matter), then other men are bound to be in the dark over it. Whom then can we employ to get to the truth of it? If we should employ a man who agrees with you, or one who agrees with me, or one who disagrees with both of us, or one who agrees with both of us; since one would agree with you and another with me and another disagree with both of us and another agree with both of us, how could any one of them get to the truth of the matter? Does it follow then that I and you and other men have not got a common knowledge? Are we then all waiting for Something [? Someone] else?

Arguing [1] is a relation (in time) of one mutable sound to another. Suppose the sounds are not relative to each other. That would be harmony (as of a chord in music).[2] The achieving of this harmony is by being a babe of Heaven. Conform to that indefinitely: thereby the passage of time is obliterated. What is the meaning of achieving harmony by being a babe of Heaven? The answer is this: 'To be' and 'not to be' are respectively 'being thus' and 'not being thus.' If to be is necessarily to be, then it is different from not to be. About this there can be no argument. Also if being thus is necessarily being thus, then it is different from not being thus. About this also there can be no argument. (That being so,) forget the passage of time, forget argumentative judgments. Be in awe of timelessness. Thus it is that you can dwell in timelessness. A penumbra asked a shadow, saying, 'There are times when you are moving, times when you are at rest: times when you sit down, times when you stand up. Why do you not work out one method and stick to it?' The Shadow said, 'Am I dependent on something else for being what I am? (If so) is the something else on which I am dependent itself dependent on

---

[1] The ensuing passage is a bugbear to the commentators, although the section on the 'law of identity' is clear enough. I follow Wang Hsien-ch'ien's order, but the grammar of this opening sentence seems to me to require a subject and the natural one is 'arguing.'

[2] The sense seems to require this addition.

something else for being what it is? Am I dependent on
the scales of a snake or the wings of a cicada? How can I
understand what makes the 'being thus' and what makes
the 'not being thus'?

Once Chuang Chou dreamt he was a butterfly, fluttering
here and there just as if he was a butterfly, conscious of
following its inclinations. It did not know that it was
Chuang Chou. Suddenly he awoke; and then demonstrably
he was Chuang Chou. But he does not know now whether
he is Chuang Chou who dreamt he was a butterfly or a
butterfly dreaming he is Chuang Chou. Now Chuang
Chou and the butterfly are in relation, so that there must
be a distinction between the two. This is what is meant by
'things being transformed.'

Chapter 3. The Master Principles for the Nourishment of Life.

    .   .   .   .

A man who was cook to Prince Wen Hui was cutting up
a bullock. The blow by his hand, the thrust from his
shoulder, the stamp of his foot, the heave with his knee,
the whish of the flesh coming away, and the whistle of his
knife going in were all perfectly in time, having the rhythm
of the Dance of the Mulberry Grove, and exactly in time
like the chords of the *Ching Shou*. The Prince said, 'How
excellent, that you should reach this pitch of perfection!'
The cook put down his chopper and said, 'The thing that
your humble servant delights in is something higher than
art, namely the Tao. When I first began to cut up bullocks,
what I saw was just a bullock. After three years I no
longer saw a bullock as a whole, and now I work by the
spirit and not by the sight of my eyes. My senses have
learnt to stop and let the spirit carry on. I rely on the
Heaven-given structure of a bullock. I press the big
tendons apart and follow along the big openings, conforming to the lines which must be followed. . . . A good cook
gets a new chopper every year; and this is because he cuts.

A poor cook gets a new chopper every month; and this is because he hacks. But the chopper belonging to your humble servant has been in use for nineteen years. It has cut up several thousand bullocks, but its edge is as keen as if it had just come from the whetstone. There is a space between the joints, and the edge of the chopper is very thin. I put this thinness into the space, enlarging it as I go; and there is bound to be plenty of room for the blade. . . . Nevertheless, every time I come to something intricate, I take a look at the difficulty. Apprehension calls for caution. My eyes dwell on it, and I act very slowly. The movement of the chopper is imperceptible, and by degrees it all comes away like bundling soil from the earth. I then lift the chopper out and stand up and look all around with the satisfaction of victory. Then I wipe the chopper and put it away.'

Prince Wen Hui exclaimed, 'Excellent! I hear what a cook has to say, and I have learnt how to nourish life.'

When Kung Wen Hsien saw a certain official he was horrified and said, 'Who is he? How is it that he has only one foot? Is this Heaven's doing or man's?' The answer was, 'Heaven's doing, not man's. Heaven's way is to create individuals. A man's outward appearance is a given thing. Thus we know that this is Heaven's doing, not man's.'

The marsh pheasant has to take ten steps for every peck and a hundred steps for every sip, but it does not beg to be kept in a cage. The food[1] there might be royal food, but it would not be good food (for the pheasant).

When Lao Tan[2] died, Ch'in Shih went to mourn over him. After three moans he went away. A disciple said, 'Were you not a friend of the Master?' Ch'in Shih said, 'Yes.' The disciple said, 'If so, then is it proper to mourn only in this fashion?' Ch'in Shih said, 'At first I took you to be Lao Tan's men. Now, no. A moment ago when I was inside to mourn, there were old men bewailing Lao Tan as if bewailing the loss of a son, young men bewailing

---

[1] The *shen* in the text seems quite impossible. I emend to *shan*.
[2] Traditionally accounted to be the first of the great Taoist Masters.

him as if bewailing the loss of a mother. The reason why
they came together, unquestionably was that they had untimely words to say, untimely tears to shed. This is to
skulk out of the sight of Heaven, to fly in the face of facts,
to forget what you have received.[1] . . . When he happened
to come, it was the right time for the Master. When he
happened to go, it was the inevitable course for the Master.
Find your peace in the right time: make your home in the
inevitable, and grief and joy cannot intrude. The ancients
said of death that it was the cutting of bonds by the Omni-
potent. There is an end to the fingers which feed the twigs
to the fire; but the fire is transmitted, and no one knows
when it will be put out.'

Chapter 4. The Human World.

Yen Hui went to see Chung Ni [2] to ask leave to go away.
Chung Ni asked him where he was going, and Yen Hui
answered that he was going to Wei State. 'With what
object?' asked Chung Ni.

Yen Hui said, 'I hear that the Prince of Wei is in the
vigour of his youth and his actions self-willed. He is
unconcerned about his country and will not see his faults.
He is unconcerned about his people dying, so that the dead
are lying everywhere all over the country; the condition of
the people is incomparably bad. I once heard you, Master,
say that one should leave the well-governed country and
go to the country which is in confusion. It is the doctor's
door which has a crowd of sick people before it. I want
to take what I have heard (from you) and think out its
basic principles. Perhaps there is some cure for Wei State.'

Chung Ni said, 'Alas, the danger is that you will go and
only bring punishment on yourself. The right way does
not allow of other things being mixed in with it. If they
are mixed in, then the right way becomes a number of

---

[1] Whether from Heaven or from Lao Tan is not clear.
[2] i.e. Confucius, referred to without any title. Yen Hui was the man
whom Confucius regarded as the best of his disciples. The incident here
is to be taken as fictitious, Confucius being made to say things which
showed that the Taoist way was better than the Confucianist.

ways. That entails confusion, and confusion harasses the mind. With a harassed mind there is no saving anything. The perfect man in the old days was first concerned about himself before he started being concerned about others. So long as there was any doubt about himself (and his true good), he certainly had no leisure to attend to the actions of violent men. Further, have you any idea what wastes the virtue in a man, or what brings knowledge into existence? Virtue is wasted through the desire for fame. Knowledge comes into existence through contention. Fame means men crushing each other, and knowledge is the tool of contention. Both fame and knowledge are indeed instruments of evil and not what should come into perfect action. Further, there may be men of solid virtue and unfailing sincerity, not permeated with mortal humours, not striving over fame, not imbued with a mortal mind; and yet they may force their rule-of-thumb speeches about moral ideals upon bragging violent men. They are rightly called calamity men, for those who bring calamities on other men are bound to bring calamities back on themselves. I am afraid that is what you [Yen Hui] will be.

.   .   .   .   .

The lust for fame! The sages failed to conquer this in other men. How much will you fail (with the Prince of Wei)? But I think you must have some plan in mind. Come, try to tell me about it.'

Yen Hui said, 'Gravity of demeanour, dispassionateness, energy, and singleness of purpose.[1] Will this be right?'

Chung Ni said, 'Terrible! How can it possibly be right? The prince is a masterful man and amply shows it. His moods are uncertain, and, since he is never contradicted by the men continually around him, he tramples on other people's feelings for the express purpose of easing his own. We can define him as a man who cannot accomplish the little daily accessions of virtue and is, therefore, all the more

[1] There is evidence, though of a little later date, that Confucianists often gave a bad impression through their pompous moral talk. It is difficult to believe that Chuang Chou is not here taking them off.

*H 973

incapable of really great virtue. He will stubbornly refuse to be converted. If he should agree with you outwardly, inwardly he will not condemn himself. How can you do anything with him?'

Yen Hui said, 'If that be the case, then I will be inwardly uncompromising and outwardly appear to compromise, and I will substantiate (my words) by appealing to the past. As for being inwardly uncompromising I shall be a disciple of Heaven; and the man who is that knows that the Son of Heaven and himself are both treated as sons by Heaven. Will a man like the prince be so individualistic as not to care whether his words win approval or disapproval from men? If he is so, then people will call him a mere child. This is what I mean by being a disciple of Heaven. As for outwardly appearing to compromise, I shall be a disciple of men, bowing and scraping with the manners of a minister. What other men do, may I not do? And when I do what others do, will they censure me for it? This is what I mean by being a disciple of men. As for substantiating (my words) by appealing to the past, I shall be a disciple of antiquity. Although I shall speak with moral authority and make actual condemnations, it will not be I but antiquity doing it. In this way although I be upright I shall not be disliked. This is what I mean by being a disciple of antiquity. Will something like this be right?'

Chung Ni said, 'How can it possibly be right? There is too much putting of things to rights and no spying out of weak spots. You may be persistent, but there will be no bad conscience resulting. However things may go, you will only come to a standstill. (The problem is,) how is it possible to make the prince change himself as if his own mind was teaching him?'

Yen Hui said, 'I can go no further. I venture to ask you for the right plan.'

Chung Ni said, 'Fast! And I will tell you that where there is fasting it is no easy matter. If a man does make an easy matter of it "the shining heavens contradict him."'

Yen Hui said, 'My family is poor. For a number of

months I have not tasted either wine or meat. May this be taken as fasting?'

Chung Ni said, 'This is the fasting in relation to sacrificing. It is not fasting of the mind. . . . Integrate your will. (Thus) do not listen with your ears, but listen with your mind. Do not listen with your mind, but listen with your vital force. Ordinary sense-hearing does not go beyond the ears, and the mind does not go beyond symbols [i.e. ideas about things not actualities]. The vital force is entirely negative and waits on things (outside one's self). The Tao brings together all negativeness (in itself), and this negativeness is the fasting of the mind.'

Yen Hui said, 'I have not begun to set this process going, and the truth is, it is because I am myself, an individual. If I had set this process going, there would have been no Hui, an individual. Is it right to speak of negativeness?'

The Master said, 'Entirely right! I will tell you. If you can go in and wander freely in this prince's cage without affecting his reputation in any way; being (caged up) inside and yet crowing cheerfully, not being (caged up) inside and yet continually there,[1] with no depression and no malice, this being your entire home in spite of your living there being because you cannot help it: (if you can do this) then you will be near to success. To take no steps at all is easy: to walk without touching the ground, that is the difficulty. Also if you act under the compulsion of men, there is no difficulty about pretending: but there is if you act under the compulsion of Heaven. We have heard of flying with wings, but not of flying without them, I have heard of knowing with knowledge, but not of knowing without knowledge. . . .

A second anecdote follows, in which Confucius appears again as the central figure. This time he is approached by an official to whom a state mission has been entrusted, and who is very worried over its difficulty. The advice Confucius is represented as giving has, of course, a strong Taoist twist to it. In some of the sentiments, however, the Confucianists' mind peeps out. The following is a good example of the two strains.

---

[1] By substituting *erh* for *tse* in these two clauses it is possible to get a likely meaning without attaching forced meanings to the other words.

Chung Ni said, 'Our human world has two moral safe-guards, the one fate, the other duty. A child's love of its parents is fate; and it is impossible for the child's heart to be loosed from this love. A subject's service of his prince is duty. Go where you will there is a prince, so that this duty is inescapable between heaven and earth. These are the two moral safeguards. Therefore, to serve one's parents in contentment without regard to the place, this is the height of filial piety. To serve one's prince in con-tentment without regard to the business entailed, this is the supreme exhibition of loyalty. So, (in any difficult business such as a state commission,) in the service of your heart to have no change in your emotions from what they were before, to know what is inevitable in the business and be content with these conditions as your fate, this is the height of virtue. As a subject or a son a man constantly has business forced on him; but in dealing with the actualities of the business he can forget his own personal concerns, and so has no leisure for loving life or hating death. It is quite possible, sir, to go forward. . . . Ride events with a free mind. Rely on the unavoidable to nourish centrality (of mind). This is perfection.'

.   .   .   .   .

Chapter 6. The Great Father of All Teachers.

The man who knows the actions of Heaven and knows the actions of men, that man is perfect. To know the actions of Heaven is to be Heaven and alive. To know men's actions is to feed what is unknown by means of what is known; and to reach the end of one's natural span [lit. Heaven's years] without being cut off half-way. This is to advance in knowledge.

(The Nature of True Knowledge is to be learnt from the Nature of the True Man.)

None the less there is cause for anxiety. For knowledge to become exact, knowledge depends on something else, though what it depends on is far from being certain. How do we know that what we call Heaven is not man, and what we call man is not Heaven? Well, there is the true man before there is true knowledge: and (the question is) what is meant by a true man. The true man of antiquity did not go counter to the few. He had no heroic achievements. He made no plans. Being what he was, when he made mistakes he did not regret them. When he was exactly right, he was not self-complacent. Being what he was, he could scale the heights without losing his nerve, could enter water without feeling wet, enter fire without feeling hot. This is the man whose knowledge can get higher in the Tao.

The true man of antiquity had no dreams while he slept and woke up without any feeling of anxiety. In eating he had no sense of the sweet. His breathing was deep; for the true man breathes from his heels, whilst in most people their breathing is from their throats, and the man who is crushed by defeat retches his words out as if he were vomiting. For a man's passions to go deep is for his instinct of vital resilience [lit. heavenly spring] to be shallow.

The true man of antiquity was not conscious of loving life and hating death. As life opened out, he did not long for joy. As he entered (the shadow of death) he did not hang back. Like a bird he flew away, just as like a bird he came: that was all. He did not forget his beginning, or have any desire about what his end might be. He received (what came to him) and took pleasure in it; and then he forgot it and received it again. That is to say, he did not injure the Tao with his (conscious) mind, nor did he supplement Heaven with man. This is what is meant by a true man.

Being what he was, he was absent-minded,[1] his manner tranquil, with a pure brow as cool as autumn and as mild as spring, in his joy and anger following the movement of the four seasons, and so fitting in with things [i.e. his environment] that he was not conscious of any limit to his

[1] Accepting Wang Mou-hung's emendation of *chih* to *wang*.

doing so. Thus it is that a sage in his employment of arms might destroy a country and yet not lose the affection of the people. His benefits might flow down through a myriad ages and yet he not be consciously fond of men. And thus it is that deliberately to rejoice in being impregnated with things is to be anything but a sage: deliberately to be attached to people is to be anything but benevolent: deliberately to wait for heaven-given opportunities is to be anything but a wise man: deliberately to make profit in one direction in order not to entail loss in another is to be anything but a man of practical principles; just as to lose one's self for the sake of one's reputation is to be anything but a good public servant, and to destroy one's character and be unprincipled is to be anything but a good private servant. Men like Hu Pu Chieh, Wu Kuang, Po I, Shu Ch'i, Chi Tzu, Hsü Yü, Chi T'o, and Shen T'u Ti were the servants of servants, were Yes-men to Yes-men and so did not say Yes to what was affirmed in themselves.

.   .   .   .

Thus it is that what the true man liked was reduced to one (thing) and what he did not like was reduced to one (thing); and, since the one and its antithesis are equally one, in the one respect the true man acts as a disciple of Heaven and in the other respect he acts as a disciple of men. In him neither Heaven [i.e. the transcendent and integrated element in Nature] nor man [i.e. the human and unintegrated element in Nature] conquers the other. This is what is meant by a true man.

Life and death are both (matters of) fate. They have the regularity of night succeeding day; for Heaven is what man cannot interfere with in the actuality of all creation. Those men who in a special way regard Heaven as Father and have, as it were, a personal love for it, how much more should they love what is above (Heaven as Father)! Other men in a special way regard their rulers as better than themselves, and they, as it were, personally die for them. How much more should they die for what is truer than a ruler! When the springs dry up, the fish are all together on dry land. They then moisten each other with their dampness and keep each other wet with their slime. But this is not to be compared with their forgetting each other in a river or a lake. The same with (everybody) praising the Sage-king Yao and denouncing the villain Chieh: it is better to forget them both and transmute their different ways.

The Great Mass loads me up with a body, gives me the labour of living, eases me off with old age, and gives me rest with death. Thus it is that that which makes my life a good is also that which makes my death a good.

A man's property is said to be safe enough when his boat is laid up in a creek and his fishing net put by in shallow water. But a strong man can come in the middle of the night and carry these things off without the sleepers knowing anything about it. In storing things, whether small ones or big, there is a question as to the right way. There is a chance of their being lost. Suppose, then, you store up man's world in man's world, is there no chance of its being lost? This is the great fact about things and their continuity. Thus, although to be patterned in the form of a man is something to be more or less pleased about, the source of joy beyond all reckoning lies in the fact that a thing like man's body has a myriad transformations, and there never has been any limit to them.

Thus it is that a sage wanders freely in the fact that things cannot be lost but are all preserved. To him to die young, to grow old, the beginning and the end of life are all good; and other men should copy them in this. How much more should they copy that which is the link of all creation, that on which the one and only process of evolution depends. The Tao has reality and evidence, but it has no (specific) action, no specific form. It can be transmitted, but it cannot be (consciously) received. It can be attained, but it cannot be seen (when it is obtained). It is self-rooted and existed before the heavens and the earth. From of old it has continued without ceasing. It is the gods, the Divine

Ruler. It produced the heavens: it produced the earth.
It is above the highest and lowest points in space, although
it is neither high nor low. Existing before the heavens
and the earth and older than the oldest antiquity, it is
neither old nor shows signs of age. Hsi Wei obtained it
and thereby adjusted the heavens and the earth. Fu Hsi
obtained it and thereby gave a double origin to matter.[1]
The Great Bear obtained it and so has never left its course.
The sun and moon obtained it and so have never ceased
(revolving). K'an P'i[2] obtained it and thereby entered
the heart of the world [lit. the K'un Lun Mountains]. Feng
Yi obtained it and thereby wandered by the Great River.
Chien Wu obtained it and thereby made his home on
Mount T'ai. The Yellow Emperor obtained it and thereby
ascended the cloudy heavens. Chuan Hsü obtained it and
thereby made his home in the Dark Palace. Yü Ch'iang
obtained it and stood by the north pole. Hsi Wang Mu
obtained it and so gained her seat on the Shao Kuang,
and no one knows her beginning or her end. Grandfather
P'eng obtained it and so lived from the age of Shun to the
age of the Five Princes. Fu Yueh obtained it and thereby became Wu Teng's minister and soothed the whole
country. (When he died) he mounted this and that constellation and put himself on a level with the stars.

Nan Po Tzu K'uei asked Nü Chü how it was that he, an
old man, yet had the face of a child. The reply was that
he had heard of the Tao, at which Nan Po Tzu K'uei asked
him whether he could learn the Tao. Nü Chü said, 'How
can you? You are not its kind of man. Pu Liang Yi
had the gifts of a sage but not the Tao of a sage, whilst I
have the Tao of a sage but not the gifts. I wished to teach
him in the hope that he might perhaps become a real sage.
. . . I held him for three days under my teaching, after
which he was able to pay no attention to the human world.
He having reached this stage, I held him for seven days,

[1] This appears to be a reference to Fu Hsi as the discoverer of the Yin
and the Yang.
[2] The spirit of the mountains, with the face of a man and the body of
an animal.

after which he was able to pay no attention to (external) objects (of any kind). He having reached this stage, I held him for nine days, after which he was able to pay no attention to his own existence. After that he was illumined. Being in a state of illumination he was able to see oneness. Being able to see oneness, he was then able to have no past and present. Having no past and present, he was then able to enter into not-dying and not-living, in which state the destruction of life is not death and increase of life is not life. As a thing himself he was always in company (with other things) and always welcoming them, always being destroyed and always being completed. The name of this state of being is "babe-like peace"; and the man with this peace is a babe on the way to completeness.'

Tzu Ssu, Tzu Yü, Tzu Li, and Tzu Lai, four men in conversation with each other, said that whoever could make nothing the head (of existence), life the backbone, and death the rump, whoever knew that life and death, survival and non-survival were all one body, that man was their friend. They then looked at each other and smiled, for they were in complete agreement. Consequently they became friends. Not long afterwards Tzu Yü fell ill and Tzu Ssu went to inquire about him. His back was all hunched up, his five viscera all raised up, his cheeks down by his navel, his shoulders above the top of his head, with a huge wen pointing to the sky, all the vital energy of the Yin and Yang in disorder in him. But his mind was not in the least perturbed by this. He limped along to a well and looked at himself and exclaimed, 'How amazing of the Creator of things to make me deformed in this way! Why should I dislike it? Supposing my left arm were to be transformed into a cock, the result would be that I should mark the time at night. Supposing my right shoulder were transformed into a cross-bow, the result would be that I should get broiled duck. Supposing that my buttocks were transformed into a wheel and my spirit into a horse, the result would be that I should ride in my carriage. How could there be anything more honourable than that? What is more, to gain is to hit the right moment, to lose is to accept the inevitable: to be content with the good fortune and to be at home with the bad is to keep sorrow and joy at a distance; and this was described of old as liberation. The men who cannot liberate themselves are entangled in material things; and, what is more still, Heaven continues, and things do not equal Heaven in that. Why should I dislike what has happened?'

[When Tzu Lai fell ill, Tzu Li went to inquire and found him at the point of death. He told the wife and children that there was no reason to be distressed over the transformation that death was, and wondered what *tsao hua* (evolution) would make of his friend, perhaps the liver of a rat or the arm of an insect.]

Tzu Lai said, 'Wherever it may be, north, south, east, or west, when a father or mother gives orders to a son, he obeys. The Yin and Yang are equally a man's father and mother. If they bring me to the point of death and I am unwilling, then I am being headstrong. They do no wrong to me. Take now a great ironsmith smelting metal; if the metal should leap up and say, "I must be made into an Excalibur," the great smith would be bound to regard the metal as ill-omened. So now, the moment there comes an attack on a man's body, to insist that it must continue as a man, this would make the Creator of things see him as a damnable fellow. So now the moment we take heaven and earth as a great melting-pot and evolution as a great smelting, how can we object to going away (to somewhere else)? Completed as we are, we go to sleep: passing out as we do, we awake.'

.   .   .   .   .

Tzu Yü and Tzu Sang were friends, and once when it had been raining for ten days Tzu Yü became alarmed lest his friend was ill; so he prepared some food to take to him. When he arrived at the door of the house, there was a sound of something between singing and moaning with the playing of a lute: 'O father, O mother, O Heaven, O man!' The voice was hardly audible and the rhythm was uneven. Tzu

Yü went in and asked Tzu Sang why he was singing in this way. The reply was, 'I am thinking who it is who has brought me to this pitch of distress; and I cannot think who it is. My father and mother surely could not wish me to be without means of living. Heaven covers all things and Earth supports all things without any partiality. Surely they could not wish me in particular to be without the means of living. I want to know who is responsible for this, but I cannot discover. But there must be somebody who has brought me to this pass. It is fate.'

Chapter 7. To Fulfil (the Government) of the (Real) Kings.

Yeh Ch'üeh[1] went to put problems to Wang Yi. He put four such, but Wang Yi did not know about any of them. Yeh Ch'üeh danced with joy over this and told Pu Yi Tzu.

Pu Yi Tzu said, 'So you only know this now? The Sage-king Shun did not compare with Fu Hsi. Shun was all for benevolence in his devotion to men, and what is more, he won their devotion, but he never began to get out into the not-man [? part of the universe]. Fu Hsi slept gently and awoke with a long stare. At one time he would take himself to be a horse, at another an ox. His knowledge was actual and to be trusted, the virtue in him immensely true; but he never began to get inside the not-man.'

Chien Wu[2] went to see K'uang Chieh Yü. Chieh Yü asked him what Yüeh Chung Shih had been talking to him about; and Chien Wu replied that he had told him about rulers and their making themselves as patterns in relation to the laws they promulgated, so that nobody dared disobey or change them.

K'uang Chieh Yü said, 'This is the very deception of moral power. All this governing of the Great Society is like trying to wade through the sea, or to bore a hole

---

[1] These three names are probably parabolical: thus Yeh Ch'üeh, Get his-teeth-into-people's-deficiencies; Wang Yi, Kingly-littleness; Pu Yi Tzu, Teacher-who-wore-clothes-of-rushes.
[2] For these names I suggest Burdened-with-himself, Made-welcome-the-weight(-of-things), and Talk-on-middles-and-beginnings.

through a river, or to set a mosquito to work on carrying a mountain. The control exercised by the sages was outside political controlling. It consisted in getting on the right basis before they did anything, in being quite certain one can do what has to be done. You see, a bird flies high to avoid injury from bolt or dart; and a mouse burrows deep into the sacrificial mound to avoid the danger of being smoked or dug out. And do sages not compare with these two creatures?'

T'ien Keng [1] was wandering in the neighbourhood of Yin Yang and came to the river Liao. There he happened to meet a man without a name whom he asked about society. The man without a name replied, 'Go away, you low fellow. Why this ill-prepared question? I was just about to companion the Creator of all. If I renounce the world, I can ride on the bird of unself-consciousness and go out beyond space, wander in the village of Nowhere and make my home in the open country of Emptiness. Why do you come troubling me with making order in society? Set your mind to wander in simplicity, harmonize yourself with non-distinction. Follow things as they are and do not give way to personal bias. Society will thus be ordered.'

Yang Tzu Chü went to see Lao Tan and said, 'Suppose we have a man, vigorous and self-reliant, far-sighted and indefatigable in learning sound principles. Would such a man compare with the wise kings (of old)?' Lao Tan said, 'Compared with a sage, such a man would be just an underling, a hand in a workshop, slaving away in a state of apprehension. Besides, because of their beautiful markings tigers and leopards are hunted down, and monkeys and dogs are kept on chains because they are clever at talking and catching rats. Are creatures to be compared with the wise kings?'

Yang Tzu Chü looked dissatisfied and begged for an exposition of the wise kings' government. Lao Tan said, 'Their government was one of achievements which covered

[1] I suggest 'the man who wanted to have his roots in Heaven,' i.e. one of those persevering people who appear as butts in this book, men who want to do the right but are conventionally-minded.

the whole Great Society but which did not appear to come
from them. They turned natural things into articles of use
so that the people could look after themselves. There
were some whose names are not even known. They just
made everything pleased with itself, whilst they maintained
their poise in the incommensurable, and wandered in the
non-existent.'

.   .   .   .   .

(The following is in the first person, presumably from
    Chuang Chou himself.)

Inaction is the real part [1] of fame, the storehouse of all
plans, the responsible head of all business, the master of
all knowledge. Identify yourself completely with infinity-
eternity and wander in the non-self. Carry to the highest
what you have received from Heaven but do not reveal
your success in this. Be empty: that is all. The perfect
man's use of his mind is like a mirror. He does not anti-
cipate (events), nor does he go counter to them. He
responds but he does not retain. Thus it is that he is able
to master things and not be injured by them.

The sovereign of the Southern Sea is called Dissatisfaction (with things as they are), the sovereign of the
Northern Sea, Revolution, the Sovereign of the Centre of
the World, Chaos. Dissatisfaction and Revolution from
time to time met together in the territory of Chaos, and
Chaos treated them very hospitably. The two sovereigns
planned how to repay Chaos's kindness. They said, 'Men
all have seven holes to their bodies for seeing, hearing,
eating and breathing. Our friend here has none of these.
Let us try to bore some holes in him.' Each day they bored
one hole. On the seventh day Chaos died.

[1] Emending the character for 'corpse' (*shih*) to that for 'real' (*shih*).

CHAPTER XIV: FIVE OTHER WRITERS IN THE 'CHUANG TZU BOOK'

The first two writings quoted in this chapter give the impression that they were written during the first decades of the Han era, the time when Taoism of one sort and another enjoyed imperial support. The second writer was obviously highly conscious of 'the Emperor' in his semi-metaphysical, semi-political theorizings. Then follows a collection of those parables which are such a feature of this book, and which show the literary influence which Chuang Chou exercised. Incidentally they are the despair of the higher critic to-day, since it is so incredibly difficult to decide what substratum, if any, of historical fact there is in them. The next quotation shows a remarkable attempt at a theory of biological evolution. The final one is the opening section of the famous *T'ien Hsia P'ien* (*Treatise on the Great Society*), in which a man of first-rate critical ability subjects 'the hundred schools' of thought to detached criticism of the most searching nature. It is greatly to be regretted that the length of this chapter makes it impossible to include the whole of it here.[1]

Chapter 12.

Vast as heaven-and-earth is, the changes in it are equally adjusted: many as the things (in Nature) are, the control over them is a single one: great as the total of the rank and file is, the thing which masters them is sovereignty. Sovereignty springs from the power of personality in a man and completes itself in Heaven. Hence this affirmation, that in the past the secret power of ruling all men was one of inaction: inaction which is nothing else than the distinctive power of Heaven.

Use speech which reflects the Tao, and sovereignty over men will be true sovereignty: have classes in society which reflect the Tao, and justice between king and subject becomes rationally clear: use the (administrative) ability which reflects the Tao, and the officials everywhere will produce peace and order. For it is by the Tao and the floating image of it that all creatures make perfect response to each other. Hence, what permeates all heaven and

[1] A very free translation is to be found in Giles's *Chuang Tzu* (Shanghai, 1900).

earth is power of personality, what is active in all creatures
is the Tao. For the control of men from above is exercised through a round of duties, and the ability to discharge
these with justice [1] is an acquired skill. For skill goes along
with a round of duties, these duties with justice, justice with
spiritual power in a man, this spiritual power with the Tao,
the Tao with Heaven. Hence this affirmation, that the
men who nourished the whole of their society had no
private desires and thus the whole of society had plenty:
that they practised inaction and all creatures changed (in
due course): that they were profoundly still and the relationships of all the clans were ordered. As the *Record* has it,
'Be permeated with unity, and all duties will be completely
discharged: have no thought for individual success, and the
names and spirits will serve your needs.'

The Master [i.e. Confucius] said, 'This Tao which works
back and forth in all creation, how overwhelming it is in
its supremacy! A man of principle cannot but cleave his
heart open (to its influence).' For we say 'Heaven' when
we think of acting without action, as we say 'spiritual
power' when we think of saying things without saying
anything: as we say 'benevolence' when we think of loving
men and turning things to their account: as we say 'great-
ness' when we think of making harmony out of discord: as
we say 'forbearance' when we think of doing nothing to em-
barrass opponents: as we say 'wealth' when we think of
possessing all sorts of things: as we say 'the start' when we
think of a man laying hold of his virtue, 'established' when
we think of his virtue going on to completion, 'faultless'
when we think of it as in accord with the Tao, 'perfect' when
we think of its never using force on anything. If the man
of principle is clear about these ten points, then they flood his
round of duties, and his mind will be enlarged; [2] they will
bubble up in his actions and all Nature be revealed [?].

A man of this kind will bury gold in the mountains,

---

[1] Emending *yi* (arts, civilization) to *yi* (justice) (Cp. Ma Hsü-lun's
comment.

[2] The connecting *erh* would seem to have got dropped out from the middle
of this sentence.

throw pearls in the sea. He will see no profit in this world's goods and will stand aloof from pomp and circumstance. He will neither delight in great age nor grieve over an untimely death. He will neither glory in prosperity nor be ashamed of poverty. (As king) he does not monopolize the gains of a generation as his private perquisites. His throne does not mean to him the splendour of fame, but the splendour of understanding that all creation is a single storehouse and in it the face of death and the face of life are the same.

.   .   .   .   .

In the Great Beginning there was nothing, and 'nothing' had no name. At the starting point of oneness [viz. the oneness of the universe] there was only oneness and no concrete form, but life might come into things. This (stage) can be described as spiritual power (at work). The formless then came to have divisions and, what is more, there was continuity in these. This can be described as 'the lot of the individual' (at work). (With these two powers) there was an uninterrupted stream of influence at work which made individual things live and brought to pass their distinctive features. This can be described as 'form.' The frame of a form protects the spirit in it, and each spirit has a pattern it should follow. This can be described as its 'nature.' When a thing's nature is developed to the full, there is a return to the spiritual power (through which it came into existence). Now this power when it is at its height is the same as it was in the very beginning. Being the same, it is unconditioned (by space and time). Being unconditioned, it is over all [lit. great] and makes 'the union of a bird's beak and its song'; [1] for the union of beak and song is part of the union of heaven and earth. This union runs through the whole system: something unconscious, beneath the surface, what is described as (divine) power which joins (everything) in a great obedience.

[1] The author apparently refers to a well-known saying. These thinkers were alive to the mystery of connection between the shape of a beak and the song which proceeded from it. Cp. above, pp. 171–2, the music from holes.

THE 'CHUANG TZU BOOK'

The Master put a question to Lao Tan, saying, 'There are men who dragoon the Tao, as if they were criticizing each other and saying that this is possible and that impossible, and this right and that wrong; like the dialecticians [1] who affirm that hardness and whiteness cannot exist together. As if you could separate things mechanically! Should men of this kind be described as sages?'

Lao Tan said, 'They are underlings, clever hands in a workshop, slaving away in a state of apprehension. They are like dogs who are clever at catching foxes and so bring trouble on themselves; like monkeys who can chatter and so are taken out of (their natural environment of) mountain and forest. Ch'iu,[2] I will tell you something which you cannot understand and which you cannot talk about. There are plenty of people who have a head and feet but no mind or ears [i.e. cannot take in the nature of the universe]; but amongst beings with bodies there is not a single one which can continue without a visible body of some kind.[3] Such a being's movement and refraining from movement, his life and his death, his rise and fall, all would be in contradiction to that whereby he is in existence. Man has some measure of control (over himself). To be unconscious of things (as outside himself), to be unconscious of Heaven (as outside himself), this means to be unconscious of oneself; and the man who is unconscious of himself, this man is to be described as entering into Heaven.'

. . . . .

Chi Ch'e [Seasonably Perspicacious] says, '. . . The great sage's government of the Great Society creates a deep commotion in the people's hearts, enabling them to put into practice enlightened principles, to change their customs, to eradicate the robber mind in them. In every

[1] This is an anachronism. There were no dialecticians in Confucius's day.
[2] Confucius's personal name. The author in thus making Lao Tan address Confucius without a title shows that he regards Lao Tan as superior.
[3] This rendering involves discarding the *yü* in the text.

man of them his individual will goes from strength to strength. It is as if the nature of the individual acted of itself, and the people do not know the source of the influence. Such a sage surely comes up to the standard of a Yao or a Shun in inspiring the people. Why should they be subservient like a girl-wife? Their desires are in agreement with the spiritual power in them, and their hearts are fixed.

Chapter 13. (Another disciple with a strong Confucian list to his mind. This meditation was probably written in the early part of the Han imperial era).

The Tao of Heaven, the Tao of an emperor, and the Tao of a sage act as a process, but not by means of lumping everything together indiscriminately. Hence the myriad varieties of creatures brought into being, and the loyalty of the whole empire to an emperor, and the universal homage paid to a sage. The man who has an understanding of Heaven and is versed in the sages' tenets, as in the natural forces (at work) in sovereign virtue, this man acts from himself, unconsciously, in entire tranquillity. The sage's tranquillity is not that which is spoken of as 'being at peace,' namely, being good and therefore at peace. No: because there is nothing in Nature which can perturb his mind, therefore he is in a state of tranquillity. If water is in a state of tranquillity, then it shows up the hairs on a man's chin and his eyebrows; and it is dead level so that the master carpenter can take it as a pattern. If still water remains clear, how much more with the things of the spirit in relation to the mind of the sage! He is the reflection of heaven and earth, the mirror of all creatures. To be in a state of tranquillity, contented, indifferent, inactive, this is the equilibrium of heaven and earth and the heart of the Tao's distinctive power. Therefore emperors and sages are at rest. At rest, then untrammelled: untrammelled, then sincere: sincere, then all-suffering. . . . Therefore I affirm that there is nothing more divine than Heaven, nothing richer than Earth, nothing greater than the Emperor. And therefore I affirm that the spiritual power of the Emperor matches Heaven and Earth. . . .

(In society) essentials are the province of the ruler, non-essentials of the ruled; (as, for example,) important decisions are the province of the master and the details the province of his minister. The use of military force is a non-essential of spiritual power. Rewards and punishments, the appeal to profit and to fear of mutilation, the Five Criminal Laws, these are the non-essentials of a country's principles. The types of the rituals and the weights and measures, account-keeping, classification, and the defining of small points, these are the non-essentials of government. The sounds of the instruments and the dressing up, these are the non-essentials of music and dancing. The prescribed periods for weeping and the distinctions in mourning clothes, these are the non-essentials of grief for the dead. These five non-essentials require the expenditure of spiritual energy and the application of the mind; but the people who in time come to obey them are merely learners of non-essentials. The men of antiquity had these things, but they opposed any tendency to exalt their importance. . . .

The men of antiquity who came to understand the Great Tao, first came to understand Heaven; the power of the Tao came second to that. Having come to understand the power of the Tao, human-heartedness and justice came next to that; and then came the maintenance of class distinctions and the classification of things . . . then the responsible use of them [?], then the examination into good and bad, then the distinction of truth and error, then rewards and punishments; and then the ignorant and the learned had each his right place, the noble and the common man their proper stations, the virtuous and the wicked each acting as he could. . . . This is to be described as a great equilibrium, the height of government.

From chapter 28. (Anecdotes, purporting to be about legendary heroes.)

(The Sage-king) Shun wished to resign his throne to Shan

Chüan. Shan Chüan said, 'I stand in the middle of the universe. In the winter I wear clothes made of fur, in the summer clothes made of grass. In the spring I plough and sow, and my body meets my requirements of labour. In the autumn I gather in the harvest, and my body meets my requirements of relaxation and food. At sunrise I go out to work, at sundown I come home to rest. I stroll in freedom between heaven and earth, and my heart is content. Why should I trouble myself with the Great Society? You distress me that you do not know me.' Accordingly he refused and went away into the heart of the mountains; and no one knew where he went to live.

T'ai Wang Shan Fu lived in Pin. When the Ti barbarians attacked him, he offered a ransom of furs and silk; but they refused to accept them. He offered them horses and dogs, and they refused. He offered them pearls and jade, and they refused. What they wanted was his territory. He then said to his people, 'I could not bear to live with a man when I had been responsible for the death of his younger brother and his son. Also I have heard that one should not use the means of nourishing life for the injury of it.' Obeying this principle, leaning on his staff [?] he went away, and the people streamed after him. The result was that they made a new state at the foot of Mount Ch'i.

Of T'ai Wang Shan Fu it may be said that his ability rose to the veneration of life; and the man who can venerate life, in spite of his high station and wealth, does not allow what should nourish life to injure his person. In spite of poverty and low station he does not allow gain to put a strain on his body. The men of to-day, high officials and members of the nobility, doubly fail in this. Once they get a sight of gain, they have little compunction about endangering their bodies.

The two fiefs of Han and Wei quarrelled and invaded each other's territory. Tzu Hua Tzu [a philosopher] went and had audience with Chao Hsi, the feudatory of Han. Chao Hsi was looking very disconsolate. Tzu Hua Tzu said, 'Suppose now that all the feudatories signed an

agreement in your presence stating that the cutting off of
the left hand would bring a fatal disease to the right hand,
and the cutting off of the right hand would bring a fatal
disease to the left hand, but the man who would cut off
his hand should rule over them all—would your Highness
cut off a hand?' Chao Hsi said, 'I would not.' Tzu Hua
Tzu said, 'Very good! From this point of view two arms
are more important than being king over the whole country.
Also, the whole body is more important than two arms,
whilst the fief of Han is less important than the whole
country. And yet your Highness is most certainly making
your body out of sorts and injuring your life by your fear
of worldly failure.'

Confucius was in dire straits between the two fiefs of
Ch'en and Ts'ai. For seven days he had no proper meal,
only some herb soup without any rice. His face showed
his great exhaustion; but he sat in the house strumming a
tune on his lute. Yen Hui was (outside) picking out the
best herbs. Tzu Lu and Tzu Kung spoke to him, saying,
'The Master has twice been ejected from his native land.
They have removed all trace of him in Wei and cut down
his tree in Sung . . . and now he is beset on every hand
by Ch'en and Ts'ai. It is no crime for any man to kill our
master, and there is no bar against his assassination. And
yet without stopping he continues to play and sing. Does a
man of principle feel in this way that no disgrace attaches to
him?' Yen Hui made no answer, but he went in and told
Confucius. He laid aside his lute and with a loud sigh said,
'These two are petty-minded. Call them to come here, for I
want to talk to them.' They came in, and Tzu Lu said, 'As
things are now, we may be said to have reached the limit.'

Confucius said, 'What are you saying? To abound in
the Tao is the meaning of abounding. To be made straight
in the Tao is the meaning of being straight. Here am I,
cherishing the Tao of human-heartedness and justice, and I
encounter the troubles of a world in disorder. What have
I done to be made straight? That being so, examine your
hearts, and do not be discouraged about the Tao. When

difficulties come, do not lose the spiritual power in the Tao. It is only in the depth of winter when there is frost and snow that we have means of knowing how luxuriant the pines and cypresses are. This crisis in Ch'en and Ts'ai is my good fortune, is it not?' He cheerfully turned back to his hut and went on strumming.

(An early attempt at a Theory of Biological Evolution.)

Chapter 18.

Master Lieh was eating by the roadside when he caught sight of a hundred-year-old skull. He plucked a blade of grass and, pointing at the skull, said, 'Ah, you and I! We know that there is no death and no life. Are you really in a bad way? Am I really all happy and jolly? A seed has a germ in it, and, when it gets water on it, this germinates [?][1]; and, if it gets an environment of water and earth it becomes the *wa pin chih yi*.[2] If life comes to it on a bank, then it becomes the *ling* [bank] *ch'iao*. If the *ling ch'iao* gets rich manure, then it becomes the *wu tsu*, and the root of the *wu tsu* becomes grubs, whilst the leaves become butterflies and after a short time are transformed into insects. When life comes to these beneath a stove, their form is like a skeleton and their name is *ch'ü to* [? a kind of cricket]. After a thousand days a cricket becomes a bird, the name of which is *kan yü ku*. The spittle of the *kan yü ku* becomes the *ssu mi*, the *ssu mi* become *shih hsi* [? food flies]. The *yi lu* are generated from the *shih hsi*, the *huang k'uang* from the *chiu yu*, the *mou jui* from the *fu ch'uan*.[3] If a *yang ch'i* be grafted [?] on to an old bamboo which has no ground shoots, it produces a *ch'ing ning*. The *ch'ing ning* produce leopards, leopards produce horses,

---

[1] Ma Hsü-lun says that we do not know the meaning of this character. 'Germinates' is, I think, a possible interpretation.

[2] The commentators appear to be unable to identify these names of plants, etc., with any certainly. Professor Giles translates *wa pin chih yi* as duckweed.

[3] The reader will notice in this sentence the change to the passive mood, also that the insects or plants mentioned do not make a line of, so to speak, evolutionary descent. The text is not above suspicion, but taking it as it is, one can only conjecture that the author wanted to show the great variety of material there was at this point for his theory.

and horses produce men. Men in time go back to the germ; for the myriad creatures come forth from the germ, and they all return to it.'

Chapter 33. The Great Society.

In the Great Society there are many exponents of the art of government; and each regards what he has as something which allows of no addition. The question is: Where in all this comes in the art of the Tao of which past ages have spoken? The answer is that there is nowhere where it is not. Again it must be asked: How does the divine (in man) descend on him, how does the light of reason emerge? (The answer is that) there is something which brings (true) sages to birth and produces (true) kings, and the source of all these is in the One.[1] To be in unbroken contact with the Parent Stem (of all life), this is to be what is meant by a 'heavenly man.' To be in unbroken contact with the germinating power (in all Nature), this is to be what is meant by a 'supernatural man.' To be in unbroken contact with the truth (about life), this is to be what is meant by a 'perfect man.' To make Heaven the Parent Stem [? of all life], power of personality the root [? of all goodness], and the Tao the door [? to all wisdom], as also to divine the changes and transformations going on (in the universe), this is what is meant by 'being a sage.' And to make human-heartedness merciful, justice principled, (the spirit of) high ritual a daily habit, and music (a power of) harmony (in society), as also in all goodwill to be kind, man to man, this is what is meant by 'being a man of principle.' Thus by means of general rules he makes distinctions, by means of names he makes indications (as to what a thing's nature is), by means of personal experience he makes proof, by means of investigation makes judgments as right as an addition sum in arithmetic. This is the bond of association

[1] Professor Giles translates 'all proceed from an original One.' So in the succeeding sentence he translates *t'ien jen*, lit. heavenly man, as 'one with God.' Both these translations in my judgment exaggerate—it may be slightly, but none the less really—the author's consciousness of what is meant in the English language by 'God.'

for the hundred officials (in society). Thus they pay strict attention to their duties, make the clothing and feeding of the people their guiding principle, with the production of surpluses and the storing of them safely away. They pay special attention to the old and the weak, the fatherless and the widow. They all have a system for the cherishing of the people.

How all-sufficient were the men of antiquity! They were 'equal to the gods.'[1] They were the good wine of heaven and earth, foster-parents to all creatures, the spirit of harmony in society, a blessing to the masses. They came to understand the basic calculations (as to the heavenly bodies and the making of the calendar) and made the connections between secondary movements, reaching out to all parts of the compass, including the small and the great, refined essences and coarse masses. The scope of their influence extended everywhere. What they made clear about the movements of the heavenly bodies has been handed down in old rules of procedure from generation to generation, and the historical records are full of references to them. What they embodied in the *Book of Odes* and the *Book of History*, the *Record of Rites* and the *Book of Music* is understood by many scholars of Tsou and Lu.[2] . . . Numbers of these men are to be found everywhere, and in the Middle Kingdom they are officially recognized.

As for the hundred schools of thought which are continually being discussed, all society is in confusion. The worthy and the sage-like do not shine forth. The power of the Tao is no longer one. Everywhere there are plenty of people who, having examined just one thing, are very proud of themselves. The situation is as if the ears, the eyes, the nose, and the mouth, each should apprehend quite clearly but could not communicate what they apprehended to each other. As if the hundred philosophers were all just artisans, each with his strong point, at all times having his use, but none the less not having an inclusive all-round

---

[1] An old expression used in sacrificing to the Sage-kings.
[2] The native states of Confucius and Mencius.

skill. There are few who have the capacity to be endowed with the beauty of heaven and earth, few who can praise the outward form of divine intelligence. This is the reason why the Tao, which in the sage is within and in the sovereign in external things, is hidden and does not shine forth, is all tangled up and cannot manifest itself. Throughout the Great Society every man takes his own desires as the rule for him. Alas, alas! The hundred philosophers all go their own way and do not return. Of course they cannot agree. Thus the students of later ages will be in evil case, for they will not see the purity of heaven and earth. The grandeur of the ancients and the great art of the Tao will be split in fragments everywhere.

PART SIX

FOUR DIFFERENT ATTEMPTS AT A SYNTHETIC PHILOSOPHY

CHAPTER XV: THE YIN-YANG AND 'FIVE-FORCES' SCIENTIFIC SCHOOL

As with early Ionian thinkers of Hellenic culture, so with the early Chinese thinkers there were some whose minds were more attuned to what to-day we regard as the field of Natural Science. Some of these thinkers followed up ideas which came from the expert diviners, others were stimulated by the work of the calendar makers, the experts on the stars, whom we hardly know whether to call astronomers or astrologers. At the beginning, however, of the third century B.C. a new school of thought came into existence under the inspiration of one Tsou Yen of Ch'i State. In spite of what some Confucianists have had to say about him, he must have been a man of remarkable intellectual gifts and amazing literary activity. Unfortunately his works have been entirely lost, and we can only learn of him through what others have written about him or works which plainly were written by thinkers of his school.

In the Han Imperial Catalogue this school figures third in the list after Confucian and Taoist schools of non-canonical philosophy, and contains names of twenty-one authors and their works. These, like Tsou Yen's, have not survived. The name given them is 'Yin-Yang Experts.' From this name it is not to be assumed that they were the first exponents of this famous dualism-in-monism, but only that they made a new rational use of the concepts, bringing in alongside of them the *Wu Hsing*.[1] This idea also had perhaps come down from a less rational age; but here again Tsou Yen's curious genius got to work and made something quite new of them. The loss of these early scientific works is not so serious to learning, for these Yin-Yang experts had a tremendous influence on Han thought, including Confucian. Indeed, for two thousand years the Chinese approach to Natural Science has been to an almost disastrous degree affected by the speculations which followed the lines laid down by this school of thought. Chinese political philosophy also suffered, as can be gathered from the final three quotations in this chapter.

---

[1] The Five Dynamic Physical Forces, wood, fire, soil, metal, water; the order varies according to theories about their functioning. The Chinese name is sometimes *hsing*, sometimes *te*.

(Ssu-ma Ch'ien's Estimate of Tsou Yen.)

In Ch'i State . . . there was Tsou Yen who came after Mencius. Having observed that those who were possessed of countries were becoming increasingly licentious and incapable of appreciating moral power . . . and of influencing the common people, he proceeded to make a profound survey of the ebb and flow of the Yin and Yang, and to write essays running to more than a hundred thousand words on their permutations and the cycles of the great sages. The language he used was vague and not normal. He could not help first investigating some small object and then making inferences as to the importance of it, this without any limit. He was first to put the present in exact relation to a past going as far back as the Yellow Emperor. He took what the learned had all narrated and made a great correlation of the ages in their rise and fall, working out their omens, both bad and good, and their institutions, and making far-reaching [? far-fetched] inferences from them. This brought him to the time before heaven and earth existed, to what is so hidden that its origin cannot be investigated.

He was the first to make lists of the well-known mountains, great rivers, and communicating valleys in the Middle Kingdom [i.e. China], of the birds and beasts and all that the water and land produce, of sports occurring among the different species of creatures. He worked out inferences on matters which even men beyond the seas cannot visualize.[1] (For example) he cited the revolutions of the Five Powers [te],[2] since heaven and earth split asunder, as

---

[1] I take these words to be a reference to the stories that became current in Emperor Wu's reign (140–86 B.C.) of a great civilization and intellectual culture beyond the southern seas and mountains of Central Asia. It looks as if for some time before this there had been communication by sea between China and India, and the Emperor Wu's great general and explorer, Chang Chien, came back from Parthia with information about India and its 'wisdom of the Buddha.' Ssu-ma Ch'ien was historian at Emperor Wu's court and died 86 B.C.

[2] In this passage, in which Ssu-ma Ch'ien is so much at his best, I take it he means what he says and that Tsou Yen was the first to coin the term Wu Te to express his idea about the Five Powers (or Forces, or ? Agents) in the history of human society. Te is the word we have met so constantly, power of personality, etc. Cp. Introduction.

instances of each power having control in its proper sphere and dovetailing with each other right down to the present day.

He regarded this Middle Kingdom (of ours)—for that is what the Confucian scholars call it—as occupying one part of eighty-one heaven-below parts. He called the Middle Kingdom 'Red-Territory-Spirit-Subcontinent,' within which are nine provinces: the 'Nine Provinces' which (the Sage-king) Yü had marked out and which are not to be counted among the subcontinents.[1] Outside the Middle Kingdom —or, as we may call it, Red-Territory-Spirit-Subcontinent —there are nine others, those which are properly called 'the Nine Subcontinents': and encircling them are seas which neither men nor birds and beasts can cross, making, as it were, one great area or one great continent. There are nine others like this, and encircling them there is a great outside sea where heaven and earth meet.

Tsou Yen's skill was entirely of this kind. And yet when we get back to essentials it rested on human-heartedness and righteousness and moderation and frugality, on the mutual influence of sovereign and subject, of high and low, of the Six Relations[2] on each other. It is the initial point (in his theories) which is extravagant. Kings and dukes and influential people, when they first got to see his skill, in fear and trembling set themselves to radical reform; but later they found it was not practicable.

The following five quotations are taken from both non-Confucian and Confucian books.[3] They show, therefore, the influence exercised by Tsou Yen's way of thinking. (Cp. Part Eight, Chapter XXI.)

The first two quotations come from the *Kuan Tzu Book*. Reference has been made to this work in the Introduction, but it is necessary to add that these two chapters illustrate not

---

[1] Obviously there was confusion in Ssu-ma Ch'ien's day on this point. This was only too possible since *chou* (province) and *chou* (continent) were still the same character at that time.

[2] Probably these were father, mother, elder brother, younger brother wife, and child.

[3] Whether they are of pre-Han date or not is very difficult to say. Personally I regard the first two quotations as late-Chou productions.

only Tsou Yen's cosmology, but also the kind of early material out of which he made his synthesis; though here again, as in the case of the early forms of the legends of the heroes and the later rationalizations of them by the Chou-Han scholars, we are not in a position to make clear distinctions between the old and the new. The old cosmological myths have not survived in recognizable form, although the agriculturists' view of life and the universe is plain to view.

The last two quotations are from the Confucian Canon. They show what the politically minded thinkers could do in the way of synthesizing Nature and Politics and Ethics. In this respect the Han Confucianists, whether conservative or liberal, proved no more enlightened than the non-Confucianists.

Kuan Tzu, chapter 40.

The royal fiats should be timely. If they are not, then there is bound to be a revelation of what Heaven in consequence brings to pass, namely outbreaks against the Five [i.e. the Five Forces] and bemusement over the Six [i.e. the Yin and Yang and the Four Seasons]. Who knows this except a sage, for he alone comprehends the Four Seasons? Should they not be comprehended, the foundation of the state is gone; for failure to comprehend (the importance of) the crops means state and family adrift. Therefore I affirm that Heaven is to be trusted for its intelligence, Earth for its wisdom, the Four Seasons for being exactly right (in their order).

The true king is to be trusted for intelligence and for his wisdom, the true minister for being exactly right (in timing measures). The question is how we know this of the true king; and the answer is that he sets men of ability to work and can be trusted to have skill in juridical decisions. To set men of ability to work means that he is intelligent: to inspire trust in his juridical decisions means that he is wise. Those who have these three (qualities) of proving oneself worthy of trust and of being intelligent and wise, in all cases receive the reward of Heaven, this being that they cannot be bemused. Those who are bemused and forget (the seasonal tasks) receive Heaven's calamities. Thus, if those in authority show success in their business and pay honour to merit, then the people with their business welcome their labours and do not scheme (for rewards). . . .

Thus it is that the Yin and the Yang are the great principles of Heaven and Earth, the Four Seasons the great Way of the Yin and the Yang and the moral power [*te*] behind punishment of crime. For, if the punishments of crime be in accord with the seasons, then comes good fortune. If, however, they be out of all reason, then comes calamity, and then there is no way of proceeding with the work of spring and summer and autumn and winter.

In the eastern quarter of the heavens there is a star, its season springtime, its vital energy [*ch'i*] the breezes (of spring) which foster wood and bone, and its virtue [*te*] one of joy in the emaciation (of winter) being nourished and in growth coming stage by stage. The work of the season has its (distinctive) words of command: to clean up the shrines of the spirits and with due respect entreat and make offerings to them: to make the Yang (power) dominant and so put the (great flood) dykes in order: to plough, harrow, and plant and tend the fields: to put the bridges to rights, reconstruct irrigation channels, repair buildings and their gutters: to get free of vendettas and forgive offences, opening up communications on all sides. For then the gentle breezes and sweet rains of spring will come, and the common people will live to a great age, and the animal creation flourish. This is what is meant by 'the Virtue of the Star.'

Thus it is that if in the spring winter measures be taken, then everything will wither: if autumn measures, they will be nipped by frosts: if summer measures, then things will grow too luxuriantly.[1] Thus it is that in the third month on the *Chia Yi* days five measures of government are required : (1) to make it a crime to do away with the helpless young (of birds and beasts); (2) to bestow honours and great emoluments; (3) to break up the ice and restore the irrigation channels and bring back those who have been banished,[2] to put blocked channels right and to repair, mark

[1] I suggest emending to *yu* (excessive) from *yu* (desire).
[2] The underlying economic motive in this and the avoidance of punishment is that man-power may be mobilized for the short northern spring.

out and strengthen roads; (4) to prohibit the killing of fawns and such tender young things and the picking of blossom and destruction of tubers (in the ground); (5) to prohibit dilatoriness. So the spring rains will come.

In the southern quarter is the sun, its season summertime, its vital energy a (pure) Yang influence which fosters fire and vapour. Its virtue is one of giving and of making joy [? music]. The work of the season has its words of command: to be generous in bestowing honours and paying emoluments and fitting in with country life, to sacrifice to the spirits with due respect, to estimate (the people's) merit and reward the good, thus setting in motion the vital energy of the Yang and bringing the ninety days of summer with seasonable rains and the five cereals and hundred fruits duly ripening. This is what is meant by 'the Virtue of the Sun.'

At the functioning centre is the soil; and the virtue of the soil actually brings about the entry and exit of the four seasons in turn. It nourishes skin and flesh and muscle, and this virtue in it is one of harmonizing peace, of impartiality in action, of righteousness without private-mindedness. . . . (So,) even when winter's cold is at its height, fief and family flourish and the neighbours on all sides are anxious to be on good terms. This is what is meant by the virtue in harvest; for the sun has rewards in its hands, rewards being [? like] the warmth of the sun, and the harvest holds harmony in its hands, harmony being [? like] rain.

In summer, if the spring regulations are carried out, then there will be wind; if the autumn regulations, then flood; if the winter regulations, then blight. Therefore in summer in the third month on the *Ping Teng* day, publish the five regulations: (1) seek out those who have been successful and have worked very hard and commend them publicly; (2) open up old graves, old houses, old granaries and pits with a view to having storing accommodation; (3) prohibit fans and rain hats, for there must be no shirking, and remove badly leaking field shelters; (4) seek out those who have been merciful on a wide scale to the people and reward them; (5) prohibit traps for birds and beasts; birds learning to fly must not be killed. If these five regulations are seasonally carried out, the summer rains will come.

Here follow similar paragraphs on autumn and winter, all written from the countryman's point of view.

Kuan Tzu, chapter 39.

Earth is the origin of all things on the earth,[1] the tender root of all life, that by which beauty and ugliness, worth and no-worth, ignorance and eminence come into being. Water is the life-blood of Earth, as it were, flowing through its muscles and veins. Thus, I say, water is richly endowed. How do we comprehend that this is so? The answer is, all water is so gentle in its purity and thus delights to steep the places man dislikes [i.e. the low-lying marshes]: this is its *jen* [human-heartedness]. We see it as black and yet white: this is its subtle nature. In measuring it, you cannot make it stop when you fill a vessel to the brim: this is its rightness.[2] It alone keeps on flowing, stopping nowhere: this is its justice. Men all make for the high places: it alone makes for the low. This is its humility; and humility is the very house of the Tao, the very instrument of true kingliness, so that the true king makes it his capital. Then there is its levelness, the basis [lit. high ancestor] of all (our) measuring:[3] its colourlessness, the raw material of all the colours: its tastelessness, the core of all the flavours. Thus it is that water is the criterion of all things on the earth, is

[1] *Wan wu*, lit. ten thousand things, including animal, vegetable, and mineral, but not 'things' in the heavens.

[2] There would seem, therefore, to be a mystic immeasurability about 'rightness,' something beyond the mere mechanical four-squareness of a square.

[3] I do not know how Western civilization first made a synthesis of measurement, but on the basis of this passage we may say that the Chinese achieved this from observation of water, i.e. of water in a tipped-up bowl staying level. From that they got the idea of the absolute straight line necessary for measurement of length and breadth, and so by extension with a T-square implement to the measurement of height. Further, the Chinese weighing implement involved a plumb hanging from a rod, and the bringing of the rod to the horizontal. Thus 'levelness' came into calculations of weight.

the *t'an* [the featureless element found] in all living things, is the substance [1] of 'warp and woof,' of what is and what is not.

The above being so, water is entirely sufficing, entirely permanent, collecting in the heavens and the earth and being stored up in all things on the earth, being produced in metals and stones, and concentrating in all kinds of living things. Therefore I say, water is a spiritual (entity). As it accumulates in plants and trees, their stems acquire their stages of growth, their flowers acquire their due number and their fruits their due quantity. As it collects in the bodies of birds and beasts, they grow fat and large, their feathers and hair luxuriant, the markings of these beautifully distinct. This amounts to all things realizing their potentialities to the full. . . .

Man is water. When the vital fluid [*ching ch'i*] of a man and a woman combine and water flows into a shape, in three months' time there is something like a sucking. How 'a sucking'? The five flavours. How the 'five flavours'? The five viscera, the sour deriving from the spleen, the salt from the lungs, the peppery from the kidneys, the bitter from the liver, the sweet from the heart. Once the viscera are all complete, the flesh can be produced; first the spleen producing partitions [?], then the lungs producing the bones, the kidneys the breast, the liver the skin, the heart the flesh. Once the various fleshy parts are complete, then the nine orifices open out, the spleen opening the nose, the liver the eyes, the kidneys the ears, the lungs the orifices.[2] In five months these are complete and in ten months' time birth takes place. At birth the eyes can see, the ears can hear, and the *hsin* [heart-mind] can think. And that through which vision comes to the eye is not only the appearance of mountain heights: the eye can also scrutinize empty space. That through which

[1] *Wu fei* is emended to *ching wei*. Assuming that to be what the author wrote, this is a remarkable, if also cryptic, statement, pointing as it does in both metaphysical directions, one that reality is substance, the other that it is relation.

[2] The text is plainly corrupt since the *chiu ch'iao* (nine orifices) include the rectum and penis, or vagina—the navel does not appear in the list.

hearing comes to the ear is not only a clap of thunder: the ear can also distinguish silence. That through which thinking comes to the mind is not only consciousness [chih] of palpable matters: the mind can also investigate the subtle and mysterious. In fact it regulates the essence [ching] of essentials [yao].[1]

Lü Shih Ch'un Ch'iu, Chüan 13, § 2.

In all cases when a high-ruling king is about to arise, Heaven is sure to reveal (beforehand) an augury of good to the common people. In the Yellow Emperor's time Heaven made huge earth-worms and mole-crickets appear, and the Yellow Emperor said, 'The vital energy of "Soil" is in the ascendancy.' That having come to pass, he consequently approved of yellow as his (symbolic) colour and made the soil typical of his reign. Coming down to the time of Yü, Heaven first made grass and trees appear, grass and trees which did not die in the autumn and winter; and Yü said, 'The vital energy of "Wood" is in the ascendancy.' That having come to pass, he consequently approved of green as his colour and made Wood typical of his reign. Coming down to the time of T'ang, Heaven first made swords to appear in water; and T'ang said, '"Metal" is in the ascendancy.' That having come to pass, he consequently approved of white as his colour and made metal typical of his reign. Coming down to the time of King Wen, Heaven first made fire appear, a red bird holding a red book in its beak perched on the Earth Altar of the Chou House; and King Wen said, '"Fire" is in the ascendancy.' That having come to pass, he consequently approved of red as his colour and made fire typical of his reign.

Water is bound to be that which takes the place of fire, and Heaven will first reveal water in the ascendancy. When that comes to pass, the approved colour will be black and

---

[1] This rendering is the obvious one, and I let it stand with all its vagueness and all its intriguing implications.

water will be typical of the administration. Should (the power in) water have arrived and not have been recognized, then, with the cycle completed, there will be a reversion back to (the power in) soil.[1]

The *Yüeh Ling* [2] in the *Record of Rites*.

In the first month of spring the sun is in the Ying Shih sector, the star at dusk being *Ts'ang*, the star at dawn, *Wei*. Its days are called *Chia* and *Yi*. Its divine ruler is T'ai Hao, and his (associate) spirit Kou Meng. Its (characteristic) creatures have scales, its (characteristic) note in music is the *Chio*, its pitch *T'ai Ts'u*, its number eight, its taste sour, its smell rank. Its special sacrifice is the threshold one, and among the offerings the spleen is foremost.

East winds loosen the freezing cold. Hibernating insects begin to stir. Fish come up to the ice. Otters sacrifice fish, and the wild geese appear. The Son of Heaven resides (for the month) in the chamber on the left of the Ch'ing [azure-coloured] Yang temple, rides in the phoenix carriage, and drives the *ts'ang* [azure-coloured] dragon horses, carrying the *ch'ing* flag, wearing *ch'ing* clothes and *ts'ang* jade on his cap. He eats (during the month) wheat and mutton. The domestic implements he uses have only slight carvings and these with a burgeoning (motif).

In this month there is the Inauguration of Spring. Three days before this is done, the Chief Recorder notifies the Son of Heaven saying, 'On such and such a day spring is to be inaugurated. The up-coming virtue [*te*] is in Wood.' The Son of Heaven then goes into retreat for purification. On the day of inauguration he in his own person leads the

---

[1] The author of this passage was working under the patronage of the First Emperor's prime minister at a time when it was still uncertain what type of regime he would inaugurate to buttress his power. Thus the author would seem to be playing for safety in case the decision should be that soil was more consonant with the dignity of so great a person as the First Emperor.

[2] The following passage has many resemblances to the first quotation from *Kuan Tzu*, but it is given as an interesting contrast showing the court attitude as compared with that of a country scholar.

Three Dukes, the Nine Ministers, and the great lords and high officers of state to greet the spring in the eastern suburb of the capital. On their return he gives largesse to them in the court. The command is given to the royal assistants to spread abroad the royal virtue [*te*], harmonizing all orders given, bringing consolation and extending mercy to the millions of the people, with the royal bounty extended in every particular as it should be. The word of command is issued to the Chief Recorder to guard the statutes [1] and maintain the laws, to give attention to the movements of the heavens, the sun, the moon, the stars of the zodiac in their transits. . . .

In this month the Son of Heaven on the first day prays to the Supreme Ruler [*Shang Ti*] for the crops and, choosing the *Yuan-ch'en* day, he, the Son of Heaven in his own person, taking the plough in his carriage of state . . . leads the Three Dukes, the Nine Ministers, the great lords, and the high officers of state to plough the field of God [2] [*Shang Ti*]. Three furrows the Son of Heaven turns up, five furrows the Dukes, nine furrows the ministers and lords. They return, and in the great chamber with the dukes, ministers, lords, and officers all in waiting, the goblet is lifted and the word given, 'The wine of labour.'

In this month the vital energy of Heaven descends, the vital energy of Earth ascends, Heaven and Earth are united, and the plants and trees put forth their shoots. The royal order is issued for the business of husbandry. The fields with an eastward aspect are to be occupied, their borders repaired, the paths between them fixed. Surveys must be made . . . to determine the right soils for the five cereals. In teaching the people the right methods, the officers must themselves take part. With the business of the fields thus prepared and the standards rightly set, the work of the husbandman does not go astray.

[1] I see in this distinction between *tien*, translated as 'statute,' and *fa* (laws) the idea of a basic constitution as distinct from the current laws of a state or the fiats of a monarch. Cp. Rousseau, *Le Contrat Social.*

[2] 'Field of God' is James Legge's translation, and coming from him should not be lost.

In this month the word is given to the chief musician to enter the college and have the ritual dances practised. The canons [*tien*] of sacrifice are re-ordered, and the word is given to make offerings to the hills and forests, to the rivers and meres, the sacrificial victims (for this month) in all cases to be males. The chopping of trees is prohibited, as also the destruction of birds' nests and the killing of the young of insects, of creatures in the womb or new-born, of birds taking to the wing, and baby animals and the eggs of birds. There must be no gatherings of the populace, no rearing of fortifications or city walls. Skeletons must be buried and bones with the flesh still on them interred.

In this month the army may not be called out, for if it is, a judgment ensues—that the battle-axes should not be raised means that war should not break out because of us. The Way of Heaven must not be altered, the ordered processes of Earth must not be broken, nor the bonds of man with man be confounded.

If in this first month the summer orders be put into effect, then untimely rain will fall, the plants and trees will prematurely decay, and the states be continually in panic. If the autumn orders be put into effect, then the people concerned will suffer from a great pestilence, violent winds and rains will come together, and weeds of all sorts will spring up together. And if the winter orders be put into effect, then the overflowing waters will work havoc and snow and frost will shackle the soil so that the first seedlings cannot enter the ground.

In the second month of spring . . .

And so on through every month of the year, each with its own special features alongside of those appertaining to its particular season.

One interesting thing is that the theory of the Five Forces has to be fitted into this scheme, and 'fives into twelve won't go.' In consequence soil (*t'u*) has a special position made for it at the end of summer and the beginning of autumn. This section is as follows:

In the very centre is the soil. Its days are (called) *Wu* and *Chi*. Its divine ruler is Huang Ti [the Yellow Emperor], and his associate spirit Hou T'u: its (characteristic) creatures those with bare skin: its musical note the *Chung* . . . its number five, its taste sweet, its smell fragrant.   Its sacrifice is in the central court, and among the offerings the heart is foremost.

The Son of Heaven resides in the great chamber of the Great Temple. . . . The implements he uses are round and capacious.

And that is all: no symbolic acts beyond those connected with his lodging and food and clothes, etc., and no 'words of command' issued to the people.   With regard to the whole scheme there is no reason for supposing that this attempt to visualize the Son of Heaven both in his personal way of life and in all his acts of government as a living symbol of divine Heaven and Earth was ever very seriously put into practice either by the First Emperor or by any Han emperor.   The whole text of this book (the *Yüeh Ling* of the canonical *Record of Rites*) appears also in the *Lü Shih Ch'un Ch'iu*.

The *Hung Fang* in the *Book of History*.

The *Book of History* (*Shu Ching*) has already been quoted in Part One, Chapter I.   This *Hung Fang* essay is entirely different in style and subject-matter from any other section of the book: to higher critics one of the major problems of a book bristling with problems.   There would seem little doubt that it was written in Han times; but when and how it came to be included in the *Shu Ching* is the question.

I have heard that in bygone times Kun by damming up the waters of the great flood confounded the Five Forces. High God was wroth and would not bestow on him the Grand Norm with its Nine Categories, for thus the unchanging relationships of men came to ruin.   Kun lay in prison till he died, but Yü [his son] took up the task and prospered.   Heaven bestowed on Yü the Grand Norm with its Nine Categories wherein were set forth the unchanging relationships of men.

Of the Nine Categories, the first is the Five Forces; the second, reverent practice of the five (daily) doings; the third, intensive use of the eight spheres of government; the fourth, harmonious application of the five arrangements of time; the fifth, establishment of royal perfection; the sixth, orderly employment of the three spiritual powers [*te*]; the seventh, enlightened practice of divination; the eighth, thoughtful application of the common lines of verification; the ninth, encouragement towards the five felicities and deterrence from the six extremes (of infelicity).

First, with regard to the Five Forces, the first is water, the second fire, the third wood, the fourth metal, the fifth earth. Water saturates and descends, fire burns and ascends: wood is crooked and straight; metal is pliant and susceptible of modification: earth fosters sowing and reaping. Saturation produces the salty flavour in foodstuffs, flames leaping up the bitter, crookedness and straightness the sour, yielding and changing the peppery, sowing and reaping the sweet.

Secondly, with regard to the five (daily) doings, the first is outward manner, the second speaking, the third seeing, the fourth hearing, the fifth thinking. Outward manner (involves) being decorous. Speaking (involves) obeying, seeing getting objects clear, hearing discriminating (sounds), thinking penetration of mind. Decorum creates majesty, obedience [? to reason] high ability, getting objects clear intelligence, discrimination of sounds the power of sizing up, penetration of mind brilliance of intellect.

.   .   .   .   .

Thirdly, with regard to the eight spheres of government, the first is food, the second commodities (of all sorts), the third the sacrifices, the fourth that of the minister of labour, the fifth that of the minister of education, the sixth that of the minister dealing with crime, the seventh entertainment of guests, the eighth the army.

Chapter XVI: Hsun Ch'ing and his Spiritual Philosophy

Hsun Ch'ing (c. 298–238 B.C.), the last of the pre-Han thinkers, was in many respects the greatest, as he was in all respects the most philosophical, of the Confucianists. For some years he was at Ch'i Hsia, the great scholar centre in the northeast. There he was brought into living contact with all the theories of his day; so that he became a man of wide learning. During the later years of his life he was a minor official, in charge of an unimportant district in the south. He was a poet as well as a philosopher and lives in the literary history of China as one of the inventors of a new form of verse which lent itself more to reflective expression than the old elegiac form. The book that comes to us under his name contains thirty-two chapters. These have suffered at the hands of his disciples, but they contain for the most part Hsun Ch'ing's ideas, as he put them into literary form.

The influence of Taoist, Mohist, and Legalist ways of thinking is clearly discernible in his distinctive tenets. Everything that came his way was grist to his philosophical mill, either to be rejected on specified rational grounds or to be reinforced on the basis of his own first principles. In the last resort, however, he was a Confucianist with an unassailable belief in the moral order of the universe. 'Heaven' was to him law, and that in the sense of 'Whatsoever a man soweth, that shall he also reap,' so that like Mo Ti he would have nothing to do with fate. Man's welfare depended on his own efforts, efforts which could and must be unremitting. Owing to the strenuous nature of the struggle for acquired personality and to the consequent need for external as well as internal discipline, the political philosophy which he evolved was a rigorous one requiring authoritarian rule and a firm repression of licence in thought as well as in deed. Yet the poet in him was highly sensitive to the aesthetic appeal in Nature and the life of man, and he saw more clearly than any other thinker before that the prime need of society was education, the making of men. In this respect he had a profound understanding of the nature and scope of education. As the quotations on *li* (religious and social ritual) will show, the business of education was to harmonize the raw instincts, and man's chief tool for this purpose was training in ritual, in a continually recurrent round of sacramental acts which made poetry of daily living.

Coming when he did, Hsun Ch'ing was profoundly conscious of the need for good logic. He thus supported the later Mohists in their attack on the sophist logicians: man could attain to a reliable knowledge of the universe and himself. In the following quotations, therefore, Hsun Ch'ing's views on Heaven and human nature are put first, and, arising out of them, his views on knowledge are put second. After them are placed his views on the indispensability of Ritual.

I. (Heaven and the Congenital Nature of Man.)

Chapter 17. A Discussion of Heaven.

Heaven's way of acting is unchanging. It did not act specially to make Yao [the Sage-Emperor] survive nor to bring Ch'ieh [the arch-criminal] to destruction. Respond to Heaven by governing well, then there will be good fortune: respond to it by governing badly, and then there will be bad fortune. If the basic industries [i.e. those in connection with agriculture] are in a flourishing state and economy is being practised in public expenditure, Heaven cannot make the country poor; and if the supply of food-stuffs is complete and energy is exercised at the right times, Heaven cannot make the people sick; and if the Right Way is being cultivated, Heaven cannot send down calamities. The fact is that (by themselves) flood and drought cannot cause famine, extremes of cold and heat cannot cause distress, nor malicious spirits bring bad fortune. If, however, the basic industries are neglected, and expenditure is extravagant, then Heaven cannot make the country rich. . . . The fact is that famine is there before flood and drought, sickness arrives before the rigours of cold and heat. . . . Observance of the seasons and good government go together, whilst calamities and good government are incompatible; and it is wrong to inveigh against Heaven because its Way is so. Thus it is that only if a man be clear as to the relative spheres of Heaven and man may he be called a man of consummate understanding.[1]

To carry to completion by actionless activity [*wu wei*], to accomplish without trying to, is to be described as Heaven's function. Deep though that function is, great though

[1] *Chih jen* is the term so often found in *Chuang Tzu* (cp. p. 181). The next sentence is also entirely reminiscent of Taoist ideas, although Hsun Ch'ing revolted against the notion that man as well as Heaven could express himself perfectly in 'actionless activity.'

it is and of vital import, the man of consummate understanding nevertheless does not consider it to any extent,
nor does he get additional ability through it, nor does he
probe into it. This means that he does not try to complete Heaven.[1] (For) Heaven has its times and seasons,
Earth its wealth, and Man his work of making order:[2] a
blending into a trinity of powers, as it should be described.

Now the man who neglected the condition on which this
blending of powers depended, hoping to be the blender
himself, would be on the wrong track altogether. The
serried ranks of stars follow their courses: the sun and the
moon take turns in shining: the four seasons successively
take charge: the Yin and Yang make their great transformations: the wind and the rain exercise their all-per-
vading influence. Thus the myriad creatures come within
the scope of this life-giving harmony (of forces) and in
every case get the nourishment which brings them to
completion. This we call a miraculous work, for we
cannot see it going on, although we see the final accomplishment. We call it Heaven's[3] accomplishment, for in
every case we know that something has brought completion, although we have no knowledge of this something in its intangibility. The true sage does not try to
know Heaven.

Heaven's function has been established once for all, its
accomplishment brought to completion once for all. Thus
man's body was prepared and the spirit of man came to
life, and with it loving and hating, delight and annoyance,
sorrow and joy: that is, the 'Heaven-given emotions' were
stored up within. Man has eyes, ears, nose, mouth, and
limbs, 'the Heaven-given (natural) pipes,' each of them in
contact with the others but not able to interchange its

[1] Modern critics are highly conscious, and rightly so, of Hsun Ch'ing's
outstanding humanism; but it is important to note how, as here, he shows
himself offended by the Taoist tendency to pantheism.
[2] Yang Liang (ninth century) interpreted this as man able to control
and utilize these times and seasons and this wealth which Heaven and
Earth provide.
[3] The temptation is to say 'Nature' as Dr. Dubs does in his translation.
Hsun Ch'ing reminds us of 'the Learned' of the eighteenth century in the
West, who substituted Nature for God.

aptitude for the others.[1]   In the central emptiness dwells
the mind [*hsin*], that is 'the Heaven-given (natural) sovereign,' controller of the five senses.[2]   The mind makes the
arrangements by which the other species are used to
nourish the human species: that is 'Heaven-given (natural)
nourishing'; for to protect one's own species is what is
called 'happiness,' to go against it is 'calamity.'   This is
'the Heaven-given (natural) system of government.'

Now to darken man's Heaven-given sovereign, to throw
his Heaven-given senses into confusion, to let go his
Heaven-given nourishment, to disobey his Heaven-given
system of governing, and to do violence to his Heaven-
given emotions, this is the supreme evil fortune.   The sage
purifies his Heaven-given sovereign, rectifies his Heaven-
given senses, prepares his Heaven-given nourishment [i.e.
by attention to agricultural pursuits], protects his Heaven-
given government, nourishes his Heaven-given emotions in
order to bring to perfection his Heaven-given merit of
accomplishment.   If this be done, then he knows what he
can do and what he cannot do, and with Heaven and Earth
discharging their responsibilities the myriad creatures are
at man's command.

.   .   .   .   .

The high-minded man [*chun tzŭ*] is concerned about the
matters in his own sphere and does not hanker after the
matters in Heaven's sphere of action; whilst the low-
minded man does the reverse.   Because the former is so,
his affairs daily go forward, and because the latter is so, his
affairs daily go backward.   There is a single reason for the
one going forward and the other going backward.   In this
lies the difference between the two.

If a star falls or a tree groans, the people of the country

---

[1] *Wu kuan*, meaning either 'the five officials' or 'the five conducting
pipes' between man and the outside world, was the name which came to be
given to the five senses.   Hsun Ch'ing seems clearly to show, both here
and elsewhere, that he had the Western idea of 'faculty' in his mind.   It
is open to conjecture whether the negative (*pu*) should not be eliminated
so that the meaning might be 'that they have reciprocating aptitudes.'
[2] For Hsun Ch'ing the mind equals the intellect plus the will.

are all in a panic.   The question is, why (this state of panic)?
The answer is, for no reason.   There is some change in
Heaven or in Earth, some Yin and Yang transformation,
something which rarely happens in the material sphere.
It is right to wonder at it; it is not right to fear it.   In
every generation there are these occurrences from time to
time, eclipses of the sun or the moon, wind and rain at
unseasonable times, strange stars appearing in groups.   If
those in authority are intelligent and their government is
equable, then in spite of these occurrences in one generation
after another there is no harm done.   If they are unin-
telligent and their government leads in dangerous paths, in
spite of there being no such occurrence they are no better off.

It follows that 'human omens' are the things to be feared,
the scamped ploughing which affects the final crop, the
sketchy hoeing which misses the weeds, the foolhardiness
in government which saps the confidence of the people.
When the fields are overgrown with weeds and the harvest
is bad, the price of corn high and the people short of food
and their dead bodies found on the roads, these are what
I call human omens.   When the official orders are stupid
ones, when public undertakings are put in hand at the
wrong times and the basic industries are not properly
organized, these are what I call 'human omens.'   If the
(sense of) ritual-and-righteousness [1] is not cultivated, if
the women's and men's apartments are not kept separate
and there is sex licence, then father and son are suspicious
of each other, rulers and ruled are at cross purposes,
tyranny and distress go hand in hand.   These I call human
omens.   They are born of disorder, and when these three
kinds come together, peace is dead in that country. . . .

The question is put: What about the special sacrifices for

[1] In Hsun Ch'ing we constantly find the two terms *li* (ritual) and *yi*
(righteousness) run together like this.   We have already met both of them
but not as a combination, *li* as a concept embracing the inward as well as
the outward motions of man's moral consciousness, *yi* ranging from the
narrow meaning of 'justice' to the wider one of 'righteousness.'   Hsun
Ch'ing combines the two terms because morality was for him an art involving the beauty of ritual.   Cp. the quotation below from c. 9.   There
he is analysing man's sense of justice, and the composite concept has to
be split up in translation.

rain and then the rain coming? The answer is that there is nothing to it. It would rain all the same if there were no sacrifices. When people 'save' the sun and moon from being devoured,[1] or when they pray for rain at a time of drought, or when they divine the omens before taking an important decision, these prayers are not to be taken as being answered. They are superfluous embellishments, for that is how enlightened men regard them, although the people generally take them to be signs of the supernatural. (Rather) it is good fortune to see them as embellishments, bad fortune to see them as supernatural. . . . Which is better, to magnify Heaven and meditate on it or to have your goods properly cared for and systematically controlled; to submit to Heaven and sing its praises or to systematize its commissions and make good use of them; to rely on things multiplying of themselves or to exercise all one's ability in developing them? . . .

It is significant that in a discussion of Heaven Hsun Ch'ing should have so much to say about man. Yet he kept the discussion strictly within limits, for he did not go into the question of the nature of man, whether it is congenitally good or genitally bad. To that topic he gave a separate essay. Comparison should be made with the Christian Church's traditional theories as to the nature of man. Hsun Ch'ing saw man rather in the way in which St. Paul, St. Augustine, and Calvin did. Cp. Mencius's opposite view of man, and the Introduction for a general approach to the question.

Chapter 23. The Nature of Man is Evil.

The congenital nature [2] of men is evil, the goodness in them acquired.[3] Let us consider now men's nature. By birth there exists a passion for profit. When men obey this passion the result is quarrelling and grabbing to the utter detriment of mutual consideration and forbearance. By birth men envy and hate. When they obey this passion

[1] i.e. do the customary rites at times of eclipse.
[2] By nature is meant nature at birth: hence my adjective 'congenital.' It is important to bear in mind that this was not for Hsun Ch'ing the whole truth about the nature of man. By birth man also has his mind-will.
[3] The ideograph wei is composed of wei (action) with a classifier jen (man). 'Acquired' and 'man-made' are both legitimate translations.

the result is killing and injury to the utter detriment of
loyalty and mutual confidence. By birth men have the
lusts of the ear and eye, have a passion for the beauty of the
human voice and figure. When they follow these lusts the
result is licence and moral anarchy to the detriment of
ritual-and-righteousness, of culture-and-reason. Thus, if
men give rein to their congenital nature and obey their
instinctive emotions, the outcome, of necessity, is quarrelling
and grabbing, a common opposing of culture and confounding of reason, and the arrival at an unmitigated state
of violence. Thus it is that there is necessity for the transformation which the teaching of example effects, a necessity
for the Way [*Tao*] of ritual-and-righteousness which alone
can produce mutual consideration and forbearance and
combine culture with reason, and so bring men to a state
of moral order. From this point of view it is clear that
the congenital nature of men is evil and the goodness in
them acquired. The fact is that a crooked piece of wood
must undergo steaming and bending before it can become
straight, that a blunt piece of metal must undergo grinding
before it can become sharp.

Assuming that men's nature is evil . . . and that consequently men are in a state of moral perversity and wanting
in control, the ancient Sage-kings recognized that men were
so and consequently all out of the true. On men's behalf,
therefore, they started [? the idea of] ritual-and-righteousness, made systematic laws with a view to straightening and
embellishing men's emotional nature and thus rectifying
them, with a view to rigorously controlling their emotional
nature and thus opening up a new way for them. For the
first time they all came into a state of order and were of
one accord in the Way. Thus to-day there are the *chun
tzu* [high-minded men], who have been transformed by a
teacher's example, have accumulated the culture of learning,
have been led on by ritual - and - righteousness. Whilst
there are men, the *hsiao jen* [small-minded men], who give
rein to their emotional nature, are outrageously harsh, go
dead against ritual-and-righteousness. From this point of

view it is clear that men's congenital nature is evil and the goodness in them acquired.

Mencius maintained that the teachability of men means that their congenital nature is good. My reply is that this is not so. Mencius failed to understand men's nature, nor did he examine into the part played respectively by the congenital nature and the acquired. What belongs to the congenital nature is from Heaven. It cannot be learned, nor can it be worked for: whereas the spirit of ritual-and-righteousness which the Sage-kings brought into existence, this is what men have to learn if they are to become morally capable and arrive at completion. . . .

Consider men's congenital nature. They are hungry and so want to be replete: they are cold and so want to be warm: they get tired with work and so want to rest. This is men's instinct and nature.[1] But consider men and their hunger: those who on seeing food do not presume to eat first, but find occasions for yielding of precedence. Consider those who being tired from work do not try to rest, but find occasions for working instead of others. Sons yield precedence to fathers, younger brothers to elder brothers, whilst sons work in place of their fathers, and younger brothers in place of elder brothers. These two lines of conduct are the opposite to nature and go counter to instinct, whilst, on the other hand, the way of the filial son implies the culture-and-reason in ritual-and-righteousness. Thus it is that if instinct and nature be obeyed, there is no mutual consideration; and if there be mutual consideration, then this is in the face of instinct and nature.[1] From this point of view it is clear that men's nature is evil and the goodness in them acquired.

Someone may put the question: If men's nature is evil, how do ritual-and-righteousness come to be? The answer is that all forms of ritual-and-righteousness are born of the acquired (character) of sage men, and do not have their origin in the nature of men. Originally a potter mixed earth

[1] This should be noted as an example of what Western logicians call a disjunctive antithesis.

and water and turned (the mixture) on a wheel and so made utensils; but then the utensils were born of the potter's acquired (skill) and not of men's nature. . . . Sages piled up purposeful thinking and practised themselves in acquired powers, and thus were able to give birth to ritual-and-righteousness and make a beginning of laws. Thus, then, these things were born of the sages' acquired (powers) and not of men's congenital nature. For example, the eye has a passion for colour, the ear for sound, the mouth for flavours, the mind for profit, the bones and fleshy parts for comfort. All this is born of man's instinct and nature. When stimulated they are born of themselves without involving deliberate effort. What is meant by 'born of the acquired' is anything which cannot come of itself and, what is more, involves deliberate effort to make it what it is. This is the evidence that the things to which nature and the acquired (character) give birth are not the same. Thus it is that the sages transformed congenital nature and made a beginning in acquired (character) and with their acquired (character) ritual-and-righteousness was born, and with the birth of ritual - and - righteousness . . . Therefore, where the sages were like the mass of people and did not differ from them at all was in their congenital nature; where they differed was in the (character) which they acquired. . . . It is because their nature is evil that man have a wish to be good. The men who have little to show for themselves would have much, the ugly would be beautiful, the niggardly generous, the poor rich, the low in the social scale the high: having no resources in himself a man necessarily seeks help from without. Therefore the rich do not aim at more wealth, the men with social prestige do not aim at more prestige. Having resources in themselves they do not go outside for them. From this point of view it is clear that it is because men's nature is evil that they have a wish to be good.[1]

Mencius has maintained that men's nature is good, but I

[1] I have my suspicions of this passage as being an insertion by a later hand. It seems to me unlikely that Hsun Ch'ing would have sandwiched so important a statement in between the arguments before and after.

maintain that it is not so. In the past and in the present the universal meaning for 'goodness' is being principled and evenly self-controlled. The meaning of 'evil' is being reprobate (in action) and morally disordered. This, I affirm, is the distinction between good and evil.

Now take men's nature as it really is. Are men mechanically rightly principled and evenly self-controlled? If they are, then what can be the use of the Sage-kings and their ritual-and-righteousness? There would be no room for the help of the Sage-kings and their ritual-and-righteousness, in adding on to men's rightly principled action and even self-control. That is not how things are. Men's nature is evil, and the fact is that because of this Sage-kings in the past saw men as reprobates and wholly out of the true . . . and therefore set up the authority of an overruling sovereign to be a blessing to men: set forth (the principles of) ritual and justice in order to effect the transformation of men: made a beginning with the rectifying influence of laws in order to exercise control over men: enhanced the severity of punishments in order to restrain men. Thus they caused the Great Society to become ordered and have a common mind on goodness. . . .

Now let us experiment with (the idea of) removing the authority of the sovereign and the transformation effected by ritual and righteousness . . . and let us watch from the side how men will treat each other. The strong would rob and maltreat the weak, the many would oppress and shout down the few.[1] In no time there would be universal anarchy, everybody destroying everybody else. From this point of view it is clear that men's nature is evil, the goodness in them acquired.

· · · · ·

What is the meaning of the saying 'a man in the street can become a Yü'? The answer is that the powers by which a Yü becomes a Yü involve his becoming both

[1] Hsun Ch'ing did not believe in the divine rightness of a democratic majority.

humane and just, law-abiding and righteous. If that be so, then humanity-cum-justice and law-abidingness-cum-righteousness are rationally learnable and practicable. But that being so, the man in the street always has the raw material (in him) from which he can get to recognize humanity-cum-justice . . . and the means at his command by which he can come to be capable of humanity-cum-justice. . . . If that be so, obviously a man in the street can become a Yü.

Now the question is whether we have to take humanity-cum-justice and law-abidingness-cum-righteousness as rational patterns [1] which in the last resort can neither be known nor be put into effectual practice. If that be so, then even a Yü could neither know nor practise them, and that would make it impossible for the man in the street to have the raw capacity and the means for recognizing and practising them. Is that not so? But then the man in the street would be unable to recognize in the family the just (relationship) between father and son, and, outside the family, the right (relationship) between sovereign and subject. That, however, is not the case. The man in the street is always able to recognize the just (relationship) between father and son, etc. If that be so, then the raw capacity for recognizing this, and the means of practising it, obviously are in the man in the street. Now if we assume that the man in the street with his raw capacity for recognizing and his means of practising is rooted and grounded in the recognized pattern of humanity-cum-justice and the practicable means for becoming humane and just, then obviously he can become a Yü. Suppose, then, a man in the street becoming a student in submission to the technique of study, concentrating his mind and integrating his power of recollection, thinking connectedly and becoming experienced in examining, daily adding to his knowledge and retaining it: if he should pile up goodness without resting, then he would become as wise as the gods

---

[1] *Li* in Hsun Ch'ing's vocabulary seems to me always to have behind it the idea of reason in the sense of the rational as opposed to the irrational. 'Principle' does not seem the right word here.

and make a trinity of power with Heaven and Earth. The
fact is that a sage kind of man is one who piles up what
(ordinary) men pile up: only he carries this to the highest
pitch.

The question now is why it is possible for a sage and not
possible for the mass of people to pile up to this extent.
The answer is that it is possible for them but it is not
possible to make them do it. The fact is that it is possible
for a low-minded man to become a high-minded man, but
he is not willing; and it is possible for a high-minded man
to become a low-minded man, but he is not willing. It has
never been impossible for such men to change places, but
they just do not do it. It is possible for them to change,
but not possible to make them. It is possible, therefore,
for the man in the street to become a Yü, but it is not
necessarily the case that he has the trained ability.[1] Although he may not have the trained ability, this does not
affect the possibility. It is not impossible for men's feet to
carry them all over the country, but no one (except Yü)
has tested his ability to do so.[2] Carpenters and farmers
and merchants have not tested whether it is impossible for
them to take on each other's jobs, but they also have
not tested whether they have the trained ability to do so,
From this point of view it follows that the possibility does
not necessarily involve having the trained ability, whilst not
having the trained ability does not affect the possibility.
So then having or not having the trained ability is vastly
different from a possibility and an impossibility, and obviously it is not possible for men to take on each other's jobs.

In some of the other essays Hsun Ch'ing does more justice to
the part which 'desire' plays in the life of man. In opposition to
the Taoist thinkers and one Sung K'eng, an older contemporary
of his, he emphasized that man's desires cannot and should
not be reduced to the minimum. Such a policy mutilates the

[1] Alternatively 'has the will-power.' It should be noted that the ideograph *chih* which came to be used for 'the will,' and probably has something like this meaning in the *Analects,* is not used in that way by Hsun
Ch'ing.
[2] The legends about Yü emphasized his trudging all over the country to
find out the lie of the land and so how to devise the right means for avoiding
floods.

whole man and is in the last resort impossible of achievement. Desires need to be both nourished and controlled. For this man depends on his mind functioning as master in him. Further, among the 'instinctive emotions' listed above—the conventional list found in all books of this period—the emotion of fear is not included. Yet fear was something Hsun Ch'ing took into account. It must suffice to quote one vivid example he gives of fear.

Chapter 22.

The theories of control which depend on the removal of desire have no way of guiding desires and so are embarrassed by the continued presence of desires. The theories of control which depend on the reduction of desires to the minimum have no way of moderating desire and are embarrassed by the multiplicity of desires. To have desires and not to have them is a matter belonging to another class of phenomena (than what the theorists think). It is a question of whether a man is alive or dead, not of whether he is subject or not to social control. To have many desires or few is a matter belonging to another class of phenomena. There are the given number of instinctive emotions. It is not a question of social control or no control. Desires exist irrespective of whether it is possible for them to be satisfied or not, but the attempt to satisfy them is along the lines of what is possible. The former is something coming from Heaven, the latter something coming from the mind. . . . What men desire most is life and what they hate most is death. And yet there are those who (think they) are acting along the lines of life and (actually) arrive at death. It is not that they do not want to live and do want to die, but that life (as they want it) is impossible whilst death is possible. The fact is that if a desire is inordinate, such that the man's energy of activity cannot fulfil it, the mind stops it. If what the mind permits hits the bull's-eye of moral reason, then, however many desires a man may have, what harm does that do to his self-control? . . . If, however, what the mind permits does not hit the bull's-eye of moral reason [li], then, however few desires a man may have, how can he stop short of moral anarchy? Thus it is that self-control and moral anarchy consist in what the mind permits and not in what the emotions wish.

Chapter 10.

Without a sovereign to keep his subjects in order . . . the whole of society is injured and unbridled desire is born. For men desire and dislike the same things. Thus desires are many and the things too few. If they are too few, then there cannot but be quarrelling.

Chapter 21.

To the south of Hsia Shou there was a man called Chüan Shu-ling. As a man he was stupid and prone to fear. Once when the moon was shining brightly he was out walking. Stooping down he saw his shadow and took it to be a crouching devil: looking up he caught sight of his hair and took it to be a forest demon. He turned and ran. When he arrived at his house, he lost his breath and died. A very distressing occurrence, this!

II. (The Problem of Knowledge.)

Hsun Ch'ing regarded the dialecticians of his day with marked disapproval. They were to him subversive of order, confounding the distinctions of right and wrong. None the less he took their work into serious account, and in many ways shows that his own mind was stimulated by their subtleties. What he thought of the Neo-Mohists and their arguments for the reality of knowledge we do not know; [1] but his own opinion was much the same as theirs.

Hsin, 'the mind,' which, in classical Chinese must sometimes be translated as 'the heart,' in Hsun Ch'ing is always the faculty with which a man knows and wills. The *hsin* stands in contrast to the instinctive emotions. Hsun Ch'ing is not free from the intellectual vice of making statements in which the mind, or for that matter the emotions, appear as acting of themselves, but in the last resort he will be found to have a singularly firm grasp of the fact that it is the whole man who does the thinking or feeling. He kept his analysing ability within bounds.

---

[1] Cp. the quotation below from c. 22. Some statements there point to his knowing their work.

Chapter 21. On Freedom from Delusion.[1]

. . . . .

By birth there is the mind and so the capacity for knowledge. There being this capacity, there is also the memory.
To remember is to store things away. On the other hand,
there is what is called emptiness, namely (the power of)
not using what has been stored away to the prejudice of
what is still to be received.

By birth there is the mind and so the capacity for knowledge. There being this capacity, there is also differentia-
tion. To differentiate means knowing more than one thing
at a time, and to do that involves duality. On the other
hand, there is what is called singleness, namely (the power
of) not letting the 'that' oneness [? of impression] interfere with the 'this' oneness. When the mind is asleep, it
dreams: when it is at leisure it goes its own way [? wanders
freely]. When it is set to work, it makes plans. The fact
is that the mind has no experience of inactivity. On the
other hand, there is what is called stillness, namely (the power
of) not letting dreams frivolously confound knowledge.

The man who has not achieved the Way but is seeking it,
he is to be described as empty, single, and so still. . . . To
have knowledge of the Way by investigation and to have
knowledge of it by practising it, this is to embody the Way.
To be empty, single, and so still, means to be supremely
pure and intelligent.

. . . . .

The mind is the ruler of the body and the master of the
spirit. It issues orders, and all parts of the body obey. It
prohibits itself: it sets itself to work: it decides for itself;
it lays hold for itself: it is self-acting, and self-stopping.[2]
The fact is that for the mouth to be forced to be silent or to

[1] The earlier common meaning of *pi* is, as Dr. Dubs has pointed out,
'beclouding.'
[2] Here, as elsewhere, is evidence that for Hsun Ch'ing the mind was what
we call 'the seat of the will.'

speak, for the body to be forced to stoop or stand upright, all that does not matter. But it does matter if the mind be forced to change its intention: what is right, that it must receive: what is wrong, that it must reject. Therefore I maintain that the mind bears the burden of its choices. What it does not forbid is bound to become apparent. Its objects (of attention) are of every kind and description, but the essence of it in the last resort is to be not double-minded. . . . If the mind diffuses itself, it will not get knowledge: if it is upside down, it will not be proficient: if it has no convictions, it will be in doubt and error. But use it to make comparative investigations and everything in the world will be embraced in its knowledge.

.   .   .   .   .

In observation of objects, if there is doubt and the centre of my mind is undecided, then (it is because) the external object is obscure. Also if my deliberations about an object are obscure, then it is impossible for me to decide what it is or what it is not. (For instance) a man walking in the dark may take a low-lying rock to be a crouching tiger. . . . It is because the darkness has deluded his intelligence. A drunken man . . . stoops his head going out of a city gate, taking it to be a low door. It is because wine has confused his spirit.[1]

If a man shuts one eye, he sees an object as if it were two . . . it is because the conditions confuse his senses. Thus it is that when a man stands on the top of a hill and looks down at a cow, it appears to be a sheep. If, however, he wanted a sheep, he would never go down and lead a cow away. This is because distance deludes as to the size of an object. When the water is disturbed and the shadows dance, a man cannot decide whether he is handsome or ugly.[2] This is because the condition of the water confuses

---

[1] *Shen*, the word for a spirit, a god. 'Spirit' seems to be the only way of translating, but I do not know precisely what is meant. For instance, what is the connection between this *shen* and *hsin*, the mind?
[2] From several references of this sort in classical books we learn that this was the mirror of those days. In Han times mirrors of polished metal came into vogue.

his vision. When blind men look up and see no stars men
do not take this as decisive as to whether there are stars or
not. . . . Now if a man at such times came to a decision
about the objects, he would be the arch-ignoramus of his
age. The decision of such an ignoramus would be one of
resolving a doubt by what is doubtful: the conclusions he
drew would inevitably be invalid. If these be invalid how
can the mind avoid mistakes? . . .

．　　　　．　　　　．　　　　．　　　　．

Speaking generally, by knowing the congenital nature of
men it is possible to know the principles at work in things
[i.e. the material world]. It is possible (apparently) to
know the nature of men and by search to know the principles at work in things, so that all men's doubts are stopped;
but then it follows that they are not able in a lifetime to
include everything. Although the process of threading
the principles together might go on for a myriad years,
it would not suffice to embrace the changes in the myriad
things, so that men generally are in exactly the same position
as the ignoramus. . . .

Chapter 22. On the Rectification of Terms.

．　　　　．　　　　．　　　　．

With regard to the power in men of making abstract
terms:[1] 'life' expresses that whereby men come to birth
as they do. 'Congenital nature' expresses the subtle
harmony of stimulus and response which is spontaneous,
not premeditated, and which 'life'[2] makes in those it
brings to birth. 'Instinctive emotion' expresses the loving
and hating, the taking delight in and being annoyed by, the

[1] The evidence of Kung-Sun Lung's vocabulary points to the meaning
here being 'abstract.' It is, however, quite likely that Hsun Ch'ing had
no clear distinction in his mind between an abstract term and a general
term. As F. H. Bradley pointed out, the distinction between the two is
very difficult to make.
[2] Emending hsing (congenital nature) to sheng (life). Four sentences
later wei (man-made attainment) is emended to wei (formative action). By
this means is avoided the inexplicable fact that the author, according to
the text, gave two different definitions of each of these two items.

sorrow and joy which belong to the congenital nature.[1]
'Purposeful thinking' expresses the power which the mind
of man, thus emotionally constituted, has of making
selection. 'Formative action' expresses the energy of
activity which can come from the mind's purposeful thinking. 'The man-made' expresses the completed result of
piling up purposeful thinking, that is to say, the capacity
for continual practising. 'The business of life' expresses
formative action taken with a view to true profit. 'Good
conduct' expresses action taken with a view to true justice.
'The power to know'[2] expresses the correspondence with
the world without which knowing can produce. 'Undeveloped capacity' expresses that in men of which they
are able. 'Competence' expresses the correspondence
[? between thought and action] which undeveloped capacity
can produce.

.   .   .   .   .

Then the question is: What are the conditions under which
similarities and differences emerge (in the mind)? The
answer is: Under the conditions fixed by the senses. With
regard to things which are of the same species or have the
same instinctive emotions, the senses get the same im-
pressions of them as objects. Thus it is that men can
compare and place things, congeal them, so to speak, and
at the same time make them understandable: and thus make
a general name for them by agreement with a view to
intercommunication.

The (sense of) difference in relation to shapes and colour
patterns comes from the eye; the difference between purity
and confusion . . . of musical notes from the ear. The
difference between sweet and bitter . . . flavours from the
mouth, the difference between nice smells and nasty . . .
from the nose, the difference between pain and itching, cold

---

[1] The temptation is to translate by 'acquired character,' and this sense
suits certain passages very well, but not some other passages. In Hsun
Ch'ing's mind congenital nature and the man-made are direct opposites.
[2] Cp. 'the faculty of knowing' in Dr. Bodde's translation of Dr. Feng
Yu-lan's *History of Chinese Philosophy*, p. 303.

and heat, smoothness and roughness, lightness and heaviness, from the limbs: and the explanation of this lies in the fact that [1] the difference between being delighted and being annoyed, between grief and joy, between liking and disliking comes from the mind, and the mind has knowledge which is based on evidence [i.e. of the senses].

For knowledge to be based on these witnesses it must be conditioned, for knowledge of sound by the ear, for knowledge of shapes by the eye, before it can pass muster. But that means that such knowledge must wait for the approximate records by the senses before its classifications can pass muster. The five senses make records, but they do not know. The mind appeals to these witnesses, but if it has no explanation to offer, then all men are agreed that it does not know. These are the conditions under which similarities and differences emerge.

.   .   .   .   .

Although 'the myriad things' merely equal a total, there are times when we want to state an all-inclusive proposition. Thus it is that we speak of 'things,' the most general of all terms, pushing out [2] with wider and wider generalizations until we (have to) stop. There are times when we want to make a classificatory proposition, and thus it is that we speak of 'birds' and 'beasts,' the two biggest of classificatory terms.

A name is not inevitably appropriate. There has to be agreement in the matter with an authoritative naming, an agreed fixing of customary speech. Then a name can be called appropriate; and if it is different from the agreed on name, then it is to be called inappropriate.

A name has no inevitable actuality [3] (corresponding to it

---

[1] The text strikes me as a little dubious, but I cannot find any help in the commentators.

[2] *T'ui* would seem to be very near the idea of induction, and it is a question whether the translation should not be 'making wider and wider inductions.' But *t'ui*, I think, was not at this time used as a technical term.

[3] The temptation is to use 'substance.' It would seem to fit here, but in other passages it does not. In view of the history of 'substantive' in the West the philosopher may conjecture here, but with care.

in the object named). There has to be agreement with an authoritative designation of the actuality in question, an agreed fixing of custom in the matter. Then the name can be called the real name. . . .

There are objects which have the same appearance but are in different places; and there are objects which have a different appearance but are in the same place.[1] The distinction passes muster. With objects which have the same appearance but are in different places, however much they may tally, this is to be called 'two actualities.' Where the appearance changes but the actuality is not in another class in spite of the (resultant) difference, this is to be called 'transformation.' Where there is 'transformation' and not separate classification, this is to be called 'one actuality.' This is the practical way in which actualities are comparatively examined and the number of them can be settled. This shows the pivotal importance of systematizing terms. . . .

As he says in another part of the chapter, 'The man of learning divides up into separate classes in order to indicate actualities.' He then deals with the paradoxes, e.g. 'to kill a robber is not to kill a man,' 'a mountain and an abyss are on the same level,' 'an ox-horse is not a horse,' which the expert logicians had made current. He classifies these paradoxes as (a) those which by the fallacious use of names throw nomenclature into confusion; (b) those which by the fallacious use of actualities throw nomenclature into confusion; (c) those which by the fallacious use of names throw actualities into confusion.

III. *The State and the Individual.*

In the light of the above two sections on Heaven and the Congenital Nature of Man and on the Problem of Knowledge, it is to be expected that Hsun Ch'ing would have authoritarian ideas on the state in relation to the individual. Living as he did in an age which at every turn flouted the Confucian idea of true kingship, he worked out a theory of sovereignty which was as extreme in its own way as Mo Ti's. His, however, was much more realistic, much more sophisticated, as also much more psychologically discerning. It was equally concerned with

---

[1] The reference would appear to be in the first case to, e.g. horses, in the second to creatures subject to radical transformation, e.g. a grub and the butterfly which comes from it.

ethical ends.   In this last connection, Hsun Ch'ing showed how
fundamentally he disagreed with the Legalists in spite of his
authoritarian tendencies.   He may be said to have been saved
from that pit through his acute appreciation of the power of
ritual in education.   Man has to achieve an acquired character
if he is to be really civilized, and not have his passions tear his
Great Society in pieces.   This character requires educating, and,
although book learning is vitally important for those who are
capable of it, since by it the ways of the Sage-kings can be
known, the practice of common rituals is the great educative
force for every member of society.   It is here that Hsun Ch'ing
showed himself very much alive to the aesthetic side of life.

The following quotations deal first with the psychological
basis of society, then with the status of the pivotal person in
society, and finally with ritual.

Chapter 9. Systematic Rule by Kings.

· · · · ·

Water and fire have the primordial energy [ch'i] but not
life: plants and trees have life but not knowledge: birds and
beasts have knowledge but not a (sense of) justice.[1]   Man
has the primordial energy, life, and knowledge, and in
addition a sense of justice.   Thus it is that he is the noblest
being on earth.   In strength he does not equal the ox, nor
in power of running the horse; and yet he can utilize the ox
and horse.   Why this is so is because men are able to band
themselves together, whilst the others cannot.   Why men
are able to do so is because they make social distinctions;
and the (efficient) cause for these distinctions being put into
effect is man's sense of justice.   Thus it is that if there be
justice, then there will be concord.   If there be concord,
then men will be united: if united, then their strength will
be multiplied: if their strength be multiplied, then they will
be powerful: if powerful, then they will conquer the world
of creatures. . . . Thus it is that they follow the order of
the seasons and exercise control over the ten thousand
creatures, and amass profit from the whole world: and this
from no other cause than that they have gained class distinctions and a sense of justice.   Thus it is that men in life
cannot afford not to band themselves together.   If they

[1] In the wide Platonic sense of equity, including a positive ethical recognition of other people's rights.

should fail and there should be no social distinctions, then they would quarrel, and if they should quarrel they would fall into a state of anarchy: if so, then they would disband: if they should disband, then they would be weak, and being weak would be unable to conquer the other creatures. . . . And all this means that men must not for a moment discard ritual and justice.[1]

The meaning of 'filial piety' is ability in serving one's parents, the meaning of 'younger brother's duty' ability in serving one's elder brother, of 'obedience' ability in serving one's superiors, of 'sovereign authority' a king's ability in settling his subjects. For to be a sovereign means to be skilled at banding people together, and if the Great Way of banding together works properly, then the ten thousand creatures will all function duly . . . and the whole association of life will fulfil its destiny. . . .

The systematic rule of a Sage-king: when the plants and trees are in their glory of bud and leaf, the axe is not allowed in the woodland, so that their life may not be cut off. . . . When the sea-tortoises and water-lizards, the fishes and the turtles and eels and sturgeon are spawning, nets and poison are not allowed in the waters, so that their life may not be cut off. . . . The spring ploughing, the summer weeding, the autumn harvesting, and the winter storing are kept to time, with the result that the five sorts of grain do not fail and all the people have food and to spare. . . . This is a Sage-king's use of natural wealth. . . . The upshot is the One communicating oneness [i.e. unity] and so being A MAN. That is what I mean by a sage man.

.   .   .   .   .

Once there were the heavens and the earth, there was the distinction between upper and lower, and when the first enlightened king made a permanent state, there was social organization (with their class distinctions). Two nobles cannot serve each other, neither can two commoners set each other to work. This is the mathematics of Heaven.

---

[1] The *li yi* here might be rendered 'ritual-and-righteousness.'   Cp. p. 230.

If people's power and position be equal and their likes and
dislikes the same so that the amount of goods is not enough
to go round, then there will inevitably be quarrelling.   And
if quarrelling, then anarchy, if anarchy, then penury.   The
early kings hated the anarchy they saw, and thus it was that
they organized rituals and social rights and thus made the
distinction of classes.   They made the people have degrees
in poverty and wealth, in nobility and commonalty to the
extent that they were all linked together by being under
someone's authority.   This was the root from which the
Great Society was grown.

    . . . Advance the worthy and competent in the service
of the state without depending on seniority, and discharge
the incompetent without depending on time (to make them
competent).   Execute ringleaders in wickedness without
depending on the (possibility of) their reform, and bring
transforming influences to bear on plain ordinary people
without depending on government measures. . . . Although a man be a descendant of the royal or ducal houses
. . . if he cannot attach himself to ritual-and-righteousness,
then put him where he belongs among the common people;
and, although a man be the son of common people, if he
pile culture on learning, rectify his personal conduct and
can attach himself to ritual-and-righteousness, then put
him where he belongs among the ministers and high
officers of state.   The people who talk outrageously and
have outrageous theories, who act outrageously and have a
capacity for being outrageous, should be given responsible
work and have a little time in which to reform.   Encourage
them with rewards and warn them with punishments.   If
they go on happily in their work, look after them: if they
do not, then exile them.   Supply the needs of the five kinds
of deformed people, employing those who have gifts, but
all without exception getting food and clothing from the
authorities.   Put the incorrigible to death without mercy.
This is what people mean by 'Heaven's moral power' [te].[1]
This is government by a true king.

[1] Hsun Ch'ing hardly ever uses *te*.

Chapter 15. A Debate on Military Matters.

· · · · ·

Ritual is the highest administrative duty,[1] the source of a country's strength, the way [*tao*] of majesty in action, the guiding principle of honour. By the practice of it kings and dukes possess the land, by failing to practise it they lose the altars they have to the gods of the soil [i.e. lose their positions of authority].

There are three sources to Ritual. Heaven and Earth are the source of its existence, our ancestors the source of its being in a class by itself, sovereigns and teachers the source of its disciplinary power. Without Heaven and Earth how could it have come to be?[2] Without our ancestors how could it have emerged? Without sovereigns and teachers how could it have disciplined men? If any of these had been lacking, there would not have been this pacifying influence among men. Thus it is that there is Ritual, the ritual serving of Heaven above, of Earth below, the reverencing of ancestors and the honouring of sovereigns and teachers.

· · · · ·

A rite in the beginning consists of a rough reproduction,[3] comes to completion with the art in it, and finishes in producing joy. Thus it is that in the most perfect form of ritual, emotion and art are completely expressed together. At a point below perfection in a rite either emotion or art gains the mastery: and below that, emotion comes (sweeping) back by reason of a reversion to excessive oneness [? identification of oneself with the rite].

Perfect indeed is Ritual (as sacramental act symbolizing)

[1] Emending *pien* to *pan*.
[2] This is not rodomontade. All great traditional rituals are sacramental representations of the nature of the universe.
[3] Following the *Shih Chi* version of the text and the standard comment there; but I suggest that it is possible Hsun Ch'ing meant by *t'o* 'escape' in the modern psychologist's sense. Cp. Malinowski in *Science, Religion, and Reality*.

the heavens and the earth in their harmony,[1] the sun and moon in their splendour, the four seasons in their succession, the stars in their movements, the rivers and streams in their flow, the ten thousand creatures in their abundance, liking and disliking in due (expression), delight and vexation with fitting (force), in the lower orders of society (the expression of) obedience, in the higher orders (the expression of) shining intelligence, with all creation (unceasingly) changing, yet without confusion, for if the unity of creation were lost, the loss would be irredeemable.

Chapter 2. *On the Cultivation of Oneself.*

In all matters relating to the functioning of the body and the mind, if they are in keeping with Ritual, there will be a far-reaching self-control: if they are not, there will be a disordering of the rhythm in living. Thus in eating and drinking, in clothing and housing,[2] in (the alternation of) energetic action with stillness, if these matters are in keeping with Ritual, then there is the harmony of moderation: if they are not, then there is physical collapse and disease. In matters of outward appearance and bearing, in meeting and parting with people, in one's style of walking, if these are in keeping with Ritual, there is the beauty of refinement about them: if they are not, then they show arrogance, surliness, vulgarity, and a barbarous spirit. Thus it is that without Ritual man cannot live, nor his business in life succeed, nor his states and families abide.

.   .   .   .   .

With regard to the art of controlling the vital energy in a man and of nurturing the mind-will: in the case of over-

[1] Dr. Dubs translates 'Li (ritual) as that whereby Heaven and Earth unite, whereby the sun and moon are bright . . .' and adds in a foot-note, 'Li (ritual) is here equated to the *Tao*.' While admitting that to Hsun Ch'in *li* was a mystic force, I find it hard to believe that he went to that length. Even in his *fu* poem on *li*, he does not.
[2] 'Housing' is a direct reference to sex hygiene. In this, as in eating and clothing, a seasonal rhythm was coming to be emphasized as having far-reaching implications of moral as well as physical health.

bearing temperaments, they need to be made gentle by learning to agree with others. In the case of conscious [1] thought-plans going too deep, they need to be integrated by the case of simple goodness. In the case of valour running to cruelty, it needs to be guided by obedience to principle. In the case of a smart kind of zeal which is out for cheap advantage, it needs to be moderated by ceasing from action of any sort. In the case of meanness and sordidness, it needs to be enlarged by (acts of) generosity. In the case of a sense of inferiority, of being slow to act, or of avarice, there is need for salvation by noble endeavours. In the case of one as common as may be, a mere drudge, there is need of violent measures, namely the most intimate contact with a fine teacher. In the case of lack of respect for others or for oneself, there is need for a man to be faced with calamity. . . . Thus in all these cases of the vital energy needing to be controlled and the mind-will needing to be nurtured, the art of it lies along no other path than that of Ritual. . . .

Ritual entails sedulous care over the ordering of matters concerning birth and death. Birth is the beginning of a man, death the end. If the end and the beginning be completely good, man's Way [*Tao*] is consummated. Thus it is that the high-minded man [*chun tzu*] has veneration for the beginning of life and is scrupulous over the end. To him the two are as one, for this is the way of the high-minded man, this is his cultivation of ritual-and-righteousness. Should there be an overestimate of life and an underestimate of death, this would mean veneration for what man has knowledge of, and blasphemy over that of which he has no knowledge. That is the way of the wicked, of profane minds; and for the high-minded man to have such a mind even in his treatment of a slave would be his

---

[1] *Chih* (knowledge): some passages in which *chih* occurs seem to get so near to what we call 'consciousness' that one can hardly refrain from translating it as such. The truth of it, perhaps, in relation to men like Hsun Ch'ing, lies in their unconsciously accepting knowledge as nothing but things consciously known, just as emotions were things consciously felt. Hence no urge to have a special term for consciousness.

*K 973

disgrace. How much more would it be so if he did service
in this manner to one he honoured and loved.

.   .   .   .   .

Expressions of pleasure and complacence, of misery and
disgust, these appear on people's faces, representing the
emotions attendant on good and bad fortune. Singing and
joking, weeping and wailing represent the corresponding
emotions in the voice.

The same symbolism is then traced in food and drink, in
clothes, and in the different kinds of rooms people live in under
happy and unhappy conditions, e.g. for filial sons mourning
their father and mother and living in a lean-to hut with firewood
for a seat and a clod of earth for a pillow. The culmination of
this argument brings Hsun Ch'ing to his contrast between life
in the raw, i.e. according to congenital nature, and life man-
made, the life of acquired (*wei*) culture and civilization. From
that he passes on to a detailed psychological analysis of mourning rites, winding up with an exaltation of the rite of memorial
sacrifice. Throughout, the recurrent theme is this dramatic
act of ritual by which the destructive tyranny of undisciplined
instinctive emotion is broken and man can become man in the
fullest as well as the highest sense.

Men at birth have in their lives the shoots of these two
kinds of emotion [viz. joy and sorrow]. To cut emotions
short and to prolong them, to give a wide and a narrow
range to them, to increase and diminish them, to assimilate
and exhaust them, to make them fine and beautiful, so that
the trunk and the branches, the beginning and the end (of
life) at all points are in accord in a way which makes a
pattern for ten thousand generations, this is what Ritual
is: and unless there be the devoted practice of Ritual, a
high-minded man has no way of being able to know it.

Thus it is that I maintain that congenital nature is the
beginning, the raw material, and the acquired is the exquisite
product of art. Without the congenital nature the acquired
cannot be added on, whilst without the acquired the congenital nature cannot of itself be beautiful. It is not until
there is the harmony of nature and the acquired that the
terms 'sage' and 'man' become one, for this is the way in
which the virtue of the Great Society is completed.

Thus it is that I maintain that as when Heaven and Earth were in accord the ten thousand creatures came to life, as when the Yin and the Yang began to follow each other (the principle of) change began to work, so when congenital nature and the acquired come to be in accord, the society of man becomes ordered. (For) Heaven can bring things to life but cannot distinguish them, Earth can sustain man but cannot order him, and beneath the canopy of heaven all species of creatures and living men depend on the Sage Man that they may find their proper stations (in life).

.   .   .   .   .

A Sacrifice to the dead is a piling up of memories and intentions, of thoughts and longings. . . . Thus it was that former kings established this beautiful cult, and the justice of honouring the honourable and loving the beloved reached its perfection.   Thus it is that I maintain that sacrifice is the height of loyalty and love, the crowning point in the ordered rhythm of ritual and in the outward form of civilized refinement, and that unless a man be a sage he has no way of knowing this.   The sages comprehend this: leaders in society put it into practice: the officials make it a matter of strict duty: the people regard it as custom: high-minded men think of it as 'the human way,' whilst the people look on it as ghostly business.

CHAPTER XVII: HAN FEI AND HIS MYSTIC MATERIALISM

Han Fei (*d.* 233 B.C.) was like Shang Yang in that he found no scope for his talents in his own country and accordingly sought for an opening in Ch'in State. There he was less fortunate than Shang Yang. He was regarded with suspicion and put under detention. The duke's minister, afraid of Han Fei supplanting him in the duke's favour, secretly urged him to commit suicide. This he did, and that was the end of him as a man. But not as an influence, for he had great literary gifts, and his writings have survived.

The *Book of Han Fei* contains fifty-five chapters, or rather essays, less than half perhaps by Han Fei himself, but all showing on the whole the typical Legalist view of man as a creature to be ruled for his own good through his material desires and his fear of suffering. There are, however, traces of something higher in the book, as we might expect, seeing that Han Fei started his career as a disciple of Hsun Ch'ing. Thus in many parts of the book we find an unconscious emphasis on the necessity of being true to the truth of things. Further, the book shows a very marked appreciation of Taoist principles as set forth in the *Tao Te Ching*.

Han Fei clearly used his exceptional intellectual powers to master the implications of this way of thinking. In the last resort, however, he was concerned with politics, the material well-being of a nation. With this as his objective he examined previous Legalist theories and made a synthesis of them. The authority (*shih*) of the sovereign was vitally important, as Shen Tao had taught: also the undeviating administration of the law, as Shang Yang had insisted. But these two were not enough. There was need for statecraft (*shu*) on the part of the sovereign, if he was to keep his team of administrators both loyal to him and incorruptible upholders of the law.

In this book the Legalist School is seen at the peak of its development, a school of thought which, as the Introduction has explained, is the nearest counterpart in China to West European post-medieval political theory.

There is so much material in this book, and some of the chapters are so long, not to say discursive, that the quotations have been grouped under headings.

I. *Concerning the Three Main Emphases in Legalist Theory.*

Nothing is more valuable than the royal person, more honourable than the throne, more powerful than the authority of the sovereign, and more august than the position of the ruler. These **four** excellences are **not** obtained from outside, nor secured from anybody else, but are deliberated in the ruler's own mind and acquired thereby. . . . This the ruler of men must keep firmly in mind.

(Chapter 4.)

Master Shen [i.e. Shen Tao, fourth century] said, 'A flying dragon rides the winds, a floating serpent wanders through the mist on the water; but when the clouds disperse and the mist is gone, a dragon and a serpent are no different from a cricket or an ant. They have lost what they depended on. Thus the reason why a man of worth may be overpowered by a worthless one is that the able man's power is weak and his position humble. And the reason why a worthless man submits to a man of worth is that the able man's power is strong and his position high. Yao [the Sage-king] as a common man could not have governed three people, whilst Chieh [the villain-king] as Son of Heaven could bring the whole of society into confusion. Thus I know that authority and position are to be trusted, ability and wisdom are not particularly desirable. . . . It was when Yao ascended the throne and was king over the Great Society that what he commanded was done, what he banned was not done. From this angle I see that worth and wisdom are not enough to subdue a population whilst authority and position are enough to overpower men of worth.'

To this the reply is made, 'In the case of a dragon . . . riding the clouds, I do not regard the dragon as not depending on the clouds. . . . None the less, if worth is discarded and reliance put solely on authority, is it enough to produce good government? If it is, I have never seen it. There is something which goes along with the particular prestige of clouds and makes the dragon able to ride them . . .; and this something is the dragon's, or the serpent's, special quality. . . . However thick the clouds and mist might be, the quality of the cricket or the ant is not up to the mark. In the case of a Chieh, seated on the throne and using the majesty of the Son of Heaven as clouds and mist, society nevertheless cannot escape great confusion; and this because a Chieh's quality is inadequate. What is more, supposing a sovereign using the authority of a Yao to govern the Great Society, how different that authority is from the kind which makes confusion! . . . The sovereigns who use their authority to make confusion are many, those who use their authority to make order are few. . . .'

(Chapter 40, on *Authority a Problem*.)

No country is permanently strong, nor is any country permanently weak. If conformers to law are strong, the country is strong; if conformers to law are weak, the country is weak. . . . Any ruler able to expel private crookedness and uphold public law finds the people become law-abiding and the state ordered; and any ruler able to eradicate individualistic action and act on public law finds his army become strong and his enemy weak. So, find out men who follow the discipline of laws and regulations, and place them above the body of officials. Then the sovereign cannot be deceived by anybody with fraud and falsehood. . . .

Now supposing promotions were made because of mere reputation, then ministers would be estranged from the sovereign and all officials would associate for treasonable purposes. Supposing officials were appointed on account of their partisanship, then the people would strive to cultivate friendships and never seek employment in accordance with the law. Thus, with the government lacking able men, the state will fall into confusion. If rewards are bestowed according to mere reputation, and punishments are inflicted according to mere defamation, then men who love rewards and hate punishments will discard public law and practise self-seeking tricks and associate for rebellious purposes. . . . Therefore, the intelligent sovereign makes the law select men, and makes no arbitrary regulation himself. In consequence able men cannot be obscured, bad characters cannot be disguised, falsely praised fellows cannot be advanced, wrongly defamed people cannot be degraded. In consequence the distinction between ruler and minister becomes clear and order is attained. . . .

Hence to govern the state by law is to praise the right and blame the wrong. The law does not fawn on the noble, (just as) an inked string [1] does not follow a crooked line. Whatever the law applies to, the wise cannot reject it nor the brave defy it. Punishment for fault never skips ministers, and reward for good never misses commoners. Therefore for correcting the faults of the high, for rebuking the vices of the low, for suppressing disorders, for deciding against mistakes, for subduing the arrogant, for straightening the crooked, and for unifying the folk-ways of the masses, nothing can match with the law: for warning officials and overaweing the people, for rebuking obscenity and danger and for forbidding falsehood and deceit, nothing can match with penalties. If they are strictly administered, no discrimination is made between noble and commoner. If the law is definite, superiors are esteemed and not flouted. If superiors are not flouted, the sovereign will become strong and able to maintain the proper course of government. This was the reason why the early kings esteemed legalism and handed it down to posterity.

(Chapter 6, on *Having Fixed Measurements*.)

The question is asked, 'Of the words of the two experts, Shen Pu-hai [2] and Lord Shang, which are the more vital to the state?' The answer is given, 'It is impossible to estimate. If for ten days a man does not eat, then he will die. Also, if the weather is very cold and a man has no clothes, he will die. If you ask which of the two, (food or clothes,) is more vital to the man, the answer is that he cannot do without either of them. They are both articles for the nourishing of life. Now Shen Pu-hai spoke about statecraft, whilst Lord Shang made laws. Statecraft consists in making awards to the officers on the basis of responsibility, of their keeping 'the name and the actuality' in

---

[1] An inked string stretched between two twigs and flicked on to the surface of a board was (and is to-day) a carpenter's device to get a straight line along which to cut.
[2] The first Legalist to emphasize statecraft (*shu*). His works have not survived.

accord. It consists in keeping in one's own hands the power over life and death and the examination of one's ministers' capabilities. A master of men [1] keeps firm hold of this.

The law is the pattern on which the orders from government offices are modelled. The penalties of the law are sure to be kept in mind by the people. The rewards of the law are kept for those who carefully observe the law, whilst the punishments are for those who wickedly disobey orders. Thus the law is a guide to ministers. If a ruler be without statecraft, there is weakness above: if the ministers without the law, there is confusion below.

(Chapter 43, on *Fixing the Law*.)

That which enables the tiger to subject the dog is his claw and fang. Supposing the tiger cast aside its claws and fangs and let the dog use them, the tiger would in turn be subjected by the dog. The lord of men controls his ministers by his personal power of punishing and rewarding. Now supposing the ruler of men to discard the two handles of punishment and reward and let the ministers use them, the ruler would in turn be controlled by the ministers.

(Chapter 7, on *The Two Handles*.)

To subdue a tiger without the help of a cage, to suppress a culprit without the help of the law, or to impede a liar without the help of the tally, would worry Pen and Yü [2] very badly and be a difficulty for Yao and Shun. Therefore, to construct a cage is not to provide against rats but to enable the weak and timid to subdue tigers: to establish laws is not to provide against Tseng Ts'an and Shih Ch'iu but to enable the average sovereign to prohibit Robber Che; and to make tallies is not to guard against Wei Sheng [a model of probity] but to make the masses never deceive one another. Thus the right way is not to rely on Pi Kan's martyrdom in the cause of fidelity, nor to count on a rapacious minister's committing no deception, but to rely on

[1] The Legalist writers all used *jen chu* for sovereign (master of men), the Confucianists used *jen chun* (men's sovereign).
[2] Pen and Yü were two warriors, famous for their strength in battle.

the ability of the timid to subdue the tiger and appropriate the facilities of the average sovereign to maintain the state.

(Chapter 26, on *The Right Way* [*Tao*] *to Guard the State*.)

The great difficulty of the lord of men is in the matter of confidence.   Confiding in men, he is limited by men.[1]

Ministers, in relation to the ruler, have no tie of kinship, but serve him solely because constrained by force of circumstances.   Therefore those who minister to a ruler always watch the mental condition of their master without stopping even for a moment; whereas the lord of men remains idle and arrogant over them.   This is the reason why the world sees cases of 'ruler-molestation' and regicide.

If the lord of men has much confidence in his son, then wicked ministers will utilize his son to accomplish their selfish purposes. . . . If the lord of men has much confidence in his wife, then wicked ministers will utilize her to accomplish their selfish purposes. . . .

Indeed, even the wife who is so near and the son who is so dear to the sovereign are not trustworthy: much less can anybody else be trustworthy. . . .

The physician sucks patients' cuts and holds their blood in his mouth, not because he is intimate with them like a blood relation, but because he expects profit from them. Likewise, when the cartwright finishes making carriages, he wants people to be rich and noble; when the carpenter finishes making coffins, he wants people to die early.   Not that the cartwright is benevolent and the carpenter is cruel, but that unless people are noble, the carriages will not sell, and unless people die, the coffins will not be bought.   Thus the carpenter's motive is not hatred for anybody, but his profits which are due to people's death.   For the same reason, when the clique of the queen, the princess, the concubine, or the crown prince is formed, they want the ruler to die early; for, unless the ruler die, their positions will not be powerful.   Their motive is not hatred for the ruler, but their profits are dependent on the ruler's death.   Therefore

---

[1] In this and the succeeding quotations emphasis is laid on statecraft.

the lord of men must specially mind those who will profit by his death. By way of illustration, though the sun and the moon are surrounded by haloes, the causes of their eclipses are inside themselves. Similarly, though the ruler guards against what he hates, the causes of his calamity consist in what he loves. For this reason, the intelligent sovereign will never undertake any inadvisable enterprise nor eat any inordinate food, but will listen to all about him and observe everybody closely in order thereby to scrutinize the faults of the interior and the exterior (of the palace): and he will reflect on the arguments for and against (brought to his attention,) and thereby learn the line of demarcation between different factions: he will compare the results of the evidence given, and so be able to insist on every utterance having an equivalent in fact. Holding that there is a parity between cause and effect, he will govern the masses in accordance with the law and gather material of all sorts for comparison and observation. Thus nobody will receive any undue reward or overstep the limits of his duties; every murderer will be sentenced to the proper penalty, and no criminal will be pardoned. If the ruler can do this, there will be no room left for villainous persons accomplishing their self-seeking purposes.

(Chapter 17, on *Internal Precautions*.)

Hold firmly to your decisions and make the (public) words and deeds of your subordinates identical with them. Cautiously take the handles (of reward and punishment) and hold them fast. Uproot others' desire of them: smash others' thought of them: let nobody covet them. If the ruler does not exercise care in keeping the gate locked and in good repair, tigers will get in: if the ruler does not take precautions for his sway, and if he does not protect his prestige,[1] traitors will make their appearance; for the man who murders his sovereign and takes his place and finds the whole people side with him in awe is rightly called a tiger, and the man who serves the country by his sovereign's

[1] Reading *shih* (prestige).

side and watches for his secret faults with villainous motives is rightly called a traitor. Scatter their partisans, arrest their supporters, lock the gate, and deprive them of all assistance. Then there will be no tigers in the country.

Be too great to be measured, too profound to be surveyed. Identify norms and names, scrutinize laws and manners, and chastise those doing as they please. Then there will be no traitors in the country. . . . Hence the saying, 'The ruler must not reveal his wants; for if he reveals his wants, the ministers will polish their manners accordingly. The ruler must not reveal his views; for if he reveals his views, the ministers will display their hues differently. If the likes and dislikes of the ruler be concealed, the true hearts of the ministers will be revealed. If the experience and wisdom of the ruler be discarded, the ministers will take precautions.' Accordingly the ruler, wise though he may be, should not bother but let everything find its proper place: talented [1] though he may be, he should not take action but observe the line his ministers take: courageous though he may be, he should not be enraged but let every minister display his prowess. So let the ruler put his wisdom aside, and he will discover his ministers' intelligence: let him put his worthiness aside, and he will discover his ministers' merits: let him put his courage aside, and he will discover his ministers' strength. In these circumstances ministers attend to their duties, magistrates have a definite work routine, and everybody will be employed according to his special ability. Such a course of government I affirm to be constant and immutable.

(Chapter 5, on *The Tao of the Sovereign*.)

II. *The Taoist Background to Han Fei's Political Theories.*

Tao is the beginning of the myriad things, the criterion of right and wrong. That being so, the intelligent ruler by holding to the beginning knows the source of everything, and by preserving the criterion knows the origin of good and evil. Therefore, by virtue of resting empty and

[1] Changing the places of *hsing* and *hsien*.

reposed, he waits for the course of nature to enforce itself so that all names will be defined of themselves and all affairs will be settled of themselves. Himself empty, he knows the essence of fullness: himself reposed, he becomes the corrector of motion. Who utters a word creates himself a name; who has an affair creates himself a form. Compare forms and names and see if they are identical. Then the ruler will find nothing to regret, since everything is reduced to its reality. . . . Tao exists in invisibility; its function lies in unintelligibility. Be empty and reposed and have nothing to do. Then from the dark see defects in the light. See, but never be seen. Hear, but never be heard. Know, but never be known. If you hear a word uttered, do not change it or move it, but compare it with the deed and see if word and deed coincide with each other.

(Chapter 5, on *The Tao of the Sovereign*.)

Virtue is internal.[1] Acquirement is external. 'Superior virtue [*te*] is non-virtue': this means that the mind does not indulge in external things. If the mind does not indulge in external things, the personality will become perfect. The personality that is perfect is to be called an 'acquirement.' In other words, true acquirement is the acquirement of personality.

In general virtue begins with non-assertion, develops with non-wanting, rests secure with non-thinking, and is impregnable with non-using. If it acts and wants, it becomes restless: if it is restless, it is not perfect. If it is put into use and thought about, it is not impregnable: if it is not impregnable, it cannot work successfully. If it is not perfect and cannot work successfully, it becomes self-assertive virtue. If virtue becomes self-assertive virtue, it is non-virtue. Contrary to this, if virtue is non-virtue, it has virtue. Hence the saying: 'Superior virtue is non-virtue, and therefore has virtue.'

The reason why men value non-assertion and non-thinking as emptiness is because by remaining empty one's

[1] This passage, of which about one-sixth is quoted, is in the nature of an exegesis of the *Tao Te Ching*, c. 38. There are ten other such passages expounding other chapters of the *Tao Te Ching*.

will is not ruled by anything. What happens is that in-
genuous people consciously aim at non-assertion and non-
thinking as emptiness, and the inevitable result is that, as
they do this, they never forget emptiness. They are thus
ruled by the will to emptiness. By 'emptiness' is meant the
state of the will not ruled by anything. To be controlled
(in one's will) by the pursuit of emptiness is *ipso facto* not
emptiness. When he who rests empty does not assert, he
does not regard non-assertion as being in a constant
direction. If he does not regard non-assertion as being in
a constant direction, he is then empty. If he is empty, his
virtue flourishes. The virtue that flourishes is to be called
'superior virtue.' Hence the saying, 'Superior virtue is
non-assertion without any pretension.' . . .

(Commentary on *Tao Te Ching*, c. 38.)

The Tao is the way of everything, the form of every
principle [*li*]. Principles are the lines along which things
are completed. Tao is the cause of the completion of
everything. Hence the saying, 'It is Tao that rules everything.' Things have their respective principles and therefore cannot trespass against each other. Inasmuch as
things have their respective principles and therefore cannot
trespass against each other, principles are determinants of
things and everything has a unique principle. Inasmuch as
everything has its unique principle and Tao disciplines the
principles of all things, everything has to go through the
process of transformation. Inasmuch as everything has to
go through the process of transformation, it has no fixed
frame. Since everything has no fixed frame, the course of
life and death depends upon Tao, knowledge of every conceivable sort conforms to it, and the rise and decline of
every kind of affair is due to it. The heavens can be high
because of it: earth can hold everything because of it: the
Pole Star can have its majesty because of it: the sun and
the moon can make constant illumination because of it:
the Five Forces can keep their positions constant because of
it: all the stars can keep their orbits right because of it: the

four seasons can control their diverse expressions because of it. . . . It was manifested in the wisdom of Yao and Shun, in the rampancy of Chieh-yü, in the destruction of Chieh and Chou, and in the prosperity of T'ang and Wu. Near as you might suppose it to be, it travels to the four extremities of the world: far as you might suppose it to be, it always abides by the side of everybody: dim as you might suppose it to be, its gleam is glittering: bright as you might suppose it to be, its body is obscure. By its achievement heaven and earth are formed: by its harmony thundering is transformed. Thus everything in the world owes it its formation. By nature the inner reality of Tao is neither restrained nor embodied.

It is either soft or weak according as the occasion is, but is always in correspondence with principle. Because of it everything dies: thanks to it everything lives. Because of it every affair fails: thanks to it every affair succeeds. Tao can be compared to water. The man who is drowning dies as he drinks too much of it: the man who is thirsty lives on as he drinks a proper amount of it. Again, it can be compared to a sword or a spear. If the stupid man uses it for wreaking his vengeance on others, calamities will happen. If the saintly man uses it for punishing the outrageous, good fortune will ensue. Thus people die of it, live owing to it, fail because of it, and succeed on account of it. Men rarely see living elephants. When they come on the skeleton of a dead elephant [*hsiang*], they imagine it alive according to the configuration of the bones. The result is that whatever people use for imagining Reality is called 'an image' [*hsiang*].[1] Though Tao cannot be heard and seen, the saintly man imagines its real features in the light of its present effects. Hence the saying, 'It is the form of the formless, the image of the imageless.'

(Commentary on the *Tao Te Ching*, c. 14.) [2]

---

[1] The ideograph *hsiang* in Han Fei's age had the two meanings, one the original pictograph meaning of 'elephant,' the other the derived metaphorical meaning of 'image' or 'symbol.' When the metaphorical usage first began we do not know as yet.

[2] Chapter 21 consists of twenty-four anecdotes about famous people in illustration of sayings in the *Tao Te Ching*.

Once Wang Shou was carrying books on his back as he travelled. He met Hsü Feng in Chou, and Hsü Feng said to him, 'Any task is any act, action arises from the needs of the time; and time has no permanent tasks. Books contain sayings, sayings arise from knowledge; and a well-informed person does not have to keep books by him. Now, why should you carry these books round with you?' Hearing this, Wang Shou burned the books and danced with joy. For the same reason well-informed persons do not teach with sayings, and intelligent persons do not fill cases with books. This is what the world ignores; but Wang Shou reverted to it. In other words, he learned to be not learned. Hence the saying, 'He learns to be not learned and reverts to what multitudes of people ignore.'

(Illustrations of the *Tao Te Ching*, c. 64.)

The King of Yüeh, after surrendering himself to Wu, showed its ruler how to invade Ch'i, this with a view to exhausting Wu's strength. The troops of Wu, having defeated Ch'i's men at the Mugwort Mound, expanded their forces from the Chiang and the Ch'i and displayed their strength at the Yellow Pool. The result was that it became possible for the King of Yüeh to rout Wu's men at Lake Five. Hence the saying, 'When you are about to weaken anything, you should strengthen it.'

(Illustrations of the *Tao Te Ching*, c. 36.)

III. *Han Fei's View of Human Nature.*

To-day of all the things which all ranks in society hold in common there is nothing like the warm feelings between sons and fathers; and any one who wants to act on the basis of public morality and issue prohibitions to those under his jurisdiction must needs take into account the intimacy of the flesh-and-blood relation. But there is something more in the relationship of fathers and mothers with their sons. If a son is born, then they congratulate

each other. If a daughter is born, they (may) kill it.[1] Both
these have come out of the mother's womb, and when it is
a boy, congratulations, when it is a girl, death! The
parents are thinking of convenience later on. They calcu-
late on long-term profit. Thus it is that even fathers and
mothers in relation to their children have calculating minds
and treat them accordingly. . . . To-day men of learning
in their attempts to please the Master of men all have a
mind in pursuit of profit, and this goes beyond the Way
[*Tao*] of loving one another. This means valuing the
Master of men's affection above the affection of father
and mother. . . .

Sage-like government is scrupulous as to the law's prohibitions. If these are perfectly clear, then the officials
keep the law. Good government of necessity involves
rewards and punishments. If these are impartial, the
people can be put to use, and the officials will be in control.
If they are in control, then the country will be rich. If the
country is rich, then the armies will be powerful, and the
business of achieving supremacy (over other states) will be
accomplished. For the Master of men to be supreme as
king is the supreme profit.

(Chapter 46, on *Six Paradoxes*.)

Eels are like snakes, silkworms like caterpillars. Men
are frightened at the sight of snakes and shocked at the
sight of caterpillars. However, fishermen will hold eels in
the hand, and women will pick up silkworms. Thus,
where there is profit, there every one turns as brave as
Meng Pen and Chuan Chu.

(Chapter 23, on *Collected Persuasions*.)

IV. *Miscellaneous*.

Take for illustration the truism that water overpowers
fire. Yet, when a tripod kettle is placed between them,

[1] There was this practice of infanticide, a practice which persisted. It
occurred when girl after girl was born. Two causes account for it, one
the religious imperative of giving birth to a son to carry on the ancestral
sacrifices, the other the poverty of a family.

then the water will be heated and boiled till it dries up over the fire, while the fire can flame with vigour and continue burning under the water. Indeed, the fact that government forbids wickedness is still clearer than this. Yet, when ministers who ought to uphold the law play the part of the tripod kettle by standing between ruler and subject, then the law, however clear in the sovereign's mind, has already lost the reason of its existence, namely, to forbid wickedness.

(Chapter 17, on *Internal Precautions*.)

By way of illustration, if a mirror is kept clear and has nothing blocking its face, then the beautiful and the ugly can be compared: if a balance is kept even and is not interfered with, then the light and the heavy can be weighed. When you shake the mirror, the mirror cannot remain clear: when you shake the balance, the balance cannot keep even. The same is true of the law. . . . The true path and the law are absolutely reliable: wisdom and ability are liable to error. In the same way, suspend the balance and you know (by) the evenness (what the weight of a thing is). Revolve the compasses and you know a circle is there. This is an absolutely reliable way.[1]

(Chapter 19, on *Pretensions and Heresies*.)

In general, anything that has a form can easily be cut and easily trimmed. How can I prove this? Well, if the thing has form, it has length [2]: if it has length, it has size: if it has size, it has a shape: if it has a shape, it has solidity: if it has solidity, it has weight: and if it has weight, it has colour. Now, length, size, shape, solidity, weight, and colour are called principles [*li*]. As these are fixed, the thing can easily be cut. Therefore, if you present discussions first in the government and draw your conclusion from them later, then thoughtful and plan-making people will know the right decisions to make. Likewise, supposing you wanted

[1] The scientist's idea of dial readings would seem to have struck this thinker.
[2] Cp. this argument with the *Mean-in-action*, c. 26. The language used there is very different, as also is the final conclusion.

to construct squares and circles and submitted to the guidance of the compasses and T-square, then you would obtain any shape which you required.   Just as every circle and square drawn is after the patterns which the compasses and T-square make, so thinkers and speakers must keep to a rigid pattern.   Sages entirely submit to the compasses and T-squares of the myriad things.   Hence the saying, 'They dare not be in advance of the world of experience.'
(Chapter 20, Commentaries on Lao Tzu's Teachings.)

Chapter XVIII: The Metaphysics of the 'Changes Scripture'

The *Hsi Tz'u* (Additional Judgments Amplification).

This amplification is the most impressive, as it has been philosophically the most influential, of the *Ten Wings* of the *Yi Scripture*. There seem to be two or more strata of thought in it; in other words, further amplification of an original amplification. The latest in date of these additions is the striking passage on the sages of old and the very practical inspiration which they derived from this diagrammatic form of thinking. The connecting thread to the various parts of the amplification is that undirected speculation about the universe gets the thinker nowhere. He requires a scaffolding of thought, and here in these sixty-four hexagrams and their symbols he has that scaffolding. Part of the Chinese fervour for logic was side-tracked along these lines.

The section on the Sage-kings reflects ways of phase (cp. p. 273) interpretation which got going in the first century B.C. and which reached their height in the first and second centuries A.D. Cp. *Ch'ien Han Shu* (*Ju Lin Chuan*) and the *Chiu Chia Yi*.

The Master said, 'The written word does not entirely express the spoken word, nor the spoken word the idea in the mind.' 'Is it then impossible to know [lit. see] the ideas of the sages?' The Master said, 'The sages made symbols in order to give complete expression to their ideas, and made the Trigrams and Hexagrams in order to distinguish absolutely between truth and error.' Here, then, are the 'Linked-on Judgments' (to these trigrams and hexagrams). By them complete expression is given to the sages' spoken words, transforming on the widest scale so that they produce the greatest public good, stimulating like drums and dances so that they bring out the divine (in man) to the full.

The Yin and Yang forces in the universe, do they not involve the tangled skein of change? With these forces coming in ordered juxtaposition the principle of change is established within their scope of operations. For, if these two forces were abolished there would be no way by which changes could emerge to view, and if changes could not so emerge, the heavens and the earth would almost cease to function.

Hence, while beyond the material realm there are what are called *tao* [i.e. controlling principles], within the material realm there are what are called *ch'i* [i.e. things serving limited ends]; and the transformation of these into selected forms is what is called 'making changes' [? progress], the application of them on a wider scale 'generalization,' the adoption of them by the whole society of men 'the business of life' [? material civilization].

Hence symbols are what the sages used for discerning the complex (phenomena) of our world of experience. By them they were able to make detailed comparisons as to forms and appearances and make emblematic representations of types of things. . . . This is why they are called 'symbols.' The sages used them to discern the energy of activity amongst men, observing the associating and inter-communicating that went with it, that so they might put into effect their authoritative institutions. Here then are the Linked-on Judgments, that so there may be a clear decision as to which bring good fortune and which evil.

Hence there are what are called the *Hsiao* [the inter-related lines] which as the full expression of the complexity in our world subsist in the Trigrams and Hexagrams, and which as the stimulators of energy in our world subsist in the Propositions. The transformations which go on according to pattern in them subsist in the making of changes (in society), and the pressing of them into actual practice subsists in their interpenetration (throughout society), whilst their superhuman brilliance subsists in the persons (who made them). (These persons) silently completed them. Thus without any speechifying on their part they were trusted, (a state of affairs) which subsisted in their practice of spiritual power.

      •   •   •   •

The sublime power [*te*] in heaven-and-earth is known by

its (giving of) life, and the sublime treasure of the sages [1] is known by their authoritative position (enabling them to exercise far-reaching influence). How then were such positions maintained? The answer is, by men.[2] How then were the population gathered round the sages? The answer is, by the production of wealth. The regulation of this wealth, the making of true judgments about it, and the prevention of the people from wrong-doing (in connection with it), these constituted (the sages') justice.

In the days of antiquity, Pao Hsi's exercise of true kingship over the Great Society was on this fashion. Looking up to the sky he observed the signs in the heavens, and looking down he observed the patterns in the earth, the distinctive ornamentation of the birds and beasts, and the adaptations of them to the different regions. Within himself he grasped (ideas), at a distance he grasped objects. This was the way in which he devised the Eight Trigrams with a view to extending everywhere the divine intelligence of his spiritual power and classifying the natural properties of all creation. He devised the knotting of cords and so made nets of various kinds for hunting and fishing. The clue to these inventions we find in the *Li* [Hexagram xxx].[3] When Pao Hsi was no more Shen Nung did his work. Axed trees were made into ploughs and bent wood into handles; and thus the advantage of ploughing and weeding was taught to our Great Society. The clue to this we find in the *Yi* [Hexagram xlii]. Also he made markets at midday, so that all the people came from all parts, assembling the goods from all parts. These having been exchanged, the people returned each with the goods he needed. The clue to this invention we find in the *Shih-ho* [Hexagram xxi].

When Shen Nung was no more, Huang Ti [the Yellow

[1] Some classical thinkers thought of 'sages' as phenomena which might appear at any time now or in the future, but the tendency was to think of 'the sages' as abnormal figures in an abnormal past. The writer here seems to think in this way.
[2] Emending the character for human-heartedness with the character for men. The two words are homonyms.
[3] In regard to both this and the following so-called clues, scholars to-day find difficulty in tracing the logical connections in the writer's mind. Cp. *Ku Shih Pien*, vol. iii, pp. 45–73.

Emperor] and Yao and Shun did their work, extending their reforms everywhere. They set the people to work on public works, but without exhaustion. Their transformation of the people was miraculous: they saw the right in what they were set to do. When one phase (in history) is exhausted, it is time for reform. When reforms are made, they must permeate (society). When they permeate, they will endure. This is the way 'help came down from Heaven on these kings, good fortune and everything to advantage.' Huang Ti, Yao, and Shun only wore their robes, and the Great Society was under control; and the clue to (all) this we find in the *Ch'ien* and *K'un* [Hexagrams i and ii].

They hollowed out trees to make boats, and cut boards to make oars: the benefit of boats and oars, meeting the need of communication, opening the way to distant parts, and profiting the whole of society. The clue to this we find in the *Huan* [Hexagram lix]. They yoked oxen and harnessed horses, carrying heavy weights to distant parts and profiting the whole of society. The clue to this we find in the *Sui* [Hexagram xvii]. They made the double gates to houses and the watchman's clapper in preparation against marauding strangers. The clue for this we find in the *Yü* [Hexagram xvi]. They cut short pieces of wood to make pestles and dug out the earth to make mortars: the benefit of mortars and pestles with which the needs of the myriad people are met. The clue to this we find in the *Hsiao Kuo* [Hexagram lxii]. They bent wood to make bows and sharpened wood to make arrows: the benefit of bows and arrows with which society is overawed. The clue to this we find in the *K'uei* [Hexagram xxxviii].

In the earliest times men lived in caves and in the wild. Then at a later period a sage substituted houses with ridge-beams and eaves as a protection against wind and rain. The clue to this we find in the *Ta Chuang* [Hexagram xxxiv]. So also the early burials consisted in covering the bodies with firewood and burying them out in the wild, not making any mound over the body or planting any trees round the grave. There were no fixed periods of mourning. Then at a later period a sage substituted the inner and outer coffin. The clue for this we find in the *Ta Kuo* [Hexagram xxviii]. So also in the earliest times men made knotted cords (for purposes of recording) and so were able to govern. Then at a later period a sage substituted written characters and written deeds. Thereby the hundred officials could be controlled and a myriad people brought under survey. The clue for this we find in the *Kuai* [Hexagram xliii].

This then is the way in which the phases (in this scripture) are symbols, that is to say images of other things . . . and the broken and unbroken lines in their relative positions are imitations of the movements in our world of experience. And this is the way in which good fortune and bad come into being and repentance and unavailing remorse are disclosed. . . .

As it is said in the *Yi Scripture*, 'Wavering between going and coming: (only) your friends able to follow out your thought.' So the Master said, 'Why take thought and why plan in this world of ours? In it everything arrives at the same end whatever the different routes they may have travelled. There is one result to a hundred plannings. Why take thought and why plan?' When the sun goes away, the moon comes; and when the moon goes, the sun comes. They push against each other, and thus light is produced. When the cold weather goes, the hot comes, and when the hot weather goes, the cold comes. They push against each other, and so the year (of the four seasons) is completed. That which is going away wanes to less and less: that which is coming forward waxes more and more.[1] Waxing and waning are mutual influences; and so profit is born. The looping up of the caterpillar as it moves is in order that it may straighten itself out. Dragons and serpents go into a winter stupor in order that they may keep themselves alive. So also when the pure essence of (a custom's) meaning comes within the range of the divine, it

[1] Accepting Lu Te-ming's emendation of *hsin* (confidence) to *shen* (waxing).

thereby becomes supremely useful; and when the utility (of a custom) enhances the peace in a man, it thereby exalts the spiritual power in him.[1]   Beyond this point it is hardly possible to have knowledge.   The limit of the divine (in man) is to know transformation, and this is the fullness of spiritual power.

(Comparison should be made between the ideas connected in the above passage with Hexagrams xvi, xxx, and lix, and the ideas connected with the same hexagrams in the *Symbolic Amplification* (cp. p. 9).   It will be found that there is no connection between the two.   One writer sees one meaning in the hexagram, the other sees another: after all, what might be expected when it is realized that the difference of outlook is that between the end of the Chou era and the beginning of the Han.   The later writer seems guilty of a serious anachronism, one which destroys the logical formulation of his theory.   If Pao Hsi only invented trigrams and it was a much later sage who invented the double-trigram system of hexagrams, how could Pao Hsi, Shen Nung, and the other Sage-kings have been inspired by Hexagrams xxx, xliv, etc.?   To this poser the writer might have replied from the standpoint of his phase-logic that the later truths and realities were implicit in the simple beginnings.)

---

[1] The Wilhelm-Baynes rendering of this and the previous sentence is, 'Thus the penetration of germinal thought into the mind promotes the working of the mind.   When this working furthers and brings peace to life, it elevates a man's nature.'

PART SEVEN

RELIGIOUS PHILOSOPHIES OF EDUCATED MEN

CHAPTER XIX: THE RITUALISTS OF THE 'RECORD OF RITES'

Under this heading quotations are taken from those constituent books in the *Record of Rites* (*Li Chi*) which betray Ch'in-Han modes of thought and tricks of composition. Some of them speak of the Chou regime in a retrospective manner, others are less candid. Confucius and his disciples are introduced into the arguments, and one or two of these books show considerable literary powers in making dialogues between 'Master K'ung' and his questioners.

The *Record of Rites* was compiled at the end of the last century B.C. by Tai Shen, who belonged to the Ritual school of thought which one Hou Ts'ang had done so much to create. Their theories, as the reader will see, are a very definite development of Hsun Ch'ing's views. They are more metaphysically minded, and in connection with music display a deep vein of mysticism. To our modern minds which tend to classify mysticism and rationalism as mutually exclusive, these thinkers are of exceptional interest, for they are both rationalists and mystics. To the ordinary rather superstitious man of their day they must have been very puzzling, but there can be no doubt that some of them upheld a standard of the spirit. Others of them are less clearly on the side of the angels, for they were vastly concerned with developing a philosophy of ritual which would commend itself to their emperor as a necessary buttress to sovereignty. None the less, they have some interesting things to say on the nature of the state and always keep fast hold of that Confucian treasure, the indefeasible right of the common man to the ordinary amenities of civilized living. Among these the ability to serve his parents both when alive and when dead stood out in the forefront.

The great question for the literary critic is whether some of these books do not contain late Chou material: a very difficult question. A somewhat easier one is whether the more ritually minded Confucianists of the First Emperor's time and their sons and grandsons in the first fifty years of the Han era are not represented in the later record of rites. My own view is that they are, so that taking the book as a whole it contains materials ranging over a period of about half a millennium.

I. *Tidying up the Universe.*

Thus there is man with his heavenly and earthly spiritual power [*te*], with his interrelating of the Yin and the Yang, with his combining of an animal and spiritual soul: [1] man, the vital energy [*ch'i*] of the Five Forces.

The heavens have the Yang power and so suspend the sun and the stars. The earth has the Yin power and so opens up the mountains and the rivers. They [i.e. the Yin and the Yang] distribute the Five Forces in relation to the Four Seasons, whereby the moon comes into being: the moon which waxes for thrice five days and wanes for thrice five days.

With regard to the Five Forces in motion, each begins as the other exhausts itself. Thus there are the Four Seasons and Twelve Months, and rotation is the basis (on which the process works). So, with the Five Notes (of music) and its fixed scale and twelve-holed pitch-pipes, [2] with the Five Tastes and their six combinations and special dishes for each month in the year, and with the Five Colours and their six variations [?] and special garments for each month in the year: all have rotation as the basis.

Thus it is that man is the *hsin* [? mind, ? heart] of heaven-and-earth, is the complement [3] to the Five Forces. Man is the agent which produces the tastes in foods, the distinctions in sounds, and the colours in clothing. Therefore sage men in making patterns (for man's life) felt bound to take heaven-and-earth as the basis (of the patterns), the Yin and the Yang as complementary to man, the Four Seasons as the controlling power in man's business, the sun and the stars as giving the daily measure of time, the moon as

---

[1] In the Chou vocabulary there was no term corresponding quite to 'soul.' With *te* expressing so much of its meaning and *shen* (self) the rest, there was no need for it; animal and spiritual soul=*kuei shen*. From meaning respectively the spirits of the dead and nature spirits, these two terms came in Han times to have the new meaning given here, at any rate for some people, if not for the uneducated.

[2] There seems to have been a set of pitch-pipes consisting of two bamboo tubes with six holes for the fingers.

[3] *Tuan* is difficult. One usage of it is that of *liang tuan*, the two ends of a stick, or of any business matter. Hence here, if the Five Forces are one end of the changing universe, then man is the other complementary end.

giving the monthly limit of time, the Spirits as 'the Associates,' the Five Forces as the raw materials (being used in the work), righteousness in ritual as the instrument (of social patternization), men's emotions as fields to be cultivated, and the Four Numinous Creatures [1] as creatures to be fed (and so prevailed on to stay).

With heaven-and-earth taken as the basis (of the patterns), it became possible to take things (in Nature) into proper account. With the Yin and the Yang taken as complementary to man, it became possible to observe the actual natures of things. With the Four Seasons taken as the controlling power (in man's life), it became possible to stir men to do (what was necessary at the right time). With the sun and stars as the daily measure of time, it became possible to arrange work methodically; and, with the moon as the monthly limit of time, the work was ably completed. With the Spirits as 'the Associates,' it became possible for the work to be under protection (from calamity). [2] With the Five Forces as the raw materials (being used in the work), it became possible for the work to be repeated (year after year); and, with righteousness in ritual [3] as the instrument, this carrying on of the work brought the achievement of its ends. With men's emotions taken as cultivatible fields, man could . . . [4] With the Five Numinous Creatures remaining, food and drink were assured. (*Li Chi*, *Li Yun*, sect. 3.)

Music expresses the harmony of Heaven and Earth, Ritual the hierarchic order in Heaven and Earth. Since there is this harmony, the hundred (species) of things (in Nature) are evolved. Since there is this order, these

[1] The *ch'i ling*, phoenix, tortoise, and dragon. The appearance of these meant peace and prosperity everywhere.

[2] How far this author and his friends really believed in the old animistic deities, I do not know. Presumably, as in the Augustan age in Rome, some believed more and some less. There were men like Virgil and men like Lucretius.

[3] i.e. the 'done things,' such as duties to family and community, done in the customary way with the due formalities of courtesy.

[4] The text seems to me corrupt. I have no worth-while suggestion to offer.

things as a whole are distinguishable among themselves. (Thus) the creation of music originates in Heaven, whilst Earth gives to Ritual its law of control. . . .

With the myriad things (in Nature) so scattered and diverse in the heavens above and the earth beneath, Ritual has its field of action. With (all Nature) in increasing flow and (the myriad things) coming together and being changed in themselves, Music has its sphere of development. . . . Thus it was that sage men created (our) music as a response to the heavens and framed (our) ritual as a partnership with the earth; and this ritual and music in their splendour of perfection are under the governance of Heaven and Earth.   (*Li Chi, Record of Music*, sect. 1.)

II. *The New Rationalizations of Death and Religious Sacrifice.*

Tsai Wo [1] said, 'I have heard the names *kuei* and *shen*, but I do not know what they mean.' The Master said, 'The breath (represents) the abundance of the *shen* (part of a creature), the animal soul represents the *kuei* (part). To be able to make a harmony of (the two concepts,) *kuei* and *shen*, is the height of philosophy.[2]

All living creatures inevitably come to die. Dying they inevitably go back to the earth. This is what is meant by *kuei* [? the material soul]. The bones and flesh moulder below, and, hidden there, make the soil of the land. But the breath soars aloft to become light, (and is found in) the fragrance and the feeling of sorrow at the sacrifice.[3] Here then is the refined essence of the hundred kinds of creatures: here is the manifestation of the *shen* in man [the spiritual soul].[4]

[1] There are terms used in this passage which make it datable as post-Ch'in, viz. a Han writing. There is no need to assume that the writer attributed to Confucius anything more than one or two sentences.

[2] In other words, extremely difficult to understand. 'Philosophy' in the early Greek sense of systematic theorizing.

[3] I assume the writer has a mystical side to him, and at the same time, like many early philosophizers, has no hard and fast distinction between the material and non-material. The interesting thing is that he regards breath, i.e. the most tenuous form of matter, as indestructible.

[4] This distinction between a *kuei* part and a *shen* part in man reminds us of the Greek distinction which survives in the expression 'body, soul, and spirit.' The reader should not draw the conclusion from this coupling of men and animals that the Han thinkers did not distinguish the two classes of living beings.

On the ground of [*yin*] this refined essence in (living) creatures, and by an extreme exercise of authority,[1] 'the two terms *kuei* and *shen* have been authoritatively fixed as a pattern of thought for the black-haired people, so that the multitude may fear and the myriads obey.' But the sages were not content with fixing terms. They built temples and established fanes in such a way as to distinguish (for a family) its near and remote kinsmen and its far-back and recent ancestors. They instructed the people to 'turn their thoughts to the past and go back to the origins and not to forget those through whom life has come to them.' Submission of the masses springs from this kind of teaching. This is why they obey, and that with alacrity.

Now that the two complementary (entities of the material and spiritual souls) have been established, the payment of man's debt is [? should be] by two rituals. One is the institution of the temple service, with burning of rank fat offered with a blaze of fragrant southernwood as recompense for the breath (we have received).

In this way the masses are taught to 'turn their thoughts back to their earliest beginnings.' The other is to offer millet and rice, savoury liver and lungs and heads and hearts (of the sacrificial beasts), mixed in with jarfuls of fragrant spirits,[2] as recompense for the animal soul. In this way the people are taught to love each other and high and low are brought to be in sympathy, which is the aim of ritual.

The man of refinement turns his thoughts back to the past, goes back to his origin, and does not forget those through whom life has come to him. This is why he calls forth all his reverence, gives vent to his emotions, exhausts his strength in discharging this service that so he may pay the debt he owes to his parents. And thus it was that in

---

[1] Is this a veiled reference to some fiat by the First Emperor? 'The black-haired people' was a term used by him for his subjects.

[2] The contrast between the offerings for this, the lower sacrifice, and those for the higher sacrifice for the breath is an illustration of the Han principle of sacrifice, that the higher the sacrifice the more simple and austere should be the ritual used in it.

days gone by the Son of Heaven lent his strength to the field
of a thousand acres and, wearing his crown and its red
silk strings, with his own hands held the plough. So also
the feudal lords lent their strength to the field of a hundred
acres and, wearing their crowns with azure strings, with
their own hands held the plough. And this they did in
order that they might do service to Heaven and Earth, to
the Mountains and Streams, to the Altars of the Land, and
to the progenitors of their lines, and in order that there
might be the new-distilled spirits and cream and vessels of
grain. This was the way they procured them, by this great
act of reverence.[1]   (*Li Chi, Chi Yi*, sect. 2.)

In organizing the sacrifices the Sage-kings laid down that,
if a man had given good laws [2] to the people, or if a man
had worn himself to death in discharge of his duties, or had
with great labour brought order to the country, or had
shown ability to stem a great calamity or ward off a great
disaster, then sacrifices should be made to them. Such
men were Shen Nung of the Li Shan family who possessed
heaven-below, who was gifted in planting the hundred
cereals: the Chou line's progenitor Ch'i who after the
Hsia line's downfall followed on Shen Nung's work, and is
therefore sacrificed to under the name of Ch'i: the son of
the Kung Kung family known as Hou T'u who when his
family lorded it over the Nine Provinces was able to reduce
them to order and is accordingly sacrificed to as the god of
the soil: Ti K'u who was gifted in (knowing) the order of
the stars and set forth their times to the people: Yao who
was gifted in the giving of rewards and making punishments
impartial and with a (supreme) act of justice made his end:
Shun who spent himself for the people and died far from
home: Yü . . . who atoned for his father's failure in not
damming the floods: Huang Ti who gave the right names

[1] There is a question whether *ching*, translated here and elsewhere as
reverence, does not in some contexts contain something of the meaning in
the words 'a worshipful frame of mind.'
[2] It has to be repeated from time to time that such statements, e.g. such
a term as 'laws' (*fa*), express the views of the writer and his school of
thought, and are not by any means always true historically.

to the hundred species of things (in Nature), thereby enlightening the people . . .: Kuan Hsü who was able to improve Huang Ti's work: Hsieh, 'the Instruction Officer' who educated the people: Ming who through devotion to duty died by drowning: T'ang who ruled the people with a benignant sway and destroyed their oppressors: King Wen who brought the rule of civilization and King Wu who triumphed in war and removed the people's calamities. All these were men whose merits shone before the people's eyes. . . . Unless a man were of this kind, he could not find a place in the Canon of Sacrifices.[1]

(*Li Chi, Chi Fa, ad fin.*)

Of all the ways of ordering the life of man none is more emotionally stimulating than Ritual; and of the Five Rituals [2] none is more important than Sacrifice. 'Sacrificing' is not a material business, or anything external. It is something from within, proceeding from the heart-mind [*hsin*]. The heart is moved and expression is given to it by ritual. This is why only good and true men have the ability to give complete expression to the righteousness in sacrificing.

The sacrificing done by such men invariably brings its own happiness: not what the vulgar would call happiness but the real happiness of being prepared. And 'being scrupulously prepared' is the name of a hundred acts of devotion: nothing left undone, meaning by this that a man has done all he can in himself, and in the outward observance subjects himself to the Way. By this a faithful minister serves his prince: by this a filial son serves his parents. The two services are at bottom one. In their higher aspects, then, they are devotion to the Spirits [*kuei*

---

[1] A very cryptic reference. When was a 'Canon of Sacrifices' made?
[2] There were 'Five Rituals' distinguished by the Han and later sacramentalists: the Ritual of Sacrifice, otherwise called the 'Blessed Ritual'; the Ritual of Congratulations, i.e. of Marriage and of Capping when a young man reached manhood; the Ritual of Entertaining; the Military Rituals; the Burial and Mourning Rituals, otherwise called the 'Cursed Ritual.'

shen], and, whilst in the community there is devotion to prince and elder, in the family there is the discharge of filial duty to parents. All this is involved in being scrupulously prepared.

Only good and true men have the ability required for this scrupulous preparation. Only when they have got this gift are they able to sacrifice. This is why in a good and true man's sacrifice he brings into play all his truth and sincerity, all his fidelity and reverence. For his expression of these (dispositions) he uses material objects, for his guidance in connection with them ritual, for enhancing the (inward) peace of them music, for blending in one whole the timeliness of the sacrificing.[1] Enlightened worship, that is what it is, without any ulterior aim; and this is the heart-mind of the filial son.

. . . All things that heaven begets and earth brings to maturity, if they can be brought as offerings, are there in the sacrifice, to show the completeness of the material side. And if that should be done without, then within there should be completeness of intention. This is the sacrificing heart-mind.   (*Li Chi, Chi T'ung, init.*)

There should be no repetitions of a sacrifice, for that would mean importunity; and importunity leads to irreverence. Neither should a sacrifice be at too infrequent intervals, for that would mean indifference; and indifference leads to forgetting (the sacred dead). That is why a man of refinement, being in harmony with the Way of Heaven, offers the spring and the autumn sacrifices (to the dead). For, when the hoar frost is on the ground, as he treads on it, he is sure to be conscious of a sadness which has nothing to do with his being cold (but with his parents being parted from him by death). Then, when the spring rains and dews fall, as he treads on the dewy ground, he is sure to have a feeling of excitement, as if he were soon to see them.

[1] The idea is that because the sacrificing is done on the right day, e.g. for recalling one's dead parents, the external act has an enormously enhanced effect on the man's ethical dispositions. I believe Christian sacramentalists would agree with this.

And since guests are welcomed with music when they come and escorted with sorrow when they depart, so at the spring sacrifice there is music and at the autumn sacrifice none.

The most rigorous vigil (before the sacrifice) is kept inwardly, though a non-rigorous one without. During those days thoughts are directed to the dead, to the places where they sat, to the way in which they laughed and spoke, to the aims and views they had, to what they took delight in and what they preferred. On the third day the man of refinement will see the one for whom he keeps this vigil. On the day of the sacrifice when he enters the apartment (in the temple), he gasps: surely there is a vision by the spirit tablet! After he has moved here and there (in making his sacrifice) and comes to the threshold, he is struck with awe: surely he hears the particular tones of the dead man's voice! Then, as he hears and listens, he catches his breath: surely he hears the sound of the dead man sighing!

(*Li Chi, Chi Yi.*)

III. *The Ritualist and Society.*

When the people approve of the orders which the ruler issues, this means that (the spirit of) harmony is (in him and them). When the upper and lower ranks in society have a family feeling for each other, this means human-heartedness (among them). When the people get what they want without special efforts, this means mutual trust. And when the injurious elements in Nature [lit. heaven and earth] are removed, this means righteousness. Now righteousness and mutual trust, harmony and human-heartedness, these are the implements of sovereignty. If it be proposed to govern the people without these implements, there will be no success.

The relation of the Rituals to the rectification of the state is the relation of a balance to weight, of (a carpenter's) inked string to crookedness and straightness, of compasses and T-squares to roundness and squareness. The reason is that provided the balance is truly suspended it is impossible

for it to be deceived over the weight: provided the inked
string is truly applied (to a surface) it is impossible for it to be
deceived over the crookedness and straightness (of a line).
. . . So with the man of principle (exercising government):
provided he is judicious in connection with the Rituals,
it is impossible that he should be deceived by traitors and
impostors.

That being so, to exalt the Rituals and be led by them
means being principled as a statesman, and to despise and
ignore them means being unprincipled as a people.   They
are the highway of reverence and courtesy; and therefore
if the Rituals be observed in the ancestral temple, then
there will be reverence, and if the Rituals be introduced
into audiences at court, then the higher and lower ranks
will be each in their proper stations.[1]   If they be part of
family life, then fathers and sons will have affection for
each other and elder and younger brothers will agree.   If
they be part of life in the country districts, then the precedence of age over youth will be maintained.   As Master
Kung [Confucius] said, 'There is no more excellent method
than the Rituals for making those in authority secure and
the people well-ordered.'   That is my meaning.

Thus the Ritual of Audiences is the means by which the
just relationship of sovereign and minister can be given
clear expression.   The Ritual of Visits and Inquiries is the
means by which the great lords can be brought to treat
each other with honour.   The Rituals of Mourning and
Sacrifice are the means by which the grateful love of
ministers and sons can be given clear expression.   The
Ritual of the District Wine-drinking is the means by which
the sense of precedence among young and old can be given
clear expression.   The Ritual of Marriage is the means by
which male and female can be clearly given their distinctive
(functions).

The Rituals are the prevention against the rise of rebellion,
just as dykes are the barriers to the advance of water.   The

[1] The first Han emperor was contemptuous of ritual, with the result that
his court became a bear-garden, and he had to turn to the Confucian
ritualists to help him out of his difficulties.

THE 'RECORD OF RITES'

man who regards the old dykes as useless and destroys
them is sure to be overwhelmed by floods; and the man who
regards the old Rituals as useless and does away with them
is sure to suffer from the calamity of rebellion. If the
Ritual of Marriage were discarded, the path for husbands
and wives would be a bitter one, and there would be any
number of sexual offences. If the Ritual of District Wine-
drinking were discarded, the precedence of age over youth
would be lost, and there would be endless litigation arising
out of quarrels and violence. If the Ritual of Mourning
and Sacrifice were discarded, then the grateful love of
ministers and sons would diminish, and the masses would
revolt against (their duty) to the dead and forget (their
duty) to the living. . . .

Thus the power which the Rituals have of transforming
by instruction is not on the surface. They put a stop to
evil before it takes on form. They cause men day by day
to travel towards the good and leave wrongdoing far
behind; and this without being conscious of doing so.
This is why the first kings exalted them. As is said in the
Yi [*Changes Scripture*], 'The man of principle is cautious
over the beginnings. To be off the true by a hair's breadth
then is to go wrong by a thousand miles.' This is my
meaning.   (*Li Chi, Ching Chieh, ad fin.*)

In bygone days there was Shun who prized the spiritual
power in man and yet did honour to age. There was Yü
who prized nobility of rank and yet did honour to age.
There were the Yin men who prized wealth and yet did
honour to old age. There were the Chou men who prized
kinship and yet did honour to old age. Shun, Yü, Yin,
and Chou, all produced the greatest kings in our Great
Society, and not one of them neglected the old. Thus long
has old age been prized among us, coming next in order of
importance to the service of parents. . . .

Filial piety and younger-brotherliness were exhibited in
the court, were practised on the roads and extended to the
hamlets in the provinces, were given free play in the royal

hunts, were cultivated in the army. The whole population would die for the principle and on no account would transgress it.　　　　　　　　*(Li Chi, Chi Yi, sect. 2.)*

Master Kung continued with the following words,'In the bygone days of the Three Eras when there was the true government of enlightened kings, a man had to reverence his wife and son. This was right, for that wife of his was hostess to his parents.[1] How could he not reverence her? That son of his was the descendant of his parents. How could he not reverence him?

A man of principle is reverent in everything and as much as in anything else reverences his own self. That self of his is a branch of the tree of his parents. How could he not reverence it? To be unable to reverence oneself is an injury to one's parents, and that is an injury to one's very root. Let the root be injured and the branches along with it will die.

These three (facts) are a symbol of life in the community. 'Self' includes other selves, 'son' includes other men's sons, 'wife' includes other men's wives. Let a man of principle put these three things into practice, and he will reach out to the whole of the Great Society.[2] They constitute the Way of a great king, and it is along this line that states and families will become docile.'

　　　　　　　　　　　(Li Chi, Ai Kung Wen.)

[1] Legge's translation has 'dead' in brackets before 'parents,' but surely there is no need for this. Her duties as a daughter-in-law corresponded to those of looking after the comfort of the family's guests.

[2] Assuming, as we well may, that this discourse was a mid-Han redaction and amplification of earlier materials, the natural conclusion is that the Mohist school of thought influenced some, at any rate, of the Han Confucianists. In an earlier paragraph occurs the expression *'ai jen!'* (love men). To *ai* men as men was Mo Ti's great discovery.

Liu An, a scion of the imperial house of the Han era, was king
of the Huai Nan area. He had a restless, inquiring spirit, and
among other pursuits set himself to be a patron of learning. He
died in 122 B.C. Thus he lived just before the political power
of the Confucian devotees began to revive. Liu An had a
catholic mind, accepting Confucian doctrines as well as Taoist;
but his main interest was in the latter. The book *Huai Nan
Hung Lieh*, from which the following excerpts are taken, was not
his own work, but the work of scholars whom he gathered
round him.

Extracts from Chapter 1. (The Universe from the Angle
of the Tao.)

The Tao covers heaven and supports the earth. It
makes the vastness of the four quarters and the eight linked
boundaries of the heavens and the earth which are so high
and so deep that it is impossible to measure them. It
enveloped the heavens and the earth, endowing them with
formlessness. (Like) a flowing fountain and bubbling
spring, empty and yet overflowingly full, both swirling and
smooth, muddy and yet more than limpid. Thus it was
that vertically it blocked out the heavens and the earth and
horizontally set the bounds to the Four (surrounding) Seas,
and made the universe eternal without rise or fall.

Thus, open out the Tao, and it envelops all space: and
yet how small it is, not enough to fill the hand! So limited
and yet able to enlarge: so dark and yet able to make light:
so weak and yet able to make strong: so soft and yet able
to make hard. It binds all space together and is the con-
tainer of the Yin and the Yang. It links the space of the
universe with the time of it and makes the sun and the moon
and the stars to shine. So delicate and rich, so fine and
minute!

By its means the mountains have height and the pools
have depth. By its means the animals can run and the
birds can fly. So also with the sun and the moon with

their shining, and the stars and their keeping of their orbits. . . .

In the very beginning of time the two Determinative Powers [i.e. the Yin and the Yang] gained the authority of the Tao and were established as the central organizing powers. Being divine powers, they transformed and stimulated in every quarter. Thus the movement of the heavens could go on in relation to the immovability of the earth, complete revolution following complete revolution without stopping. Water flows without ceasing, unceasingly, (yet) like all things it ends as it begins. The wind rises and clouds are numerous. Everything gets its response: there is the thunder-clap and then the rain falls; (things in creation) complementing each other to a limitless degree. . . . As the potter's wheel turns, the hub makes a complete revolution, and the circular process is repeated. Materials which have been carved and polished turn back to their original state.

All this is action by inaction, which harmonizes with the Tao, speech by not-speech,[1] which is pervaded with spiritual power. Thus gladly, without anything exalting itself, with everything achieving harmony, there are the myriad differences in things, but agreement with everything's nature [i.e. natural proclivity]. The Tao is divinely entrusted to the tip of a faded grass stalk; and at the same time it makes the wholeness of the vast universe. Its power tranquillizes the heavens and the earth, harmonizing the Yin and the Yang, making the regular intervals of the seasons, and co-ordinating the Five Forces. As it warms with its breath and gently instructs, overshadows, and nurtures, all creatures of every kind receive life. It imbues grass and tree, metal and stone, makes the robustness of bird and beast, giving the sheen to feather and scale, bringing forth horns and antlers. It is the Tao which makes the beasts' wombs not to miscarry and the birds' eggs not to addle: so also with fathers saved from the grief of losing their sons, elder brothers saved from mourning their

___
[1] I suggest *wei* should be *yen*.

younger brothers, children not becoming orphans and wives not becoming widows, no baleful influence in rainbow or comet: all this, wherever the all-containing power of the Tao regulates.

The supreme Tao brings all creatures to life: but it does not own them. It produces all the changing phenomena in the world, but does not play the prime minister over them. . . .

(And so forth, following the line with which the *Tao Te Ching* has made us familiar.)

Chapter 2. (The Beginning of the Universe from the Angle of Being and Non-being.)

(Take the following statements,)[1] (first,) since there was such a thing as 'a beginning' (to the universe as we see it), then, second, there was a pre-beginning stage in which 'something' had a beginning, and (third) there was a pre-beginning to the aforesaid pre-beginning and in it 'nothing'[2] had a beginning. (Fourth,) since there is such a thing as 'something,' then (fifth) there is such a thing as 'nothing,' and (sixth) in the pre-beginning stage there is both 'something' and 'nothing,' and (seventh) in the pre-beginning to the aforesaid pre-beginning stage, there was 'something' and 'nothing.'

With regard to the (first) statement that there was such a thing as a beginning (to the universe as we see it): when no complex energy had put forth any sign of coming shoots and no stock had any body with which to germinate, there was a state of negativeness, and mere wriggling about which was on the point of producing development but in which there were none of the species in creation.

With regard to the (second) statement that there was a pre-beginning stage in which 'something' had a beginning: when heaven's vital energy began to descend and the earthly vital energy to ascend, the male and female forces

[1] Cp. *supra*, *Chuang Chou*, c. 2. This later author has important changes in the second, third, sixth, and seventh statements.
[2] The text says *yu* (something), but the explanation below points to *wu* (nothing) as being what the author had in mind

came together in some sort of fashion, wandering everywhere the one with the other, struggling and interpenetrating in the midst of space and time; and driven by power
inherent in them, these forces embodied harmony. There
was a state of confused huddling together in which the two
forces wanted to establish relations with things; but even
the signs of their individualization were not yet completed.

With regard to the (third) statement that there was a pre-
beginning to the aforesaid pre-beginning and in it 'nothing'
had a beginning: when the harmony which Heaven contains
had not yet descended and the vital energy which Earth
cherishes had not yet spread abroad, there was a state of
emptiness, of silence, a desolation like the mist over hoar
frost. Non-existence was like a flow of vital energy and
greatly penetrated the complete darkness.

With regard to the (fourth) statement that there is
'something': it refers to the myriad things in creation combining to scatter down roots and stems and branches and
leaves with the different shades of green, along with fungi
and water-weeds and rushes with their shining colours;
and refers to locusts flying and silkworms [1] creeping and
spiders walking, all gulping and breathing. It is possible
in accordance with the handling (of these tangible things)
to count and measure them.

With regard to the (fifth) statement that there is 'nothing':
if you look at it, you see no form, and, if you listen for it,
you hear no sound. If you try to feel it, it is impossible
to get hold of it; (and) if you try to visualize it from a distance, it is impossible to set any limit to it. It is auxiliary
to something else and goes along with fusion (of things).
It is like a desert, something featureless, measureless,
transparent.

With regard to the (sixth) statement that in a pre-beginning stage there is both 'something' and 'nothing': fold up
the heavens and the earth together, and put all creatures
into a state of fusion: there will be a great interpenetration

---

[1] The text is slightly emended to follow the indication of meaning
afforded by 'spiders walking.'

of chaos and darkness, so deep and wide that there can be nothing spatially outside and (at the same time such) that a split hair or point is too big to be contained in it.   There can be no boundary wall to space, but the root for producing both 'something' and 'nothing' is there.

With regard to the (seventh) statement that in a pre-beginning to an aforesaid pre-beginning stage, there is both 'something' and 'nothing': if the heavens and the earth have not sundered, the male and female forces have not split into two.[1] If the four seasons have not become distinct, the myriad creatures have not come to life.   That is a state of vacancy like 'uninterrupted quietness,' a state of in-stantaneousness like 'pure transparency' in which no shadow appears.   It is like the (parable of) Light asking Non-existence (about 'nothing')[2] and then retiring and losing consciousness of himself.   He then said, 'I can manage both 'something' and 'nothing,' but I cannot manage 'nothingness of nothing.'   Even if we assume that 'the nothingness of nothing' is the final mystery, how would it be possible to get from the That to the This (of existence)? 'The Great Mass loads me up with a body, gives me the labour of living, eases me off with old age, and gives me rest in death.'

Chapter 3. (The Beginning of the Universe from the Angle of Speculative Astronomy.)

Before the settling down of the heavens had produced their form, there was a state of mounting like the beating of wings, of resisting and cutting into rings.   Hence the statement, 'The Great Beginning was the beginning of the Tao in emptiness.'   The emptiness produced the space-time (nexus) and the space-time (nexus) the vital energy, and the vital energy had layers to it.   The purer, more dis-persive layers forced themselves out and made the heavens.

[1] The sun and moon were taken as symbolizing the male and female forces.   There is probably a reference to them here, for, as in the last paragraph the abolition of space is considered, so here is the abolition of time.

[2] The parable comes in *Chuang Chou*, c. 22.

The heavier, more turbid ones solidified and made the earth; and, since the union of pure and less material (substances) is easy and the solidification of heavy and turbid ones is difficult, hence the heavens were finished first, and the earth was composed later. The continuative vitality in the heavens and earth made the Yin and the Yang, the concentrative vitality in which made the Four Seasons, the dispersive vitality in which made the myriad creatures. The warm energy of accumulated Yang generated fire, the vital essence of which made the sun, whilst the cold energy of accumulated Yin made water, the vital essence of which made the moon. The overplus of energy from the sun and the moon made the stars.

Then follow some descriptions of the Yin and Yang forces at work producing wind and rain, frost and snow by various processes. The same forces make the basis of distinction between creatures which fly and walk—these make a *yang* genus—and those which burrow and are prostrate—a *yin* genus —all of them in their characteristic movements fitting their environments of sun and moon and fire and water. There is a harmony of living creation in which man's actions have their place. Thus, e.g., when there are executions of violent men, violent winds abound. Incidentally it may be noted that the heavens are distant from the earth 510,000 *li* (a *li* being one-third of a mile). Some details in further descriptions are similar to those in the *Yueh Ling* of the *Record of Rites*. A semi-physical, semi-chemical schematology of the Five Forces (wood, fire, earth, metal, and water) is also fitted into this harmony of which the sun and moon and the stars in their fixed courses are such important symbols.

PART EIGHT

THREE HAN CONFUCIANISTS DOGMATIZING

CHAPTER XXI: TUNG CHUNG-SHU

Tung Chung-shu (? 179–? 104 B.C.) has a double interest and importance. In the first place he engaged the confidence of the great Han emperor, Hsiao Wu (*d.* 87 B.C.), who established Confucianism as the state religion. Tung Chung-shu seems to have had a great deal to do with this decision: a momentous decision, since it was never actually reversed until A.D. 1912 (the foundation year of the Republic of China). Legalistic ideas were still rife among government officials, so that, although the emperor himself did not adhere solely to the Confucianist system, the decision was a great triumph for 'the Scholars.' In the second place, Tung Chung-shu was a student and teacher rather than a statesman. He also wrote on a wide variety of subjects, cp. the Imperial Catalogue, in which he figures as author of a book of one hundred and twenty-three essays.[1] Judging from those which are extant, his Confucianism was a very different kind of system from that which Confucius more or less vaguely conceived. The Taoist element is more strongly marked than in Hsun Ch'ing. Above all, Tung was greatly preoccupied with straightening out the current muddled thinking about the Five Forces. Opinions differ as to whether he succeeded. On the whole, he was not very consistent, though his treatment of the Five Forces from a dozen different angles reveals one thing clearly enough, that he took the idea of each of the Five Forces 'conquering' the one before it as not the fundamental principle in the process. 'Conquering' might happen, and indeed did happen when kings and ministers worked wickedness: then any of the Five Forces might conquer any other, and anarchy result among 'the ten thousand creatures' and in the society of man.[2]

The following quotations taken from his book, the *Ch'un Ch'iu Fan Lu* (String of Pearls on the *Spring and Autumn Annals*),[3] are chosen to show (1) his treatment of the Yin-Yang and Five Forces theories, (2) his philosophy of history, one in contrast to Tsou Yen's, (3) his theory about man's nature, (4) his reinforcement of the *Hung Fan's* emphasis on royal virtue as vital to the welfare of man—a development of Hsun Ch'ing's theory of sovereignty.

---

[1] A number of these are not extant.
[2] Cp. e.g. cc. 58 and 59, not quoted below.
[3] The *Annals* had by now become a symbol of ordered historic time.

Chapter 42. The Spiritual Principle of the Five Forces.

Heaven has Five Forces, first Wood, second Fire, third Soil, fourth Metal, fifth Water. Wood comes first in the cycle of the Five Forces and water comes last, Soil being in the middle. This is their order which Heaven has made.

Wood begets Fire, Fire begets [i.e. from the ashes] Soil, Soil begets Metal, Metal begets Water, and Water begets Wood. This is their father-and-son (relation). Wood dwells on the left, Metal on the right, Fire in the front and Water behind, with Soil in the centre.[1] This is their father-and-son order, each receiving from the other in its turn. Thus it is that Wood receives from Water and Fire from Wood. . . . As transmitters they are fathers, as receivers they are sons: an undeviating dependence on the father to set the son going. This is the Way of Heaven.

That being so, Wood having begotten Fire nourishes it, whilst Metal having died is stored up in Water. Also Fire delights in Wood and through the Yang power at work is nourished by it, whilst Water having conquered Metal, through the Yin power at work buries it. Also in the service which Soil renders to Heaven it 'uses all its loyalty.'[2] Thus it is that these Five Forces correspond to the actions of filial sons and loyal ministers. Putting 'the Five Forces' into words, they appear as five kinds of action [*hsing*]: is that not so?

The result of this, namely that definite propositions can be made about them, is that sage men can get to know them and thereby increase their own loving-kindness and decrease their severity, lay stress on the nourishing of life, and take care in the funeral offices for the dead, in this way being in keeping with the ways of Heaven. Thus, as a son welcomes the completion of his years of (nurture), so Fire

[1] Other thinkers always seem to visualize the Five Forces as strung out in a time-sequence. Hence the interest of this alternative visualization of them as in a bunch, an image which profoundly affects our thinking about them.

[2] Tung Chung-shu admittedly has a tendency to anthropomorphic, or rather anthropopathic thinking, but if we remember that this phrase 'using all loyalty' was a common one for a servant doing his duty, i.e. fulfilling his function as a servant with undeviating fidelity, our author is not so fantastic as he may appear at first sight to be.

delights in Wood; and, as (the time comes when) the son buries his father, so (the time comes when) Water conquers Metal. Also the service of one's sovereign is like the reverent service Soil renders to Heaven. Thus we may well say that there are Force men and that there are both Five Forces, each keeping its right turn, and Five-Force officials, each doing his utmost.

That being so, Wood has its place in the eastern quarter and has authority over the vital energy of spring: Fire has its place in the southern quarter and has authority over the vital energy of summer: Metal has its place in the western quarter and has authority over the vital energy of autumn: Water has its place in the northern quarter and has authority over the vital energy of winter; and that being so, Wood takes charge of life-giving and Metal of death-dealing,[1] Fire of heat and Water of cold: so that men must needs go by this succession and officialdom must needs do its best; for this is the fate ordained by Heaven.

Soil has its place at the (functioning) centre and is the very fattening dew of Heaven. Soil is Heaven's thighs and arms, its virtue so prolific, so lovely to view that it cannot be told at one time of telling. The fact is that of these Five Forces and Four Seasons Soil is what brings them all together. Each of the five has its own office: nevertheless, if they did not rely on Soil at the centre, they would collapse. In similar fashion is the reliance of sourness, saltiness, pepperiness on sweetness. Without that the others could not make 'flavour.' The sweet is the root of the five flavours. Thus Soil is in control of the Five Forces; and their unifying principle is the vital energy of Soil, just as the existence of sweetness among the five flavours cannot but make them what they are. That being so, among the actions of sage men there is nothing equal in value to fidelity—fidelity which I have described as the virtue in Soil. . . .

[1] The Yin-Yang and Five-Force theorists emphasized what may well have been a very old custom, that executions should only take place in the second half of the year. Cp. *Kuan Tzu*, c. 40, and banished men being brought back in the spring. (See p. 216.)

Chapter 23. The Raw Material and the Finished Product of the Reforms of State Organization made in the Three Sage-king Eras.

The *Spring and Autumn Annals* says, 'The King reformed the monthly calendar,' and an amplifier asks which king, and answers King Wen. . . . A true king must get a commission from Heaven before he becomes king, and as king he is sure to correct the time of New Year's Day and change the colours of (ceremonial) clothes, and reorganize the Rites and the Music. (In these matters) he makes uniformity throughout the Great Society, for this is a means of showing that the changing of the royal family is not just a handing down of (an ineffective) human-heartedness but is pervaded with what has been (newly) received from Heaven.[1] . . . The king's reorganization of the First Month in the year [2] was in response to a radical change . . . and in doing this he paid homage to Heaven and Earth. . . . Each of the Five Ti [Sage-Sovereigns] . . . used his pattern as a symbol [*hsiang*] of his following his destiny . . . removed his capital to a new place, changed the titles of his officers. . . .

Of the Three Regimes the black is to be taken as the one which came first. On the first [i.e. rectifying] day of the first [i.e. rectifying] month, with the new moon in the *Yun-Shih* star sector, and the *Tou* constellation taken in the fifth watch at the Yin point of time, Heaven marshals the vital energy and begins the transformation of everything everywhere, and everywhere the shoots display their colour black. That is why a court conforms to this colour, wears black (ceremonial) head-dresses and black clothes, has carriages made of black materials, with the horses black and black trappings and black flags; with the great precious jade of office black, black victims for the sacrifice in the suburbs. . . . The (administration of) the law should imperceptibly

---

[1] This sense of a Heaven-directed revolution occurring from time to time is a vital element in Confucian political philosophy, indeed in the political consciousness of the Chinese people generally.

[2] Different dynasties changed the beginning of the calendar, e.g. from one season to another.

bear the tender shoots of a new birth. Thus in this month there should be no killing. Trials in the courts should not be held under the new moon, and the judgments should minimize the characteristic power [*te*] of punishment The descendants of the two previous dynasties should not be exterminated. . . .

Then how is the rectification made to a white regime? This is done by passing over to the rectifying [i.e. first] day of the rectifying [i.e. first] month fixed with the new moon in the Hsü sector and the Tou constellation taken in the fourth watch. Heaven marshals the vital energy and begins to make the transformation of moulting for all creatures. New feathers and down begin to come, white in colour. That is why a court conforms to this colour, wearing white head-dresses and clothes. . . . (The administration of the) law should imperceptibly bear the tender burden of a new body.[1] Thus in this month there should be no killing. . . .

Then how is the rectification made to a red regime? . . . The spiritual principle in this rectifying originates in homage done to Heaven.[2] An ancient king, having received his commission and become king, reformed the system and adopted a (new) emblem. He fixed the colour before he reported to Heaven and Earth at the altars in the suburbs. He also reported to the whole company of Spirits and far back along his ancestral line. Only after doing this did he publish the news throughout the realm. The great lords having received the news . . . reported it to the gods of the soil and grain, to their ancestors in (their temples), and to the mountains and rivers. By the influence of these acts the whole administration became a unity. As to radical changes effected by the Three Regimes among the nearer barbarians and very distant parts, there were no more murderers among them. Yet it is only in the Middle Kingdom that there have been three (sage-king) eras (namely, the Hsia, Shang, and Chou) with their reforms.

[1] Emending the text to make it fit with the parallel passage in the previous paragraph.
[2] Emending *yuan* to *t'ien*.

Chapter 35. A Deep Examination as to Names [ming] and Emblematic Designations [hao].

The necessary condition of order in the Great Society consists in discrimination as to supremacy; and the necessary condition for making this discrimination consists in a deep examination of 'names' and 'emblematic designations.' Names are the first items (to be examined) in any reasoned synthesis [*ta li*]. If their meanings can be noted so that we can observe the scope of them, then truth and error can be arrived at and their consistency and inconsistency become clear of themselves. Such is the pivotal importance of terms in relation to heaven-and-earth.[1] The criterion of truth is to be found in consistency, the criterion of consistency in (the distinction between) names and emblematic designations, the criterion for names and emblematic designations in heaven-and-earth; for heaven-and-earth is the logical basis [*ta yi*] of both names and emblematic designations.

The sage men of antiquity were patterning themselves on heaven-and-earth in the cries [2] which they gave—what we call 'emblematic utterances.' They authoritatively disseminated these utterances among the people, (making them) what we call 'names.' [3] A name taken as a word is utterance plus convention. An emblematic designation taken as a word is a cry, and so a copy. Thus the cry which comes in imitation of heaven-and-earth is an emblematic designation. (Only) the utterance which is made through convention is a name.

Names and emblematic designations have (as words) two different sounds, but they come from the same root. They all are emblematic utterances and so convey Heaven's

[1] i.e. Nature, the materially objective as distinct from the spiritually objective, Heaven, and from the subjective which, as the succeeding argument points out, is a characteristic feature of 'names,' though 'names' have to be considered in relation to the objective.

[2] *Ho* is 'an excited cry.' Clearly Tung Chung-shu has in mind the idea of an emotional intuitive response to direct experience of heaven-and-earth as reality.

[3] Cp. *Hsun Ch'ing*, p. 244. Tung Chung-shu accepts his theory about convention, but he goes beyond it and in the last resort against it.

meanings. Heaven does not speak, (mechanically) propelling man into expressing its meaning. Nor does it act,
propelling man into preserving its Mean in their actions.
If, then, names are the means by which sage men express
Heaven's meanings, then these meanings must on every
account be deeply observed.

'A sovereign [*chun*] with a heavenly commission,' these
words are a communication of Heaven's meaning. The
result is that the emblematic designation 'Son of Heaven' is
perfectly right. The Son of Heaven looks to Heaven as if
it were his father. He serves Heaven as a filial son. Take
the great feudatories: their emblematic designation, *chu
hou*, is perfectly right, since they are careful to look to
[*hou*] the one to whom they do homage, namely the Son of
Heaven. . . .

An emblematic designation gives a general idea, a name
particularizes; and the particulars given make distinct the
practical nature of the thing named. A generalization
involves a particular statement of that practical nature.
(For example,) with regard to making offerings to the dead,
the emblematic designation for these is *chi* [1] [sacrifice], an
abstract [2] term for sacrificing, since the spring sacrifice is
called *tz'u*, the summer one *yo*, the autumn one *chang*, and
the winter one *cheng*. . . . There is nothing which has not
a general emblematic designation, and no emblematic
designation which has not an abstract term alongside
it. Thus in this matter each emblematic designation
should be in conformity with the name and each name in
conformity with Heaven. This is a Heaven - with - Man
dispensation.

When the royal fiats make unity, when they are in agreement and are impregnated with reason, when they stir to
action and produce mutual benefits, when they conform to
and give and take from (heaven-and-earth), this is what is

---

[1] Presumably the author had in mind the component parts of this ideograph, viz. two hands held up and the *shih* character which is found in so
many characters dealing with religious matters.
[2] A different expression has just been used for 'generalization' and the
san of *san ming* has the basic meaning of 'broken loose.' But cp. Bradley's
Principles of Logic (1932), pp. 81, 82.

meant by 'the Way of Spiritual Power.' And when we examine deeply into the high significance of the royal emblematic designation, we find contained in it five divisions. . . . Thus it has been said, 'There is no (need) for any protection outside Heaven's, and the ways of Earth embrace all in love. The wind carries his commands and makes a unity of his majesty. The rain diffuses the virtue in him abroad to all alike.' This is the (high) art of being a king.

From this Tung Chung-shu goes to a study of *chün*, the name for 'sovereign.' He reckons that *chün* can be used of monarchs deviating from the norm, whilst Son of Heaven should only be used of those plainly with the heavenly commission. Having thus opened the way for the discussion of good and evil, he then comes to the question of man's congenital nature, the question to which Mencius and Hsün Ch'ing had given apparently diametrically opposite answers.

In this age there have been people avowing different positions about man's 'nature' [*hsing*], people who are not at all clear about it. Why do they not go back to the name *hsing*? Is it not to do with birth?[1] Thus the raw material which man has mechanically, as it is when he is born, that is what we call his congenital nature. *Hsing* is raw material. Now, how can it fit the facts to insist that this raw material in our nature is equivalent to the term 'good'? It cannot. How then is it possible still to speak of the raw material as good? The name *hsing* cannot afford to get away from (the idea of) raw material by a hair's breadth. If it did, it would not represent congenital nature. This must on all accounts be examined into.

The *Spring and Autumn Annals* distinguished the real features in all objects with a view to rectifying their names, so that names and the things they name might exactly correspond. . . . Now, it is the mind which prevents all the evil inside a person from revealing itself outside. Thus it is that the term 'mind' is equivalent to a mat (protecting the person sitting from the dirt of the floor).

[1] The *hsing* ideograph is composed of *sheng* (birth, life) and *hsin* (heart-mind).

Unless there was dirt in what comes to us in the vital
energy, what need would there be for the mind to act as a
mat? I regard the term 'mind' as expressing a real feature
in man. That reality is that there is both inordinate desire
and human-heartedness. The vital energy of both is in the
self; and this true 'self' is taken from Heaven, for Heaven
has the two outgoings of the Yin and the Yang. So also
the self has two parts to its congenital nature, that of
desire and that of the human-hearted. As Heaven has the
Yin prohibited in (the sphere of) the Yang, so the self
works in the same way as Heaven, having emotion blocked
[lit. protected by a mat] in (the sphere of) desire. . . .[1]

Since Heaven's prohibition of the Yin is like this, the
question is how to avoid injuring desire and yet to have a
rest from emotion, and thus fit in with Heaven, with the self
prohibiting what Heaven prohibits. I affirm that if the
self is like Heaven, prohibits what Heaven prohibits, and
does not [2] run counter to Heaven, it must be because it
knows Heaven. (That is to say,) if the congenital nature
does not take advantage of authoritative teaching [chiao],
then it can never get a mat [i.e. a protective apparatus]. . . .

What evidence is there that this is so? The fact is, the
congenital nature is to be compared to growing rice, goodness to the grain in the growing rice, and it is not possible
for all the growing rice to be good (to eat). Goodness
comes from the congenital nature, but it is impossible for
the congenital nature to be all good. In both cases, namely
of goodness and of the grain, that with which man follows
up Heaven and which he completes in the external sphere,
is not that which Heaven does in its internal sphere. What
Heaven does reaches a point; and there it stops. Within that
limit is what is meant by the expression 'the Heaven-given

[1] That is what the logical parallelism of the two halves of the sentence
produces; but this introduction of emotion (ch'ing) and desire (yü) is not
easy to link on to the previous affirmation about inordinate desire and
human-heartedness. The key to the difficulty is that inordinate desire is
to Tung Chung-shu evil, but desire at the right time to the right extent
is not.
[2] There would seem to be half of a double negative which has dropped
out of Sun Kung's text.

congenital nature.' Outside that limit is what is meant
by the expression 'man's part': and man's part is outside
the congenital nature so that the congenital nature may
not fail to become virtue.

The emblematic designation of the people [min] is to be
taken as 'purblind.' [1] If the congenital nature be already
good, then why should 'purblind' be made the emblematic
designation? For, speaking from the angle of ruinous
perversion from the norm, that designation could never
be to induce a coming madness of destruction. How can
a wholly good congenital nature have, as it were, eyes?
Eyes are darkened in sleep and become purblind, waiting
for the awakening with the subsequent seeing. So long as
the awakening has not come, it is permissible to speak of
the raw materials for seeing, but not permissible to speak
of actual seeing.

Taking the myriads of the common people to-day, and
speaking without any special investigation, apart from
what the men of enlightenment [chun tzu] are, what is to
be made of them? Some say the congenital nature possesses
the (motivating) condition of goodness, the mind the raw
material of goodness. Very well, but how does the opposite
to goodness fit in with these (notions)? The reply is that
it does not. A cocoon of silk contains a thread of silk,
but it is not (equivalent to) the thread. An egg contains
a chick, but it is not a chick. Follow this up in relation to
any species of being, and there will be no more doubts.
The Heaven that gives life to the people has Six Scriptures
[Ching], [2] and where they speak of congenital nature, they
do not disagree. And yet some say that it is good, and
others say it is not good, whilst those who describe it as

[1] The temptation is to think that mere similarity of sound was the
ground for Tung Chung-shu's accepting min(g), 'purblind,' as the emblematic designation of min (the common people); but his remarks on the
sages and their intuitive utterances rules this idea out. On the other hand,
I have not been able to discover any statement of this kind by a sage. The
Shuo Wen is interesting under min (common people): 'springing up everywhere but without understanding (shih).'
[2] Presumably the Odes, the History, a book of Rituals, i.e. which does
not include the Record of Rites, a book on Music, the Changes, and the
Spring and Autumn Annals. Mencius was not in the Canon at that time,
nor for a very long time after.

good have, each of them, different ideas. (For example,) the congenital nature means the welling up of love for father and mother, something better than is found in birds and beasts, and on this hypothesis the congenital nature is to be described as good. These are Mencius's words, guarding the Three Ties (of sovereign and subject, father and son, husband and wife) and the Five Relationships [1] and the Eight Shoots of fidelity and truth-speaking, all-embracingness and love, honesty and generosity, courtesy and the passion for it: which, of course, may be described as good. These, however, are the goodnesses of sage men, so that Master K'ung said, 'A good man I have never succeeded in seeing. To see one who was continuously so, that would do.' What the sage calls goodness is not easily matched. It is not the goodness of birds and beasts which may be called goodness.[2] Only if the stirring of the shoots of goodness be better than in the case of birds and beasts, may it be called goodness. How, then, was it he [Confucius] had never seen this? Further, if goodness in birds and beasts does not pass the test of (human) goodness, it is much the same with plants and trees, so that they do not come up to the level of the name.

We know that the congenital nature of the people is better than that of birds and beasts, and yet its goodness does not come up to the level of the name. We know that the name assumes sageness, that what sage men authoritatively lay down for the Great Society is to be taken as right. As the man who wants the right direction either in the morning or in the evening looks to the North Star, so the man who doubts what is right looks to the sages; and the sages held that in an age without a king, in teaching without (right) names, the people have no chance of matching goodness. Such is the difficulty of matching goodness; and it is in consequence wrong to say that the congenital nature of

[1] *Chi* more often refers to the divisions of time, but here surely to the Five Relationships, in which total there is added on to the three already mentioned the relationship of elder and younger and of friend with friend.

[2] This interpretation forces the grammar. The only alternative is to suppose a *pu k'o* has been dropped out and then to translate, 'If it be not better than that of birds and beasts, it may not be called goodness'

the myriad people in all cases does match it. If the raw material (under discussion) be that of the congenital nature of birds and beasts, then the nature of the people is good; but if it be in relation to the goodness of man's Way, then the nature of the people definitely falls short. . . . The raw material which I maintain to be the congenital nature is different from that of Mencius. Mencius thinks of a low-level raw material in relation to what birds and beasts do. Therefore he affirms that the congenital nature is good. I (think of) a high-level raw material in relation to what the sages make good, with the result that I maintain the congenital nature is not good.

Goodness goes beyond the congenital nature, (just as) the sages go beyond goodness, and consequently the *Spring and Autumn Annals* which are the great source take care to rectify names. Names are not congenital nature. The congenital nature has the raw material in it, but it has not woken up, to use the illustration of a purblind person waiting for awakening teaching before he can be good. . . .

Examine this slowly with a quiet mind, and these words will become clear. With only the congenital nature there is purblindness which has not yet been awakened to what Heaven does. A patterning of oneself on Heaven (you will remember) brought about the emblematic designation. Therefore I call the people 'the *min*' [common people], a term which inevitably means purblind. Follow out this name and emblematic designation by entering into the process of reason in them, then you will understand. It is a rectifying of names and designations in relation to heaven-and-earth.

What heaven-and-earth give birth to is to be called congenital nature and natural emotions: the two together constitute the whole act. Purblindness pertains to the emotions and also to the congenital nature. If you say the congenital nature is good, what about the emotions? Therefore the sages never compromise the name by declaring that the congenital nature is good. The self has both a congenital nature and natural emotions, just as Heaven has the Yin and the Yang. To speak of men in

the raw being without their emotions is like speaking of
Heaven having the Yang and not the Yin—but there is no
time for an exhaustive discussion of that. To name the
congenital nature (rightly), we do not use too high or too
low a meaning, but one exactly in the middle. The name
'congenital nature' is like a cocoon or an egg, an egg
awaiting the change which brings the chick: a cocoon
awaiting the winding which brings the thread. The congenital nature awaits the authoritative teaching which
brings goodness.

Chapter 57. *Things of the Same Genus Energize Each Other.*

Take the levelling of the ground drawing water to it, the
removing of dry heat attracting the damp, the spreading of
the sticks dispersing the fire, the removing of the damp
attracting dry heat. All things reject what is different
and follow what is akin to them. Thus it is that if the
(respective) vital energies are similar, then they coalesce:
if notes harmonize, they make a chord. The experimental
proof [*yen*] of this is extraordinarily clear. Try tuning
musical instruments . . . and the *kung* note and the *shang*
note struck from a drum are answered by the *kung* note
and the *shang* note from the other instruments. This is
nothing miraculous, but the Five Notes being in relation
and giving spontaneous utterance: they are what they are
by destiny. Lovely things summon the whole genus of
lovely things, repulsive things summon the whole genus
of repulsive things. This arises from the complementary
way a genus responds, as, for instance, if a horse whinnies,
another horse whinnies in answer, and if a cow lows, another
cow lows in response.

When a high-ruling king is about to ascend, his lovely
omens appear first. When one is about to be destroyed,
baleful omens also appear first. Things indeed summon
each other, like to like, a dragon[1] bringing rain, a fan
driving away heat, the place where an army is being thick

[1] The dragon from time immemorial was associated with great clouds
banking up.

with thorns. In all cases both of the lovely and of the repulsive there is a following movement which makes a fate,
the abiding place[1] of which no man knows.   When Heaven
is about to make the Yin descend, men begin to fall sick;
that is, there is a movement prior to the actual event.   It is
the Yin beginning a complementary response.   Also when
Heaven is about to make the Yin descend, this makes men
feel sleepy. This is the Yin vital energy at work.   There is
also grief which makes men feel sleepy—complementary to
the Yin demand—and there is delight which does not make
men feel sleepy — complementary to the Yang demand.
At night time water floods more by several degrees.   When
there is an east wind, wine soaks in more.   Sick men are
very much worse at night.   Just before a chick emerges
from the egg it in all cases gives a cheep and so in complementary fashion thins down the vital *ch'i* in it and makes it
more exquisite. Thus it is that Yang reinforces Yang, and
Yin reinforces Yin, and the two vital energies of the Yang
and Yin follow on each other in classifiable fashion with
complementary (processes) of reinforcement and the reverse.

Heaven has the Yin and Yang, and so has man.   The
Yin vital energy of heaven and earth rises, and the Yin
vital energy of man responds by rising also.   Man's Yin
energy having risen, Heaven's Yin energy also must by
rights respond to it by rising.   That their way [*tao*] [i.e.
the way of heaven and earth and of man] is one is made clear
by this: If the rain is to come, then the Yin must move and
set its influence to work.   If the rain is to stop, then the
Yang must move and set its influence to work.   The fact
is, the coming of rain is not a beginning which should raise
the question of its being miraculous; but its rationale is
profoundly mysterious.[2]

[1] That is a literal translation.   For those who wish to verify what early
Chinese views of cause and effect were, these few sentences would seem
to be of the highest importance, more particularly because of the emphasis
on like with like and the sense of a mystery lying beyond.   It is possible,
since he refers to an army and thorns, that Tung Chung-shu had in mind
the *Tao Te Ching*, in which the problem of a First Cause is raised.

[2] Note this interesting contrast between the miraculous, i.e. phenomena
due to the intervention of spirits and so quite clear in their way, and the
big mystery attaching to the real working of cause and effect.

It is not only the two vital energies of the Yin and the Yang which advance and retreat in classifiable fashion. Calamities, however calamitous, and blessings in their way of happening also are classifiable. Not one but has something beforehand which begins it and by being classifiable is complementary to it and reacts on it. The truth is that men of unearthly brilliance turn from looking out for (what may happen) to listening judiciously to (what is there); and speech becomes sagely brilliant by its looking out for the inside (meaning) and turning to judicious appraisement.[1] The result is that it is only sages in their enlightenment who know the bottom of their minds; and in all cases their knowledge consists in this. When the note *kung* is struck forth from a lute, the other *kung* strings (near by) reverberate of themselves in complement: a case of comparable things being affected in classifiable fashion. They are affected by a sound which has no visible form to it; and when men can see no form to what is having an effect, they describe the phenomenon as spontaneously sounding. Also, when there is a mutual reaction without anything visible (to account for it), they describe this as spontaneously so. In point of fact there is no 'spontaneously so.' There is what propels man to such and such a pass; and things inevadably have a real propelling power, invisible though this may be. As the tradition of the *Book of History* affirms, when the Chou House was about to rise, there was a great red bird with a grain of corn in its beak which settled on the roof of the royal dwelling. King Wu was delighted, and so were all the great officers. Duke Chou said, 'Prosperity! Prosperity! A revelation from Heaven.' By this they were encouraged. . . . In their fears they trusted to this.

There may seem to certain types of educated religious minds no great harm in this form of reasoning and its main conclusion —a very common one in the sphere of monotheistic religion. But it was not long after Tung Chung-shu when this kind of

[1] A difficult passage, but the meaning apparently is that two complementary actions are needed, the one a looking out for any sign that may appear, the other a sizing up of what is bound to have appeared and to need right appraisement.

thinking was carried to the most fantastic lengths of logic, and a grossly superstitious kind of Confucianism came into vogue. The first steps towards this are discernible in the following passage.

Chapter 64. The Five Forces and the Five Daily Doings.[1]

If the king and his ministers do not practise the ritual courtesies; if there be no majesty (on the one hand) and no reverence (on the other), then the trees will not grow crooked or straight (as they should), and in the summer there will be an excess of high winds: for wind is the vital energy of Wood and the wind's piercing blast corresponds with the (piercing) *chio* note in music which is the characteristic note of Wood.

If the king's speech be not in accord (with reason), then the metals will not be pliant and susceptible of modification, so that in the autumn there will be an excess of thunder-claps: for thunder-claps are the vital energy of Metal, and their crashing peals correspond with the *shang* note in music which is the characteristic note of Metal.

If the king's seeing fail to get objects clear, then the fires will not burn, so that in the autumn there will be an excess of lightning; for lightning is the vital energy of Fire. . . .

If the king's hearing fail to be discriminating, then the waters will not saturate or descend, so that in the spring there will be an excess of violent rain; for rain is the vital energy of Water. . . .

If the king's mind fail to be penetrating, then the sowing and reaping will not be completed, so that in the autumn there will be an excess of rumbling thunder; for rumbling thunder is the vital energy of Soil. . . .

[1] Cp. the *Grand Norm* in the *Book of History.*

CHAPTER XXII: PAN KU AND THE 'PAI HU T'UNG YI'

The lengthy quotations from Tung Chung-shu have shown how at the very time when the Confucian tradition was made into a state religion the mind of the man who had much to do with this was working freely in its own way. The appeal to authority can be found in Tung Chung-shu's writings, but the appeal to reason is also very much there. This was towards the end of the second century B.C. When we come down to the later (Eastern) Han dynasty, we find an intellectual situation of a considerably different complexion. To bring this home to the reader, two quotations are taken from the official histories of the two Han dynasties. Both quotations illustrate official scholar opinion in the second half of the first century A.D., i.e. when the later Han dynasty was in full swing. The first quotation is from Pan Ku's *Ch'ien Han Shu* (*History of the Former (Western) Han Dynasty*), and constitutes his preface to the Imperial Catalogue (cp. Introduction, p. xxxv). The statement is taken as his redaction of Liu Hsin's report on the cataloguing. The second quotation leads on to the *Pai Hu T'ung Yi* by Pan Ku. It was because of the bitter contentions among the leading scholars that Emperor Chang called a conference in A.D. 79.

Is it too much to say that there is clear evidence of the dangerous, some would say unholy, alliance between religion and politics which has figured so frequently in the history of monarchies throughout both the ancient and the modern world? Religion having achieved its sacred scriptures and its experts in exegesis looks to the state to buttress the cause of righteousness and truth. The sovereign having achieved his supreme position looks to the leaders in religion to buttress his authority by lending to it the numinous sanctity of religion.

In the days that are past when Chung Ni [Confucius] was no more and his profound words were cut short, and when his seventy disciples came to be buried, then his main principles were contradicted. Thus it came about that the *Spring and Autumn Annals* became five different books, the *Odes* four, and the *Changes* had several different schools of amplification. Then in the Warring States era with its north and south and east and west divisions, when truth and falsehood both made schism, at that time the words of the philosophers caused utter confusion. So we come to

the calamity of Ch'in [i.e. the First Emperor] when literature
and culture were destroyed by fire so that 'the black-heads' [1]
might be kept in (the darkness of) ignorance. The Han
then arose and rebuilt the ruin which Ch'in had left. They
made a great harvest of writings, opening a wide road for
the collection of books.

Then came the age of Emperor Wu [140–87 B.C.]. Books
were still lacking, and pages [lit. bamboo tablets] missing
from them, the ritual all to pieces, and music dead. The
Holy One above [2] groaned and gave utterance, 'Our
Royal Self being grieved herewith devises plans for the
preservation of books. . . . As for the expositions of the
philosophers, let them all be stored in a private library.' [3]

In Emperor Ch'eng's time [32–7 B.C.], since books were
to a considerable extent scattered and lost, the Emperor
sent a special messenger, Ch'en Nung, to search out neglected books throughout the Empire. He gave orders to
the Superintendent of Palace Officers, Liu Hsiang, to collate
(the texts of) the Scriptures and their amplifications, and
the various philosophers and works of poetry; to Infantry
Commander Jen Hung to collate the texts of books on
military matters; to Chief Historian Yiu Hsien to collate
the texts of books on mathematics and science; to Physician-
in-waiting Li Chu-kuo to collate the texts of the books
on technical skill. When each copy was finished with, Liu
Hsiang was straightway to detail the number of sections to
each and the titles, to extract the essential meaning of each,
and embody it all in a report to the Throne. When Liu
Hsiang died, Emperor Ai [6–1 B.C.] empowered his son,
Hsin, to complete his father's work.

Liu Hsin thus brought together all the different kinds of
books and reported them to the Throne under seven main
heads. Thus it came about that there are (1) the Class of
Compilations, (2) the Class of the Six Arts, (3) the Class of
the Philosophers, (4) the Class of Poetry, (5) the Class of

---

[1] The First Emperor's contemptuous name for his subjects.
[2] A common title for the Emperor.
[3] i.e. not for public consumption because of deleterious doctrines which
might be found in them.

Military Matters, (6) the Class of Mathematics,[1] (7) the
Class of Technics.   Here I edit his more important points
and give the list of books in full.

There then follow the titles of the books in each class, each
class being divided into a number of subdivisions.   Pan Ku
gives a postscript to each class, and to some of the subdivisions.
Space forbids more than the quotation of those on the different
schools of philosophy.   With regard to the statements he makes
about each school having published (so to speak) its works
under the aegis of a department of state, he speaks entirely
theoretically without any historical warrant, as far as we can
see.   That is the significance of those statements: to Pan Ku's
bureaucratic mind that was what must have happened in the
era of the Chou philosophers.

On the right are recorded 53 Ju (Confucianist) authors
with a total of 836 sections to their works.   These authors
as a class issued their works under the Ministry of Education; for they helped rulers to conform to the Yin and the
Yang, to understand the transforming influence of authoritative teaching.   They made roving dissertations on the contents of the Six Scriptures.   They kept carefully within the
confines of human-heartedness and righteousness.   They
recorded Yao and Shun, as if they were their ancestors.
They upheld the rulings of King Wen and King Wu, and
they made Chung Ni their revered master, attaching great
importance to his words.   With regard to the *Tao* [the
Truth], they stand highest (of the philosophers). . . .

On the right are recorded 37 Taoist authors with a total
of 993 sections to their works.   These authors as a class
issued their works under the Ministry of Historical Records;
for they wrote down in order the causes of success and
failure in the state, of survival and of ruin, of calamity and
blessing, of the Way of the past and the Way of the present.
From this they came to know how to grasp the pivot
and maintain the root, in purity and emptiness to guard
themselves, in humility and weakness to teach themselves.
This is the skill required for the sovereign so that he should

[1] Dr. Bodde in his translation of Dr. Weng Yu-lan's *History of Chinese
Philosophy* translates this by 'divination.'   I agree that it includes divination,
but I think the wider term is more correct.

merely sit facing the south in harmony with the Sage-king Yao, who had the power in him to abdicate. . . .

On the right are recorded 21 Yin-Yang authors with a total of 369 sections to their works. These authors as a class produced their works under the Ministry of the Seasons; for they reverently conformed to the vast heavens and the ordered emblems, the sun, the moon, the constellations, and the stars, reverently transmitting the people's times and seasons. . . .

On the right are recorded 10 Legalist authors with a total of 217 sections to their works. These authors as a class produced their works under the Ministry of Crime; for they trusted in rewards and made punishments unevadable as aids to the regulating power of the Rituals. . . .

On the right are recorded 7 Logicians with a total of 36 sections to their works. These authors as a class produced their works under the Ministry of Ritual; for in ancient times, when names and positions were different, the rituals differed accordingly. Master K'ung said, 'It is a matter of necessity that names should be right. If they be wrong, then speech is inconsistent, and if speech be inconsistent, then no business can be successfully completed.' . . .

On the right are recorded 6 Mohists with a total of 86 sections to their works. These authors produced their works under the guardianship of the Pure Fane [i.e. the sacrifices to King Wen]; for a rush hut and uneven rafters is being economical, the feasting of the aged is all-embracing love . . . to look up to Heaven with filial reverence is the way for subjects to identify themselves with those over them.

(Pan Ku, *Ch'ien Han Shu*, chüan 30.)

And so on with more subdivisions of the Philosopher Class, the exponents of inter-state policy making 12, miscellaneous writers 20, writers on the theory of agriculture and agricultural economy 9, and imaginative writers 15. Each of these has a ministry behind it. The grand total of philosophical authors runs to 189 with 4,324 sections. Our first-century guide, Pan Ku, estimates that out of ten of them nine are worth studying, but he criticizes them as a whole as emphasizing one end of the truth to the exclusion of the other end.

In the fourth year of Emperor Chang [A.D. 76–88] . . . in the winter there was a great pestilence among the cattle. In the eleventh month on the Jen-Hsü day, the following order was promulgated: 'Let it be known that in the direction of mankind which came from the Three (Sage) Eras, the learned study of the Truth [1] was of basic importance. When the Han, following on tyrannical Ch'in, came to display the glories of the trained art of the Confucianists [Ju], they set up the Five Scriptures in the care of five departments of learned experts. . . . In each case this was to the end that these learned studies might be advanced and the spiritual culture of the Truth be honoured and extended.' In the Chung-Yuan year [A.D. 56] of Emperor Kuang Wu there was the fiat issued for the Five Scriptures to be copied with the chapters and sentences (clearly marked); and there was all the trouble of discussions over the pruning of the text. In the Yungp'ing year [A.D. 58] of Emperor Ming, the Military Intendant of Ch'ang Hsüeh urgently memorialized the Throne: 'The great practice of the early sovereigns was to take opportune and extensive measures so that the scholars [Ju] generally might as a body be right as to the meaning in the Scriptures and to a certain extent be able to give definite instruction to students, and they be able to aid themselves. Master K'ung said, "It is the failure to expound matters of learning which distresses me." He also said, "To be extensively learned and so whole-hearted, keen in inquiring and so near to thinking (effectively): human-heartedness lies just there!" How marvellous was this exhortation of his!' Thus the fiats were issued to the various Great Officers and doctors of learning, advisers to the throne and other such officers together with their disciples and scholars (not in office), to meet at the White Tiger Belvedere (Pai Hu Kuan), there to expound and to discuss where the Five Scriptures are in agreement and where they are not. Superintendent Wei Ying was made the referee in cases of doubt, Officer-in-waiting Shün

[1] *Chiao*, viz. the basic truths in Confucianism, that is in the kind of Confucianism which was emerging from the various traditions and becoming the Great Tradition of the Chinese people.

Yü-kung petitioned the Emperor in person to attend the
meeting, as Emperor Hsüan had done in the meeting of
the Kan-lu year [52 B.C.] in the Shih Ch'ü Council Chamber.
The White Tiger Decisions were presented to the Throne.

(Fan Yeh, *Hou Han Shu*, chüan 3.)

The above decisions were summarized in the book known as
the *Pai Hu T'ung Yi*. Extensive quotations from this important
document are not necessary. The decisions represent a position
much the same as that of Tung Chung-shu; but two references
are required, one to show the tendency in official scholar circles
to a theocratic view of the monarchy, the other to show the
age's adherence to the Five Forces Theory.

Chüan I. Degrees in Noble Station.

I. '*Son of Heaven*' *as a Title.*

The term 'Son of Heaven' is a title of noble station.
How came it about that this term is used as a title? The
father of the true king is Heaven, the mother Earth, and
he is Son of Heaven. Thus it is that the *Yüan Shen Ch'i*
says 'Heaven covers, Earth sustains,' and this refers to the
Son of Heaven. In the heavenly regions his model is the
North Star. The *Kou Ming Chüeh* says, 'Son of Heaven is
a title of noble station.'

The virtue in Emperors being abundant, in Kings scant,
why is it that they are all designated Sons of Heaven?
It is because they were all commissioned by Heaven and so
held sovereign sway within 5,000 *li* of territory. The *Book
of History* says 'The Son of Heaven, acting as the father and
mother of his people, becomes ruler of all under heaven.'

How do we know that Emperors (should) also be desig-
nated Sons of Heaven? Because they are the models for
all under heaven. The *Chung Hou*[1] says, '(I) the Son of
Heaven, thy servant Fang Hsün.' The *Lost Chapter of the
Book of History* says, 'He inaugurated the rank of Son of
Heaven.'[2]

---

[1] The citation from this apocryphal work has been traced by Dr. Tjan.
Emperor Yao is addressing Heaven.

[2] The passage as a whole shows the dogmatic mind at work, e.g. using
proof texts, yet the phrasing is not logically artless.

How is it we say 'absolute ruler' as well as 'Son of Heaven'? Because his words are equivalent to Heaven the all-covering, Earth the all-sustaining, all of them together constituting royal sway throughout the world.

There seems to be no mincing of words here. It only remains to add that other tendencies of Confucian thought went in a different direction, and the theocratic idea did not succeed in establishing itself as the supreme principle of government.

Chüan II, 2. The Five Forces.

What is the explanation of 'the Five Forces'? The explanation is as follows: Metal, Wood, Water, Fire, Soil are called 'forces,' the wish being to express the principle of Heaven in action as vital energy. The supplementary relation of Earth to Heaven is like the service a wife renders her husband or a minister renders his sovereign. This is explained by the position being a humble one and the humble person being able to render intimate service. The result of this is that Earth identifies itself with one (function) and (thereby) pays (due) honour to Heaven.

The *Book of History* says, 'First Water, second Fire, third Wood, fourth Metal, fifth Soil. Water's typical position is in the north where the Yin vital energy (masses?) below the Yellow Springs. Water bears the responsibility of nourishing all creation. Thus in (our human) speech it is equivalent to levelling, for it nourishes all impartially and is the criterion of the level (horizontal?).

Wood[1] is in the eastern region, that is the region where the Yang vital energy (as seen in spring) begins to stir and the whole creation begins to give birth. Thus Wood in (our human) speech is equivalent to pushing forth, for the Yang vital energy leaps up, pushing forth from the earth.

Fire is in the southern region, that is the region where the Yang energy is in the ascendancy. The whole (vegetable) creation has its branches and stalks hanging down (heavy with fruit). Fire in (our human) speech is equivalent

---

[1] The author introduces a third order of treatment. Speculation in this field varied considerably, and the order varied according to the theory.

to bearing the burden of compliance, by which is expressed (the idea) of all things spreading and spreading. Thus fire in (our human) speech is equivalent to transforming: with the Yang energy functioning all creation is transformed.

Metal is in the western region, that is the region where the Yin energy begins to rise. The whole creation comes to a standstill. Thus Metal in (our human) speech is equivalent to being blocked.

Soil is in the functioning centre, for the functioning centre is Soil. Soil holds sway over giving forth, including all creatures in its sway. Thus in (our human) speech it is equivalent to giving forth. How do we know that the eastern quarter is equivalent to (new) life? In the *Yo Chi* it is written, 'In the spring birth, in the summer full growth, in the autumn harvest, in the winter the store.'

That Soil is not the name of any one of the seasons is because it is another name for the earth. Amongst the Five Forces it holds the most honourable place. Thus it will 'not admit of being departmentalized.'

The *Yüan Ming Pao* says, 'Earth has not relative position, and the *Tao* is present (everywhere). Therefore, (as) the Supreme Oneness (of the universe) has no share in (processes of) transformation, (so) the *Jen Chu* (Lord of men) [1] does not admit of being departmentalized.' [2]

---

[1] *Jen Chu:* the term constantly used by the Legalist school and implying exercise of autocratic powers.

It is rather breath-taking, this achievement of the dogmatic mind arguing to a foregone conclusion. It reveals, of course, a strong theocratic trend in the thinking of the Second Han court. The inevitable inference is that Confucianism plus Legalism plus Taoism plus Mohism produced just that, a theocratic state. On the other hand there is strong evidence that during the two Han eras there was developed an imperial constitution of the 'unwritten' kind. The Emperor, ostensibly a Confucianist monarch, was expected to toe the line of strict rules of what were held to be ancestral procedure. The bulk of these came under the heading of *Li Chiao* (the Principles in the Rituals). The neglect or transgression of them caused a feeling of outrage among officials and people.

[2] My renderings in this passage contain some different emphases from those in Dr. Tjan's translation.

CHAPTER XXIII: WANG CH'UNG

Wang Ch'ung (c. A.D. 27–97) makes a curious and fascinating study. He belonged—if he can be said to submit to any but his own very individual way of thinking—to the rationalist wing of the Confucianist school. The critical powers of his mind were exceptionally strong, so that he spent himself in combating and exposing the superstitions and other erroneous beliefs of his age, and it is clear that by so doing, as also by a rather disagreeable egotism, he made himself very unpopular. In his lonely later years he gave himself to writing and produced a book of eighty-four essays, the concluding one of which was a short sketch of his own life and career with an appraisement of contemporary tendencies of thought and of his personal reaction to them. This autobiography, the first in Chinese literature, reveals the trend to authoritarianism, the belief that because a statement came in an old book with the name of a famous teacher attached to it, therefore it must be true.

The title which he gave his book, *Lun Heng* (the weighing up of critical discussions), is an apt description of its nature. He is first and foremost a critic, all his energies are used in working out accumulative arguments in which, after the pattern of Kung-sun Lung's dialogues, contentions for and against are considered. His chief bugbear was the anthropomorphic ideas about 'Heaven'; for he would allow no element of design in the order of the universe. Yet his distinctive kind of realism drove him to an acceptance of ethical values as an integral part of the human pattern of life: values which could not be explained by any Mohist or Legalist theories of utility. For Western students of classical philosophy he is interesting for the affinities he displays with both Stoic and Epicurean thought.

Wang Ch'ung was not a first-class metaphysician, and as a logician his chief contribution to knowledge is the dialectical ingenuity with which he was able to fight his opponents. There is nothing of the simple-minded dogmatist about Wang Ch'ung. Further, his book was written in popular style. It is, therefore, the more significant, particularly as its command of the language of dialectical logic demonstrates how much the late Chou dialecticians had contributed to the scholars' tools of reasoning.

The Scholars at the present day have a passion for believing that what their teachers say is (genuinely) old, and they regard the words of worthies and sages as all of the very essence of truth. In expounding and learning these words off by heart, they do not realize that there are any difficulties requiring explanation.

Worthies and sages, when they take up their pens to write, are greatly concerned with ideas which they have examined in great detail; nevertheless it is not admissible to say that they always get hold of the truth. How much less can we say it of all their fragmentary utterances! People to-day have no sense of criticism, and if any statement be true but its meaning deep and difficult to perceive, they do not know to inquire. I maintain that the words of worthies and sages are in many cases mutually incompatible, their writings very often mutually contradictory: a fact which the students of Confucianism to-day are unable to realize.

In discussions people continually make the statement that the Seventy Disciples of Confucius's Door were much more talented than the present exponents of Confucianism. This statement is false. People of that sort visualize Confucius the teacher as a sage man passing on the Tao and therefore of necessity imparting it to exceptionally talented men, who are in consequence described as unique. The talents of the men of old are those of the men of to-day. What we call men of genius to-day, in ancient times were regarded as divinely inspired; and so it is said that in subsequent ages there have hardly been any like the Seventy Disciples.

Suppose there were a teacher like Confucius now, then the Scholars of to-day would be disciples like Yen Hui and Min Tzu Ch'ien. Suppose there had been no Confucius, the Seventy Disciples would be like the Scholars of to-day. How do I prove this? By the fact that in learning from Confucius they would be unable to press questions home. And yet, if they did not completely comprehend the Sage's words, if in expounding his principles they could not formulate them clearly, it would be their duty to ask him to make them clear; and if then they still did not completely comprehend them, it would be their duty to criticize right up to the hilt.

Kao Yao in setting forth principles (of policy) in (the Sage-king) Shun's presence spoke superficially and in extremely sketchy fashion. When Yü criticized him his words became deep and his sketchiness changed to a demarcation of his subject; for a critical demand to know what is meant brings out the depth of meaning there may be, and exigent opposition makes things clear. . . . There were few disciples such as Tzu Yiu with his raising of difficulties with Confucius. The result is that Confucius's words have become inexplicable, the reason being that the Seventy Disciples were unable to raise difficulties. Thus the Scholars to-day cannot verify whether what Confucius taught is true or not.

The standard of scholarship [1] is not made by lack of ability and the difficulty of opposing one's teacher. It entails getting at the heart of his tenets and verifying his principles, obtaining evidence and ascertaining whether they are true or not. And the method of critical inquiry is not restricted to the lifetime of a sage man. Those who to-day unravel the expositions which have been made of a sage [2] do not of necessity require a sage to teach and inform them before they dare speak. If there be questions on knotty points and thereby the creation of difficulties for Confucius, what harm will there be to right principles? Words exist in order to [3] pass on knowledge of the sacred heritage. What contravention of reason lies then in a critical exposition of Confucius? The expression 'inquire what Confucius himself said' involves probing into those passages which are knotty; and from one generation to another men of outstanding gifts and great knowledge, men born with the ability to answer questions and solve problems, these will certainly approve the words which come from our generation as to the truth or otherwise (of Confucius's teaching).

Chüan ix, c. 1.

Wang Ch'ung then embarks on a critical examination of such passages in the *Analects*. He does not set out to 'debunk'

---

[1] *Hsüeh wen*, lit. learning (predominantly from a teacher) and inquiring. The two words came in the Han era to be run together to mean 'scholarly learning,' as in the English expression, 'a man of scholarship and learning.' It is the common expression to-day for learning in the academic sense.
[2] Emending *shuo* to *sheng*
[3] Adding *yi* to the text.

Confucius, but he does rather demolish the saint's halo round
his head. He does not sum up at the end of the essay. In
another essay, dealing with Mencius, he sets his detective ability
to work to discover in him moral faults and things which are
inconsistent with reason. In a third essay entitled *Denunciation
of Han Fei* (the great Legalist, see Part Six, Chapter XVII), Wang
Ch'ung goes farther than criticism. He not only denounces;
he also takes the opportunity to state his convictions about the
vital importance of the ritual mind and the necessity of governing
with a view to encouraging the real virtue that is at any rate in
some men.

Han Fei's policy consisted in making the laws very clear
(to the people) and in exalting practical achievement.
Where moral and intellectual worth was not of utility to
the state, it was not to be rewarded, and where lack of
morals was no harm to public order, it was not to be
punished. The piling up of achievement brought great
rewards, whilst the function of punishment was discharged by the death penalty. Thus it was that in his
treatment of scholars (in his book) he described them as
men who without being producers were consumers and
compared them with the whole class of grubs. . . .

Now in speaking of utility, ritual-and-righteousness [1] is
not equal to food and drink; but, supposing Master Han
were kindly invited to eat in the presence of his sovereign
or his father, would he be willing to do so without bowing
to them? Yet to do so would be after the pattern of ritual-
and-righteousness and would be of no actual bodily utility.
Master Han, nevertheless, would in the end not be one to
omit the bow: he would not give up ritual-and-righteousness
for slovenly utility.

The Scholars represent ritual - and - righteousness, the
farmers and fighting men food and drink. To ennoble the
farmers and fighting men and bring the scholars to ruin is
equivalent to (society) abandoning ritual-and-righteousness
and devoting itself to food and drink; and if ritual-and-
righteousness were gone, the foundations of society would

---

[1] 'A civilized code of morals' would perhaps convey the meaning of
li yi as well as the very literal 'ritual-and-righteousness,' but the idea of
'ritual' here goes deeper than 'civilization.' Cp. Hsun Ch'ing (p. 230),
who almost certainly coined the term.

be destroyed and the upper and lower ranks be in confusion, whilst the Yin and the Yang would get out of gear, the wetness and dryness of the seasons be out of order, the five cereals not be giving good harvests, the myriad populace dying of starvation, with the farmers having no means of tilling the soil and the soldiers no means of fighting.

When Tzu Kung wished to abolish the sacrifice of a sheep at the announcement of the new moon, Confucius said, 'You love the sheep in this matter: I love the rite.' Tzu Kung hated the waste of a sheep, whilst Confucius was concerned about the abandonment of ritual. The fact is that if an old dyke is taken to be of no use and is let go, there is sure to be a disastrous flood; and if old rites are taken to be of no service and are let go, there is sure to be disastrous anarchy. The existence of the Scholars down the generations amounts to the old dykes of ritual-and-righteousness. To have them is of no (apparent) utility: not to have them is definitely harmful.

The foundation of academic institutions has existed from ancient times, a paying of deference to (society's) root and of honour to (civilization's) beginning. From this has arisen the appointment of officers of state and the employment of their assistants; and officers must not be dispensed with, the High Way (of society) must not be abandoned. The Scholars are assistants to the officers of the High Way, and if they are taken to be useless and discarded, this is equivalent to discarding the High Way. The Way does not itself produce results in men, but those who do produce such results need the Way for the production. The foot marches on the road and so moves on: but the road which is marched on needs to be a non-marching thing, for the body needs hand and foot if it is to move and thereby depends on something which does not move. Thus it is that sometimes the thing which is useless and yet useful is needed to produce results, and the non-production of results is, as it were, what (everything) depends on. The Scholars are what the farmers and the fighting men must

depend on. What would happen if they were abolished
and did not survive in society?

After giving instances of Scholars whose moral influence won
the respect of kings and the like, Wang Ch'ung produces evidence
of the double strand in life to which justice must be done in any
theory of human nature or policy of government.

The principle of state control entails the cultivation of
two things, namely moral power [*te*] and physical force.
The cultivation of moral power means the cultivation of
men of lofty repute and thereby indicating one's ability to
reverence true worth. The cultivation of physical force
means the cultivation of soldiers full of vigour and thereby
showing one's ability to use troops. This is what is meant
by 'civil and military measures in full working order,
moral power and physical force both adequate.' Affairs
of state may be carried out sometimes by the gentle persuasion of moral influence, sometimes by the pressure of
force. In international relations the use of moral power
may bring independence, in internal affairs the use of
force may bring self-preparedness. Those who respect
moral power come to terms without war, whilst those who
flout moral power take note of portentous military strength.

King Yen of Hsü practised human-heartedness and
justice, and thirty-two states sent envoys by land to pay
their respects. When Ch'u State heard of this, it sent
troops and destroyed Hsü: a case of having moral power
as a protection but no force in reserve.

Moral power cannot be the sole means of keeping control
of a country, and force cannot be the direct means of driving
away an enemy. Master Han's policy of not cultivating
virtue and King Yen's practice of paying no attention to
force, both were one-sided and open to objection. Both
were defective. . . .

Consider the congenital nature with which men are
endowed: it is both pure and (alternatively) impure, selfish
and (alternatively) disinterested, each nature having its own
habits of living—as plants and trees have different raw
material and cannot be taken back to the beginning and

changed.   Kuang Chueh and Hua Shih[1] refused to take
office in the Ch'i Fief, as Tuang Kang Mu refused in Wei
State.[2]   Their nature was pure and disinterested: they had
no lust for wealth and honour: they went against the spirit
of the times: their sense of justice could brook no com-
promising service of the state.   Although men of this kind
escape execution, their actions are such that they can get
no great following.   (As it was,) the Great Duke did execute
them, and Master Han maintains that he acted rightly.
That is equivalent to saying that men have no congenital
nature, plants and trees no raw material.

In regard to the Great Duke's execution of Kuang Chueh
and Hua Shih, supposing there were men of this stamp in
Ch'i, they would not, because the two suffered the death
penalty, refrain from purifying themselves; and supposing
there were no men of this stamp in Ch'i, however much
attempts might have been made to cultivate them, there
would in the end have been no transforming influence from
that quarter. . . . The Marquess Wen of Wei State bowed
as his chariot passed Tuan Kang Mu's homestead, but all
Wei did not therefore close its doors (and refuse to take
office).   Arguing from these instances, if the Great Duke
had not executed the two worthies, all Ch'i would not have
refused to serve; and the reason is that the practice of
purity and disinterestedness is not what men generally can
achieve.   What men cannot do, they cannot be forced to do
even by the power of moral persuasion.   Try putting men
to death in order to prevent them: they cannot be stopped.
So then the Great Duke's execution of these two worthies
was useless in regard to the transformation of men's minds.
It was meaningless murder of innocent people. . . .

In Sung State there was a charioteer.   If a horse refused
to budge, he cut its throat and threw it into a ditch.   He
took another horse, and, if it refused to budge, he cut its

[1] Two legendary worthies at the beginning of the Chou era who refused
to recognize the new government and were accordingly executed.   Wang
Chung's attitude to them is that virtue may result in death, but the injustice
of their death is a seed of calamity for a more or less distant future.
[2] This worthy moved the hearts of kings and saved his country, but he
got no reward for it.

throat and threw it into a ditch. He would do this a third time: an instance of extreme intimidation applied to horses. This, however, was not the method used by (the famous charioteer) Wang Liang. When he stepped into a chariot, the horses lost their wild humours, just as under Yao's and Shun's government the people were not wild and rebellious. Wang Liang soothed the hearts [*hsin*] of his horses, and Yao and Shun complied with the wishes of their people.

Now we men have a common nature whilst horses belong to a different species. Yet Wang Liang was able to pacify these creatures of a different species, whilst the Great Duke was unable to give free course to men of a common nature. . . . Supposing Master Han were called on to decide the merits of these cases, he would without a doubt say that Wang Liang was right and the Sung man wrong; for the former's action was constructive, the latter's destructive, and destructive action is not so good as constructive in relation to horses. So also with the people: that they should die is not so good as that they should live. Supposing, however, that Master Han should say that Wang Liang was wrong, he would be making himself out the same kind of person as the Sung man, for he would destroy the good. Again, supposing he should say that the Sung man was wrong: since that man's method was the same as the Great Duke's, to count the one wrong and the other right would mean that Master Han was in a state of uncertainty as to what he approved and what he disapproved.[1]

2. *Criticism of Current Superstitions.*

Two quotations out of a very large number of possible ones must suffice under this heading.

At the height of summer thunder and lightning come with tremendous force, splitting trees, demolishing houses, and from time to time killing people. The common idea is

[1] The passage illustrates incidentally the technique of dialectic for which these later classical thinkers were under so great a debt to the Dialecticians of the fourth and third centuries B.C.

that this splitting of trees and demolishing of houses is Heaven setting a dragon to work. And when the thunder and lightning rush on people and kill them, this is described as due to hidden faults, for example, people eating unclean things, and so Heaven in its anger striking them and killing them. The roar of the thunder is the voice of Heaven's anger, like men gasping with rage. Ignorant and learned alike talk like this, making inferences [1] from the ways of men in order to make sense of what happens.

This is all nonsense. The genesis of thunder is one particular kind of vital energy [ch'i], one particular kind of sound. Its splitting of trees and demolishing of houses is one with the rushing on men and the killing of them. At the same time as the killing occurs the splitting and demolishing occur. Are we then only to ascribe the splitting and demolishing to Heaven's setting of a dragon to work; and the killing of men to hidden faults? A dragon at work is auspicious,[2] something very different from an inauspicious event. For the two to be at the same time and have a common sound cannot be true.

The people who thus make sense of it regard the roar of the thunder as Heaven in anger making a gasping noise. This fits with punishment of faults, but it does not fit with setting a dragon to work. Thus the punishment of faults and the anger of Heaven, this is admissible: but where can the dragon come in with faults and anger? . . . So then the theory about the dragon being set to work should not be listened to, nor should the words about the punishment of faults be believed.

(Chüan vi, c. 4, on *Thunder and Lightning*.)

The Scholars have handed down a writing in which it is said, 'In the days of Yao ten suns came out at the same time, and the myriad things were all being burnt up when Yao

---

[1] *T'ui* has occurred in previous quotations, but I have been slow to give it the full force of 'inference.' Yet here *t'ui* seems without a doubt to mean this.

[2] Whatever may be the significance of a dragon in the myths and legends of other cultures, in Chinese folklore it is predominantly auspicious: numinous yet beneficent.

shot an arrow at the suns and nine of them disappeared, only one remaining.' This statement is false. With regard to shooting with a bow and arrow, at not more than a hundred paces the arrow loses its force entirely. The course of the sun, however, is that of the stars in the quarters of the sky, and the distance between the sky and men (on the earth) amounts to ten thousand miles [*li*]. How then could Yao succeed in shooting those suns? If in Yao's day the sky and the earth were near to each other, not more than a hundred paces apart, then Yao could have shot those suns, for the arrow could have reached them. Anything beyond a hundred paces would have been impracticable. But even on the assumption that in those days the sky and the earth were near to each other and Yao could manage to hit those suns, he still could not have injured them.

If he had injured them, why should they have been willing to disappear? Fire is light.[1] Suppose a torch kindled by earthly fire and a man shooting it from the side: although he hit it dead in the centre, would he be able to extinguish it? If, then, earthly fire cannot be extinguished by an arrow shot, why should heavenly fire disappear because of one?

This story aims at saying that Yao shot the suns by means of the essence of truth in him. Wherever such truth is applied, metal and stone fade away, for if there be nothing materially solid about truth, neither is there anything beyond its range. Now, water and fire go together, each having its own particular nature. If there be a power to shoot fire and extinguish it, then there must be a power to shoot water and remove it. In the days of the Great Flood, when all the Middle Kingdom was inundated and the people suffered great injury, why did not Yao extend his essence of truth and shoot the flood and so remove it? He was able to shoot the sun and prevent fire from being an injury. If he could not remove water by shooting, then

[1] Probably *kuang* should be *huo* (fire). The two characters resemble each other.

we know that this talk about shooting suns is false and not based on facts.

Some say that the sun consists of *ch'i*,[1] and although an arrow cannot reach it, the essence of truth can destroy it. Now, the sky is also a great distance away. If it is to be taken as *ch'i*, then (according to this theory) it is the same as the sun and the moon: if it is to be taken as being material, then it ranks with metal and stone. In that case, if Yao's essence of truth destroyed the sun and worked injury on metals and rocks, then in shooting the sun it was able to pierce the sky: is not that so? But the world attributes wickedness to Chieh and Chow, since they 'shot the sky and mauled the earth.' . . . So Yao was wicked in the same way as Chieh and Chow. How then could any essence of truth in him get a response from Nature [lit. Heaven]?   (Chüan v, c. 2.)

Rather faulty arguing, and chop-logic stuff at that. But Wang Ch'ung is like this on occasion. Nevertheless, his contention in this essay is a sound one in its way: he will not allow that any action on man's part can have a miraculous effect (*kan*)[2] on Nature. The idea that it could was widely held in his day, not only by simple people, but also by a strong section of the Confucianist school who carried it to great lengths. Wang Ch'ung belonged to an opposing and more rationalistic section which ultimately got the upper hand.

3. *Wang Ch'ung's Ideas about the Universe and Man's Place in it.*

The heavens and the earth having united their vital energies, the myriad things (in Nature) came naturally into existence, just as, a man and woman having united their vital energies, children come naturally into existence. With regard to the myriad things in Nature, the species which contain blood are conscious of hunger, conscious of cold. Having perceived that the five cereals are edible, they take

---

[1] *Ch'i*: interpreted in other passages as 'vital essence' (? vital fluid). I confess I have no clear idea as to what Wang Chung meant by *ch'i*, and can only suggest that, generally speaking, in very late Chou and in Han writers *ch'i* belongs to that class of phenomena which the Greeks recognized as 'meta-physical.' Cp. the next quotation.

[2] A technical term which came into use in Han times.

them and eat them. Having perceived that silk and hemp
are wearable, they take them and wear them.

Some people have the theory that Heaven brought the
five cereals into existence in order that they might be food
for men, and brought silk and hemp into existence in
order that they might be clothing for men. This means
Heaven acting as farmer and mulberry girl to the human
race, and it is incompatible with the naturally so [*tzu jan*]
(in Nature). Therefore the principle of the theory is
dubious and cannot be our guide. Let us trust to the
Taoists in making sense of this matter. They said, 'Heaven
discharges vital energy, and amongst the myriad things in
Nature grain relieves hunger and silk and hemp save from
cold. Thus it is that men eat grain and wear silk and hemp.
The fact that Heaven does not deliberately bring the five
cereals and silk and hemp into existence in order that men
may eat and wear them is like the fact that there are calamitous changes (in Nature), and these are not aimed at repri-
manding men. Things come into existence naturally, and
men eat and wear them. Vital energy changes round (in
its incidence) naturally, and men are frightened of that.
To make sense of this along the lines of the other theory is
repulsive to the mind of man; for, once we recognize the
token of Heaven's authority as 'intention,' where does
'natural process' come in, where is there a place for
'inaction'?[1]

Why should we assume natural process in relation to
Heaven? Because Heaven has no mouth and no eyes. I
make the judgment: the existence of action is in the field
of mouths and eyes. Mouths want to eat and eyes want
to see: within an appetite, without the manifestation of it.
Mouths and eyes go searching for things, and the obtaining
of them is action for the satisfaction of desire. Suppose
now that there were no desire of the mouth and the eye
and that in relation to things there were no link of searching; how then could there be action?

---

[1] The Taoist idea of *wu wei* (actionless activity) as the characteristic of
'Heaven.'   Cp. Part Four, Chapter IX.

How do we know that Heaven has no mouth and eyes?
We know this from Earth; for with the soil Earth becomes
a body,[1] and soil, speaking basically, has no mouth and
eyes. 'Heaven' and 'Earth' equals [2] 'husband and wife.'
Since Earth has no mouth and eyes, we also know that
Heaven has no mouth and eyes; for, if we assume Heaven
has a body, it can only be like Earth's body. Assuming a
vital energy of Heaven, that energy is of the nature of
cloud and vapour. How can things of that kind have
mouths and eyes?

Someone may say that every kind of movement has its
origin in non-action: there is desire with the result movement; if movement, then there is action. Supposing
Heaven's courses of movement are like men's, how is it
possible there should be inaction? The reply is: Heaven's
courses of movement are equal to the discharge of vital
energy. Its body moves, and vital energy comes forth, and
things come into existence. When vital energy is set in
motion through men, the body moves and the vital energy
comes forth and a child comes into existence. As for men's
discharge of vital energy, it is not true that they desire in
order to bring children into existence: the vital energy is discharged, and children come into existence by natural process.
(So) Heaven in its movements does not desire in order to
bring things into existence, but things come into existence by
natural process. This then is the 'naturally so' (in Nature).
The discharge of the vital energy is not a desire to make
things: things, on the contrary, make themselves. This
then is 'inaction.' The statement that Heaven is naturally
so and inactive refers to vital energy, something which is
tranquil, without a ripple of desire, inactive, with no
business in hand. . . .

The question is asked: Man's life being in relation to

---

[1] Did he mean 'body' (*ti*) in a literal or metaphorical sense? I do not
know, and, further, I am not sure that from a wider point of view it matters,
for there surely can be no question but that Wang Ch'ung was conscious
he was using the argument from analogy.
[2] This is an excellent instance of how the Chinese puts two ideas in juxtaposition with no indication whether the connecting link is an existential
'is,' or such a meaning, e.g., as 'amounts to.' Cp. Introduction.

Heaven and Earth and they being inactive and man a
creature endowed with a heavenly nature, how can it be
right that he is active as well as inactive? The answer is
that a man whose whole being is imbued with moral power
is endowed with a large quantity of heavenly vital energy.
Thus it is that he is able to pattern himself on Heaven, be
naturally so, be inactive. Where a man is endowed with
only a slight amount of vital energy, pays no attention to
the Virtue of the Tao, and bears no resemblance to Heaven
and Earth, the result is that he is called an unconscionable fellow: [1] 'unconscionable,' that is, not conforming to
Heaven and Earth, not of the same class as the sages and
worthies. The result is that he is (full of) activity.[2]

.   .   .   .   .

The Scholars expound the right way for husband and
wife as one patterned on Heaven and Earth. They know
this. They do not know how to extend the way of husband
and wife in order to consider the nature of Heaven and
Earth. In this, we may say, they are misguided.

Heaven covers (everything) from above, earth dykes up
(everything) from below. The vital energy below vapori-
zing, the vital energy above descends, and the myriad
things come naturally into existence in the space between.
Whilst they are coming to be, there is no need for Heaven
to cherish them, just as a father cannot know his son while
he is in the mother's womb. A thing comes naturally into
existence, a child naturally to completion: how could
Heaven and Earth and a father and mother know about
them? Once a child is born, however, man's right way
involves the principle of instruction, Heaven's right way
that of inaction, a giving of full play to the natures of
things. The result is that (Heaven) lets the fish go free in
the rivers, the wild beasts on the mountains, each following
the desires of its own nature. It does not force the fish

---

[1] *Pu hsiao* denotes primarily a son being unlike his good father. Cp.
Tao Te Ching, c. 67, foot-note.
[2] The technical term 'creaturely activity' used by the Society of Friends
is a good parallel.

to the banks nor drive the beasts into the watery depths.
How could it? It would be violation of their natures, a
sacrifice of what is right for them.

The human society is in the same class as the fish and the
wild beasts. The highest virtue in ruling them is equal to
frying small fish, doing just what Heaven does.

   .   .   .   .   .

Heaven and Earth cannot be active, also they cannot
know (how to be so). When there is a stoppage in the
stomach and it aches, it is not anybody that makes it do
so, but the vital energy acting by natural process: the vital
energy which just as much fills up the space between heaven
and earth as it does the space in a man's back and stomach.
If we say that 'Heaven' is the author of calamitous re-
visions, then every kind of prodigy, small and great, is due
to 'Heaven's' activity: is not that so? If a cow were to
give birth to a horse, or a peach tree produce a plum,
according to this line of argument, a heavenly spirit enters
the cow's stomach and makes a horse and sticks a plum
on the peach tree!

           (Chüan xviii, Essay 1, on *Naturally So*.)

   .   .   .   .   .

There is an old saying that Heaven and Earth have no
purpose in bringing men into existence: men just get born
by natural process. Now for what reason [*ku*] would a
man who argued in this fashion say that Heaven and Earth
are a (kiln or) a furnace, the myriad things the copper in
the furnace, the Yin-Yang the fire, and the transformation
brought about the work done? My judgment is as follows:
The foundryman or potter's use of fire is for the smelting of
copper and the fixing of the crocks. His activity has a
purpose. The argument, however, with regard to Heaven
and Earth is that they have no purpose in bringing man into
existence, that men just get born by natural process. Is
it (logically) admissible to describe the potter and the

foundryman as having no purpose in making utensils and
so to describe the utensils as without premeditation completing themselves?

Where a comparison does not really accord with the
matter under consideration it may not be called an analogy:
where the words do not designate actualities [1] they may not
be called true. I maintain that the above analogy deals
with men as endowed with vital energy and not able to be
completely uniform, just as there are different moulds into
which the smelted copper runs and the fire acts on the
(different) utensils being burnt. The analogy does not
say that Heaven and Earth bring men into existence in the
same way as the potter and the foundryman. . . .

An analogy about man should in all cases cite man's
business. Now man's business may not logically be cut up
into unconnected sections. . . . When the eyes try to look
at the head, the head cannot avoid turning,[2] and when the
hand hovers over the foot, the foot cannot avoid moving.
The eyes and the head and the hand and the foot belong to
the same body. Suppose now the potter or foundryman
preparing the new material for various utensils: he is
certain to have moulds for the different forms. These he
makes with a purpose in view. In lighting the charcoal
and making up the fire he is certain to regulate the furnace.
This he does with a purpose in view, although not all the
molten copper can become utensils, not all of the crocks
made turn out well, for we are unable to bring into existence
(exactly) as we purpose.[3]

Heaven and Earth cannot bring men into existence
(exactly) as they purpose, and that being so, then bringing
of the myriad things into existence is also what they cannot

[1] A passage like this shows proof how, in spite of the feeling of moral
disapproval which came to be held about the fourth and third-century
logicians, the terms which they coined, and to a certain extent the habits of
exact reasoning which they inculcated, became part of the heritage of
educated men.
[2] Instinctively the head turns in the same direction as the eyes, as they
vainly try to see the head.
[3] The idea of 'factors in a situation' appears to be beyond the range of
Wang Chung's powers of expression, but he clearly is thinking of 'un-
controllable factors.'

do as they purpose. Heaven and Earth unite their vital energies and the myriad creatures just bring themselves into existence.

The preparation of the soil and the sowing of the seed is done with a purpose, but when we come to the crop and the question whether it ripens, that is just as it happens to be. The proof of this is that, if Heaven brought the myriad things into existence with a purpose in view, it would have had to command them to love each other, and not command them to prey upon each other. Here some may say: There are the (respective) vital energies of the Five Physical Forces and Heaven brought the myriad things into existence by filling them with the vital energies of the Five Forces, and they (not Heaven) prey on each other. The reply is that Heaven should have used the vital energy of only one force in bringing things into existence, and should have commanded them to love each other, and not have commanded the vital energies of the Five Forces to do the exact opposite, namely prey on each other.

At this some may say: It is desirable to make the Five Forces to be of use, and therefore they are commanded to prey on each other, for by so doing they complete each other. For this reason Heaven uses the vital energies of the Five Forces in bringing the myriad things into existence. Man uses the myriad things to accomplish myriad ends. If these vital energies cannot control each other, man cannot set each to work on the other: if they do not prey on each other, they cannot be made of use. If metal [i.e. the axe] does not prey on timber, timber cannot be of use: if fire does not smelt metal, metal cannot be made into tools. Thus it is that the different things prey on each other and bring profit to each other. All living creatures fight for victory over each other, biting and devouring each other, and it is the vital energies of the Five Forces which makes them so.

My reply is: If Heaven in bringing the myriad things into existence wants to command them to be of use to each other and in consequence they inevitably prey on each other, then Heaven brought tigers and wolves, snakes and all the venomous insects into existence in order that they might prey on man. Does Heaven want man to be of use to them? Further, one man's body contains the vital energies of the Five Forces, therefore in the individual's conduct there exists the practice of the Five Everlastings [*Wu Ch'ang*].[1] These are equivalent to the *tao* [? spiritual element] of the Five Forces. With these and the Five Organs [2] the vital energies of the Five Forces are all present. If, according to the objector's own words, all the creatures with blood in their veins, because of the vital energies of the Five Forces in them, forthwith start preying on each other, then in the individual man's body in which the Five Organs lie so tranquilly, there must be a preying of one on the other.

(Chüan iii, Essay 5, on *The Tendencies in Things*.)

Sometimes one is inclined to suspect Wang Ch'ung of being prepared to use any handy stick in order that he may beat his opponents. E.g. he accepts the 'Five Everlastings' with an ease which we should hardly expect, although, as a matter of fact, he does generally agree with those who maintain that there are spiritual values. That he does manage to square this with his fierce objection to any *telos* to the universe or the life of man, is the main interest to him as a philosopher. In this connection his views on 'Fate' and 'Good luck,' and on the man's survival of bodily death, need to be considered.

Whenever men happen to meet with and get embroiled in trouble, it is in all cases due to fate. There is fate in relation to dying and being born, in relation to a long life and a short one. There is fate also in relation to high station and low, and poverty and wealth. From kings and dukes down to the common people, from sages and worthies to the most ignorant, every man belongs to the class of beings which have heads and eyes and blood in their veins and not one of whom but has a fate. If a man's fate is to be

[1] Viz. human-heartedness, justice, the ritual mind, wisdom, and mutual trust. *Wu ch'ang* was a Confucianist expression which became current at any rate by Han times. The *ch'ang* (abiding unchanged) has the force of 'values' in modern Western philosophy.

[2] Viz. liver, heart, lungs, spleen, and kidneys.

poor and low in rank, however rich and high he may be, he will none the less become involved in disaster. If a man's fate is to be rich and high in rank, however poor and low he may be, he will none the less happen on worldly bliss. . . .

All this being so, it is by no means certain that wealth of talents and nobility of conduct can guarantee that a man will of necessity be rich and of high station; neither is it by any means certain that poverty of talents and slenderness of moral worth can guarantee that a man will of necessity be poor and of low station. There are times when the fate of the talented and noble man is a hateful one and he has no way of climbing the social tree, and other times when the untalented and ignoble man has a good [shan] fate and rises again and again.

Thus it is that wisdom and folly in the conduct of affairs, purity and impurity in daily life, these are connected with the congenital nature and the talents (of individuals): the high and low rank of officials, the poverty and wealth of family fortunes, these are connected with fate and the times. Since there is fate it cannot be avoided: since there are the times, they cannot be changed by force; and wise men leave everything in heaven's keeping, contented and unconcerned, tranquil and forgetting it all, even though their poverty should change to wealth.

(Chüan i, Essay 3, on *Fate and Prosperity*.)

When a number of people are attacked at the same time, those who can conceal themselves are out of the fray. When a number of people encounter frost on the same day, those under cover suffer no injury. Those who are in the fray and those who suffer injury are not necessarily wicked, nor the others good. It is luck one way or the other.

(Chüan ii, Essay 1, on *Good Luck*.)

The common idea is that the dead become ghosts, have knowledge, and can injure people. Let us subject this to proof in relation to other kinds of things [wu].

(I maintain that) the dead do not become ghosts, have no consciousness, and cannot injure people. How do I prove my position? By means of other beings. Man is a being and other creatures also are beings. When they die, they do not become ghosts: why then should man alone when he dies be able to become a ghost? If in this world the distinction can be made between men and other creatures by the ability [1] and the inability to become ghosts, then becoming or not becoming a ghost is still difficult to discriminate clearly. If the distinction cannot be made, then also there is no way of knowing that men can be ghosts.

That by which a man lives is rarefied vital energy. When he dies that energy is wiped out, for the beings which can make rarefied vital energy are such as have blood in their veins. When a man dies, the blood in his veins is exhausted; that being exhausted, the vital energy in him is wiped out: this energy being wiped out, the parts of the body decay: the parts of the body decaying, it becomes dust and ashes. What then can it make use of to become a ghost?

Without the senses men have no means of getting knowledge; and thus it is that deaf and blind people are to be compared with plants and trees. Are not men whom the rarefied vital energy has left, no more than what the deaf and blind are? Since they are in decay, they then dwindle away to nothing.

Because (an object) is all indistinct and not really visible to the eye, therefore it is spoken of as a ghost or spirit. When men see the shape of a ghost or a spirit, it is therefore not the essence of a dead man. What then? This, that 'ghost' and 'spirit' are only the names of something indistinct and not really visible. When a man dies his essence rises to heaven and his bones go into the keeping of the soil. (Chüan xx, Essay 3.)

[1] Adding *yi neng* to the text.